THE SHARPSHOOTERS

The Sharpshooters

A History of the Ninth New Jersey
Volunteer Infantry in the Civil War

EDWARD G. LONGACRE

POTOMAC BOOKS
An imprint of the University of Nebraska Press

Library of Congress Cataloging-in-Publication Data
Names: Longacre, Edward G., 1946– author.
Title: The sharpshooters: a history of the Ninth New Jersey Volunteer Infantry in the Civil War / Edward G. Longacre.
Description: Lincoln: Potomac Books, an imprint of the University of Nebraska Press, 2016. | Includes bibliographical references and index. | Description based on print version record and CIP data provided by publisher; resource not viewed.
Identifiers: LCCN 2016018626 (print) | LCCN 2016018247 (ebook) | ISBN 9781612348070 (cloth: alk. paper) | ISBN 9781612348834 (epub) | ISBN 9781612348841 (mobi) | ISBN 9781612348858 (pdf)
Subjects: LCSH: United States. Army. New Jersey Infantry Regiment, 9th (1861–1865) | New Jersey—History—Civil War, 1861–1865—Regimental histories. | United States—History—Civil War, 1861–1865—Regimental histories. | United States—History—Civil War, 1861–1865—Campaigns.
Classification: LCC E521.5 9th (print) | LCC E521.5 9th .L66 2016 (ebook) | DDC 973.7/3—dc23
LC record available at https://lccn.loc .gov/2016018626

Set in Minion by Westchester Publishing Services.

In memory of
John T. McNulty
(1926–2013)
Past Commander
Joel Searfoss Camp #273
and
Color Bearer Emeritus
Pennsylvania Department
Sons of Union Veterans of the Civil War

CONTENTS

ILLUSTRATIONS

ACKNOWLEDGMENTS

This book could not have been written without the assistance of various institutions and individuals, each deserving of my gratitude and thanks. Research material came from many sources, including the New Jersey State Archives, the New Jersey Historical Society, the libraries of Rutgers and Princeton Universities, the historical societies of Burlington and Hunterdon Counties, the Historical Society of Pennsylvania, and the Wilson Library of the University of North Carolina at Chapel Hill.

While I am indebted to the staffs of each of these repositories, I extend particular thanks to Albert C. King, Curator of Manuscripts, Special Collections and University Archives, Rutgers University Libraries, who expedited my search through the hundreds of regimental documents, principally soldiers' correspondence and diaries, contained in the library of the State University of New Jersey. Other persons offered equally valuable assistance. Joseph G. Bilby of Wall Township, New Jersey, a leading light of New Jersey Civil War studies, placed at my disposal a wealth of material gathered during his research for *"Remember You Are Jerseymen": A Military History of New Jersey Troops in the Civil War*, coauthored with the late William C. Goble and published in 1998. Gilbert V. "Skip" Riddle of Greenville, North Carolina, not only answered my numerous questions about the North Carolina area of operations but gave access to his compilation of contemporary newspaper articles pertaining to the Ninth's service in the Tar Heel State. John Kuhl of Pittstown, New Jersey, provided the majority of the illustrations from his vast collection of New Jersey Civil War documents and artifacts, as well as copies of the Andrew J. Little letters in the Hunterdon County Historical Society. Bradford Verter of Princeton, New Jersey, lent me copies of the Symmes H. Stillwell letters, excerpts of which were cited in Verter's illuminating article, "Disconsolations of a Jersey Muskrat," published in the *Princeton University Library Chronicle* for Winter 1997. Still others who rendered research assistance include Tom Ankner, Newark, New Jersey; Joseph M. "Marty" Boa, Tinton Falls, New Jersey; Brett Bondurant, Raleigh, North Carolina; Bill Godfrey, Hampton, Virginia; Willard B. Green, Carneys Point, New Jersey; Philip Koether, New York City; David Martin, Hightstown, New Jersey; John M. McNulty, Glenside, Pennsylvania; Laura Mosher of the United States Military Academy Library, West Point, New York; Tom Mullusky of the Gilder Lehrman Institute, New York City; and Steve Shaffer, New Bern, North Carolina.

It should go without saying that none of these persons is responsible for the themes, interpretations, or conclusions of the author.

INTRODUCTION

Civil War unit histories can provide invaluable insight into the dynamics of mid-nineteenth-century soldier life. The best examples of the genre convey to the reader what the fighting men, North and South, experienced, processed, and remembered: hunger, thirst, fatigue, sickness, physical and psychological pain, the comforts of comradeship, of being part of a corporate endeavor in a worthy cause; the alternating routine and chaos of military duty; the terrifying sights, sounds, and smells of combat. It takes time, however, to provide perspective, balance, and context to soldiers' reminiscences. Those histories written soon after war's end by the veterans themselves tended to produce a highly romanticized picture of regimental life and military service. Men known for their unsavory character or unsoldierly conduct were, in a sense, missing in action. The writers filled their pages, instead, with high-toned expressions of patriotism, vignettes of officers and men acting nobly in a noble cause, dramatic depictions of courage under fire, and poignant examples of hardships stoically endured in furtherance of national or sectional goals.

There were, of course, exceptions to this rule. These include the two published histories of the Ninth New Jersey Volunteers, compiled by former members of the regiment, Pvt. Hermann Everts in 1865 and Lt. J. Madison Drake, twenty-four years later. Both works, which contain an almost day-by-day account of regimental activities and a more or less complete roster of officers and men, are treasure troves of information for latter-day historians. Drake's much larger volume also includes copies of official reports, veterans' reminiscences, biographies of notable officers and men, and other pertinent material.[1]

Not surprisingly, the veteran-historians highlighted the military prowess of the Ninth and the virtues of its soldiers. Yet neither depicts the Ninth as a bastion of exemplary intent or pristine conduct. The authors are unusually candid in describing soldiers who ran amok, looting the property of army sutlers and enemy civilians—upon occasion, though usually by order, torching the homes of avowed secessionists. Everts and Drake hinted at a few officers and men who failed to measure up to the expectations of their comrades and their government. And they pulled few punches when characterizing members of the high command for whom the Ninth had little regard. For example, while the regiment applauded Ulysses S. Grant's rise to command of all the forces of the Union in the spring of 1864, it did not think much of the strategy he applied to those campaigns in which the Ninth participated and suffered heavily. When their corps came under command of William T. Sherman during the closing weeks of the war in North Carolina, the soldiers of the Ninth clearly preferred serving under "Uncle Billy."

But candor has its limits. Everts and Drake chose to overlook some of the more objectionable qualities and activities of those who followed the flag of the Ninth New Jersey through three years and ten months of arduous, debilitating, and often exasperating campaigning. They generally ignored the enlisted men who shirked duty, got drunk on a regular basis, and quarreled and fought with comrades over sundry matters. Nor did they identify the officers who administered needlessly harsh discipline, tended to their own comfort at the expense of their men, and hid behind trees during battle. Such traits characterized every body of fighting men, Union or Confederate. If Everts and Drake downplayed them it was undoubtedly due to a desire to avoid offending still-living comrades and to spare their families from chagrin and embarrassment.

A major theme missing from both works, although hinted at more than a few times, was the generally low opinion the men of the regiment entertained toward the enemy's people. They regarded the poorly clothed, poorly armed, underfed soldiers of the Confederacy as ragamuffins and scarecrows even as they praised their fighting spirit and combat performance. They were scarcely less disdainful of Southern civilians, most of whom they considered slovenly, dissipated, and dense. Yet these views paled in comparison to their distaste for the great majority of the African Americans they met in large numbers almost everywhere they were stationed.

Race prejudice was not the exclusive possession of the officers and men of the Ninth New Jersey. It could be found in every Union regiment, even those from New England, a wellspring of abolitionism and other liberal causes. Yet the Negrophobic attitudes of the Ninth were unusually consistent and the soldiers especially vocal in expressing them. Although they approved of the freemen and runaway slaves who provided enemy intelligence; sought employment as guides, teamsters, and officers' servants; and succored escaped prisoners, the regiment derided most black civilians as "pampered," "sassy," "fat, well-dressed and indolent," the undeserving beneficiaries of government-fostered "negroism." The black soldiers they encountered in the Carolinas and Virginia they denounced as poorly disciplined and skittish under fire, often a disgrace to the uniform they shared with their white comrades. For the unwanted presence of United States Colored Troops (USCT) they blamed Abraham Lincoln's Emancipation Proclamation. Referring to that document, a member of the Ninth declared that "there is scarcely a man in the ranks . . . who approved of it" and did not wish to see it rescinded. One member of the Ninth put it plainly in a letter published in a Newark newspaper a few weeks after the proclamation took effect: "Who ever heard of a Jersey man and a nigger living in harmony together?"[2]

The regiment's scorn peaked in early 1863, when it served under Maj. Gen. David Hunter, a Virginia-born abolitionist whose support of black troops antagonized the majority white soldiers of his Department of the South. When transferred to Virginia for the 1864 campaigns, the men of the Ninth gave only slightly more allegiance to Maj. Gen. Benjamin F. Butler, another prominent patron of black men in uniform. Late that summer, however, when the USCT began to shoulder a greater share of the combat burden and proved themselves to be competent soldiers and staunch fighters, regimental perceptions of their right to bear arms begin to moderate. Even so, numerous members of the rank-and-file clung to preconceived attitudes of African American inferiority.

This much said, Private Everts and Captain Drake were entirely justified in highlighting the valor and skill of the soldiers of the Ninth. Arguably the most distinguished of the forty regiments of infantry New Jersey contributed to the Union armies—the only one to reenlist, at the close of its three-year service term, for the duration of the conflict—the Ninth saw action in forty-two battles and engagements, lost 261 of its officers and men to combat wounds or disease, and marched or sailed some 7,600 miles through three states in the performance of its duties. Recruited as a sharpshooter unit and clothed in distinctive uniforms of green trim, the handpicked regiment is said to have outperformed in target competition a team from Berdan's Sharpshooters, the most celebrated marksmen in the Union ranks. In battle the Ninth's firepower took a heavy toll of every Confederate unit opposed to it. Present-day historians have characterized the regiment as "one of the most unique military units ever to serve under the state of New Jersey's banner," while lamenting that the story of "the outdoorsmen and target shooters of the Ninth . . . was largely lost to the general public during the war and afterward. . . . Then and now, they have always deserved better."[3]

One reason for the regiment's unjustified neglect is that it did most of its soldiering in North Carolina. The war in that department has long been overlooked; given its strategic influence on other, more well-publicized theaters of operations, it merits greater attention. As historian John G. Barrett has noted, Gen. Robert E. Lee's well-documented operations in Virginia "were controlled to a large extent by conditions in North Carolina. The historian's failure to record adequately the fighting in the Tar Heel state, therefore, has left incomplete the story not only of the conflict in North Carolina but of the larger war in the eastern theater."[4]

Well-publicized or not, the Ninth New Jersey distinguished itself almost as soon as it took the field as a member of Gen. Ambrose E. Burnside's expedition against the Carolina coast. In its first two battles—Roanoke Island (February 8, 1862) and New Bern (March 14)—the regiment attacked through waist-deep swamps considered impenetrable by the enemy and helped make the Confederates' position untenable. For its marked ability to simultaneously swim and fight the regiment won the enduring nickname "Jersey Muskrats."

Historical inattention can also be traced to the Ninth's later service in two other secondary theaters of operations: Charleston, South Carolina, in the spring of 1863, where naval blundering produced a failed attempt to capture that historic city, and Southside Virginia in mid-1864, where Butler's ill-starred Army of the James attempted to seize the enemy capital at Richmond. Under Butler's erratic leadership the regiment— now christened the Ninth New Jersey Veteran Volunteers—took part in a series of poorly conceived and mismanaged engagements. The deadliest of these took place at Drewry's Bluff, south of Richmond, on May 16, where the regiment was placed on the far right of its army, a mile from the banks of the James River. When thousands of Confederates bypassed the unanchored flank on that foggy morning, the Ninth was surrounded and overwhelmed. It suffered heavier casualties in this fight than in any other engagement. During the month of May alone it lost two officers and sixteen enlisted men killed in action, two officers and 153 men wounded (several mortally), and three officers and fifty-five men missing, most of them captured. The majority of the latter would die of disease or starvation at Andersonville and other prison camps in the Deep South.

After enduring the discomforts and hazards of life in the trenches at Cold Harbor and Petersburg, the Ninth was returned to North Carolina to recruit its strength. Brought back to fighting trim by an influx of recruits, substitutes, and a minimum of draftees, it served with consummate skill through the last eight months of the war. Generals who praised the Ninth as their "right arm" and "the flower" of their commands consistently gave it the post of greatest importance and danger during field movements and expeditions. By the time of its discharge in July 1865 the Ninth had fairly won its reputation as the most honored regiment New Jersey sent to the war. Its story deserves to be told again, in greater detail and broader context than in 1865 and 1889.

THE SHARPSHOOTERS

1   Attention Riflemen!

When the North mobilized for war in the spring of 1861, patriotic men from all corners of every loyal state rushed to their local recruiting offices. Yet New Jersey's initial response to the bombardment of Fort Sumter, the spark that set the nation ablaze, was decidedly uneven. On April 14, the day that the battered U.S. Army garrison in Charleston harbor surrendered to local attackers, unidentified citizens of Belvidere, the seat of rural Warren County, decorated their town with flags bearing the Palmetto emblem of South Carolina. The editor of the local newspaper, the *Warren Journal*, put his astonishment in bold print: "SECESSION IN BELVIDERE."

Whether a juvenile prank or a political statement, the banners were quickly torn down and the Stars and Stripes were raised, first over the county courthouse and then atop homes and business places throughout the town. Two days later Edward L. Campbell, a future officer in no fewer than three New Jersey regiments, began recruiting a militia company known as the Warren Guards. Before month's end rallies in support of the war effort were held throughout the county, and on the twenty-ninth the Warren Guards left Belvidere for a training camp in Trenton, the state capital. The company would later become a component of the state's Thirty-first Infantry Regiment.[1]

These pro-Union activities aside, Belvidere's early display of Southern sympathy suggested a statewide ambivalence toward the unfolding hostilities. Even the lowering of the U.S. flag over Fort Sumter did not silence a number of editors and politicians who blamed the Republican Party in general and Abraham Lincoln in particular, rather than the "fire-eaters" of the Deep South, for the coming of war. Most of the antiwar rhetoric emanated from the industrial centers of the North. The *Paterson Daily True Register* declared that "the contest . . . has been forced upon us by the Administration . . . and because it can terminate in no beneficial results, it is the more to be deplored." The *Newark Daily Journal* doubted that Republicans had the stomach to wage a war and the skill to prosecute it effectively. Three days after Sumter's fall the *Hunterdon County Democrat* wondered "whether New Jersey will consent to remain divided by the arbitrary lines of black Republicanism, or adopt a Constitution which as sacredly regards the rights of others as it protects her own."[2]

Fiery editorials in opposition to the Lincoln administration did not seem out of place in such a politically conservative orbit as New Jersey. By 1861 the state had become a bastion of Democratic Party influence, so much so that the Republicans had taken to calling themselves the Opposition—that is, in opposition to the majority party. With few exceptions, the results of the recent national and state elections had affirmed the Democratic ascendency. In the general election Lincoln had failed to win a majority of New Jersey's votes. He fared especially poorly in the northern counties, where Democrat candidates won three of five vacant seats. On the national level, the only Opposition victors hailed from South Jersey, where an antislavery Quaker heritage remained influential and liberal social and racial attitudes were relatively prevalent. The Opposition's candidate for governor, Charles S. Olden, a moderate Republican, had won office in Trenton but primarily because the Democrats had run a candidate with an unsavory personal reputation who alienated voters of every political persuasion.[3]

New Jersey's economy was a major factor in its political orientation. The state had long enjoyed close commercial ties to the South. For decades industrial centers such as Newark, Jersey City, and Paterson had supplied Southern markets with all manner of goods and services for farm and home (a famous saying held that the South "walked on Newark shoe leather"). Largely due to the Southern trade, so important to New Jersey's economy, at war's commencement prominent politicians including a former governor as well as the editors of newspapers in Newark and New Brunswick called for the state to ally itself with the Confederate States of America. If unwilling to take so drastic a step, New Jersey should stand alone, independent of both North and South.

Cultural and social ties also lent New Jersey a Southern perspective. Large numbers of Southern-born students matriculated each fall at the College of New Jersey (now Princeton University) and hundreds of Southerners vacationed every summer at the Jersey seashore. Confederate president Jefferson Davis's second wife was descended from a distinguished New Jersey family. Census records indicate that by 1860 the state was home to more than 6,000 native Southerners. As many as several hundred Jerseymen would serve in the armies of the Confederacy, while four natives or longtime residents of the state would become Confederate generals. Although present-day historians have effectively refuted earlier descriptions of New Jersey as the "northernmost border [slave] state," a small number of slaves toiled within its borders. Loopholes in the state's 1844 act that supposedly eradicated the institution meant that not until the Thirteenth Amendment became law in 1865 was slavery expressly prohibited in New Jersey. Little wonder that when the time came to proclaim one's allegiance, Jerseymen at first felt somewhat conflicted and torn.

But the period of indecisiveness was brief. War fervor has a way of uniting peoples of disparate views in a common cause. In the weeks and months following the events in Charleston, a large measure of political opposition to the war was swept away as Democrats and Republicans alike confronted a crisis of almost biblical proportions. By assaulting federal property and firing on the nation's flag, the South had forfeited much of the political capital she had stored up through decades of cooperation with the Democratic Party. The need to rally to the nation's defense silenced or at least muted much of the criticism aimed at Washington by the editors and politicians of North Jersey. In some cases this was the result of a true conversion to the cause of saving the Union; elsewhere it was brought on by compulsion and pangs of self-preservation. When a Unionist mob threatened to ransack the offices of Newark's nay-saying *Journal*, its editor quickly decided that the Lincoln government deserved his support, however conditional he might make it. Other antiadministration journals just as speedily altered their editorial slant, especially when it became clear that support of the true patriots who rushed to enlist led to increased readership.[4]

And rush they did. During the three and a half months between the war's opening shots and its first sizable land battle—First Bull Run (or First Manassas), on July 21—recruiting in New Jersey was a growth industry. In mid-April Lincoln called to the colors 75,000 militia to combat "combinations too powerful to be suppressed by the ordinary course of judicial proceedings." This was a patently inadequate number to coerce the South to return to the Union, but Lincoln's hands were tied by statutory restrictions. At this same time he called for a special session of Congress to meet on July 4 to lay the groundwork for a more realistic basis on which to wage war.

Along with almost every loyal state, New Jersey responded eagerly to Lincoln's call. Though its once-thriving militia system had been allowed to decay over the past decade and more, the state easily met its initial quota of four regiments of citizen-soldiers. Led by a militia stalwart from Newark, Brig. Gen. (of state troops) Theodore F. Runyon, this motley but eager aggregation of 3,000 left the state capital at Trenton for Washington DC on May 3.

Early-war enthusiasm was so strong that New Jersey's supply of soldier material far exceeded the demands placed on it by the War Department. Long after the militia departed, Trenton teemed with recruits for the "Jersey Blues" (a traditional name for the state's military forces, dating to the Revolutionary War). There were so many would-be warriors that when the government called for additional volunteers Governor Olden quickly formed three regiments of three-year men.

Before the end of June, following a perfunctory training period in Trenton, the First, Second, and Third New Jersey Volunteers were off for the nation's capital. Formed into a brigade along with a New York regiment under a former regular army officer, Col. William R. Montgomery, they were integrated with the state's four militia outfits and constituted a division under Runyon.[5]

Although Runyon's command was a part of the army that attacked the Confederate defenses at Bull Run, the poorly armed, indifferently trained division was fragmented to guard various depots and outposts well in rear of the battlefield. Only two of its components, the First and Second Volunteers, were called to the scene of fighting late on the day of the battle, by which time the defeated Federals were in full retreat. Although the First New Jersey stayed long enough to help cover the withdrawal, the Second turned about and without orders rushed back to Washington. Here was a most inauspicious start to New Jersey's effort to help save the Union.[6]

The debacle of July 21 cast a pall on state recruiting, as it did almost everywhere in the North. In the immediate aftermath of the battle Lincoln issued another call for volunteers. This time New Jersey's assessment—like the original quota, based on the state's population—was five regiments. By late September enough recruits had come forward to meet the quota. Some enlisted from patriotic motives, others to avail themselves of the bounties paid by the various counties and communities of the state. In some cases these bonuses amounted to more than one thousand dollars, paid in monthly amounts throughout a soldier's term of service. Yet whereas the First, Second, and Third New Jersey had gone to war at or close to their ordained strength of 1,000 officers and men, the Fourth through the Eighth Regiments numbered 900 men each, or slightly fewer. According to a recent wartime history of the state, "the burnished glory of arms had begun, ever so slightly, to tarnish."[7]

Because no large-scale engagements took place through the rest of the year to enable the Union forces to redeem themselves for Bull

Run, the apparent statewide decline in volunteerism might have been expected to continue. Instead, when the War Department on September 5 authorized the raising of additional regiments, New Jersey experienced an unexpected burst of patriotic enthusiasm. In contrast to the ten-company structure of the state's earlier organizations, the Ninth New Jersey Volunteer Infantry attracted enough volunteers to fill twelve companies. Here was an almost unheard-of anomaly, one that would not be resolved until November 1862 when the excess companies were disbanded, their officers discharged, and the enlisted men transferred to other units of the regiment that needed filling up.[8]

One reason for the wave of recruits was that from the outset the Ninth New Jersey was publicized and promoted as an elite organization, a regiment of skilled marksmen. Dating from Bunker Hill and the Battle of New Orleans, sharpshooters had held an honored place in the annals of American warfare. Their skill with the long arm enabled them to take an especially heavy toll of the enemy. At extreme distances they could decimate advancing troops, shattering their formations and, by picking off the officers, depleting their leadership. To honor their special prowess and enable them to blend in with terrain and foliage, sharpshooters wore distinctive uniforms of green. The envy of lesser mortals, they carried themselves with a proud bearing, one justified by their carefully honed expertise.

Even before recruiting for the Ninth formally got underway, rumors spread through the northern counties of the state that New Jersey was looking for skilled riflemen. On August 20 a notice in the *Newark Daily Mercury* announced the recruitment of a company of sharpshooters for attachment to "Colonel Berdan's Company." This was a reference to the imminent formation of what would become the most celebrated body of marksmen to participate in the war. The creation of Hiram Berdan, a mechanical engineer from New York acclaimed as the finest rifle-man in prewar America, the supposed "company" would evolve into a full-size regiment formally known as the First U.S. Sharpshooters. Composed of picked men from five states, dressed from head to toe in stylish green, Berdan's men would set the standard for crack shots in the ranks of the Union armies. The widespread publicity they attracted would spawn the raising of a second regiment of marksmen which, though smaller than the First and not commanded by Berdan himself, would benefit from its identification with him.[9]

Attentive to the powerful influence of the term, state officials, in raising the Ninth New Jersey, prevailed on the War Department to authorize its recruitment as a rifle regiment. On September 17 Charles Scranton of Warren County published a broadside headed "ATTEN-TION RIFLEMEN!," which solicited 101 men "to form a company of Sharp Shooters" for the Ninth Regiment. Scranton, a prominent member of Governor Olden's staff, sought men "between 18 and 36 years of age, medium height, all good marksmen." The company was to be headed by Capt. James S. Nevius of New Brunswick, whom Scranton had recommended highly to New Jersey's adjutant general (for unrecorded reasons, however, Nevius never commanded the unit). Two weeks after Scranton's appeal was published, Elias J. Drake of Newark, who would become captain of Company K of the Ninth, was appointed by state officials to raise a second company of sharpshooters "as a flank company" of the Ninth.[10]

The Ninth Regiment was recruited to a large extent from among the rural communities and coastal areas of the state, which abounded in experienced woodsmen and watermen. As J. Madison Drake commented, more so than the majority of Northern recruits, the men of the Ninth were "accustomed to the use of the rifle from boyhood." Company D, which drew from the wildfowlers and baymen of northern Ocean County, was especially blessed with good marksmen. Two other companies of the Ninth would consist of German-born target shooters from Newark, several of whom were veterans of European wars.

As soon as recruiters for the Ninth enlisted the requisite number of men, they were sent by train to Trenton where they commenced training. Thanks to the overflow of recruits, Camp Olden, on the outskirts of the city, quickly became a bustling place. The War Department had decreed that the outfit should be "ready for marching orders" within thirty days of rendezvousing in the state capital, which meant that the men would be something less than polished soldiers by the time they left Trenton for Washington. But there was no help for it; the war would not wait for them to learn more than the basics of military life. The balance of their education would consist of on-the-job training.

Looking back almost forty years later, historian Drake offered a pleasant, if perhaps overly poetical, description of the men who flocked to the regimental rendezvous in early September 1861. He recalled "bright-faced men, in the hey-day of youth," who had left "their happy homes on the mountains, as well as from hamlets embosomed in picturesque valleys, where freemen grow stalwart and their souls are fired with love of country. They came from the cabins which dot the sandy beach from Monmouth to Cape May . . . from cottages by the riverside, and among those artificial streams [that is, canals] by which commerce avoids the perils of our treacherous coast; from the lines of the railways which their sinewy arms assisted to construct; from the mines where ores were being delved to forge instruments of war; and . . . from college, office, workshop, mill and factory, determined to lend their best efforts in resisting the reckless men who were striving to subvert the nation's liberties."[11]

The first group of approximately 100 men, most of them German immigrants and second-generation German Americans—reached Camp Olden on September 13. That same day they were mustered into federal service by 1st Lt. Charles H. Brightly of the Fourth United States Infantry; logically enough, the unit was designated Company A. Its first commander, Capt. Frederick Rumpf, one of the European veterans, presumably had the support of the men under him, yet he would remain in command for less than three months before abruptly resigning his commission and leaving the regiment.[12]

If Rumpf lacked the wherewithal to shoulder the responsibilities required of him, the same could not be said of the camp's commander, Maj. Charles Adam Heckman. Pennsylvania-born, a resident of

Phillipsburg, New Jersey, and of German parentage (he spoke with a noticeable accent), Heckman had been handpicked for the job by the camp's namesake. Although not a professional soldier, he looked and behaved like one. The governor had been impressed by his military background, which included Mexican War experience as a sergeant in the celebrated Regiment of Voltigeurs (a French term for riflemen). During the earliest days of the present conflict Heckman had served as a company officer in the First Pennsylvania Volunteers. Between wars he had clerked in a hardware store and been a conductor on the Central Railroad of New Jersey. Heckman was also a dedicated musician; according to nineteenth-century New Jersey historian John Y. Foster, "his flute was scarcely less precious to him than his sword."[13]

The multitalented Heckman also possessed engineering experience that had enabled him to lay out and oversee the functioning of the regiment's training camp. Drake declared that "a better selection of commandant could not have been made." Drake believed that the distinguished record the Ninth would make was owing in large measure "to the excellent instruction received from the pains-taking major." A born leader and destined for higher command, Heckman quickly won the trust and respect of the rank and file, as much for his unceasing efforts to better the living conditions of his men as for his skill and bravery under fire.[14]

Heckman may have been the first field-grade officer to reach Camp Olden but within a fortnight he was subordinated to the newly commissioned colonel of the regiment, Joseph W. Allen. The newcomer was, like Heckman, a nonprofessional soldier. Unlike him, Allen had no military education or experience—in fact, he lacked military credentials of any kind. A benefactor of the all-too-prevalent process by which politically connected civilians were offered high rank in the army of 1861, the forty-nine-year-old Allen was a civil engineer from Bordentown, well known for managing railroads, water works, and other infrastructure projects. For six years he had represented Burlington County in the state senate and since the war began had been serving provisionally as New Jersey's quartermaster general. According to Drake, the colonel "possessed qualifications of a high order," but when in camp he "gave his attention to the equipping of the men, leaving the administration and instruction of the regiment to his able and indefatigable major."[15]

While fielding a dozen companies instead of the regulation ten, the Ninth was beset by another organizational anomaly: for the first four months of its service it lacked a second-in-command. Evidence suggests that Governor Olden intended to appoint as the regiment's lieutenant colonel 1st Lt. Richard Lodor of the Fourth United States Artillery, a West Point graduate with family ties to New Jersey. Olden considered the posting a mere formality, but for unknown reasons the army refused Lodor's request for a wartime transfer to the volunteer service. Not until early December would Major Heckman be promoted to fill the all-too-prominent vacancy. Since the men of the Ninth knew nothing of Lodor but to a man were convinced of Heckman's qualifications for the higher rank, they rejoiced over the turn of events that had surprised and chagrined the governor.[16]

The outfit was also pleased when, two months after Heckman's elevation, the Ninth's highly respected adjutant, Abram Zabriskie, a twenty-year-old lawyer from Jersey City, was commissioned major. One biographer notes that Zabriskie "was lineally descended from one of a family honored in Polish history. . . . The blood of the Huguenots and Hollanders also flowed in his veins. Contemplating the example, and imbibing the spirit, of an ancestry devoted to civil liberty, may have stimulated his devotion to his country when in peril."[17]

While the top echelon of the Ninth was being filled, its company-level officers received their commissions and reported to Camp Olden. As was the norm in hundreds of regiments North and South, many gained their positions through family and professional connections as well as from an ability to recruit a suitable number of enlisted men. On September 30 Colonel Scranton announced in a letter to Joseph Thompson, a judge of the Hunterdon and Somerset County courts, that Company H of the Ninth would be commanded by Scranton's brother-in-law Joseph J. Henry. Thanks to Scranton's high position, two of his close acquaintances, James Stewart and Joseph B. Lawrence, would be commissioned, respectively, first and second lieutenant of the company. Henry would lack enough of an opportunity to demonstrate his mettle, but Stewart and Lawrence would prove to be two of the most capable officers the Ninth ever knew.

In the same missive Scranton assured his correspondent that the latter's son, Augustus Thompson, was also officer material, but he recommended that the young man join the quickly filling ranks of Company H as its second or third sergeant. Scranton made a point of declaring that in choosing officers for the Ninth, "we are paying special attention to having men of good moral character in every respect." Since young Thompson fit that description, and because he had personally persuaded several men to accompany him to Camp Olden, he was not compelled to wait his turn. In mid-October Capt. William B. Curlis of Pennington, commanding Company F, welcomed Thompson into the ranks of his unit and saw to it that he was appointed its first lieutenant. The arrangement by which these men, none of whom had prior military experience, obtained positions of rank and responsibility may seem haphazard and perhaps also detrimental to military efficiency. Even so, Thompson too would prove himself an able officer, respected for his leadership in camp as well as in battle.[18]

At the outset, before the boredom of routine and the drudgery of near-constant drilling began to sap morale, life at Camp Olden was a pleasant experience for a majority of its inhabitants. Colonel Allen's background as quartermaster enabled him to keep the regiment well-equipped, while the state authorities ensured that its rations were abundant. J. Madison Drake, now a sergeant in Company K, assured the readers of his hometown newspaper, the *New Jersey Journal* of Elizabeth, that he and his comrades "have more food than we can possibly eat—all of which is of the best quality." He added heroically that "there is no grumbling" at Camp Olden, "and the boys, determined to let the world wag as it will, endeavor to make themselves comfortable, and are resolved to do their duty." It would appear, however, that not every member of the regiment felt comfortable, especially when rations were not distributed in a timely manner. In mid-October Pvt. David C. Hankins of Company D petitioned his sister in Burlington to send him a few dollars, apparently to purchase victuals from a source outside camp. Not only had the regiment yet to be paid, "the dam butcher hant bin here to day."[19]

Drake took pains to describe the regiment's rations as good, presumably meaning both nutritious and tasty. At least one comrade testified to this. Writing to his mother in early November, Corp. Symmes H. Stillwell of Company M, a twenty-one-year-old native of Cranbury, described a visit by friends from neighboring Princeton: "They enjoyed themselves very much and was very much taken with a soldgers dinner." Even so, most men agreed that there was a certain dreary sameness to the daily fare, whether in camp or, later, in the field. In both venues the soldiers' diet relied heavily on such unexciting staples as dried beef and dried pork, a few "desiccated" (dehydrated) vegetables, and a bread ration known as hardtack, all washed down with copious amounts of coffee. Hardtack was one culinary item that engraved itself in the psyche, memory, and humor of the soldiers. Veterans would never forget the strength required to masticate the notoriously thick cracker. It came in boxes marked "B. C." for "Bureau of the Commissary," but men swore that was the time period it had been baked. As it frequently became infested with weevils, hardtack came to be known as "worm castles." Some wag recommended that it be consumed only at night to avoid close inspection of the contents.[20]

The handiest alternative to unpalatable rations was the sutler, a civilian merchant licensed to travel with and sell to the army. Too many sutlers were notorious for charging exorbitant prices and, for cash-strapped customers, usurious interest rates. They profited from supplementing government fare with such gastronomic luxuries as apricot pies and lobster salads, though many did much better by selling liquor to enlisted men in violation of army regulations. While most regiments were assigned a single sutler, two purveyors, both from Burlington County, were initially licensed to sell to the Ninth New Jersey. Although Messrs. J. B. Forker and A. M. Tilton and their successor, Walter Fuller, appear to have dealt fairly enough with the men of the Ninth to win their approval, the same could not be said of those who replaced them in later months. One of these sought to make a 300 percent profit from his wares, only to pay an even higher price for his greed.[21]

Although it took a few weeks for complete uniforms to be issued, the Ninth New Jersey was fully clothed by early October. The regiment's ensemble no doubt disappointed those recruits who had expected to be garbed from head to toe in sharpshooter green à la Berdan's men. Instead, the Ninth wore the standard dark blue tunics and sky-blue pantaloons of the volunteer army. Distinctive green coloring, however, was visible on the seams of the enlisted men's uniforms, on the shoulder straps of the officers, and on the chevrons of sergeants and corporals. Another unusual addition to every man's uniform was a pair of brass shoulder scales. The men would quickly discard these relics of the prewar army, supposedly effective at warding off saber blows but obsolete and uncomfortable.[22]

Camp life was enlivened not only by visits from friends and family members but by the appearance of citizens and soldiers with a vested interest in organizing and equipping the regiment and placing it in the field as expeditiously as possible. State and local political officials and, upon occasion, officers from the War Department came to confer with Colonel Allen and Major Heckman. At the same time, patrons of the regiment from all over the state arrived at Camp Olden bringing gifts. Various organizations and individuals donated, or pledged to donate, such nonstandard equipment as rubber blankets to ward off rain and frost and mittens to prevent marksmen's hands from the numbing cold. The blankets arrived in sufficient quantity to supply almost the entire regiment but only after Captain Henry publicly scolded "the good people" of Warren County who had been slow to redeem their pledge. "The nights have been freezing cold for a month past," Henry informed the editor of a Belvidere newspaper on November 16, "and the men have but a blanket apiece. Besides we have had driving rain storms which are the most disagreeable of all the different varieties of bad weather and during which our guards are exposed to all their fury on the open plain both by day and by night."[23]

The mittens, the gift of a privately staffed soldiers' aid society and delivered by "four-horse load[s] of very pretty girls," were not late in coming but were found to be several sizes too large for most of the men. They did not, however, go to waste; many were large enough to be worn on the soldiers' heads as they slept in their chilly tents. Another piece of headgear—and a fashion statement of some note—made an espe- cially popular gift at this early stage of the war. This was the havelock, a strip of cloth which, when fastened to a soldier's cap, shielded his neck from the sun and wind. It was a thoughtful gesture, but because many men considered the havelock a cumbersome appendage that stimulated perspiration and accumulated dirt, it never caught on with the regiment.[24]

Benefactors including the Young Men's Christian Association donated reading material of both a religious and a secular nature. Members of the grand lodge of the Odd Fellows of Newark brought various other gifts and were rewarded by being allowed to attend one of the Ninth's evening parades. Highly impressed by the spectacle, the Noble Grand declared that he "had never before looked upon a more robust or patriotic body of young men." A beaming Colonel Allen "thanked the distinguished gentlemen for their visit as well as for the kind words uttered."[25]

One especially popular event was the arrival of citizens bearing battle flags that had been purchased or hand-sewn for presentation to the various companies of the Ninth. These banners were intended to supplement the regimental and state colors every New Jersey regiment received from Trenton. Two of the most memorable presentations occurred in November when the men of Company K received a flag donated by the citizens of Elizabeth and Company F accepted an especially colorful banner from a Mercer County delegation headed by the Reverend George Hale of Pennington. Kindly intent was behind these donations, though the gestures were misplaced. As Sergeant Drake noted, "shortly afterwards we found we had no more use for the flag[s] than for the mittens, as a regiment is permitted to carry but two colors, and they were provided by the state. But we took everything that was offered, even if we had to throw the articles away after reaching the field of action."[26]

Flags would go a long way toward sustaining regimental morale, but the firearms to be issued to the Ninth were critical to its performance in battle and skirmish. It appears that a number of enlisted men brought their own rifles with them when they entered the army, for by early October, before the regiment was fully armed, several members of the Ninth were testing their proficiency during a shooting competition held in an open field in rear of a Somerset County hotel. Weeks would pass before government-issued arms reached Camp Olden. By month's end the governor was informing Secretary of War Simon Cameron that although the regiment was well along to being fully organized, it lacked weaponry of any type. "Requisition for arms has been made some two weeks since," Olden reported, "but they have not been received." War Department assistance was imperative, for the state's coffers were running perilously low. At Olden's behest Colonel Scranton had written directly to President Lincoln to request relief. Scranton lamented that, having already raised nine regiments for federal service including five apportioned to the state less than three months ago, "we are about broke," although "no state has worked harder to fill her quota than New Jersey."[27]

Lincoln and Cameron sympathized with the plight of the Ninth New Jersey, but hundreds of regiments across the North were clamoring to be armed from the finite supply of rifles at the War Department's disposal. Eventually the Ninth received a shipment of Belgian-made muskets, part of a cache of modestly priced arms that government purveyors had located in Europe and bought up in quantity (some 60,000 Belgian arms would be purchased by war's end). From the start the Ninth found this antiquated shoulder arm—a flintlock converted to the percussion ignition system—"cumbersome and unreliable." Its gravest deficiency was that, being a smoothbore, it had a maximum effective range of only 200 yards. Even so, it was no less serviceable than the majority of the weapons available to the War Department at this period. Of the 500,000 shoulder arms stored in federal and state arsenals at war's outset, 400,000 were 69-caliber smoothbores. Most of the regiments, North and South, that went to war in 1861 carried these less-than-impressive tools of war.

An obsolete musket was hardly the proper armament for an outfit that had been recruited as a team of dead shots. Fearing that the men's morale as well as their expertise would suffer for want of a better fire-arm, Major Heckman, with the support of Colonel Allen, urged the governor to pressure the War Department to arm the Ninth, instead, with the rifle. This arm benefited from the bullet-steadying influence imparted by the spiral grooves carved inside its barrel. Loaded with a soft-lead 58-caliber "minie ball," whose hollow base expanded upon firing to grip the rifling, a so-called rifle-musket could be effective at distances of 600 yards or more from the target. In the minds of the regiment's crack marksmen, this was more like it.[28]

Eventually the combined efforts of officers and governor paid dividends. At first it was rumored that the Ninth would be allowed to exchange their muskets for British-made Enfield rifles, large quantities of which were being purchased by Northern and Southern arms merchants. Reportedly, by mid-November a shipment of these long-range rifles, to be allocated to the Ninth, had been stored at the Bridesburg Arsenal in the suburbs of Philadelphia. However, the weapons never found their way to Camp Olden.[29]

Less than a month before it was transferred to Washington for field service, the Ninth received the shoulder arm it craved. For some weeks state officials, with the rather lukewarm support of Secretary Cameron, had been gnawing away at the reluctance of the army's chief of ordnance, Brig. Gen. James Wolfe Ripley, to release to volunteer outfits the Model 1861 Springfield Rifle, then in relatively short supply. For the Ninth success came in late November when more than a thousand stand arrived in Trenton. Sergeant Drake reported that "officers and men were delighted at the change of arms, and when the regiment appeared on dress parade for the first time with the new and handsome rifle, a feeling of intense pride took possession of all—the glistening of the bright barrels in the setting November sun adding to the general joy."

The regiment immediately tested the new weapon. A target range was set up in camp, rounds were fired, and scores were tallied. Having been accustomed to use of the rifle from boyhood, erstwhile deer and duck hunters regularly struck the bull's eye at distances of up to 500 yards. The Ninth's general proficiency was in sharp contrast to the dearth of shooting experience among the majority of recruits from the Mid-Atlantic states. It would pay dividends in the months ahead, when human targets took the place of forest animals and water fowl.[30]

The regiment grew by leaps and bounds, with a particular spurt in mid-autumn. By the first week in October it numbered only 700 officers and men but little more than a week later, upon the muster in of its twelfth company, the Ninth neared its peak strength of 1,159. Some companies exceeded their mandated strength of 100 by more than 30 percent. Only five weeks after its first company was sworn into federal service, the regiment was more than strong enough to take its rightful place in the field.

Throughout that period there had been "no relaxation from duty" at Camp Olden. Strict adherence to regulations served to keep it that way. Corporal Stillwell, who for a time served as sergeant of the camp guard, noted that recruits were prohibited from leaving the premises for longer than forty-eight hours and that no more than five men could be gone at one time. Passes signed by the officer of the guard and probably countersigned by Colonel Allen were required for leave-taking. Although this practice was more or less rigidly enforced, the craftier and more nimble soldiers managed to evade it, usually by prevailing on Stillwell's men to look the other way when they took off. On October 18 no fewer than twenty members of Capt. Cornelius W. Castner's Company B managed to slip away for some unauthorized socializing at home. All returned quickly enough once Colonel Allen branded them as deserters and released their names to the local newspapers.[31]

At least one member of the Ninth committed crimes of a much graver nature. Early in November one "W. J.," otherwise unidentified, was ceremoniously drummed out of camp for what Sergeant Drake called "conduct unbecoming an American soldier." He described the unique event in dramatic detail: "The regiment was formed on the parade-ground. . . . In a moment the ranks were opened, and the front rank faced to the rear, when an ear-piercing fife and a couple of drums, heard on the left of the line, announced that the doleful ceremony had commenced. The prisoner, with shaved head, pinioned arms and downcast look, marched between files of men carrying their rifles in an inverted manner so that he was encircled with bayonets. Not a sound broke the stillness of the beautiful forenoon, save the strains of the musicians who played the 'Rogue's march' with astonishing vigor. As the fellow passed the men in either rank fastened their eyes upon him, but none looked with pity—all believing that he merited the signal disgrace, and that the command was better off without him. As he passed out of camp at the guardhouse a number of hoodlums from Trenton saluted the recreant with contemptuous cries." Drake added that "never again was it found necessary to carry out such a sentence in the Ninth regiment."[32]

W. J.'s comrades were kept too busy to entertain thoughts of committing similar offenses and sharing his fate. Drill, at both the regimental and company level, consumed several hours of every day. To increase the men's stamina Major Heckman led them on excursions far from camp, one being a three-mile hike to the village of Sandtown on November 13.

The men were frequently drawn up on the camp's parade ground for reviews and inspections. The day before the hike to Sandtown Colonel Allen assembled the Ninth to celebrate a Union victory in South Carolina, the capture of Port Royal Harbor and Hilton Head Island by an army-navy force under Brig. Gen. Thomas West Sherman and Flag Off. Samuel F. Du Pont. The gaining of this strategic foothold between Charleston and Savannah prompted "several national airs" from the Ninth's embryonic band and the firing of signal-guns. To this martial accompaniment more than a thousand soldiers "rent the air with cheers."[33]

Other regimental events provided excitement for the local citizenry. As reported in the *State Gazette* and *Republican* of Trenton, on November 20 a group of civilian teamsters employed by the Ninth "made quite a display—all turning out with their teams and driving through the streets" under the direction of the wagon master, Isaac W. Eayre. "Then came an ambulance drawn by two horses, each containing a trumpeter . . . followed by two hospital wagons drawn by four horses each; then came a two horse ambulance and three ambulance carts each drawn by one horse. Then came the heavy four horse baggage wagons, ten in number. The horses were all large, strong, fine-looking animals, and everything about the men, horses and wagons was in the best order. The 'parade' attracted very general attention."[34]

Unwilling to be outperformed by the hired help, two weeks after the teamsters made conspicuous display the officers and men of the Ninth paraded as a body through the city. Recalling the event almost thirty years later, Sergeant Drake described the event as "a spectacle . . . that has had no parallel since. No such body of men had ever before been banded together in New Jersey, and when company after company with perfect precision filed past, the populace had nothing but favorable comment and genuine applause." Drake noted that the regiment was accompanied part of the way by a company of home guards assigned to the state arsenal. At some point the regiment accelerated its march, leaving their escorts far behind, whereupon the affronted guardsmen returned to their barracks. Drake added that "the 'slight,' as the militia-men afterwards called it, was never forgotten by the heroic men who sacrificed so much for their country by serving a few weeks at the arsenal."[35]

Two days after the parade, the men of the Ninth awoke to the blar-ing of bugles. They downed a Spartan breakfast of coffee and hardtack, then packed their belongings and struck their tents. In the cold, murky dawn of December 4 they shuffled into line and answered roll call. After enduring vexatious but unexplained delays, they commenced a slow march to the train that would carry them to the nation's capital. Many considered the movement weeks overdue. As early as November 17 Camp Olden had been alive with rumors of an impending mass departure. By then the luster of soldiering had been worn off by weeks of dull routine and strenuous labor, and as a whole the outfit was "in great glee at the prospect of soon leaving" Trenton behind. The leave-taking had been scheduled for the twenty-first before being delayed for another two weeks by the late arrival of enough rifles to arm all twelve companies. When December came in, everyone from Colonel Allen down to the lowliest private was nearly frantic to get to the scene of active duty—or so they claimed in their letters to family members and friends.[36]

The regiment's trip to Washington was a long one; so too was its mode of conveyance. Three trains of passenger, box, and flat cars on the Camden and Amboy Railroad were required to accommodate the men of the Ninth as well as twenty-five supply wagons, five ambulances, and eighty officers' horses. Despite the early hour and the raw weather, hundreds of well-wishers—local citizens as well as family members who had traveled to Trenton from outlying points to see their loved ones off—were at the depot to wave and shout farewell. "As the cars moved away," Drake remarked, "bells were rung, whistles blown, hand-kerchiefs waved and cheers given." To this raucous accompaniment the forty-four officers and 1,115 enlisted men of the Ninth New Jersey Volunteers began their long-deferred journey to Camden, Philadelphia, Baltimore, Washington—and war.[37]

2   Down to the Sea in Troopships

The Ninth's southbound odyssey got off to an unpropitious start when, a short distance outside Trenton, one of the trains "run off the tract," as Pvt. Hankins put it, although the accident "dident hurt any body." It did, however, keep the steam-powered caravan from making good time toward its final destination. Once moving again, the trains wound through familiar venues including Bordentown and Burlington, where neighbors of Colonel Allen had gathered to bid him farewell as the lead train rumbled past. None would have supposed that the sight of him waving from the rear of his passenger coach would be the last they would ever see of him.[1]

From Burlington the railroad veered southwest to Camden on the Delaware River opposite Philadelphia. Arriving there near sundown, hours later than expected, groups of soldiers were laboriously ferried across the river by steamboat. The regiment's first stop outside its home state was at the Cooper Shop Volunteer Refreshment Saloon, a soldiers' rest that patriotic Philadelphians had established opposite the Washington Street wharf to refresh the troops heading for Washington from points north and east. In operation for only a few weeks, the saloon had already succored thousands of fresh-faced recruits eager to reach their new campgrounds on the Potomac.[2]

The Ninth's arrival drew mixed reviews from the local media and the citizenry. One of the city's leading newspapers applauded its coming: "The men looked finely, as though amply fed and cared for, and are just that kind of material that the rebels will most have occasion to avoid." Yet not every resident hailed the Ninth so warmly. As the regiment marched through cobblestone streets to the Cooper Shop, it was greeted with hoots and curses and called "a pack of thugs, thieves and other 'nice' names." Even so, as a Jerseyman wrote, at the saloon "we had a fine supper—one that a soldier don't get every day."[3]

Having eaten, rested, and availed themselves of toilet facilities, the men regained their stacked arms and were marched through the dark streets of the lower city to the intersection of Broad and Prime Streets. At the depot of the Philadelphia, Wilmington and Baltimore Railroad, they boarded the train that would carry them to a city that on April 19 had witnessed a bloody clash between soldiers bound for Washington and a pro-secessionist mob of civilians. Lurid stories of the "Baltimore riots" were fresh in the minds of the officers and men of the Ninth as they traveled southward, at only a few miles per hour, through the early morning hours of December 5. To the relief of everyone, when at 9 a.m. the train reached the city's President Street Station, vocal supporters of the government were the only citizens on hand to welcome it. As the regiment, flags flying and band playing, trudged a mile or more through the city to the Camden Street Station of the Baltimore and Ohio (B&O) Railroad, it was cheered by well-wishers who, "no matter from what cause, vied with each other in welcoming the defenders of the national government." Curiously, it seemed that the farther south the regiment went, the more cordial its greeting.[4]

There was no refreshment saloon in Baltimore but there were plenty of vendors hawking sweetmeats, pies, cakes, and other delicacies. When they reached the B&O depot the men experienced a long delay in returning to the cars. To keep them in a positive frame of mind they were permitted to break ranks and purchase whatever they desired. This they were able to do because the Ninth had answered its first pay call only days before leaving Trenton. According to an enlisted man from Belvidere, the nongovernment fare "came very acceptable, for we were hungry just about that time," and they had no wish to resort to the soldier's morning fare of hardtack and coffee.[5]

At noon the men reassembled and finally boarded the down train, many of whose cars reeked of sheep recently hauled to market. If the trip to Baltimore had been slow, the pace of the Washington leg was glacial. Not until 2 p.m. did the train begin to move, and it seemed to stop at a crossing every five minutes or so. The "dreary all-night ride" did not cease until daylight on Friday, the sixth. By now the passengers were in the poorest spirits, most having found it impossible to sleep thanks to the stinking, unheated cars, the ear-splitting noises emitted by an aged, overworked engine, and the jouncing and jostling produced by rickety tracks and an absence of shock-absorbing springs. The men were placed in no better spirits when, upon alighting from the coaches, they were marched through streets mired in mud and jammed with troops. They finally perked up when they reached the local Soldier's Rest. Sgt. Drake recalled that the regiment took "great satisfaction" from the accommodations they found there, especially the "cheering blazing fires" that helped relieve the bone-numbing chill they had been enduring for so many hours.

At about one in the afternoon, the final leg of the Ninth's journey got under way, a two-mile march through downtown Washington and then out the northeast quadrant of the District of Columbia. The arduous hike finally ended in an open field along the turnpike to Bladensburg, Maryland, where a camp had been laid out for the new arrivals. The bleakness of the venue was disheartening: no standing tents or roaring fires greeted the cold, weary newcomers. Still, everyone prepared to make the best of the primitive conditions, the first of many they would endure in the years ahead. They stacked arms, unslung knapsacks, and settled in as best they could. "We were almost as comfortably situated as at Camp Olden," Drake boasted heroically. "True, we had no straw with which to fill our [bed] ticks, but readily adapting ourselves to the situation, procured an abundance of dried leaves on which we reposed with satisfaction and genuine pleasure, sleeping as tranquilly as though our beds were composed of down."

The sergeant admitted, however, that when buglers awoke the regiment "bright and early" on December 7 the men "answered roll call in no very cheerful frame of mind, being cold and quite stiff in the joints." For many, the stiffness was a prelude to years of suffering from rheumatoid arthritis. One so affected was Pvt. Noah Jeffrey of Company D, who dated the onset of his arthritic condition from this very week. Like numerous comrades who suffered the same fate during their war service, however, Jeffrey would faithfully complete his three-year enlistment with the Ninth.[6]

Although tired and achy, the men set to work pitching tents, erecting supply facilities, and building a guardhouse to confine recalcitrants and truants—the first occupants being those few who refused to labor alongside their comrades. Within a day or two, Camp Allen (per custom, named in honor of the regimental commander) began to assume at least a semipermanent appearance. Soon the officers were taking up their duty as tactical instructors. The most conspicuous and energetic was the Ninth's new lieutenant colonel, Major Heckman having been promoted to fill that anomalous vacancy the day before the regiment left Trenton.[7]

Heckman's old position was promptly filled, but it was not an in-house promotion. The new major was James Wilson, formerly the senior company commander of the Second New Jersey Volunteers, an outfit already on duty in northern Virginia. Although details are sketchy, the fact that Wilson came to the Ninth from another regiment suggests that he was a political appointee. This may have explained why the Ninth failed to welcome him with open arms and instead considered him "unfitted for active campaigning."

Wilson's principal disqualification appears to have been physical in nature; Sergeant Drake described him as "rotund," claiming that the man tipped the scales at nearly 300 pounds. It may be that the sergeant was exaggerating, for an officer that portly would have had a difficult time finding a horse able to carry him comfortably. Drake added that Wilson had a reputation as a "thorough company drill-master," but from the day he took charge of tactical instruction he made little impression on regimental proficiency. This was so, Drake wrote, because by the time they reached Washington the men of the Ninth had already mastered the basic infantry tactics of the day as set forth in a number of drill manuals published or authorized by the War Department. This, too, seems an exaggeration, for the instruction provided at Trenton over a nine-week period would not have qualified the Ninth as tactically astute. It is true, however, that the regiment had drilled often enough to acquire a distinctive "long swinging step" that would characterize it throughout the war.[8]

Drake claimed that the lessons the men of the Ninth were taught came from the tactics manual compiled by Brig. Gen. Silas Casey, who happened to command the sector of the Washington defenses that included Camp Allen. However, Casey's *Tactics* was not made available to the Union recruits until 1862. As for the effectiveness of the work, basically a translation of a French manual, present-day historians note that although widely consulted by the army throughout the war it added little to existing tactical theory.[9]

If some considered Major Wilson an inadequate instructor, Colonel Allen was even less prepared to supervise the men. Within days of the Ninth's arrival in the capital, the colonel found himself commanding not only his own troops but also three New York regiments whose camps adjoined the Ninth's. Neither experience nor ability qualified the former state senator for brigade command, but it devolved upon him because he was senior to the New York colonels by date of commission.

While Allen's ascension was a misguided effort in conformance with army customs and regulations, the Ninth flourished under the sure hand of his ranking subordinate. Camp discipline tightened up noticeably on Heckman's watch. "We were kept strictly within the limits of the camp," Drake noted, "neither officers [n]or men being allowed to leave." Some Jerseymen, especially those who would have enjoyed sightseeing in the capital, considered the restrictions excessive. The semiliterate Pvt. Hankins, who wished to visit the city in order to have his "likeness" taken by a local photographer, informed his sister that "we cant get a pass [to leave camp] even to go out after a cantean of water let alone going to Washington." Since the dawn of American warfare, new recruits, unwilling to admit they had forfeited the prerogatives of free men by signing their enlistment papers, had complained bitterly of being confined to a military compound like so many felons. As had the many thousands of soldiers who had preceded them, this latest generation of citizen-soldiers would soon learn to accept their fate, but the process would take time and generate the customary amount of grumbling.[10]

Lieutenant Colonel Heckman had helped lay out the regiment's campsite, situated on what Pvt. Albert R. Thomas of Company F called "a beautiful hill" about two miles northeast of the capital. The eminence afforded the regiment "a fine view of the surrounding country," including Washington City, Georgetown farther to the west, and, on the south side of the Potomac, Arlington Heights. But the pleasant vista was available for little more than a week. On a mid-December morning the Ninth was ordered to pass in review before General Casey, his staff, and a bevy of government officials. After two hours of scrubbing dirt from coats, pants, and shoes, the Ninth was marched to Meridian Hill, a remote location in the northwest sector of the District where a training facility known as Camp Cameron had been established. There a dozen other regiments—all of them units of Casey's division—had already assembled.[11]

A dramatic sight met the regiment's eyes on Meridian Hill. "But few in the Ninth had ever seen so many troops in line," wrote Sergeant Drake, "which made the spectacle all the more brilliant and wonderful to them." The Ninth did its best to appear worthy of so grand an event. With pride the sergeant observed that "no command in that host was so strong as the Ninth, and as it passed in review . . . a buzz of admiration was heard among the staff and the hundreds who had gathered to see this magnificent sight."[12]

One of the more prominent spectators was Gen. Ambrose E. Burnside. A celebrated participant of Bull Run, the handsomely bewhiskered brigadier was on the verge of receiving authority to lead an expedition to sever Confederate communications along the coast of North Carolina, and he was looking for seaworthy outfits to add to his command. By all accounts, Burnside was impressed by the size and poise of the Ninth as it passed the reviewing post he shared with General Casey. Soon after the review Burnside made personal application to add the Ninth—so many of whose recruits had lived and worked on the water—to his U.S. Army Coast Division. Other attendees at the review, reporters from the big-city newspapers of the North, also took note of the Ninth. In their dispatches they commented not only on the size of the regiment but on its evident proficiency at drill.[13]

When the review was over the men returned to their camp along the turnpike, exhilarated by the favorable impression they believed they had made on every spectator. When in subsequent days rumors of a permanent movement began to circulate, the Ninth supposed it was on the verge of crossing the Potomac, testimony to its readiness for field campaigning. Almost daily since the regiment's arrival in Washington, the sounds of cannon and sometimes of musketry had wafted up from the south side of the river, suggesting a need for additional combat troops in that sector. The real reason for the upcoming move, however, related to regimental health. A polluted stream was the principal source of water along the Bladensburg Pike, and on its hilltop perch the regiment was subjected daily to cutting winds and snow showers. Thus far only one-quarter of the regiment had been supplied with rubber blankets for protection from the weather. According to Private Hankins, within two weeks after reaching Washington 200 members of the Ninth had come down sick; every day several were relieved from guard and sent to the camp hospital. Hankins had been told by the Ninth's chief surgeon, Dr. Frederick S. Weller, that "if we dident move we would all dy [die]."[14]

When orders to pack up arrived on the nineteenth, the outfit broke camp with a sense of excitement and anticipation, only to be disappointed when the route of march led back to Meridian Hill. There it took over the camp of one of General Casey's regiments that had relocated to Virginia—apparently, other troops were deemed more prepared to occupy the war zone than the Ninth. The men took pride, however, that during the movement, which took them through downtown Washington, they were "smilingly observed" by a distinguished spectator. According to Sergeant Drake, President Lincoln had specifically requested to view the regiment that had attracted so much attention during the recent review.[15]

At first the Ninth's new campsite—located near Columbian College on even higher ground than the old—appeared a pleasant place, one in keeping with the temporarily "delightful weather." But conditions deteriorated rapidly when a raging storm struck the area on the nineteenth and continued for two days. By the twenty-second the rain had turned to snow and the camp was, in Hankins's words, "a very wet place," with mud "about nee deep." Even so, Hankins considered Camp Cameron, which the Ninth shared with as many as 9,000 other troops, a better location than the old one. For one thing, "we have plenty to eat," portable stoves having been moved inside the men's tents to ward off the cold as well as to prepare meals. Then, too, new uniforms would soon be on hand to replace the rather shoddy attire the soldiers had been issued at Trenton.[16]

More than one of Hankins's comrades agreed with his assessment of affairs. A homesick recruit from Company F, James Van Fleet, found life on Meridian Hill "a great deal better . . . than I though[t] it would, but I would like to have been home." So too would Zachariah Hankins, the cousin of David Hankins, who from another camp outside Washington expressed in a letter to David's sister a desire he undoubtedly shared with many members of the Ninth: "I wish we had some Jersey girls here to sleigh ride with. It has been so long since I saw a girl that I think it would do my eyes good to see one, and more yet to hug her head well." Yet even a life so far from home had its compensations. Pvt. John Nymaster of Company F insisted that "down hear we have good times. We have plenty to eat, plenty to ware."[17]

Nymaster was quick to add that there was also "plenty driling to do" at Camp Cameron. Weather permitting, such exercise was a daily and, at times, an hourly chore. When not on the drill plain the men kept their target eye sharp with regular rifle practice. The results—the bull's-eye hit squarely and consistently at distances of up to 500 yards— were so impressive they soon caught the attention of observers from neighboring units. Supposedly the publicity the Jerseymen attracted led to a competition with Berdan's Sharpshooters, whose camp on Meridian Hill sat adjacent to the Ninth's.

There are two versions of what happened next—neither is verifiable but each seems credible enough to invite acceptance, at least by the men of the Ninth and their loyal supporters. According to an account incorporated into Drake's history, the officers of the Ninth challenged Berdan's best marksmen to a target shoot, but the green-clad riflemen, fearing an embarrassing outcome, declined. According to other sources including the *State Gazette and Republican* of Trenton, the challenge "was accepted, and the match to a trial of skill took place, resulting in the victory of the Ninth." Wherever the truth lies, the anecdote served as a long-lived testimony to the Ninth's facility with shoulder arms. On numerous occasions over the next three and a half years its men would prove themselves eminently worthy of this reputation.[18]

On at least one occasion daily drill was interrupted by a somber ceremony, one new to the regiment but with which it would become all too familiar. One day after the Ninth spent its first Christmas of the war—a quiet, introspective occasion, with only the camp guards on duty—regimental drill came to a sudden halt at the shouted command of Lieutenant Colonel Heckman. Seconds later came "a piercing fife and muffled drums, followed by a small company of soldiers, [who] approached with measured tread." No advance word of the funeral procession had been received, but without missing a beat Heckman had the men present arms to honor the fallen soldier. Sergeant Drake observed that "it was by such thoughtful acts that the men had learned to love the commandant, whose constant aim was to win their esteem and confidence."

The holiday season seemed to call for additional displays of military pageantry, for on December 28 the Ninth again joined the other regiments in Casey's division for a gala inspection. The event was followed by another march through the heart of Washington, "to the joy and satisfaction of thousands who lined the wide thoroughfares," although whether the spectators included the president is not known. Two days later yet another such exhibition, this on a smaller scale, impelled General Casey's inspector general to praise the clothing, arms, and equipment of the Ninth. The event sent the camp abuzz with rumors: "Knowing ones in the regiment" claimed that active campaigning usually followed closely on the heels of inspections and reviews. These and other reports of an impending transfer to the south side of the Potomac stirred the hopes of many men too young or too naïve to contemplate the consequences of such a movement.[19]

Portents of one kind or another were there for all who had the keenness to perceive them. During the night of the thirtieth, a military stable half a mile from the Ninth's camp caught fire. Private Nymaster reported that of a lot of 1,000 officers' and cavalry horses, some 220 perished in the flames. Those animals that escaped bolted in panic through the capital's streets. It took several hours to round them up, and for some time afterward anxiety gripped the seat of government, as if in anticipation of additional calamities.[20]

The city was still on edge two days later when the new year came in with a bang—a cannonade at midnight from the forts on Arlington Heights. Providing sweeter accompaniment—a program of "patriotic airs"—were the brass bands of several of the outfits at Camp Cameron. The concert went on for a half hour or more before ceasing to allow the men the sleep they needed. The concert makers included ten musicians of the Ninth New Jersey under the baton of bandmaster Peter Gahm. For the next eight months they would accompany the regiment on active campaigning. During combat they would lay aside their horns and fifes to assist the Ninth's medical staff, most often as litter-bearers. Their services would be dispensed with in August 1862, one month after Congress repealed the law authorizing bands to be attached to every Union regiment. In early 1864, however, the band would be reconstituted on an unofficial basis, its instruments being furnished through the largess of Abram Zabriskie, then colonel of the Ninth. Under the direction of Pvt. Gottlieb Hoyer, a German-born professional musician from Newark, it would accompany the regiment until dissolved in June 1865.[21]

Not only music greeted the new year in the camp of the Ninth New Jersey. Prayer meetings were held in the officers' mess tent. Perhaps as a result of the regiment's recent exposure to the military funeral rite, these were well attended. It was said that many of those on hand "implored the Redeemer to inspire them with a firm determination to love and serve Him while life endured." The local weather had moderated considerably (Pvt. Henry Cook of Company K considered January 1 the "warmest New Year I ever seen"), but the only activity in camp was an afternoon dress parade. The men spent the remainder of the day visiting the other occupants of Meridian Hill, including members of a unique organization, the Sixth Pennsylvania Cavalry. The Philadelphia regiment had gone to war armed not with rifles or carbines but with a spear, eight and a half feet in length—a relic of wars past that, although unwieldy and unsuited to latter-day campaigning, fostered a sense of elitism in its bearer. The visitors were suitably impressed by the quaint instruments. To a man, however, they preferred shooting their enemy at long distance to striving to impale them at close quarters.[22]

Drill resumed on January 2. At first the men maneuvered while toting only their rifles; later they toiled under full knapsacks. On the third the regiment was mustered for pay for the first time in the field.

Each private soldier received two months' pay, twenty-six dollars. The majority of the pay was slipped inside the letters the men sent home via military agents. Henry Cook noted that he and his father, James, also a member of Company K, entrusted a combined total of forty dollars to be carried to New Jersey by the state agent, Col. Jonathan Cook (no relation to them). Men without loved ones to support were promptly relieved of their earnings by comrades more proficient in games of chance, especially draw poker.[23]

Orders read during dress parade on January 3 informed the regiment that it was no longer attached to General Casey's command. Along with three outfits from Massachusetts, New York, and Pennsylvania, it was now part of the brigade of Brig. Gen. Jesse Lee Reno, a West Pointer with fifteen years' experience in the regular army. Born in western Virginia and reared in Pennsylvania, Reno had received two brevet promotions for gallantry during the Mexican War. He had already gained an enviable reputation in the volunteer army. The Ninth would come to view him as a fair and considerate man as well as a dependable leader in combat.[24]

More "welcome news" was received a few days later: Reno's troops would form part of the expedition being outfitted for service in North Carolina under Ambrose Burnside. The army's contingent, to be towed south by transports, would be supported by a formidable array of navy craft, the same combination that had reaped rewards at Hatteras Inlet. Burnside's initial effort was the defeat of the enemy garrison on Roanoke Island, followed by the seizing of strategic points on the Neuse and Pamlico Rivers including the communications hub and deepwater port of Beaufort. This was only the latest in a series of army-navy strikes at the Carolina coast. It would follow not only the Port Royal expedition but also the October capture of Forts Hatteras and Clark on the Outer Banks of North Carolina by an army command under Maj. Gen. Benjamin F. Butler and a naval force led by Cdr. Silas H. Stringham. Though ultimately successful, both operations had experienced major difficulties, but Burnside's project would top them in terms of dangers encountered and hardships endured.[25]

At 8 a.m. on the fourth, the Ninth struck camp for the third time in its brief existence. Buffeted by bitter winds and a snow storm that made everyone increasingly miserable, the regiment trudged back through the streets of the capital. At the B&O depot they boarded cars that, while providing minimal warmth, at least shielded the men from the weather Sergeant Drake called "colder than any we had experienced" since leaving Jersey.

By noon the train had reached Annapolis, the jumping-off point for Burnside's expedition. That city at the mouth of the Severn River served not only as Maryland's capital but as the home of the United States Naval Academy, yet it failed to impress its unwilling visitors. To Sergeant Drake it was "a dingy town." Henry Cook considered it "a poor looking city." To their dismay, they would linger here far longer than anyone expected. The transports assigned to carry the Ninth and the rest of Burnside's troops down the Atlantic coast would not be on hand until the following day, and they would not be casting off any time soon.

Most of the men spent that evening aboard the cars, although Companies F and K sought refuge in the Naval Academy barracks. The building was vacant, the student body having been relocated at war's start to Newport, Rhode Island, but apparently no bunks were available, for the men of Capt. Curlis and Drake were forced to sleep on the bare floor. Everyone was achy and ill-tempered when roused from sleep in the predawn darkness of January 5, but at least the snow had ceased.

Marched down to the local docks, the men noticed that many of the stores in town, especially the saloons, were closed and the premises under guard. They learned that the previous night a soldier from a Massachusetts regiment had been killed during a round of drunken horseplay in one of the city's ubiquitous oyster bars; afterward Burnside had shuttered every establishment that might invite repetition of the incident. Fortunately, some members of the Ninth were granted liberty to shop in the stores that remained open. Men with cash loaded themselves down with all manner of paraphernalia, much of it neither useful nor convenient for a march.[26]

Later in the day the Ninth learned that it would be the first unit in Burnside's 15,000-man command to shove off for North Carolina. Given the regiment's size, no one transport was large enough to accommodate it; thus Colonel Allen loaded the outfit's right wing—Companies A, C, D, E, H, I, and M—aboard the *Ann E. Thompson*. Allen, Lieutenant Colonel Heckman, and most of the regimental staff accompanied this contingent. A few hours later the other companies were herded aboard the brigantine *Dragoon* under the supervision of Major Wilson. The men expected to get under way momentarily, but it turned out that no ship would set sail until all the others in the army's flotilla—almost eighty, all told—were ready to leave. Since it was the first to board, the Ninth would have the longest wait. When the men heard the news, the corporate mood nosedived.[27]

The limited space available aboard ship, and how that space was allocated, was yet another detriment to morale. Still new to soldiering, the men had yet to accept military custom, which among other things accorded certain privileges to the officers. While the latter lounged in furnished staterooms, most of the men were confined to the ships' holds. There was precious little room for sleeping, and to find it often required the most strenuous contortions.

Not until the snowy morning of the sixth were the ships carrying the troops of the Ninth unmoored and towed out of the harbor and into the Severn. By now everyone was tired, frustrated, and hungry. According to Henry Cook, almost every passenger on the *Dragoon* was complaining about the daily ration, which consisted of a "sea biscuit, piece of pork, and cup [of] coffee." Early that evening the noncombat dangers of a soldier's life came vividly to mind when a wayward steam lighter crossed the path of a rowboat returning to shore from a ship in the harbor. The ensuing collision sank the troop-laden boat. The prompt actions of another steamer managed to rescue all but one occupant, who would be officially listed as killed in the line of duty but not "in action."[28]

The complaining only increased during the next two days, for the transports remained stationary throughout the eighth, when the last contingent boarded its ship. Floating about listlessly under cold skies and intermittent rain and snow was enough to try the patience of even the most Job-like soldier. Fortune smiled on only a few, to whom shore leave was granted. On the seventh a famished Henry Cook climbed into a lighter that deposited him back in Annapolis, which he found still "full [of] soldiers, some drunk." After patronizing a local eatery, he took another boat back to the fleet, where he visited some of his comrades aboard the *Thompson*. The following day Cook returned again to shore but only briefly. Upon returning he learned that some of his companions on the *Dragoon* had evaded Burnside's restrictions to secure liquor and smuggle it aboard ship.[29]

On the eighth, with the flotilla apparently ready to weigh anchor, the commanding general climbed aboard the steamer *George Peabody*, only to relocate at the last minute to the smallest craft in his command, a propeller-driven gunboat. Burnside's most recent biographer theorizes that he did so to show the men that he could rough it with the best of them, thus fostering "both courage and confidence by personal example." Both commodities would be needed en route to the fleet's destination, for several of the ships were reported to be something less than fully seaworthy and rough weather was building on the horizon. The following day the general occupied a surf boat and was rowed about so that the men aboard every transport could see and cheer him. The men of the Ninth heartily joined in the huzzas for their chieftain, who at this early stage of the war represented the cream of Union leadership.[30]

To the relief of everyone involved, the grand expedition finally weighed anchor on the rainy morning of the ninth. As the *Dragoon* steamed out into Chesapeake Bay, Henry Cook not-so-fondly "bid good by[e] to Annapolis." Though it was a "splendid sight to see the fleet under way," the southward journey proved to be anything but splendid, defined as it was by fits and starts. By the morning of the tenth the fleet had anchored to wait out a dense fog. As of 1 p.m. the sky was clear enough to start again, and by sundown the Ninth's ships were within sight of "grim-visaged" Fortress Monroe at the tip of the Virginia Peninsula, one of only two U.S. Army installations in the South with a Union garrison. By 7 p.m. on the tenth the ships were anchoring for the night just off the Old Point Comfort Lighthouse.[31]

The well-strung-out flotilla, which Sergeant Drake compared to a "huge anaconda," lay off the masonry stronghold during the eleventh. The next day it got under steam and started out into the broad Atlantic toward Hatteras Inlet and, farther south, works that remained in enemy hands. By mid-afternoon the Ninth's vessels were passing the Cape Hatteras lighthouse. Early that evening they dropped anchor alongside what remained of a side-wheeler that had met an unhappy fate on the local shoals. By then the surf, ominously choppy, was heralding a coming squall. Soon the transports were bobbing about like corks in a tub. On the *Ann E. Thompson* the men of the right wing were pitched from one side of the hold to another. Symmes Stillwell wrote that "we had to anchor about 2 miles out [to sea] for fear of being stove to pieces." Seasickness kept Henry Cook and many of his comrades on the *Dragoon* up all night. Even had they been able to keep down an evening meal, there was "nothing to eat but biscuits, fat slimy pork, and coffee." In fact, throughout the voyage rations were so scarce that angry soldiers broke into the ships' galleys to steal flour, molasses, sugar, and other provisions, which they shared with equally famished comrades.[32]

If the twelfth was an ordeal, the next two days were a horror for every unwilling seaman. "Blowing a perfect gale," wrote Henry Cook on the fourteenth. Barely able to scratch out a diary entry, he reported himself "very, very, very sea sick, cant eat anything, cant vomit." At times he felt so wretched that he would "just as leave die." The weather not only created hardship and suffering but posed both an immediate and a constant threat to the safety of the flotilla. So too did the fact that many of the ships drew too much water to ensure a safe passage through the barrier islands into Pamlico Sound, the primary route to Roanoke Island. The most daunting obstacle was the narrow channel through the sandbank that separated the sound from Hatteras Inlet. The shoal-topped bar at the mouth of the channel and the "swash," a crooked waterway a mile or so inside the inlet, ran about eight feet deep; most of Burnside's troop-crammed vessels drew ten feet or more.[33]

The navy's contingent was in better condition to overcome these hazards. When the transports and supply ships left Fort Monroe, Flag Off. Louis M. Goldsborough had moved south from his fleet's rendezvous in Hampton Roads. Goldsborough, one of the navy's most experienced officers, was commanding the largest aggregation of warships ever seen in the western hemisphere. These included twenty ships from Goldsborough's North Atlantic Blockading Squadron, mounting a total of sixty-two guns; nine light-draught gunboats; and five floating batteries. Eight more gunboats were waiting to link with him off Hatteras.

The navy sailed under sealed orders; twenty miles out of Hampton Roads these were opened and Goldsborough's subordinates learned that "your first point of attack will be Roanoke Island and its dependencies." The objective was highly valuable to the invading forces. Approximately twelve miles long and three miles across, Roanoke nestled between the North Carolina mainland and Nags Head on the 200-mile chain of barrier islands known as the Outer Banks. The land mass (home to the "Lost Colony" of English settlers who had vanished without a trace almost 300 years ago) dominated the sea approaches to strategic Albemarle Sound and blocked entrance to the Chowan and Roanoke Rivers. With the island in his possession, Burnside could move inland via these waterways to threaten the enemy's railroad link to Virginia as well as the communications hub at Norfolk. A Union presence on Roanoke would also bar the enemy from attempting to recapture the forts at Hatteras Inlet.[34]

Throughout the fourteenth, the weather had its way with Burnside's transports including those carrying the men of the Ninth, lying at anchor some three miles outside Hatteras Inlet. As Sergeant Drake put it, "the gale continued with increasing violence, the cold wind howling fiercely, as it hurled the sea mountains high, tossing our gallant vessels with precious cargoes in a manner adapted to incite the fears of the most intrepid." More than a few Jerseymen feared they would share the fate of that luckless Massachusetts soldier, killed before getting into combat.[35]

On the morning of the fifteenth the wind abated, but only briefly. Fearing that his ships would need help clearing the bar, Colonel Allen seized the opportunity to report the regiment's situation to Burnside, who along with his staff had reached dry land. Accompanied by Lieutenant Colonel Heckman, Adjutant Zabriskie, Surgeon Weller, Quartermaster Samuel Keys, the captain of the *Ann E. Thompson*, and a crew of six, Allen climbed into a boat; soon the party was being rowed through the breakers to shore. Reporting at expeditionary headquarters, where he also found General Reno, Allen announced the proximity of the Ninth and sought help to have it towed into the anchorage.

It is not known what level of assistance was promised but by noon Allen's party had started back to the *Thompson*. The surf was running dangerously high, but after some difficulty the rowboat reached deep water and the passengers believed they were "out of all danger." Then, about a half mile from shore, the party encountered angry breakers. Their boat withstood several waves, but one struck so suddenly and with so much force that everyone was tossed overboard. "Scattered hither and thither," most fought their way back to the vessel, which they found overturned. Some clung desperately to the hull; others flailed about in the water with nothing to hold on to.

Of the Ninth's officers, Allen, Heckman, and Zabriskie were considered good swimmers. The adjutant was the strongest of the three, having demonstrated as much during an excursion to the bathing beach at Long Branch, New Jersey, in the summer of 1860 when he saved his sister from a riptide that had carried her far from shore—two would-be rescuers died in the same attempt. Although Zabriskie was described as possessing "quick, cool discernment," he did not expect to survive this latest predicament. As he wrote to his father two days later, "Our condition was perfectly hopeless. As for myself I had no idea, whatever, of being saved."

Some of the others had even less of a chance. Allen, weighted down by a tight-fitting uniform including a coat made of India rubber, soon exhausted himself. At length he called out to his subordinates: "I cannot stand this much longer—take care of yourselves!" Despite the efforts of Zabriskie to hold Allen's head above water ("I could not do it long"), the colonel was soon floating face down in the surf. Minutes later the adjutant heard Dr. Weller gasp, "Oh, I am gone!" Before the surgeon could sink Zabriskie grabbed him and managed to manhandled him onto the overturned boat, but then "a wave broke over us . . . and threw us off, and that was the last I saw of the poor Doctor alive." Along with the ship's second mate, who also disappeared below the waves, Allen and Weller became the first fatalities of the Burnside expedition upon reaching North Carolina.

For a time it appeared that there would be additional casualties. "After tossing about this way nearly an hour," Zabriskie wrote, "our strength perfectly exhausted, yelling all the while to some schooners in the offing, though hopeless of being heard, we were at last picked up by the boats of the United States schooner 'Highlander,' which was being towed inside the inlet by a tug boat." The rescued soldiers and sailors eventually recovered from their ordeal, though in Heckman's case recuperation was slow and uncertain.[36]

The fate of Allen and Weller cast "a general gloom" over the officers and men of the Ninth, who considered their unexpected demise "a great loss." Allen may not have been a military man in the strict sense of the term, but he had taken care of the men, ensuring that they received adequate food and clothing as well as effective firearms. Dr. Weller, who had been the impetus for moving the Ninth's first camp in Washington to a healthier location, had won the trust and respect of everyone he ministered to. Their bodies and that of the drowned seaman were recovered late that same afternoon. The following day, "enwrapped in canvas, completely coated with tar and sand" and escorted by a detachment of Company B, they were rowed to shore through calmer waters for temporary interment on Hatteras Island. Afterward Captain Castner led his men of Company B in a brief funeral service.[37]

A few days later, a delegation of the officers aboard the *Ann E. Thompson* convened a shipboard meeting to put into writing their reactions to their colleagues' deaths. The gathering produced a series of resolutions that expressed "the deep sympathies of soldiers and friends" toward "the sad fate which has deprived us of their services and friendship. . . . They have left to their children noble names, and a fame in which they may be proud." Copies of the resolutions were sent to the families of the deceased, to Governor Olden's office, and to the editors of the state's major newspapers.[38]

The following month the bodies of Allen and Weller were exhumed and, accompanied by the Ninth's chaplain, Reverend Thomas Drumm, were returned by ship to New Jersey. At Trenton their flag-wrapped coffins were conveyed to the state capitol through streets lined with bowed heads and doffed hats, a militia regiment serving as an escort. Placed in repose in the senate chamber, the remains were viewed by thousands of citizens including family members and friends of the Ninth's soldiers. After properly solemn rites, the bodies of colonel and surgeon were transported by rail to Bordentown and Paterson, respectively, for interment.[39]

Soon after recovering from his near-drowning, Heckman would be promoted to fill Allen's position. Assistant Surgeon Lewis Braun took over Weller's duties but he remained with the regiment for only two months before resigning his commission. Soon reports had Braun being replaced by a civilian surgeon, Dr. J. R. Riggs of Paterson, but Riggs declined the appointment. In a move more acceptable to the regiment, on February 8 Assistant Surgeon Addison W. Woodhull was promoted to succeed Weller. Although he would not join the regiment until mid-March, Woodhull would serve ably in that capacity for the next three years, assisted by Drs. Fidelio B. Gillette and John M. Davies. The care the surgeons displayed toward their patients would be validated by results. Service in a venue replete with swamps, thickets, and miasmic vegetation would impair regimental health from time to time. Even so, the Ninth New Jersey would fare better than the majority of those regiments relegated to years of service in coastal North Carolina.[40]

Hard on the heels of suffering their first casualties, the Ninth New Jersey faced a series of ordeals that tried the souls of officers and men as never before or afterward. By January 16 both the *Dragoon* and *Ann E. Thompson* were still being buffeted by dangerous winds and a violent surf miles from the security of the harbor inside Hatteras Inlet. Many of those aboard *Dragoon* had lost faith in the ability of their captain to negotiate a path to safety. Late that day, however, rescue appeared in the guise of the steamer *Patuxent*. Although experiencing much difficulty in breasting the tossing waves, her crew managed to attach a hawser to the struggling brig. By dusk the *Patuxent*, bobbing wildly, had slipped over the bar into Pamlico Sound, but when *Dragoon* reached the whitecaps in advance of the inlet a mighty wave lifted the vessel into the air and slammed her against the sandy bottom of the ocean. The force of the blow not only split the hawser but snapped the *Dragoon*'s masts and side ribs. If she remained on the bottom the brig would be torn apart by the churning sea. With *Patuxent* out of sight and night coming on, the left wing of the Ninth, including future historian Drake, keenly felt the "terrors of our situation."

The imperiled passengers had to think and act quickly, and they did so. Under the direction of 1st Sgt. Thomas W. Burnett the men of Company B assembled forward of the main deck, loaded their rifles, and unleashed nine volleys. It took an hour ("it seemed like an age" to those aboard) before the firing attracted the attention of comrades on land. At once army headquarters sent Burnside's own vessel to the rescue. Upon nearing the *Dragoon*, the general himself was seen clinging to a rope ladder on her starboard side, shouting encouragement to the brig's passengers. Eventually another hawser was attached and the transport towed back across the bar into deep water. When far enough out to make another attempt, the ship was steered back toward the harbor. This time she passed the breakers and reached smooth water. Pvt. John Clark of Company F, writing in his hometown newspaper in Somerset County, described the mood of the left wing during the barely averted crisis: "Although soldiers are generally called hard cases, I tell you there were many very penitent ones among us when we found ourselves in this predicament, and they continued so until aid arrived." Henry Cook had a different perspective on the regimental response: "Officers were much excited while on the bar," he wrote in his diary. "Men behaved well."[41]

A few days after the *Dragoon* reached safe haven, the *Thompson*, carrying the larger portion of the Ninth, endured her own trial by fire—literally. Early on the eighteenth the transport remained well out in the ocean, "tossed like a chip upon the maddened waves." Around noon one of the breakers heaved from its fastenings a stove in the galley of the forward deck, spilling hot coals on the woodwork and igniting a fire that a greasy floor carried into the ship's hold. Believing the entire ship to be on fire and lacking an exit from the flames, the passengers panicked. Men tried to reach the upper deck by climbing on the shoulders of those crushed beneath them. The "shouting, swearing, and praying" continued for several minutes until the fire on deck was brought under control.[42]

As if this near catastrophe was insufficient to jangle nerves, it became evident that the *Thompson* was too heavily laden to cross the bar. She would have to be lightened by dumping ballast, including excess cargo. The task of directing the operation fell to Sgt. Charles Hufty of Company D, a Camden resident and Bull Run veteran. Two or three days were given over to tossing overboard everything that could be dispensed with—extra rigging, bars of pig iron, and more than eight tons of provisions. By discarding excess weight, however, the *Thompson* invited other dangers. As Corporal Stillwell remarked in a letter home, the troopship sat atop "a sandy bottom and our anchor would not take any hold but kept dragging about. . . . We knowed if we went ashore our vessel would be smashed to pieces and the men drowned in the rageing surf and we knowed if we went to sea the vessel would shurely capsize because there was no ballast to hold it down."[43]

By the morning of the twenty-first the *Thompson*'s captain feared that the pounding waves would soon destroy his ship. They had already torn apart one transport, whose passengers had been saved through a last-minute transfer to a more sturdy vessel. Then, too, a supply ship had sunk with the loss of 100 horses. When the *Thompson*'s skipper signaled his ship's distress to shore, Burnside's headquarters again responded by sending a "huge steamer" to the rescue. By noon a hawser had been attached to the *Thompson* and both ships were heading for the inlet. As on the eighteenth the rescue ship made it safely into deep water but the vessel in her charge did not. As Corporal Stillwell wrote, the towing rope parted and the ship stuck fast on the bar, "thumping and pitching and rolling and . . . crac[k]ing, we expecting to be smashed every moment."[44]

In fact the surf was less damaging this day, but from her precarious perch the *Thompson* continued to endure the brunt of the sea for hours until additional help came. Unlike three days earlier when the *Dragoon*'s rescue ship effectively abandoned her, the steamer that had hauled the *Thompson* onto the bar returned with a new hawser. Once the usual difficulties were overcome the rope was attached, and after one unsuccessful attempt the transport was finally hauled into the harbor. Although the Ninth had yet to set foot on solid ground, through the quick thinking and heroic efforts of the men themselves and their army and navy comrades, the regiment had been spared from a watery grave. Now at last it would have the opportunity to add its weight to an important effort ashore.[45]

3 Jersey Muskrats

The mettle the Ninth displayed during its recent crises was not confined to those aboard the *Dragoon* and *Ann E. Thompson*. Ten days after the latter was pulled to safety, Corp. Samuel J. Dilks of Company K, recently detached from the regiment, rejoined it at Hatteras. Because Dilks had been assigned to duty aboard the *Pocahontas*, the supply ship that had been lost during the gale of the thirteenth and fourteenth, his comrades had despaired of seeing him again. Not only had Dilks saved himself when his ship went down, he had saved every other passenger. The vessel had lost engine power, and lacked intact lifeboats. As it was being swept toward the rock-strewn shore, Dilks proposed to swim to the beach with a line attached to his waist. Divesting himself of overcoat and brogans, he plunged into the surf and by paddling furiously managed to reach dry ground. He had just enough energy left to tie the end of the rope to a stake which he sank into the ground. The line enabled him to grasp a hawser that was run out from the steamer, which he fastened to the ground on the end of an old but sturdy spar. Once the hawser was secured, the *Pocahontas'* crew tightened it until it could bear their weight. One by one they hauled themselves across the water via the rope bridge. Almost miraculously, every man made it through the breakers, "although the passage was far from being safe or pleasant."

But not every crewmember escaped that way. When the wind died down cries of help could be heard coming from the listing ship. Dilks was informed that one person was still aboard, and in great peril—the ship's cook, an elderly black woman. No one else was willing to return to the vessel to save her, so Dilks, who had recovered the strength his recent labors had cost him, pledged to "bring her to the shore, or sink with her." The rescued crewmen tried to dissuade him, believing the effort to be suicidal; in her panic the cook would surely drag both of them down.

Dilks refused to listen. Grabbing the hawser with one hand, he paddled back through the waves with the other. Displaying the same vigorous effort he had demonstrated in swimming to shore, he reached the supply ship and found the stranded woman. At first, fearing that she would drown, she refused to accompany him through the raging waves. Dilks "thought the woman ungrateful; but, ungrateful or not, he was determined that she should go back with him." Snatching up a piece of rope, he strapped the cook to his back and jumped with her into the heavy surf. The return trip was difficult in the extreme, but the pair made enough progress that when halfway to safety some of the crewmen swam out to help them the rest of the way. Finally deposited safely on the beach the cook, once she caught her breath, loudly and repeatedly thanked God and her rescuer for her deliverance.

Dilks's daring and selfless act demonstrated that, no matter the attitude of some of his comrades toward people of color, not every member of the Ninth was a bigot, even by the rigid standards of twenty-first-century American society. As Sgt. Drake noted, the corporal's heroics "formed the theme of conversation around many a camp-fire for years afterward." Dilks's later service was no less worthy of admiration. He served through the war with his company, "being foremost in battle—never shirking duty, however unpleasant or dangerous." He survived to return to his home on the Jersey shore where for years afterward, fittingly, he had charge of a government life-saving station. In that capacity he assisted in the rescue of many endangered swimmers but none of them under such perilous conditions as when saving the storm-lashed crew of the *Pocahontas*.[1]

Even with its ships ensconced inside Hatteras, there were obstacles to overcome before the Ninth New Jersey could set foot on solid ground.

By January 19 Flag Officer Goldsborough's fleet, with the exception of one gunboat that had sunk after running afoul of her anchor, had passed safely into Pamlico Sound prior to turning north to assault the western flank of Roanoke Island. It took two more weeks, however, to get the army's transports and supply vessels across the swash and into position for a land attack. Throughout that period the troops were kept aboard ship. Most were confined to the hold, which emitted what Henry Cook called an "awful stench" that threatened to sicken every passenger.

Stomachs as well as nostrils suffered throughout the enforced layover. Even inside the inlet the churning waves produced seasickness, but those who could force down food had little to digest. The niggardly ration that had plagued the regiment since leaving Annapolis continued to generate complaints. The men were lucky to receive a single meal per day, and the diet ran heavily to salt pork, crackers, and coffee. At exorbitant prices they could buy additional rations from civilian crewmen including a "detestible negro cook" who offered meat and fruit pies baked in the *Dragoon*'s galley along with a dubious mixture of crackers, water, and sugar passed off as pudding. The men became more restless and listless than ever, and there were few means of escape from the corporate misery. Private Cook fumed that anyone caught playing cards to pass the time was punished more or less severely. When his card game was broken up one of the sergeants cursed his company commander and immediately lost a stripe.[2]

The severest hardship was the scarcity of good drinking water. The destructive weather had influenced Burnside to send his several water-supply ships far out to sea. For weeks they were not readily accessible to the transports, whose water tanks quickly ran dry. The water shortage soon became critical throughout the fleet, and the problem was felt no more keenly than aboard the *Ann E. Thompson* and *Dragoon*. Angry at being issued only a half pint per man per day, those aboard the latter ship began to accuse Major Wilson of deliberately withholding the water. According to Cook, the major and the other officers got "good and plenty water" while the enlisted men were reduced to catching rainwater as it ran off the ship's rigging and forecastle. By some means Wilson's alleged dereliction was brought to the attention of General Reno, who threatened to report him to Burnside unless he increased the daily ration. "From that [time] out," Cook reported, water was available "in abundance."[3]

Yet it was not always fit to consume. Once the *Dragoon*'s three water tanks were refilled and the men began to drink, the substance was found to have a nasty taste; Cook and his comrades held their noses as they consumed it. This was bad enough, but strands of variously colored hair began to turn up in cupful after cupful. One of the enlisted men determined to find the source of the filament. Climbing to the top of the most accessible tank, he inspected its contents by the light of a sulfur match, then called for a pail and scooped up enough to make a thorough survey. Descending to the deck, he refused to allow anyone to view the result until the assistant surgeon was on hand. Dr. Braun arrived, inspected the bucket, and exclaimed: "Yes, boys, those are pieces of dead rats. . . . It's a wonder you are not all sick."

Further investigation revealed that before the ship left Annapolis a multitude of rodents had crawled into the empty tanks only to drown when they were filled. It is not known whether any member of the left wing fell ill from drinking the polluted water (although some may have been sickened to learn what they had drunk). Nor is it known whether those aboard the *Thompson* or the other ships in Burnside's fleet were similarly affected. It is a fact, however, that at least on the *Dragoon* the water ration thereafter improved. A crew from Company B was sent ashore each day, returning with enough potable water to supply passengers and crew throughout the length of their stay aboard ship.[4]

In the last days of January the volatile weather at Hatteras moderated enough to pass Burnside's vessels through the swash and into Croatan Sound, the body of water that separates Roanoke Island from the North Carolina mainland. On the twenty-seventh some of the few tugboats in Burnside's armada attempted to tow *Dragoon* over the swash. To improve the chances of success, the entire left wing was taken off the ship and placed aboard the tugs. But it was of no avail; the tide was not high enough to float the brig, even with her reduced draft, over the vexing obstacle, so the men returned to the ship. The next day the tugs reappeared and the process was repeated. This attempt also failed, even as General Burnside came alongside in his flagship to urge the tugs to further effort. Finally, on January 30 the passenger-laden tugs pulled the brig through the swash.[5]

The remainder of the Ninth New Jersey was not towed across the inner bar until February 5 and then only after several failed efforts. Some of those aboard the *Thompson* had to change ship no fewer than three times. On January 31 the seven companies were transferred to a familiar craft, the steamer *Patuxent*, and then, for some reason, to the transport *George Peabody*. Because the latter was already loaded down with soldiers and baggage, the Jerseymen endured severely cramped conditions until February 1, when Companies D and I were offloaded onto the schooner *George A. Smith*. Not till the fifth was *Dragoon* safely inside Croatan Sound. By then the men were writing home to warn their families of the falsehoods some New York newspapers were printing. These included a report, probably inspired by news of the deaths of Allen and Weller, that due to some catastrophic accident the entire regiment had been dumped into the ocean and drowned.[6]

As if the men of the Ninth had not endured enough adversity en route to battle, sixty of them were cheated, as they believed, out of money lawfully owed them. All were experienced sailors with a knowledge of the duties required of active-duty seamen. For that reason they were detailed to alleviate a shortage of gunboat crewmen. All appeared pleased with the transfer, especially as it came with the promise of additional pay. For unspecified reasons, however, the money was withheld. The plight of the quasi-seamen does not appear to have evoked sympathy from comrades who, lacking their nautical skills, would be confined to duty on land—once they finally got off their swaying, reeking transports. As Sergeant Drake noted with more than a hint of reproach, the underlying motivation of the transferred men had been to "escape hard marching and accompanying exposures and fatigues." Such men deserved to be cheated, if that is truly what happened.[7]

Marching and exposure seemed imminent by February 6. At 9 a.m. all of Burnside's vessels got underway, churning up Roanoke Sound behind a dozen heavily armed gunboats. The movement had an almost festive aspect: "The vessels, gaily trimmed with bunting, bands playing and men singing, impressed all alike, nerving us for the fray, which could not be far distant." The northward passage was unopposed, and by sundown the fleet had anchored about twelve miles from the island.

Aware that fighting would commence come dawn, perhaps earlier, the men "sought their bunks at an early hour," not only to gain sufficient sleep for the fight but, as Drake believed, "to mediate upon the blessings which had so far been vouchsafed, and to supplicate for a continuation of God's favor and a happy issue in the coming contest." Those blessings, especially of hearth and home, were thrown into sharp relief when late on the sixth the men answered a shipboard mail call. With thoughts of imminent combat in mind—and all too aware that this might constitute their last contact with parents, siblings, relatives, and friends—the readers devoured the tidbits of local and family news from correspondents who routinely expressed hopes and prayers for the continued safety of their loved ones under arms.[8]

Roanoke Island was a position the Confederacy could not afford to lose; curiously, it was defended by a force so small that Burnside and Goldsborough could probably have captured it with one-third the combined force at their disposal. Writing after the war, the local military district commander, Brig. Gen. Henry A. Wise, nicely summarized the strategic importance of the island as "the key to all the rear defenses of Norfolk. It unlocked two sounds, Albemarle and Currituck, eight rivers . . . four canals . . . [and] two railroads." Because it commanded access to so many transportation facilities as well as to areas where food and forage were abundant, Roanoke, Wise added, "should have been defended at the expense of 20,000 men and many millions of dollars." Instead, it was held by slightly more than 1,400 effectives under Col. Henry M. Shaw of the Eighth North Carolina Infantry (Wise, Shaw's immediate superior, was then on sick leave as he had been for some five or six weeks). The dearth of defenders seems incongruous, given the inroads that any force taking possession of the island could make, but the situation was reflective of the second-class status the Old North State held in Confederate strategy. Only 13,000 poorly trained and armed troops were on hand to protect the whole of North Carolina's 400-mile coastline.

Other than Shaw's men, Roanoke provided little defensive punch. Apart from a few guns that bore on the island from across Croatan Sound at Redstone Point, the position was protected by five water batteries mounting fewer than three dozen cannons. One of these emplacements, twelve-gun Fort Huger at the northern tip of the island, was situated too far from the scene of the coming fight to have an effect on the outcome. So too was a battery on the eastern side of the island at Ballast Point. Theoretically, a naval squadron under Flag Off. William F. Lynch also defended Roanoke, but the force was unworthy of its name, consisting as it did of five tugs and two side-wheel steamers imperfectly transformed into warships, with a total armament of nine guns. The only other means of defense were the vessels and pilings that had been sunk in hopes of obstructing the channel between the island and so-called Fort Forrest—a waterway that Goldsborough's gunboats would not have to negotiate. Perhaps more significantly, neither Wise nor Shaw had erected guns capable of sweeping the marsh-infested channel Burnside's troops had to pass to enter Croatan Sound.[9]

Amid these conditions, the naval attack began at about noon on the seventh when the gunboats in the advance commenced an eight-hour bombardment of Fort Bartow, the most effectively located of the island's water batteries. Bartow's nine guns replied as rapidly as possible, but they were no match for the firepower directed at them on many sides. One of the ships targeting this battery, the USS *Southfield*, commanded by navy lieutenant Charles F. W. Behm, included a seventeen-man gun crew from the Ninth New Jersey under Acting Master's Mate William F. Pratt. In his official report of the fighting Behm lauded the Jerseymen, who "behaved remarkably well, considering that they were not used to the handling of large guns. Mr. Pratt made excellent shots wherever he could get the range, clear of other vessels." The men of the Ninth expected to return to the regiment after the engagement, but according to newspaper reports Goldsborough vetoed the move on the grounds that "the Jersey Blues had shown themselves too good managers of the big guns to allow him to part with them."[10]

Given the preponderance of Union firepower, Fort Bartow ought to have been overwhelmed, but the shells from Goldsborough's gunboats did surprisingly little damage beyond setting fire to some wooden barracks. Corporal Stillwell attributed the result to the presence of Flag Officer Lynch's little armada, "which kept up a continuous fire on our gunboats all day." The Rebel gunners scored several hits on their enemy and even forced one ship to quit the fight for repairs.

In the end, the contest was a standoff but it might have been otherwise had the defenders been able to fling shells at Goldsborough's ships instead of a steady diet of less destructive round shot, the only ammunition at their disposal. Perhaps nettled by their inability to raze the land defenses, the Federals vented their frustration on Lynch's fleet and nearly obliterated it. Of the seven Confederate vessels operating in Croatan Sound, two were sunk by gunboat fire, two were disabled and scuttled by their crews, and one was captured. The remaining steamers retreated toward Elizabeth City to replenish ammunition, but three days later they were overtaken by a fleet of gunboats and destroyed.[11]

Burnside's foot troops, anxious to be committed to the fight, finally went into action late on the afternoon of the seventh. A runaway slave had alerted the general to an advantageous landing site at Ashby's Harbor, midway up the island's west side. The information turned out to be inaccurate: the position was covered by Confederate sharpshooters ensconced in a nearby woods, but an adjacent stretch of beach was virtually unguarded. The intelligence did, however, give Burnside the impetus to launch his carefully detailed plan of operations. At 4 p.m. he sent up Croatan Sound the transports carrying the first of his three brigades under his senior subordinate, Brig. Gen. John Gray Foster. Behind each of the vessels came a queue of surf boats loaded with detachments of each regiment in the brigade.

Foster, detecting the Rebel force at Ashby's, swung his ships farther to the north and out of harm's way. At a predetermined point the steamers released the small craft they had been towing, and the boats, carried on the current, were steered in toward land. As soon as they grounded, the soldiers jumped out and waded ashore. Within a half hour Foster's entire command, 4,000 strong, had negotiated the coastal marshes to reach dry ground and, unopposed, press inland.[12]

As soon as the towed boats could be rowed back to Burnside's fleet, General Reno's Second Brigade clambered into the vessels and pushed off for shore in the weakening light. For the men of the Ninth, the maneuver put an end to thirty-five continuous days of service aboard ship, a period filled with mind-numbing tedium and abject terror. After setting foot on land Corporal Stillwell wrote his mother: "I could not tell you one half the hardships that we went through" aboard ship.[13]

By the time the Ninth was rowed to the beach, it was dark, a sharp wind was blowing, and rain was pouring down. The conditions posed enough of a hardship, but even after they left their boats the men could barely feel solid ground beneath their feet, stumbling as they did across bog holes and through patches of mud and sea grass. Pvt. George Stout of Company H wrote that the regiment "marched through mud knee deep for half a mile, when we came to a little field" mired in wet sand. Sergeant Drake recalled that "it seemed for a time as if we would never again reach dry land, and in our ignorance wondered why our commander had not constructed a board walk through the swamp for our accommodations. But, by and by, we reached an open space, which proved to be a plantation, and on this, without shelter of any sort, in the midst of a cold, drizzling rain, we encamped for the night."

The rain persisted for hours, making everyone thoroughly miserable. "We had no shelter nor no blankets," noted Corporal Stillwell. "We left our knapsacks and blankets on the boats. We took nothing with us but haversacks and canteens." Their contents, "hard crackers and water . . . was what we had for our supper and breakfast and the wet ground for our beds."[14]

In this uncomfortable venue—the first it could accurately call a bivouac in the field—the Ninth made contact with Reno's other regiments, which had already connected with the first wave of troops under Foster. Before midnight the last third of Burnside's force, the brigade of Brig. Gen. John G. Parke, had landed north of Ashby's Harbor. Only two of Parke's regiments would join in the attack, one being the most publicized outfit in Burnside's entire force, the "Hawkins's Zouaves," otherwise known as the Ninth New York Volunteers.[15]

Even before Parke's troops reached dry ground, the conquest of Roanoke Island was a fait accompli. Although the nearest Confederates had opened a desultory skirmish fire as soon as their opponents waded ashore, they failed to effectively contest the landing. Lessons learned during subsequent army-navy expeditions would confirm that once an amphibious force of sufficient size gained a foothold on an enemy's shore, the operation could not fail. In almost every case, as here at Roanoke, the defenders, if forced to retreat, had little room to run and nowhere to hide.

February 8 came in cold and foggy, but more quiet than the previous night. Reconnaissance parties reported that the Rebel force that might have menaced a landing at Ashby's Harbor, perhaps 450 strong, had abandoned the area. The Federals suspected correctly that the defenders had fallen back to join the balance of Shaw's force. This consisted of the colonel's own regiment plus the Thirty-first North Carolina, three companies of the Seventeenth North Carolina, and elements of two regiments from the Wise Legion, the brigade-sized force raised and commanded by the absent district commander. Though hardly a formidable body even in its original form, Shaw's command had been depleted by the assignment of dozens of infantrymen to man the island's batteries, including those that lacked the range to fire on the approaching bluecoats.

Burnside's initial objective was an imperfectly constructed earthwork that stretched for almost 300 yards across the width of the island. Anchored on both ends by what Shaw and his engineer officers considered impassable swamps, it had at its center a battery consisting of three obsolete smoothbore guns, one of Mexican War vintage and another for which ammunition of the proper size and weight was lacking. The guns would be of little help; Shaw's principal hope for resisting the enemy lay in his three groupings of infantrymen. Six companies, drawn from four North Carolina and Virginia regiments, were stationed behind the breastwork and on the edge of the swamp on the work's left flank to prevent an attack in that quarter. Another body of defenders comprised a mobile reserve at a point some 250 yards farther north. How much faith the colonel could have entertained in this heterogeneous assortment is a matter of debate especially considering that a large portion was armed not with rifles but with double-barreled shotguns, flintlock muskets, and other short-range weapons.[16]

Through the night, Burnside and his subordinates had fine-tuned the plan of attack. Simple enough, it called for an advance by Foster's brigade with Reno's in close support; Parke's regiments would remain in reserve unless or until needed. About 7:30 a.m. Foster's lead element, the Twenty-fifth Massachusetts, sloshed forward through mud, pools of stagnant water, and rain-sodden thickets toward Shaw's works. A limited number squeezed themselves into what Lieutenant Colonel Heckman called "a narrow cart road" that straggled across the length of the island—actually, a causeway through wetlands that had been turned into a "muddy pulp" by the recent rains. The advancing troops drew fire from the Rebel cannons at a distance of about 700 yards. To respond Foster had the Twenty-fifth take position to support a mobile battery of six boat howitzers dragged forward by a crew of sailors and marines and commanded by a seventeen-year-old midshipman who would become one of the war's early heroes, Benjamin H. Porter.

The battery was also supported by an infantry detail including several of those who had transferred from the Ninth New Jersey to naval service. Some served in the role of riflemen; others helped maneuver the howitzers into firing position. In the fighting to come five privates would become casualties, one of them, James Herbert of Company C, being killed. Another detachment of ten Jerseymen detailed to naval service had hit the beach that morning, cast off from the gunboat *Delaware* "for the purpose of reconnoitering." This force, under Acting Master Luke B. Chase, relayed intelligence to Flag Officer Goldsborough throughout the subsequent fighting.[17]

The firepower of Porter's battery notwithstanding, Foster's advance quickly bogged down, forcing him to send two other Massachusetts regiments to try to turn the enemy's left via the swamp on the right of the road. But as the Bay Staters struggled through the waist-deep water they became mixed up and thrown into confusion under fire from the force opposite them. At this point, sometime after 8 a.m., Burnside ordered up Reno's brigade. The latter surged forward in a long, single column, the Twenty-first Massachusetts in the lead followed by the Fifty-first New York, the Ninth New Jersey, and the Fifty-first Pennsylvania Volunteers.

Reno saw at once that he could not follow closely behind Foster— maneuvering room was lacking—so he informed his colleague that he would veer to the left and try to turn the enemy right via the swamp in that sector. The two leading regiments plunged into the morass, which was even deeper and covered with more and thicker undergrowth than the one on the other flank. In some places the brackish water threatened to rise to shoulder height. Men dodged trees and vines that hung just above their heads. Shorter men lost their footing, tumbled beneath the surface, and came up gasping for breath and spitting mouthfuls of slime.[18]

The regiments preceding the Ninth New Jersey made indifferent progress and took a number of casualties. What lay ahead looked ominous, but gestures of bravado characterized the Ninth's advance to this point. Some men loudly expressed impatience to get into the fray; others tried to make light of their situation to the extent of cracking a feeble joke or two. But now, as wounded men stumbled back down the line or were carried past on stretchers, the men came face to face with the horrors of the battlefield. Few of those who survived ever forgot the experience. As Sergeant Drake put it, "the sight of the maimed men, who had, but a few moments before, been in the full possession of bodily vigor and strength, as they were borne back past our slowly-moving column, caused the stoutest hearts to shudder." Pvt. John Kitchen of Company F admitted that "it made me feel bad for a while to hear the wounded groan and bel[l]ow," but, like the majority of his comrades he strove to control his emotions and concentrate on the job ahead. Drake agreed that once the initial shock wore off, "there was no more levity—all felt that a great responsibility rested upon them—and they nerved themselves for their fearful task."[19]

Shaken or not, the Ninth chafed at the delay in getting into a position to challenge the enemy. Experienced in negotiating wetlands, they looked disapprovingly at the progress of the regiments in front of them and told themselves they could do better. Sometime after 8 a.m. they finally got the chance to prove it when Reno ordered his advance to speed up. At his call to "enter the swamp to the left by company front," Lieutenant Colonel Heckman led the Ninth forward, passing the Fifty-first New York, which was lingering at the edge of the morass, and the Twenty-first Massachusetts, which was struggling through the turgid water.[20]

In division front (two companies abreast) Heckman's column plunged into the swamp, which in places rose to one's midriff or even higher. As the men slogged through the muck they struggled to keep rifles clean, ammunition dry, and their brogans from being sucked off their feet. For one man at the head of the column, "it was the hardest kind of work to wallow through the mud, and [as] I (as file closer) had much responsibility in keeping the men together, of course I had a good deal of wading to do. . . . The boughs of trees and brushes were continually falling on our heads."

Upon passing their struggling comrades, the Jersey soldiers perceived that their leader was acting "in the most intelligent and skillful manner" in contrast to some of the other regimental commanders. Drake attributed the difference to the combat Heckman had seen in Mexico. By acting "in a heroic manner," another Jerseyman wrote after the battle, "he gained the love and won the admiration" of everyone in the regiment. Yet another member of the Ninth marveled at the unconcern with which Heckman exposed himself to the enemy's fire: "He stood up and faced a shower of balls thicker than any hail storm you ever saw." At length the head of the column reached firmer ground at a tree line some 100 yards from the enemy's works. "We now had gotten in a dense thicket," a member of Company K recalled, and "we could hardly penetrate the undergrowth. . . . The scene was awfully terrible, and yet sublime, and such as no man need ever wish to experience again."[21]

Apparently Heckman had taken steps to ensure that the vanguard included some of the best shots in the Ninth, for when the regiment's first division drew bead on the earthwork it did considerable damage. Although some of the shooters undoubtedly experienced some apprehension at unleashing their weapons for the first time at fellow human beings, others claimed the experience bothered them little or not at all. Corporal Stillwell told his mother: "I felt just as cool and no more excited than if I had been shooting birds in the woods."[22]

The effect of the Ninth's fusillade was immediate and severe. It stunned the nearest Confederates, who had not expected to draw fire from that quarter, and they were shocked by the casualties it inflicted. As soon as his right flank came under attack, Colonel Shaw had one of his guns pivot in the Ninth's direction and open fire. Lieutenant Colonel Heckman responded by directing his "dead shots" to pick off the gunners, while "the part of the regiment not engaged were ordered to squat in the water, securing their ammunition from damage." The tactic proved effective; within minutes the cannon was firing intermittently and causing scant damage. When the first division's ammunition began to run low, its men displayed almost parade-ground precision by filing off to right and left as the next companies in line took their place, maintaining a "well-directed fire" on earthwork and battery. Their commander was pleased to observe that the return fire continued to be sporadic and ineffective.[23]

If one Rebel had his way, the Ninth's advantage would not last. Through field glasses Heckman saw an officer—later identified as Lt. William B. Selden, a member of Shaw's staff—struggle to send a better-aimed round at his assailants. Reloading the cannon slowly and deliberately, careful not to expose himself unnecessarily, he aimed, sighted, and fired. By then, however, three Jerseymen had done the same and a split second after the blast died away Selden fell dead across the trail of his piece.[24]

Selden never observed the terrible effect of his final shot. Fragments of shell struck no fewer than four men, killing two and maiming the others. The fatalities were Pvt. Isaac V. D. Blackwell of Company F and Company H's commander, Joseph J. Henry. Blackwell's death inspired an anguished letter from the executive officer of his unit, Lt. Augustus Thompson: "When within about fifty yards of the fort, we were ordered to kneel down in the bushes and then the 9th opened their fire. . . . About five minutes [later] . . a shell from one of the enemy's guns struck and killed the man in my company that stood right before me. As he fell I caught him in my arms and held him until the men came up and carried him off. . . . Oh, who can imagine my feelings as I stood there in the water up to my waist, holding one of my own men just dying, and the balls flying thick around!"[25]

Captain Henry may have been the fourth victim of Selden's shot, but he became the first New Jersey officer to lose his life in combat. Highly respected by colleagues and enlisted men alike, the twenty-seven-year-old native of Warren County, son of a coal and iron magnate, had been a practicing lawyer in Belvidere and for two years had served as secretary to his kinsman, U.S. congressman George Whitfield Scranton. Henry's brother had preceded him into the army, being appointed adjutant of the First New Jersey Volunteers. So eager was Joseph to fight that in the war's early weeks he had joined the Frontier Guards, an ad hoc bodyguard to President Lincoln, reportedly the target of assassins and kidnappers. When the Ninth New Jersey began organizing, young Henry secured a captain's commission but only after declining a lucrative State Department appointment as consul to the island nation of Minorca.

Remarkably, when struck Henry sustained no external injuries. His brother-in-law, Colonel Scranton, explained that the shot "which had nearly spent its course struck him just above the [waist] sash. . . . The contusion from the missile left only a livid spot as the cause of his death. No wound was visible elsewhere, but this proved sufficient." The captain may have had a premonition of coming death. In his last letter home, written aboard ship a few days before the fighting on Roanoke, Henry had begged his sister: "Do not cease to pray for me, for mercy—forgiveness—and should it be ordered that I shall perish on the field, that through the merits of the blessed Savior, I may obtain an entrance to the abode of the Redeemed on High."[26]

Two days after the battle, the officers of the Ninth convened a meeting to provide a fitting memorial for the fallen officer. As they had following the deaths of Colonel Allen and Surgeon Weller—and as they would for every officer to die in action over the next three years—the committee voted resolutions of respect and sympathy for the loss of "our beloved associate and friend." Copies of these were sent to Henry's family as well as to the editors of Warren County newspapers. The *Belvidere Intelligencer* responded with an eloquent obituary that ended with a flourish both military and religious: "Beloved young soldier, rest in peace! . . . . May we all imitate his devotion and love of country, and be prepared to go *home* whenever the *Master* calls."[27]

The enlisted men who were wounded by the shot that killed Henry and Blackwell, members of Company K, were disabled for life. The second to be struck, Pvt. Jonathan A. Bural, lost a leg. Both legs of Corp. John Lorence, who as the first to be hit absorbed the full shock of the blast, were so fearfully mangled they had to be amputated below the knee. Fully conscious while being carried on a litter to the rear, Lorence inspired his comrades with his spirit, proclaiming, "I'm done for, boys, but go in—the day will soon be ours!"[28]

Despite suffering greatly, the Gloucester County farmer survived his wounds and the surgeries that followed. As he came out from under chloroform word of Roanoke's capture reached the field hospital; reportedly, he "raised himself up on his arm, and, with an enthusiasm which thrilled the bystanders, waved his cap in the air and gave three hearty cheers for the Union." Lorence was later visited by Generals Burnside and Reno and other high-ranking officers, who shook his hand and thanked him for his service and sacrifice. A reporter who interviewed the corporal's comrades wrote that "all speak in eulogium of his pluck." A comrade of Lorence's, writing to his hometown newspaper, observed proudly that "this is the material of which the Ninth is composed."[29]

Even after Lieutenant Selden's demise, the Jerseymen absorbed enough cannon and rifle fire ("one continuous peal," as one man wrote, "without hardly a cessation") to sustain an alarming number of casualties. Corp. Daniel W. Shoemaker of Company H wrote that the enemy "plowed lanes through us." As comrades fell around them, some feared the worst. "I expected my turn to come every minute," wrote Private Kitchen, "but I escaped unharmed. . . . The lord is merciful [and] in him I put my trust." Yet despite its rough handling, the Ninth gave better than it got. For almost two hours the regiment targeted the right flank of Shaw's position, inflicting unacceptable losses. Finally, inevitably, the line cracked and broke apart.[30]

The Ninth was the first outfit to discern the turning point. Demonstrating resourcefulness and athleticism, Lt. Samuel Hufty, Jr., second-in-command of Company I, had shimmied up a pine tree to gain a long, unobstructed view of the action. Shortly after 11 a.m. he shouted down to Adjutant Zabriskie, at the base of the tree, that the Rebels were evacuating their works. Zabriskie relayed the news to

Heckman, who informed everyone within range of his voice: "Now, my boys, we've got them; we'll do the charging!" At his command several companies broke formation and made for the line of defense. Some men thrashed through swampland, ducking repeatedly to avoid low-hanging boughs; others pounded across solid ground replete with roots, vines, brambles, and some of the rankest vegetation they had ever encountered. Not surprisingly, men tripped and fell, but not all ran afoul of natural obstacles. Soon after the Ninth swept forward, volleys of small-arms fire ripped into its rear ranks, causing casualties and an understandable degree of disorder.[31]

Few experiences on a battlefield produce more confusion and distress than being shot at from behind. The victims must have supposed that the Rebels somehow had outflanked them and had unleashed an enfilading fire. After a few minutes, however, it became apparent that the Ninth had been hit by friendly fire, delivered by one of General Parke's regiments charging up the causeway from its initial position in the rear. Their gaudy attire identified the wild-charging troops as Hawkins's Zouaves, as did their celebrated battle cry of "Zou! Zou! Zou!"

While some of the newcomers delivered an indiscriminate fire, others were running the other way, panicked by a return fire coming from Shaw's center and left flank. More than a few Zouaves halted in mid-flight, turned about, and unleashed a second volley into the rear of the Ninth New Jersey. Then everyone in a fez and baggy pants was scrambling for the safety of the rear, a move reminiscent of the disgraceful rout of the previous July. When a handful of fear-crazed New Yorkers dashed into the ranks of the Twenty-fifth Massachusetts, they were turned back by bayonets and sabers brandished by officers and men who shouted: "No Bull Run here!"

According to historian Drake, "the Ninth New Jersey never forgot this lamentable affair. There was no excuse for the blunder on the part of the New Yorkers, who had not been engaged (and were *not* engaged) in the battle." Some of their victims considered the Zouaves' behavior deliberate. In a letter home Corporal Stillwell fumed that they "knowed at the time we was Jerseymen. They wounded several of our men and would have killed half of us if we had not fell on our faces." Like many another observer, Drake blamed the Zouaves' behavior on the incapacity of their commander, Col. Rush C. Hawkins, an inexperienced, self-serving, and politically motivated officer who had failed to check his men's tendency to run wild. Its conduct caused the regiment to be excluded from further participation in Burnside's campaign through transfer to the Virginia theater.[32]

As if they had not done enough damage, after the battle Hawkins, his military and political cohorts, and some New York City reporters loudly declared that the Zou-Zous had won the battle by delivering the day's critical assault, wresting the works from the enemy through a combination of skill, fortitude, and iron discipline. Nothing was said of the regiment's unauthorized advance, the damage it inflicted on friendly forces, or its disgraceful skedaddle. To make matters worse, the New York papers omitted any reference to the Ninth New Jersey's role in the fight. Three weeks later Pvt. John N. Smith of Company F wrote Judge Thompson that "I suppose you heard that the Zouaves alone [did] the most fighting but that is not so, they were in the rear and after they saw the Rebels leaving the battery then they ran and hollored as ho[a]rse as they could."[33]

Remarkably, the fire from the rear did not prevent the main body of the Ninth—Companies D and I in the advance—from being among the first troops to reach and occupy the Rebel defenses. According to Drake, the regiment was *the* first to take possession of the earthwork and its cannons, the latter having been abandoned after their battery horses were shot down. This claim was advanced by numerous members of the Ninth both at the time and in later years. However, the timing of its arrival at the works remains a matter of debate. Most accounts of this part of the battle have the Twenty-first Massachusetts or the Fifty-first New York being first to take possession. At least one unidentified Jerseyman conceded as much: writing in the Trenton newspapers, he admitted that once the works emptied and the Federals charged,

Massachusetts soldiers got there ahead of the Ninth. "Our boys also made tracks," he added, "but they were up to their middle in the water and mud, and could not get there so soon." Two factors account for this: the friendly fire that caused the charging men to halt and fall on their faces to avoid quick death, and "a deep ditch" in advance of the enemy line that stymied the regiment for a time. When its color bearer, Sgt. Clark N. Burroughs of Company F, came up, the regiment at least had the satisfaction of signaling a change of possession. "The Stars and Stripes was soon aflying where theirs was," wrote David Hankins, "and theirs were trampled under foot."[34]

Although only one-fourth of his men had held the breastworks at any point during the battle, Colonel Shaw had been unwilling to bring up his reserves, fearing that they would have been cut down while crossing the open ground to their front. When forced to fall back, Shaw consolidated the two bodies and led them to the north end of the island. This dictated Burnside's next move: a concerted pursuit to cut off the enemy's retreat. Elements of Reno's and Parke's brigades took the lead, the former shifting to the right to snatch up would-be escapees before they could cross the sound to Nags Head, the latter turning in the other direction to occupy the now-silent Fort Bartow. Meanwhile, Foster's troops pushed north along the other side of the island until they met Confederates flying a truce flag. Foster halted his pursuit long enough to demand his opponents' unconditional surrender; Shaw, lacking any viable alternative, complied. The lopsided but desperate battle of Roanoke Island was over, a fight in which the Ninth New Jersey Volunteers had done its fair share, and more, to secure the outcome.[35]

Although the published record provides few details, the Ninth took part in the devastating pursuit of Shaw's troops. "After the rebles left the fort," Corporal Stillwell wrote, "we followed them to some houses [converted into hospitals] where we found 20 of their wounded and with them General Wise['s] son, that was wounded in 5 places." This was Capt. O. Jennings Wise, commanding Company A, Forty-sixth Virginia Infantry. The former editor of the *Richmond Enquirer* succumbed to his wounds before day's end. A comrade of Stillwell's wrote that "all told, there were some hundred of the rebels in the hospital, and several dead. Along the road which we pursued, heaps of dead rebels could be seen."[36]

Stillwell added that "we kept on until we came to a reble . . . barracks [large] enough for all our army here." Taking possession, the famished men quickly repaired to the cook shack, where they made good use of the food the former occupants had left behind, some of it still on the fire. "We were very nicely quartered," wrote Corporal Shoemaker, "having good barracks, plenty of sweet potatoes and fresh pork"—a blessed relief from the monotony of hardtack and salt beef. Next to the barracks was a half-constructed facility for slaughtering cattle. "They thought they were building a slaughterhouse for us," the corporal joked, "but their labor was in vain—the prisoners acknowledge that they can't stand [against] the Yankees."[37]

The men of the Ninth, "tired out, wet through and cold" in the words of Private Cook, spent the night in the barracks, which, while "commodious," was also "a trifle unclean." Even so, it represented "a great improvement upon what we had been favored with the previous night." The regiment ventured forth only once, to join in a giant "jollification" during which some of the leading officers of the division were serenaded and persuaded to make speeches. Flushed with victory, one unidentified officer (probably General Reno himself) declared that the military might of the Confederacy had been broken and that the coup de grâce would soon be delivered right here in the North Carolina department. The men of the Ninth, captivated by the prospect of a climactic triumph in what was generally considered a secondary theater of operations, were entirely willing to accept this prediction. As Sergeant Drake put it, "if our little army was shortly to end the war, as our general had promised we should, the other armies would no doubt envy us." The soldiers of the Coast Division could think of no better way to return home than bathed in the glory of having personally dealt rebellion and treason a fatal blow.[38]

Having shared in a victory that would further their careers and might make their names household words in the North, the ranking officers could afford to be generous and complimentary to the men who had done the heavy lifting. In the aftermath of the battle no regiment received greater praise—or a more fitting nickname—than the Ninth New Jersey. There is no disputing that the moniker "Jersey Muskrats" derived from the regiment's vividly displayed ability to swim and fight at the same time. However, there are varying claims as to who conferred the title, and when. Corporal Stillwell, writing six weeks after the fighting, claimed that General Burnside himself "called us Jersey muskrats when he seen us in the mud up to our necks." Something about this assertion fails to ring true, although it is a fact that high-ranking officers applauded the Ninth's ability to shoot down Rebels at long distance while struggling to keep their heads above water.[39]

In his history Drake asserted that captured Confederates, impressed by the Ninth's aquatic abilities, were the first to describe them as "muskrats." Another account attempts to corroborate this claim. In a letter to his family almost exactly one year after the fight, a member of the regiment who identified himself as "W. R. K." of Company K (evidently Pvt. William R. Knapp), noted that on the eve of a later battle a Confederate colonel who had been captured at Roanoke Island and later paroled and exchanged learned that the men of the Ninth were among those confronting his outfit in its position on the edge of another swamp. "They are in the advance then," the officer supposedly told some of his officers. "The quicker we get out of here, the better, for them damned *musk rats* will go through that swamp in spite of hell."[40]

For his part, Symmes Stillwell agreed that the prisoners taken on Roanoke spoke highly of the regiment; he maintained, however, that they referred to it as "the Bloody Ninth." By the time Stillwell wrote this anecdote had made its way into print, initially in the *Newark Daily*

Advertiser. Still another account suggests that the men conferred the coveted title "Muskrats" on themselves. Private Kitchen wrote that he and his comrades lost many of their rations and some of their ammunition to the swamp waters, "but we waded through like mus[k]rats." Regardless of its origins, the term had much meaning for the men of the outfit, especially since they were destined to fight over many another piece of swampland during the next three years, and they never tired of referring to themselves that way.[41]

4   "Charge, Ninth, Charge!"

Members of the Ninth who described the fighting on Roanoke Island in letters home could not determine the number of comrades killed, wounded, or missing—some had a hard time tallying the losses in their own companies. The figure most often cited for the regiment was approximately thirty casualties. Many of the big city newspapers listed six killed and twenty-seven wounded. The New Jersey press offered a pared-down lit of eighteen casualties. Some papers, including the august *New York Times*, named the victims and described their wounds. The *Hunterdon Democrat*, given its political orientation, may have relished copying the *Times'* list, which graphically depicted the human toll of the Lincoln war effort: "Three fingers amputated," "shot in the groin," "shot in face," "shot in mouth," and "leg amputated, [condition] dangerous." Originally the *Democrat* claimed that there had been no deaths in the regiment, "although one or two may die of their wounds." In a report published one month later the paper provided an equally erroneous listing of four fatalities and fifty-eight wounded.[1]

Exact numbers, compiled at a later date by army officials and included in the *Official Records of the Union and Confederate Armies*, reveal that the Ninth New Jersey had one officer and six enlisted men killed (the highest-ranking among the latter being Company H's Sgt. Austin Armstrong, from Blairstown), twenty-eight men wounded, and two men missing and presumed captured. This total, thirty-seven, amounted to about 14 percent of the number of casualties suffered by Burnside's command, a proportion in keeping with the fact that at least seven Federal regiments saw action on Roanoke Island.[2]

The casualty figures suggest that the Ninth had contributed materially to the fighting and had suffered accordingly. "We all felt proud of our victory," wrote J. Madison Drake, "the Ninth being especially pleased at having been the first regiment from New Jersey to do battle in defence of the flag." To a large extent the corporate pride derived from the valor and spirit displayed by men such as John Lorence. Other members had performed just as gallantly even if they had not sacrificed as much as the corporal from Mullica Hill.[3]

Several Jerseymen had their battle stories told in the state's news-papers, although their names were not always recorded. A prevalent virtue highlighted by the press was an all-consuming desire to continue fighting even under daunting conditions. One account highlighted a private "wounded by a bullet through the head . . . [who] walked alone back to the hospital tent, as he said 'to get something to keep the blood out of his eyes, when he would come back to his company.' The poor fellow fell dead just as he got to the tent." Another man "was shot through the body, and was being attended to by the surgeons, [when he] asked to be 'carried back where he could fire upon the enemy.' Still another, belonging to Co. K, when required by the Surgeon to stay and assist him in dressing the wounded, cried like a child, and begged to be permitted 'to go into the fight, not play *mom*.'"[4]

Missing from the newspaper coverage was the revelation that not every soldier had played the hero's part on Roanoke. In the wake of the victory Color Sergeant Burroughs was stripped of his post of honor for unspecified "neglect of duty"—the implication being that he had shirked his responsibilities by remaining out of the fight. Burroughs was at first replaced by Edward S. Carrell, and then, in early March, by George Meyers, who would retain the position through the rest of the war. An even more egregious case of dereliction of duty was 1st Lt. Thomas J. Smith of Company M, whose offense was revealed by an anonymous Jerseyman in the March 7, 1862, edition of the *State*

Gazette and Republican. Smith's conduct was also the subject of a let-ter written two weeks later by Corporal Stillwell, possibly the source of the newspaper article. At a critical point in the fighting Stillwell heard his captain, Joseph McChesney, call his subordinates to his side. Only one responded, prompting McChesney to shout: "Where is my [other] lieutenant?" An enlisted member of the company piped up: "Yonder is the other one, behind a tree." While neither article nor let-ter recorded the upshot, Smith resigned his commission and left the regiment, presumably in disgrace, early in March. Stillwell, who had a sharp eye for the failings of his leaders and comrades, would report a similar incident in a later battle, this one involving the unbecoming conduct of an entire company of the regiment.[5]

Proud of the Ninth's overall performance, Lieutenant Colonel Heckman put his emotions on display when composing his first official report of operations as regimental commander. In fact he prepared two reports, both dated February 9. The first, which was transmitted to General Reno's headquarters, was relatively brief. It described the regiment's movement toward the enemy's right flank and its subsequent deliverance of "an oblique fire upon the battery . . . by successive divisions." Significantly, he did not claim for the Ninth the honor of being first inside the enemy's abandoned works, instead remarking that it entered the battery "in company with the Twenty-first Massachusetts Volunteers." Overlooking the behavior of Lieutenant Smith, he added that "the officers and men of the regiment conducted themselves with courage and coolness, and I am perfectly satisfied with them."[6]

The second, much longer and more detailed, account of the Ninth's participation went to Governor Olden's office in Trenton. Sending reports of the operations of volunteer regiments to their state capitals was something of a convention, especially in this early period of the war. The practice helped strengthen the bond between the political officials and the military units that were the beneficiaries of state patronage. In this document Heckman, no longer constrained by a perceived need to placate his superiors and colleagues, unequivocally stated that members of the Ninth were the first to take possession of the Rebel position whose defenders they had forced to evacuate. He stated that the commander of the Twenty-first Massachusetts and the major commanding the main body of Hawkins's Zouaves, upon entering the works, "gave us a short, impromptu speech, and each claimed to have captured the fort." He added sarcastically, "it must have been so, for those of us who were in the battery when they arrived declined to contradict them."

As he had when reporting to General Reno, Heckman heaped praise on the regiment, the "gallant behavior" of whose officers and men, "in this its first engagement, prevents my making mention of individual bravery." Even so, he singled out Abram Zabriskie, "who during the whole of the battle manifested the self-possession of a veteran." Supported by subordinates such as the adjutant, Heckman was certain that "the future of the Ninth will be replete with brilliant deeds . . . and that the honor of the country and our flag will not be tarnished by any act of hers. From first to last its conduct was, in the highest, courageous."[7]

Heckman's appeal to state pride had the desired effect. When the news of the Ninth's dramatic performance reached Trenton three days after the battle, it prompted "great rejoicing" throughout Jersey but especially in the capital. From an artillery position in rear of the state house, a local militia outfit fired a salute of 100 rounds. The first salvo was the signal for bells in the towers of city hall and several churches to begin pealing. Bonfires were lit and drum corps pounded away in the city's streets. A correspondent for the *State Gazette and Republican* reported that "all over the town, in every public place and in every street, men were shaking hands and congratulating each other over the brightening prospects, and everywhere we saw the signs of rejoicing, patriotism and devotion to the Union. If there were any persons who did not join heartily in these rejoicings they had the prudence and good sense to keep themselves out of sight."

The state, and especially its seat of government, had not experienced such joyous times since war's outbreak. Thrilled by the results of Roanoke Island, especially coming as it did on the heels of word of Brig. Gen. Ulysses S. Grant's well-publicized capture of Fort Henry on the Tennessee River, the New Jersey Assembly passed a series of resolutions in support of the war. Burnside and Grant were the men of the hour, but the main source of the glad tidings, on the local level, was the Ninth New Jersey Volunteers.[8]

The aftermath of victory brought a measure of relief and relaxation to a regiment and an army that had suffered more than its share of privations and hardships since setting sail from Maryland one month earlier. Corporal Shoemaker reported his company "very nicely quartered" in the barracks the Ninth had acquired from the enemy. An unidentified member of the Ninth, writing in the *Newark Daily Advertiser*, pronounced the accommodations "splendid." He described them as consisting of thirty-some buildings, "108 × 40 [feet] each, just completed, showing the number of troops which would probably have been concentrated on this island." Other reviews of the Ninth's living conditions were not as positive. Drake, for one, recalled the barracks as "filthy and filled with vermin." This was a criticism leveled almost every time a Union force occupied quarters that had once housed Rebel soldiers.[9]

On February 12 life got more comfortable for the regiment when seven of its companies marched to the main wharf to collect the knapsacks containing dry clothing, rubber blankets, and other precious items that they had been compelled to leave aboard ship. Presumably, the rest of the outfit received the same opportunity once relieved of its priority duty, guarding prisoners.[10]

Their contact with the prisoners of war enabled the Jerseymen to take the measure of their opponents. The interrogators were quite pleased when their charges—either sincerely or to curry favor with their captors—lauded the regiment's role in the battle. "The prisoners have acknowledged," one enlisted man reported, "that it was the fire of the Ninth New Jersey that not only drove them from the battery, but scattered the reserve which was posted in the rear." The Confederates appear to have been especially impressed by the marksmanship of the picked riflemen at the head of the regimental column. Not every prisoner could identify the Ninth as his primary assailant, though more than one admitted that "the regiment in the swamp gave them 'fits.'" Another way of saying this had come from General Reno, who after the battle declared that the Ninth "did the business for the rebels."[11]

The Jerseymen, who were not at all impressed by their prisoners, refused to return any compliments. The victors hardly resembled fashion plates after hours of fighting in mud, dirt, and a swamp, but they were fully armed and accoutered. By contrast, the Confederates had no uniformity of clothing or weaponry. Many wore civilian attire, without a single piece of uniform to identify them as soldiers. They carried an odd assortment of firearms including carbines, shotguns, fowling pieces, and flintlocks. In place of effective shoulder arms, almost every Confederate carried a bowie knife with a blade from six inches to two feet long. Instead of knapsacks, as Pvt. Henry Cook observed, many carried their belongings in suitcases and carpetbags; some had extra clothing strapped to their backs.

Cook tried, without much success, to elicit the prisoners' motivation for taking up arms against the national government: "As a general thing they are ignorant" and close-mouthed about their military service. Eventually, he made the acquaintance of more talkative prisoners, members of Wise's legion. It was obvious that these better-clothed and -equipped Virginians were higher on the social scale than their North Carolina compatriots and considered themselves better soldiers: "They curse the NC soldiers for having sold [i.e., betrayed] them," Cook wrote in his diary. "The[y] think the NC did not fight good enough."[12]

Like soldiers in every war, the men of the Ninth spent a certain amount of time hunting for souvenirs of the battles in which they had taken part. "Many of the boys secured valuable prizes," wrote a Jersey-men named Charlie; he himself "picked up a double barrelled shotgun when following up their retreat. I will send it home if I get a chance." Some of Charlie's comrades discovered a huge cache of knives, several of which were sent home by express post to relatives and friends. "What the Confederates intended doing with the ugly-looking weapon we could not ascertain from them," wrote Sergeant Drake, "but a darkey told us they were to be used in 'chopping off de Yankees heads.'" Within a few weeks the souvenir takers had done so much damage to themselves and their comrades that Colonel Heckman confiscated the weapons and handed them over to Quartermaster Keys for safekeeping. Many gave them up willingly; they had tired of lugging around the oversized weapons and had come to see how worthless they would be in battle.[13]

The thrill of victory and the pangs of sympathy toward those who had suffered in gaining it soon gave way to more mundane emotions, notably hunger and fatigue. By February 17 the Ninth's store of fresh beef had run out. Because no cattle were available on Roanoke, everyone had to subsist, as before, on hardtack and salt pork (or "salt junk," as many called the sometimes inedible ration). Predictably, the men began to grumble. "Rashions poor," wrote the disgusted Private Cook. "Each man receives a small piece of dough, the size of an egg, which he has to bake himself." Frustrated by the lack of palatable food, a committee of soldiers got up the nerve to complain. They marched directly to the colonel's tent only to find him indisposed with an unspecified ill-ness. Unwilling to wait for him to recover, the grievance committee carried a sample of the prevalent fare to General Reno's headquarters. Undoubtedly to their surprise, Reno not only granted them a hearing but inspected the unappetizing mounds of dough they had brought with them. He further surprised them by inviting them inside his tent where he displayed the same barely digestible meal that had been pre-pared for him. Forced to admit that he was eating no better than they were, the group departed, "wiser if not happier men."[14]

More than a few men suspected that the scanty, poor-quality rations were undermining the overall health of the regiment, whose medical tents were already crowded with measles and typhoid fever sufferers. In mid-February Private Cook visited some of the patients, whom his father, a hospital steward, was ministering to and called the scene that met his eyes "a sorrowful sight." With the regiment minus a chief surgeon—Dr. Woodhull's arrival was still weeks away—medical care was clearly lacking. Corporal Stillwell, among many others, believed that "if a man gets sick here he does not get much care. . . . several of our reg[i]ment died since we have been here from wounds and fevers." By late February at least two or three funerals were held every week for those who had succumbed to various lowland maladies. For the Ninth, as for virtually every other regiment in the Department of North Carolina, the parade of death would continue at a more or less steady pace throughout the conflict.[15]

Presumably the troops were put in a better frame of mind when Flag Officer Goldsborough visited the army's camps on February 13 to the cheers of soldiers who appreciated the navy's contribution to the recent victory. Other spurs to morale occurred over the next few weeks. On the twenty-fourth mail was distributed to the regiment and a few days later everyone received a new issuance of clothing including pants, underclothes, and shoes. These items were supplemented by the receipt of "a handsome donation of socks, towels, &c." courtesy of the ladies' aid society of Bridgeport, Gloucester County.[16]

The war news in other theaters continued to be heartening. On February 16, ten days after seizing Fort Henry, General Grant captured a Confederate army inside Fort Donelson on the Cumberland River. The victory would make Grant, the most successful field commander in the West, a major general, while the terms he demanded of the garrison—"unconditional surrender"—gave him a new and resonant nickname. (Little publicity had been paid to the same demand, which General Foster had made to some of Shaw's troops on February 8, more than a week before Fort Donelson fell.) Then, on March 1 word reached the troops on Roanoke Island of the occupation of strategic Nashville, which would become a base of operations for the Federal armies in the West. The several news reports caused "great excitement" in the camps of Burnside's troops, whose occupants cheered, lit bonfires, set off fireworks, and prodded their bands into playing patriotic tunes.

The victories in North Carolina and Tennessee made many soldiers believe that similar success was imminent on the Virginia Peninsula, the new, major theater of operations in the East. According to Sgt. (later 2nd Lt.) Charles Bayard Springer of Salem County and Company I, the prevalent sentiment among the troops on Roanoke was "Next to Richmond, then for home." Symmes Stillwell was one of those who believed that "the back of the rebellion is broken. The rebels are panick stricken. They cannot stand their ground any longer."[17]

In this hopeful frame of mind the men tended to their ordained duties. A few days after the fighting on Roanoke, the Ninth resumed regimental, division, and company drill. The exercise was conducted on the grounds of the plantation on which the regiment had landed the evening before the battle. Regimental drill took up much of the morning, while drilling by battalion began at 5 p.m. As of February 25 evening dress parade was reinstated. All the elements of a semipermanent camp seemed to be in place, suggesting that the regiment would be confined to the island for an indefinite period.[18]

But appearances deceived; before the close of February rumors were afloat that the Ninth, and many another regiment under Burnside, would soon pack up and move—somewhere. To Private Cook, the prospect of imminent combat appeared to coincide with the decision of several officers to resign their commissions. In mid-month, 2nd Lts. Joel W. Clift of Company C and Francis A. Adler of Company L followed the disgraced Lieutenant Smith into civilian life. Three weeks later 2nd Lt. William H. Benton of Company G and Capt. Henry F. Chew of Company I left the regiment; so too did Company M's 1st Sgt. Andrew Cause, Jr. Within another month, 2nd Lt. James V. Gibson of Company F and Capt. John P. Ritter, commanding Company G, would follow suit.

On the surface the multiple resignations may have hinted at less than honorable intentions, but there is no reason to suspect that they were prompted by the fear that another battle was approaching or were the result of bad conduct in camp or field. Sickness and disability appears to have occasioned some of the defections, and in other cases—notably Captain Chew and Lieutenant Clift, who within a few months would join the newly formed Twelfth New Jersey Volunteers—they were career-enhancement moves.[19]

Henry Cook and his news-mongering mates were correct to predict an upcoming movement. Early on March 3 the regiment received orders to evacuate its borrowed quarters. Having packed their possessions the night before, under Lieutenant Colonel Heckman's supervision the men were marched down to the wharf. There seven companies boarded the steamer *Peabody* (General Burnside's erstwhile flagship) while the other five trudged up the gangplank of a familiar but not fondly remembered vessel, the brig *Dragoon*. Due to overcrowding, almost immediately the seven companies aboard *Peabody* were transferred to two other ships, the *H. F. Brown* and *Albany*.[20]

Although chancy weather kept the men aboard ship for a week before sailing, in comparison to the journey that had brought the Ninth from Annapolis to Roanoke Island, this trip, made in company with the bulk of the Coast Division, was brief if not especially comfortable. Though the southward journey covered almost 150 miles, this time there was little grumbling about a scarcity of food and water. The men were irritated, however, by the secrecy behind the operation. As Private Cook reported, by March 7, with their ships still lying off Roanoke, the men remained "at a loss to know w[h]ere we are going," but two days later he heard an accurate rumor that the movement was aimed at the North Carolina mainland near New Bern.[21]

The state's second-largest city, New Bern was a major base of enemy operations, a link in the communications chain that extended into Virginia. Situated at the confluence of the Neuse and Trent Rivers, it was a haven for privateers—sleek cruisers capable of evading the ships of the North Atlantic Blockading Squadron with cargoes critical to the sustenance of the Confederate war effort. The move against New Bern was comforting news for it indicated that, having secured the coast of North Carolina, the army was now in a position to move inland against larger objectives. On the tenth, the day before the fleet finally sailed, Cook jotted in his diary that everyone was "discussing the coming contest. Boys eager for the fray." He saw no signs of anxiety or trepidation among the men in the hold. Nor did any emanate from the officers' quarters, where Lieutenant Colonel Heckman could be heard tooting merrily on his flute.[22]

Early on the twelfth the transports finally left Hatteras and, convoyed by a fleet of gunboats, tacked southwestward. Around mid-afternoon they entered the mouth of the Neuse, and by 8 p.m. the vessels had anchored near the mouth of Slocum's Creek. The warships went on ahead to engage the local defenses. With the comforting support of the navy in mind, that night the men of the Ninth fell asleep with "no misgivings as to the result of the contest, whatever or wherever it might be, for we had absolute faith in our leadership and in ourselves."[23]

At daylight on the thirteenth the men were awakened by gunboats shelling some woods on the right bank of the river thought to be occupied by the enemy. When the fire was not returned, the transports began to offload, the men being carried to the beach in rowboats. Once on land they were formed into columns and led along a sandy road under a steady rain. The fourteen-mile trek took the Ninth and the rest of Reno's brigade through low, marshy ground past a deserted barracks and an empty earthwork along the tracks of the Atlantic and North Carolina Railroad. At a point known as Otter Creek the columns diverged. Foster's brigade, followed by Parke's, took "the county road" with the intention of attacking the enemy's left and front, while Reno's troops moved farther west along the line of the railroad, aiming for the Rebel right flank.[24]

The rain was still coming down when at 9 p.m. the men were permitted to bivouac within hailing distance of opposing pickets who were keeping up an intermittent fire. As a well-drenched Sergeant Drake put it, "nobody at home would have envied us" that night. The men of Company D had it even tougher than the rest of the Ninth, being assigned to help a crew of sailors lug around those boat howitzers that had helped win the day on Roanoke. "We felt a breath of relief on seeing the guns with their hardy crews arrive," Drake recalled, "but owing to the proximity of the enemy, welcomed them in silence."[25]

As they had during their first night on Roanoke, the men huddled around their fragile campfires, trying but in the main failing to keep warm and dry. Some blamed their plight on a detail composed of slaves who had been liberated from the Confederates on Roanoke Island and had been attached to the Ninth in a multifaceted support role. According to a soldier writing in a Jersey City newspaper under the pseudonym "Alf," the former chattels had been assigned to fetch the overcoats and blankets the men had left on the troopships but to the caustic disgruntlement of the soldiers failed to do so. Certain it is that the regiment awoke on the morning of the fourteenth in sorry shape; a member of Company K believed that "one good man would be a match for five of us," but whether they lacked protection from the rain is a matter of dispute. An account by 1st Sgt. James B. Goldsmith of Company B, published in the *Paterson Daily Guardian*, described at least some as bedding down under both rubber and woolen blankets that permitted them to sleep despite the elements.[26]

Some men might have harbored grievances against their black assistants but the officers were quite pleased by the intelligence gleaned from the liberated slaves as to the nature and extent of the New Bern defenses. Although the informants were not familiar with every logistical detail, Burnside and his subordinates gained a general picture of the main works, which were situated at a point about six miles south of the city. They consisted of entrenchments and small earthen forts protected for some distance by an abatis of fallen trees. The line ran westward from Fort Thompson, an earthen work anchored on the Neuse that mounted thirteen guns, only three of which bore on the land approaches to the city.

Many of the Rebels were dug in on the north side of a swampy stream known as Bullen's Branch, but the extent of their line was unknown. Originally, the Federals believed it did not protrude far from the railroad; in fact, it ran westward for almost another mile. This was a considerable distance for the local Confederates to secure, but they placed much reliance on the swampy barrier below their position. Reminiscent of Colonel Shaw's faith in the swamps that guarded his flanks on Roanoke Island, New Bern's defenders considered any effort to cross Bullen's Branch, especially under fire, "impracticable."

As with the one on Roanoke, this position was held by a force too small—some 4,500 troops of all arms—to make it impregnable. Its thinly held left-center was especially vulnerable, although the ground around the right flank was occupied by a well-trained and well-led regiment, the Twenty-sixth North Carolina. The outfit supported a two-gun battery that was further protected by ravines, thickets, and those felled trees. Manned by members of Capt. Henry Harding's company (the "Beaufort Plow Boys"), the guns covered the sector toward which Reno's brigade was advancing. All of the defenders were under the command of Brig. Gen. Lawrence O'Bryan Branch, a former lawyer, editor, and congressman who headed the Confederate District of the Pamlico, while the Twenty-sixth North Carolina was led by Col. Zebulon B. Vance, a future governor of the state.[27]

At daybreak on the fourteenth Burnside's advance resumed. As soon as the men were awakened they were made to check the reliability of their rifles, which had been compromised by the continuing rain. As Sergeant Drake wrote, everyone "withdrew the loads from our rifles, wiped our rifles carefully, reloaded, partook of a cold and hasty meal, and at seven o'clock moved back to the railroad track and commenced our march toward the city of Newbern." Some men were not as lucky as the ones the sergeant described, having been put on the road without being permitted the time to boil coffee or devour a cracker or two. Wet and mud-spattered, the troops of all three of Burnside's brigades trudged through the sand and mud in the general direction of New Bern.

Rifles at the ready, hugging the left side of the railroad, the men of the Ninth had covered a few hundred yards when the shooting started. Word drifted back that the enemy's works were in sight, though their exact position and strength remained unknown for some time afterward. Cautiously but surely, Reno's brigade moved up on the left flank, keeping pace with Parke's brigade in the center and Foster's command to the right. Shortly before 8 a.m. the principal fighting began on Foster's part of the line. It slowly swept westward under a fog so thick that, according to Sergeant Goldsmith, "we could not see fifty yards in front of us." General Reno agreed that "it was almost impossible to see the rebels," but they could be heard quite plainly. By 9 a.m. their fire was lacing Reno's position, where the Twenty-first Massachusetts, at the head of the brigade, was pushing to within 200 yards of Branch's works.[28]

Now the fog began to lift and Reno could discern that the Rebels were manhandling a gun into position to lay a barrage on the railroad and its environs. Before this could occur he ordered the Twenty-first Massachusetts to charge the entrenchments including a strongly held position on the grounds of an old brickyard. The New Englanders, who had made the initial attack on the Rebel right on Roanoke, again went forward against the same sector. But although they did so with verve and spirit, this time they were met by overwhelming opposition. After briefly seizing a small fort at the railroad, the attackers were driven out at bayonet point by desperate defenders.

Their repulse was the result of an imperfect understanding of the enemy's position, the intelligence supplied by local blacks notwithstanding. As General Burnside explained in his official report of the battle, Reno "soon found that instead of the enemy's right being on the railroad it extended to a point some three-quarters of a mile beyond, and they were posted along the whole line in a series of redans [small,

V-shaped forts] separated from him by fallen trees and an almost impassable swamp."[29]

Reno's belated discovery forced him to attack frontally. It was at this point that the Ninth New Jersey, the next regiment in his column, came into line and unleashed what the brigadier called a "well-directed fire" on Harding's company and the battery it was serving. The marksmanship was remarkable for the fact that, as Company K's Thomas Freeman wrote, "we could only see their heads [above the works], while we were entirely exposed to them. Some of them got up the trees and picked off a good many of our men before they were discovered, but as soon as we saw them [they] come down, some of them head foremost."[30]

Other Confederates resolutely returned fire and quickly got the advantage of the still-arriving Jerseymen. Corporal Stillwell wrote that "the balls came so thick and fast we had to fall on the ground and jump up and run up a little wase and fall again." Lacking good cover and at first outgunned, the Ninth discovered that its opponents were trying to gain a position from which to deliver an enfilade. Suddenly the regiment's left—the left flank of the entire Union line—appeared in danger of being turned. Responding to the threat, Lieutenant Colonel Heckman swung his left wing into position to block the maneuver. Applauding Heckman's move, his colleague to the immediate rear, Col. John F. Hartranft, hustled up his Fifty-first Pennsylvania to prolong the line and shore up the embattled sector.[31]

According to Sergeant Drake and Pvt. Hermann Everts, by dint of constant effort the Ninth silenced Harding's battery, which was emplaced in a ravine about 100 yards from the regiment's front. Another version of the battery's demise was offered after the war by Pvt. John Houck of the Twenty-sixth North Carolina. According to Houck, after firing two rounds Harding's crews discovered that their remaining ammunition was too large to fit the barrels of the cannons, "and these guns were useless." This was a disheartening outcome especially considering that Houck and his comrades had "toiled the greater part of the [previous] night in rain and mire, dragging the guns . . . from the railroad across the ravines and spurs towards the right, cutting roads through the thickets and making bridges and causeways to keep the guns from sinking in the spongy soil." After the fight Lieutenant Colonel Heckman, who appears to have had no knowledge of the actual cause, took credit for overpowering the guns, and Reno endorsed the claim in his own report of the action.[32]

The fighting on the Ninth's front continued fast and furious. To break the stalemate, at one point Heckman attempted a ruse of war. Now that he had secured his flank against attack, he considered encouraging the Rebels to strike it, convinced they would suffer heavy losses. He therefore directed the the men of the left wing to "cease firing and lie down" in order to give the impression they had been knocked out of action. The stratagem failed, prompting the colonel to order the men to resume firing from a standing position. Minutes later, Captain Curlis noticed that one of his men in Company F, William Suydam, had not risen from the ground. Supposing the private had been felled by a bullet, Curlis knelt over Suydam's inert form only to discover the man had fallen sound asleep.[33]

By noon the fighting had been going on for more than four hours, and the ammunition of several of Reno's regiments was running low. The situation was especially critical on the Ninth's part of the line, where the men had been firing as fast as they could reload and aim. Now, however, they were ordered to husband the last ten rounds out of the sixty each man had been issued, and "not to fire unless the rebels exposed themselves." When Heckman sent an aide to inform his brigade commander of the fact, Reno advised him to fall back to the rear for resupply—Hartranft's Pennsylvanians, he said, would cover the withdrawal. But Heckman had no desire to quit the fight even temporarily; he begged his superior for authority to charge the Rebel right where the defenders, despite lacking artillery support, were holding on for dear life. After a quick inspection of the ground in front of the Ninth, Reno gave his permission.

Heckman leapt at the opportunity. He ordered Companies C and E to remain behind to secure the rear and guard the regimental colors. Then, placing himself at the head of the remainder of the Ninth, he shouted for all to hear even in the din of battle: *"Charge, Ninth, charge!"* At these words, his men vacated the inadequate field works they had hastily erected and raced into the teeth of an enemy fusillade. Heckman tried to keep pace with them, although, as Drake noted, "older than most of his men, and consequently a little stiff in his joints," he failed to maintain his position at the head of the column throughout the charge. Another reason for his less than sprightly gait was a lingering pain in his side and hip, where a Rebel bullet had carried away the scabbard of his saber.

Less encumbered by the impediments of age, Heckman's troops, shouting at the top of their voices, passed him on their way forward. One portion of the regiment burnished its "Jersey Muskrat" credentials by wading Bullen's Branch, that "almost impassable swamp" that protected the enemy's works. Penetrating seas of muck and mire had become a specialty of the Ninth. "As we advanced through the woods and swamp," Sergeant Drake wrote in a letter published in the *State Gazette and Republican*, "the enemy poured upon us grape [i.e., shrapnel], canister and shell, but with little effect. Nothing daunted, we continued to press on through mud and water sometimes climbing over fallen pines, sometimes jumping over ditches." Having cleared these obstructions, they pounded up a steep incline to the works beyond, vaulted over their "blood-stained, slippery sides," and landed inside just as the Twenty-sixth North Carolina abandoned the position.[34]

Corp. Henry V. Van Nest of Company F called the works in the Ninth's front "an awful place to charge," but the North Carolinians' hold on them could not withstand the frenzied attack, which was bolstered by the fire of the boat howitzers farther to the rear. Private Houck, who clambered up a hill to safety, wrote that "the bullets seemed to be drifting around me. Reaching the top of the knoll completely exhausted, I leaned for a few moments against a tree for protection and looking back saw Reno's brigade sweeping down into the felled timber, flaunting their flags and hopping over the logs and . . . peppering the trees around me."[35]

Other points on the line having fallen to comrades farther to the east, the Ninth spread out to consolidate its gains. These included dozens of prisoners, many of them wounded, and not two but six pieces of artillery. One of the guns had been served by a team commanded by Capt. William H. Martin of Houck's regiment—an officer who looked quite familiar to one of his opponents. Prior to the regiment's charge, Capt. James Stewart had instructed some of the members of Company H to try to pick off the enemy's gunners. On this occasion the regiment's vaunted marksmanship appears to have faltered, for at least one Confederate escaped being struck. Seizing the rifle of Pvt. Augustus Lott, Stewart sent a carefully aimed bullet through the Rebel's skull, an event that recalled the fate of Lieutenant Selden on Roanoke Island. The assailant recalled that "I fired and saw him throw up his hands and fall backward. We were then ordered to charge and when we entered the fort he was lying there dead."

Inspecting the fallen officer, Stewart claimed to have recognized him as Martin, whom he had known before the war when the man was a resident of Washington, New Jersey, near New Brunswick. Stewart's assertion was picked up by a reporter and printed in numerous newspapers both in New Jersey and in the larger cities of the North; its dramatic retelling would survive the war. But because critical evidence is lacking and some details of Stewart's story are inconsistent (in a postwar account he claimed to have found Martin not dead but "gasping his last"), it is impossible to verify his claim. For this reason, the story of a New Jersey Confederate killed in battle by a former acquaintance is best regarded as one of countless fascinating but apocryphal anecdotes of the war.[36]

General Branch later reported that having been "assailed by overwhelming forces," he had no choice but to withdraw. First the center of his line, between the railroad and the Old Road to Beaufort, held by some unreliable militia, caved in, and then the rest of his position was rolled up from east to west. "My troops," Branch admitted, "were much scattered in retreat." A member of the Twenty-seventh North Carolina, on the extreme left of Branch's line, wrote that when his regiment was ordered to fall back, "such a mess I never saw. . . . We were scattered through the woods and every man took care of himself."[37]

The Twenty-sixth and other units on the Rebel right were among the last defenders to depart. Unhinged by the pounding of the Ninth and its supporting units, Colonel Vance's men fled west in the general direction of Kinston. Those who avoided being shot down or overtaken reached that place on the sixteenth, where they finally rallied. But by giving up his original position—even though he burned the railroad trestle and dismantled the machinery of the drawbridge that gave access to New Bern—General Branch ensured the city's occupation by Foster's brigade.[38]

Though the Confederates had fought with what Sergeant Drake called "the courage of despair," having inflicted nearly 500 casualties on their antagonists, their failed attempt to protect New Bern cost them dearly: sixty-four officers and men killed, 101 wounded, and 413 missing (Burnside reported taking more than 200 prisoners). In his report the Union commander noted that "the rebel loss is severe, but not so great as our own, [they] being effectually covered by their works" while the attackers had fought mostly on open ground. The defenders also lost eighteen field guns and great quantities of ammunition and equipment. Adding the heavy weapons of Fort Thompson that had been neutralized by the Union army and navy, no fewer than sixty-four artillery pieces passed into Union hands. Still other spoils fell to the Federals. Sergeant Drake confiscated the war horse of a North Carolina officer who had been killed during the retreat. As a noncommissioned officer Drake was not authorized to keep a mount, so he paid to ship the animal by train to his home in New Jersey for his postwar use.[39]

The Ninth New Jersey had suffered more or less heavily for its accomplishments. In a March 16 letter David Hankins informed his sister that "our Regiment was pretty well cut up." The same expression was used by Symmes Stillwell, writing to his mother two days later. Demonstrating the extent of its involvement, the Ninth had suffered sixty-two casualties, about 13 percent of the Coast Division's total. The number included 2nd Lt. William Z. Walker of Company A, who was either killed or mortally wounded. Walker had compiled a colorful pre-war career: the thirty-four-year-old native of Massachusetts had mined gold in California before joining the famous vigilante committee that helped pacify lawless San Francisco. Returning east, he had graduated from the Columbia University law school, in 1861 giving up his practice in Manhattan to join the Ninth. Known among his fellow officers for combining "true courage and indomitable energy," Walker would be sadly missed as would the enlisted men of perhaps lesser pedigree but no less courage and fortitude who had fallen around him in the battle.[40]

As at Roanoke Island, the Ninth had its share of heroes, including several who, though badly wounded, either refused to quit the field or fled the hospital to return to the fight. One of these, Company G's Sgt. Joseph A. Schnetzer, fought throughout the fight propped against a tree, having been shot through the thigh. Though he escaped unhurt, Captain Curlis, who was known as "one of the bravest officers in out gallant Regiment," exposed himself so recklessly that his tunic was riddled with bullets. Some men fought not only fearlessly but also cheerfully. A comrade in Company E marveled at the behavior of Pvt. Lorenzo Cummings, noting that "it does him so much good to get a shot at the rebels. . . . [After] every shot he made he would dance and laugh, and shake his head," enthralled by the savage effervescence of combat.[41]

Once again, not every member of the Ninth had fought with becoming gallantry. On the rainy march from Slocum's Creek to the battlefield several fell out, supposedly due to fatigue, and failed to return until long after the fighting ended. More reprehensibly, an entire company apparently contrived to remain out of action. During the Ninth's climactic attack, Captain McChesney of Company M, who had sustained a leg wound, was being carried to the rear. On the way he encountered a unit huddling in some ditches and ravines well behind the front. From all appearances, when the Ninth had charged these men had held back. Corporal Stillwell described them as "cowardly Dutchmen," a derogatory reference to soldiers of German ancestry. The apparent target of his scorn was Company L, which had the largest percentage of German Americans, including dozens of recent immigrants, in the regiment. (Stillwell's use of the epithet was unintentionally ironic, for his state's earliest settlers had emigrated from Holland; by the mid-nineteenth century their descendants were heavily represented among New Jersey's social, political, and cultural elite.)

According to Stillwell, Captain McChesney, upon discovering the fainthearted soldiers, searched about for their commander, whom he hotly berated. At one point he had the men carrying him "set him down and drawed his pistol and said go on you coward or I will shoot you. Our men grabbed his pistol or he would have shot him on the spot." Then McChesney's men "charged on the coward and drove him and his Company on until Col Heckman [came up and] threatened to run the sword through him."[42]

Stillwell's account lacks corroboration and sufficient detail to be pronounced fully accurate. Then, too, the presumed source of McChesney's and Heckman's condemnation, Capt. Charles H. Erb, rather than resign his commission in the manner of Lieutenant Smith after Roanoke Island, remained with the regiment until the fall of 1862 when mustered out as a supernumerary. Erb's senior subordinate, 1st Lt. Henry M. Heinold, did resign around the time of the fighting at New Bern. His motives, however, remain obscure.[43]

In addition to several prisoners and the guns manning the three captured redans, the Ninth came away from the battle in possession of two highly prized trophies. The first Jerseyman to enter the work that had shielded Harding's battery, Sgt. David C. Bradford, a New Brunswick resident in Company B, seized a fallen banner, in size three feet by six feet, that bore the inscription "Beaufort Plow Boys." As this unit had been positioned in the Ninth's front and had lost a number of its men apparently including its color bearer, the capture was nothing particularly remarkable.

More unusual was the Ninth's seizure of a second enemy banner. Well after the fighting another member of Company B, Pvt. William Danbury, ranged eastward toward the abandoned Confederate camps beyond the railroad and happened upon the silken flag that had been carried by a member of the "Scotch Riflemen," Company C of the Thirty-fifth North Carolina Infantry. Each member of this unit had been presented with such a flag, the gift of a prominent resident of Moore County. Though smaller than the Beaufort Plow Boys flag, this one was more ornate, bearing the lines of a poem:

Our cause is just
Our duty we know
In God we trust
To battle we go.

On the reverse side was a poignant motto: "We are sending our boys, our best and bravest / Oh! God protect them, Thou who savest." Why no Federals who fought on that part of the field discovered the fallen color is a mystery.[44]

Presumably, both banners were presented to higher headquarters for inspection and returned to the regiment with congratulations on their capture. Subsequently they were sent under escort to Trenton and delivered to Governor Olden prior to being put on display in the state house. The Plow Boys flag remained there for the next forty-three years. In May 1905 it was returned to North Carolina authorities upon the dedication of a monument to the Ninth on the grounds of the national cemetery that had been established at New Bern. Details of the disposition of the flag of the Thirty-fifth North Carolina have been lost to history.[45]

5   Working on the Railroad

The fruits of victory at New Bern were still fresh when Burnside plotted his next move. While Foster's brigade did occupation duty in and just outside the city, the expeditionary commander had Reno's men picket the railroad from the drawbridge the Confederates had rendered unusable (but which would soon be repaired) southward to the area around the recent battlefield. Parke's brigade was sent down the coast to prepare for an attack on Fort Macon. Situated on the eastern end of Bogue Banks, the twenty-mile stretch of barrier islands that gave access to Beaufort Inlet, Macon controlled the only entrance through the Outer Banks not yet in Union hands. Its capture would enable Burnside to take the next step in his carefully calculated campaign: an advance on Goldsboro, headquarters of the Confederate Department of North Carolina and northern terminus of the Atlantic and North Carolina Railroad.[1]

As Reno's men spread out to pacify their assigned area, the Ninth New Jersey set up its camp—which it prudently named for its brigade commander—on the south bank of the Trent River less than a mile below New Bern. Because no garrison equipage was on hand, the going was rough at first but by evening some tents had been hauled ashore. The rest arrived the next morning and were quickly erected, giving Camp Reno an atmosphere of stability. The impression was heightened when on March 16 Addison Woodhull, formerly assistant surgeon of the Fifth New Jersey Volunteers, arrived to fill the long-vacant post of chief surgeon of the Ninth. "He came highly recommended," J. Madison Drake noted, "and the confidence reposed in him from the start was fully justified throughout the war."[2]

Over the next several days members of the regiment secured leave to visit New Bern on official business. Pvt. Henry Cook accompanied Lt. Jonathan Townley and two other enlisted men of Company K to see to the embalming of a comrade who had died at sea, Pvt. Theodore Denman. Many residents had evacuated upon the Yankees' approach; Cook found the "nice looking town" to be "all deserted." Two days later he joined almost every member of his unit in visiting the camp hospital, which had been set up on the grounds of the old brickyard. Nearby they buried Corp. Levi Dupue, who had been wounded slightly on Roanoke Island and mortally at New Bern. Cook wrote: "Lieu. Townley read the Funeral service. Boys all sad, return to camp. First death in company from wounds." That evening Captain Elias Drake penned a letter of condolence to Dupue's widow in Newark ("he was a Christian and a good soldier. He was among the foremost in battle.... I loved him from the first acquaintance for his modest and upright conduct"). Drake would hand-deliver the heartfelt message, for in a matter of days he would resign his commission and leave the regiment for home, citing health reasons—rheumatism and a liver condition. Officially Drake's resignation was "much regretted." Private Cook wrote, however, that "the boys did not like him . . . [and are] glad to get rid of him." Drake would be succeeded by Lieutenant Townley who, though a strict disciplinarian, commanded more respect among the company.[3]

Regretted or not, there was a worrisome aspect to Drake's departure, the most recent of a series of several such actions. A few weeks after he left, an unnamed enlisted man, writing to the editor of the *Newark Daily Advertiser* under the heading "Reduced Strength of the 'Ninth,'" commented that "for six weeks but one of the twelve Camp Olden Captains has been able to do duty. Some have resigned, who have found themselves utterly unable to endure this life; others have gone home on furloughs, either wounded or sick; and still others remain with their commands, though at present unable to do duty. In other regiments it has been much the same, though perhaps most of them were used less roughly in battle. Exposure, it is thought, has had more to do with this state of affairs than any other matters."[4]

The Ninth's mood was brightened by subsequent events. It became known that both Burnside and Reno had commended the Ninth for its role in the recent fight while singling out Lieutenant Colonel Heckman for conspicuous leadership. Around the same time word was received that Gen. Joseph E. Johnston's Confederate army had evacuated the camps it had occupied at Manassas since the battle of the previous summer. (Johnston's move constituted a long-planned withdrawal to a more defensible position closer to Richmond, but the Northern papers hailed the event as a great victory and the Ninth accepted it as such.) Cheering news was also received on the evening of the eighteenth, when the Ninth held its first postbattle dress parade. Orders read during the ceremony announced Charles Heckman's promotion to colonel.[5]

The news came as a great relief to the regiment; for some weeks there had been rumors that despite Heckman's demonstrated aptitude Governor Olden was considering appointing a regular army officer to lead the regiment, a move that would have found favor with few at Camp Reno. The esteem with which the regiment's commander was held by his subordinates and his "gallant and unflinching bravery in battle" would earn him a gift sword, "of the finest Damascus [steel] beautifully inlaid in gold," as well as a "richly chased" scabbard to replace the one shot away at New Bern. The entire ensemble cost the officers who subscribed to it no less than five hundred dollars. The saber would be presented to Heckman during dress parade at sunset on June 21. (Two months later, Captain Stewart, whose heroics at New Bern were likewise much admired, would also receive a presentation sword, a gift of the men of Company H.)[6]

The orders read on the eighteenth also conveyed Major Wilson's promotion to lieutenant colonel to succeed Heckman and Adjutant

Zabriskie's elevation to major to replace Wilson. The competent, energetic, and unassuming Zabriskie was a popular choice for high station even though he had missed the fighting at New Bern due to illness. There were mixed opinions as to Wilson's ability to shoulder his new responsibilities; even so, all three officers received repeated huzzas from the assembled regiment.[7]

Still another cause for celebration emanated from Trenton, where on March 20 the state legislature unanimously adopted a resolution of appreciation for the Ninth's performance at Roanoke Island and New Bern. The proceeding lauded the conduct that officers and men alike had displayed since the inception of the Burnside expedition, highlighting "their patient endurance under privation and fatigue" and the "courage evinced by the havoc made in their own unwavering columns" in both battles. Through such behavior the Ninth had "sustained the high reputation which, since the days of the Revolution, has belonged to the soldiers of New Jersey." The lawmakers further authorized Governor Olden to "have prepared and forwarded to said regiment a standard on which shall be inscribed these words: 'Presented by New Jersey to her Ninth Regiment, in remembrance of Roanoke and Newbern.'"[8]

The encomiums kept coming. Two weeks after New Bern General Burnside issued General Orders No. 23, Department of North Carolina, which conveyed a letter from the army's adjutant general, Lorenzo Thomas: "The President and Secretary of War have specially instructed me to express their high appreciation of the bravery and skill displayed by the 9th New Jersey regiment of volunteers—their success being at once glorious and fruitful. They have not failed to notice also a sure sign of high discipline in the cheerful spirit, with which obstacles briefly alluded to in reports have been overcome in the field."[9]

These were glorious times for the regiment, but the honors bestowed on it would have to sustain the Ninth for quite some time. More than two years would pass before it took part in an engagement of the size and scope of Roanoke and New Bern, and the experience would produce no laurels for anyone involved.

For two weeks after New Bern, life in the countryside of southeastern North Carolina was placid, and in quick time camp routine became boring in the extreme. J. Madison Drake, now first sergeant of Company K, observed that "everything being quiet," many officers secured furloughs and left the regiment for a few weeks at home. Before March ended Colonel Heckman and Major Zabriskie sailed for Jersey via New York City along with the recently resigned Captain Drake. Their departure left Lieutenant Colonel Wilson in command of the regiment for the first time.[10]

In their absence, few events of any note roiled the steady flow of camp life. Guard and picket duty, even in the enemy's country, was as tedious as it was ubiquitous. Companies E and I escorted a foraging detail that swept the area for rations as well as for hay and grain for the army's horses. Generals Burnside and Reno dropped in to observe the regiment on drill and, according to reports, came away impressed. Chaplain Drumm distributed copies of *The Soldier's Prayer Book* to every member of Company K, although how many recipients took the time to read it is unknowable.

Drumm would not lead any prayer services for long. Late in May he would break a leg when thrown from his horse; soon after limping back to Jersey to recuperate he resigned his position. Seven months would pass before he was replaced by the Reverend John J. Carrell, father of Edward S. Carrell, erstwhile color bearer of the Ninth and now second lieutenant of Company H. The new chaplain, a Pennsylvania-born Presbyterian, was a graduate of Lafayette College and the Princeton Theological Seminary. During the period prior to his appointment, religious services would be organized by the men themselves. At irregular times they held prayer meetings and hymn fests, sometimes in coordination with local representatives of the Young Men's Christian

Association (YMCA) and delegates of the YMCA-sponsored U.S. Christian Commission.[11]

To an increasing degree the regiment interacted with local whites who appeared dazed and lost in the aftermath of Confederate defeat, not to mention penniless and hungry. Symmes H. Stillwell, now wearing sergeant's stripes, found many of them "at the point of starvation. They have nothing to do and nothing to eat." Many begged food from the regimental commissary and were fed surreptitiously from excess rations. Some observers believed charitable acts of this nature would have a beneficial effect on the way Southerners regarded their invaders. Captain Curlis was convinced that "the masses of the South are deluded and misguided by their leaders, and as soon as they are informed of the true sentiments of the North, they will lay down their arms and return their allegiance to the Constitution which our forefathers fought and bled for."

Every day local "contrabands" entered the camps of the Ninth and neighboring regiments, seeking food, shelter, and employment. Stillwell found them "flocking here by hundreds, running away from their masters for 20 miles around the country. We give them houses to live in and plenty to eat and set them to work for the goverment." The sentiments of a few Negrophobes in the ranks notwithstanding, during this early period of adjustment, the regiment and African Americans appear to have intermingled without discord or tension. One Sunday a black minister was invited to preach to the churchgoers of the Ninth; the service was well attended by soldiers and contrabands alike.[12]

On the last day of March the regiment's service outside New Bern abruptly ended thanks to General Burnside's decision to send the Ninth down the railroad toward its terminus at Morehead City. Various companies would be dropped off at points considered worthy of being patrolled on a daily basis. From these locations the Ninth could support the operations of General Parke against the port of Beaufort. By the end of April Parke's brigade, to which the Ninth had been attached, had invested Fort Macon. Though held by a determined garrison, the pentagonal fortification was obsolete and in disrepair; it would fall following an eleven-hour barrage by rifled cannons, mortars, and naval guns that breached its masonry walls. The deepwater ports of Beaufort and Morehead City, now firmly under Union control, represented stepping-stones to Burnside's contemplated invasion of the North Carolina interior.[13]

On April 1 Camp Reno was partially dismantled, most of the regiment's tents being struck and supplies packed for travel by sea and land. Early that morning eight companies (B, C, D, F, I, K, L, and M) under Lieutenant Colonel Wilson marched to the local wharf, where the "wheelbarrow" steamer *Union* was waiting. The vessel carried the men down the Neuse to Slocum's Creek, where the Ninth had disembarked prior to advancing on New Bern. Going ashore under a torrid sun, they trudged to the hamlet of Shepardsville, thirty miles from New Bern and eleven miles from Beaufort on the north bank of the Newport River.

A half mile from Shepardsville was Newport Barracks, a log structure the Confederates had erected the previous winter. There, for the third time in less than two months, the men of the Ninth occupied captured enemy housing. They did so upon relieving Parke's rear guard, a New England regiment that was moved eight miles down the railroad to Carolina City, Parke's headquarters during his operations against Fort Macon. Carolina City, a place with which the Ninth would become quite familiar, was grandiosely misnamed; much less than a city, it consisted of a few ramshackle dwellings and the ruins of a once-prominent hotel. Seven miles northwest of Beaufort, the seedy settlement—home to fewer than eighty residents—squatted on the north shore of Bogue Sound, which an anonymous member of the regiment described as "a narrow neck of water running between the mainland and a small barren island of the same name . . . about half a mile in width, very shallow except a narrow channel about 40 feet wide. It extends from Beaufort . . . some 20 miles."[14]

Throughout April, the regiment settled into its new area of operations, one warmed by a tropical-like sun; cooled by sea breezes; abounding in towering pines and moss-hung sycamores; infested with swamps, quicksand, guerrillas, and bushwhackers; and lacking sources of palatable water (one soldier described the local water as "unfit to drink in most localities, unless made into tea or coffee"). The local fauna were sources of unease. Sergeant Stillwell wrote that "there are plenty of wild animals and reptiles and serpents of different kinds. Aligators and wild cats make all kinds of noises around our camp at night." Insect life was even more discomforting. An enlisted man of Company F found it "pretty hard sleeping here, [what with] mosquitoes and fleas as big as roaches. There is no kind of loathsome insects but what may be found here."[15]

In this rather inhospitable country the regiment took on many responsibilities but the principal task was guard duty. Lieutenant Colonel Wilson stationed three companies (initially I, L, and M) to secure the barracks and the surrounding country, while placing a fourth company (F) seven miles to the north on low, swampy land near Havelock Station, and a fifth (D) midway between those points. The other three companies covered a couple of roads that led to Swansborough, twenty-some miles west of Beaufort. An anonymous member of Company K described the strategic nature of the larger of the two : "The possession of this road is of great importance and utility to us, and in no way could the enemy harm us more than by gaining even temporary possession of it."[16]

At each of these several locales, the men picketed for twenty-four hours at a time before being relieved. When not on guard the men drilled (four hours a day for those at Newport Barracks) and labored to erect twelve-foot-tall earthworks, felled-tree abatises, and blockhouses to protect the railroad against roving Confederates. Other soldiers helped expand Newport Barracks to include stables, a hospital, and numerous storehouses. As one Jerseyman wrote, "the steady stroke of the axe has resounded through the forest, and trees have been landed prostrate, forming a barrier to prevent the impetuous 'skedaddle,' for which Southrons are so notorious when we happen to be at their heels." Although this man admitted that the regiment's job was arduous and dangerous, in off-duty hours "the boys amuse themselves fishing, catching clams and crabs, sailing and swimming." A comrade agreed that "we have good times here and don't care about leaving. We live on chickens, eggs, butter, corn bread, clams and sweet potatoes, and have all the milk we want at ten cents a quart." David Hankins declared that "the picket duty we have to do is easier than camp duty."[17]

The local civilians—for the most part, poor whites—appeared harmless enough. Many were, or professed to be, strong Unionists. They readily took the oath of allegiance to the U.S. government, and they sought accommodation with the occupying force. Considered "white trash" by their upper-class, secessionist neighbors, most of the men folk appeared slovenly, unintelligent, and indolent, while the women were anything but models of feminine beauty and charm. As one soldier noted disdainfully, they "don't look much like the Jersey girls." One reason for this, according to Private Hankins, was that, like the men, every female had "a chewed stick in their mouth and that full of Snuff."[18]

The other portion of the civilian population—escaped or liberated slaves—was a major source of regimental support. By summer men and boys were coming into the regiment's lines in droves, eager to help cut timber for a large blockhouse going up on Bogue Sound and to dig wells and erect defenses for it. Meanwhile, female contrabands washed the Ninth's clothes at the rate of five cents per item. To some members of the Ninth the newcomers presented a spectacle both sorry and diverting. According to a man in Company K, "a more forlorn looking set of beings never met the gaze of Union soldiers before; but for all their look they afford us an endless source of amusement in their quaint songs and comic dance." A more sympathetic view was expressed by a comrade who described the majority of the fugitives as "intelligent men and women . . . [who], though laboring under many inconveniences, are exultant at having obtained their freedom."[19]

Alligators and mosquitoes might wreak havoc on the regiment's peace of mind but more enduring threats were posed by those armed Confederates who inhabited the country between New Bern and Beaufort and continually sniped at the Ninth's outposts. Less than a week after the outfit's arrival, portions of three Confederate cavalry companies totaling some 120 men swept down on two picket posts about five miles from Newport, held by detachments of Company B. Taken by surprise, the guards "[with]stood the attack," in the words of Lieutenant Colonel Wilson, "and returned the fire" but managed to inflict only one casualty—on a Rebel's horse. In return, it suffered one casualty: Pvt. Warren W. Sweeze, mortally wounded.

A greater loss, in a sense, was the capture of three noncommissioned officers and six privates. Carried off by the attackers, they became the regiment's first prisoners of war. Their comrades, incensed by their seizure, begged permission to pursue the captors. 2nd Lt. Edgar Kissam of Company D offered to hunt down the raiders if it took two or three days and to destroy any of their facilities he happened upon. Though Kissam plead his case passionately, Lieutenant Colonel Wilson "would not let us go, so now the opportunity is lost."[20]

Wilson was undoubtedly correct to refuse permission, not only because the current whereabouts of the raiders could not be determined but also because he had been ordered to keep a firm hold on the railroad, which remained intact. The only act approaching retaliation that he permitted was the burning of some local bridges to hamper future attacks. The work was done by elements of Companies B, C, and I led by the recently promoted Capt. Samuel Hufty. Another upshot was the arrival at Newport Barracks one day later of Companies A, E, G, and H, which had been released from Camp Reno by General Parke to bolster the railroad's defense. With the exception of about 100 wounded and sick still in the camp hospital under the supervision of Captain Castner, the Ninth was again intact. By the end of May, by which time the hospital at Newport Barracks was up and running, the last of these patients had been sent down by train from New Bern.[21]

For several days following the April 7 raid the regiment was on high alert. On the evening of the eighteenth a member of a picket post manned by a detail from Company L heard noises that suggested the nearness of enemy forces. The panicky soldier responded by firing wildly into the darkness. Reacting to the shots, the "long [drum] roll" was beaten to turn out the garrison. Men clambered from their bed-rolls, grabbed their weapons, and rushed to the threatened site, only to discover the cause of the commotion: a cow from a nearby farm had wandered into the regiment's lines. Learning of the false alarm, a disgusted Sergeant Stillwell berated the German Americans who had raised it, whom he called "the greatest cowards in the world." But the fancied attacks continued; as Sergeant Drake admitted, "almost every day there were alarms at some point along our line," and not every perpetrator was a "damned Dutchman."[22]

Sometimes officers were to blame. One May day the troops at Newport Barracks turned out in mass at the sound of firing before learning that the officer of the day, 1st Lt. Edwin S. Harris of Company C, had carelessly discharged his pistol. Had an enlisted man been the culprit he might have been punished severely; Harris merely "received an admonition from Colonel Heckman for his indiscretion."[23]

In the wake of Fort Macon's surrender, the men of the Ninth learned that in his official report General Parke had cited the regiment for rendering "most efficient service in completely protecting our line of communications from raids of the rebel cavalry, who were constantly prowling about the country." Although the Ninth had not taken a direct part in the reduction of the fort, Parke authorized the regiment to add the battle honor "Fort Macon" to its colors along with the inscriptions "Roanoke Island" and "New Bern." Drake noted that the men received "the gratifying announcement" with much enthusiasm. The Ninth would continue to add the names of battles and major skirmishes to its flag over the next two years.[24]

Fort Macon's surrender was yet another feather in the cap of the Coast Division, and its members fully appreciated its importance. The only drawback, as many saw it, was Burnside's decision to parole the captured garrison, which raised concerns that some or all of those soldiers would retake the field in violation of their pledge not to fight until properly exchanged. Private Hankins, for one, complained that "if they would keep all the prisoners that they take and send all of the dam nigers to Africa, w[h]y this war would soon come to a close."[25]

Such criticism was perhaps symptomatic of a sense of discontent that appeared to be spreading through the Ninth at its far-flung duty station. As early as the regiment's first week on the rail line, Company I's Lieutenant Springer had detected "some dissatisfaction prevailing among the officers." Sergeant Drake agreed that the entire regiment was "dissatisfied and long[ing] for a change" of station. Rumors were afloat that instead of continuing to operate on the Carolina coast the better part of Burnside's command would be ordered to the Virginia front. This prospect, which portended heavy fighting and consequent suffering, may have concerned some of the men, but most appeared eager for a change of scenery, especially as major successes were occurring in Virginia on a regular basis, soon to include the capture and evacuation of Norfolk and Portsmouth.[26]

Those who did not wish to stay where stationed were troubled by another rumor making the rounds—that local Unionists had petitioned Burnside to assign the Ninth to permanent duty in their midst, so secure had the regiment made them feel. Likewise troubling was a third rumor, this regarding the disbanding of two of the Ninth's companies, their men to be distributed among the remaining ten. Supposedly this was the result of the difficulty of obtaining enough recruits to fill vacancies in all twelve companies caused by sickness or battle wounds. Some feared that the reduction, even if strictly an organizational action, would lessen the perceived strength and effectiveness of one of the Union's premier sharpshooting outfits. This rumor, at least, was based on fact: the Ninth's consolidation to the infantry regimental standard of ten companies would come to pass, although not for another six months.[27]

The declining state of regimental contentment was not reversed by a series of spirit-raising events including the long-delayed coming of the departmental paymaster, bearing two months' pay for every officer and enlisted man, and the return to the field of Colonel Heckman and Major Zabriskie. Both officers had been unwell upon leaving the regiment in March but now appeared "greatly improved in health and strength." The continuing "dissatisfaction among the officers" may have been directed at Lieutenant Colonel Wilson, who had served competently in command during Heckman's absence but appears to have lost some confidence and respect for failing to pursue the April 7 raiders. Undoubtedly the rank and file felt more secure with their senior officer, whom they trusted implicitly, back in the fold.[28]

Upon his return Heckman saw for himself the troubles that were disturbing the temperament of the Ninth. After being wounded at New Bern Captain McChesney had gone home to recuperate. By late May he had been away from the regiment for two and a half months. Because his wound did not appear to be severe, the men of Company M did not understand why their leader's recovery was taking so long. Sergeant Stillwell suspected that McChesney cared more for his own well-being than that of his company.

On previous occasions Stillwell had spoken highly of the captain's mettle, but now he accused McChesney of antagonizing the men through strict discipline and harsh punishment meted out for various infractions. Shortly before the captain's return Stillwell decided that "it does not make much difference to me wether he comes back or not and the most of the Company wishes he would not come at all. One thing certain the Company has got along better since he has bin gone than it ever has before. Captain Macchesney is as brave a man as ever drew a sword but that is not the thing altogether, as [a] man must have principle to get along at anything. I do not believe in using men so. He has to lock them up in the guard house before going into battle for fear they would shoot him. I could mention many things that he done wrong . . . but I do not wish to disgrace him." Stillwell preferred that his company be led by 2nd Lt. Thomas B. Appleget, whom he considered "the best . . . Officer we ever had in the Company and a brave officer to[o]."

Others, including the captain's fellow officers, had their own problems with him. Soon after finally rejoining his company, while serving as regimental officer of the day McChesney was accosted by several colleagues including 1st Lt. William Zimmerman of Company G, most or all of whom had been drinking. (Alcoholic beverages were regularly available to commissioned officers but off bounds to enlisted men, an inequality that the latter deeply resented.) An argument ensued and quickly escalated. Heated words were exchanged, then some punches. The result was the arrest of McChesney's assailants for conduct unbecoming, specifically for "resisting and abusing" a fellow officer while on duty. At least one of the accused, Lieutenant Zimmerman, was thrown in the guardhouse. When details of the row became known, members of Zimmerman's company threatened to release him and Stillwell's company was called out to restore order.[29]

For weeks afterward the effects of the confrontation simmered throughout the ranks. Apparently it was not diffused by the spread-out nature of the regiment's various components, for late in June a troubling story, precipitated by the incident, made the rounds of several North Jersey newspapers. On June 27 the *Paterson Daily True Register* published the accusations of a German American member of the regiment—otherwise unidentified—that "the officers [of the Ninth] are intemperate in their habits and are guilty of bad conduct." That same day Trenton's *State Gazette and Republican* circulated "reports of quarrels among the officers and consequent insubordination," all precipitated by drunkenness.

According to the *Gazette*'s editor, it was bad enough that an occasional enlisted man should be in the same condition, but when "half of the officers [are] drunk and fighting among themselves, what can we expect from a private, when they set such an example?" The editor was quick to point out that "we do not like to publish such an exposure of the conduct of the officers of so fine a regiment as the Ninth, but without it there can be no reform, and that a reform, and a sweeping one, is needed, is but too plain. The men, under the circumstances, have conducted themselves in an exemplary manner, and if the officers cannot conduct themselves in a manner becoming 'officers and gentlemen,' we trust their places will be supplied by others, selected, as far as possible, from the ranks."[30]

The commanders of the regiment, seeking to salvage its hard-earned reputation for order and efficiency, undertook damage control. Within a few weeks the anonymous complainant had been identified as a private in Company A but his name was not publicized. In mid-July he was conveyed under guard to New Bern for court-martial. A comrade who refused to credit the man's claims told the Paterson editor that "I only hope he will get what he deserves for circulating such a foul lie. It is hardly necessary for me to add that the regiment is not demoralized." Other Jerseymen agreed. An enlisted man from Camden, writing to his local paper, asserted that since the regiment left New Jersey, "I have never seen but two officers and privates intoxicated," even in places where liquor was easily obtainable. This man claimed that "there is far less drinking in the 9th than in any other regiment, and some of its officers refrain from touching liquor of any kind, even wines." But the accuser had his defenders. Pvt. Andrew J. Gafney of Company K claimed that a number of officers, including Captain William B. Boudinot, were frequently drunk and insisted that the arrested comrade "was punished cruelly . . . for speaking the truth loudly." Gafney may have been the source of other newspaper accounts that the enlisted men of Company K were "addicted to gambling and drunkenness."[31]

Presumably, the Camden soldier's refutations assuaged the concern of soldiers' relatives that the safety of their loved ones lay in the trembling hands of alcoholics. McChesney's confrontation with his tipsy associates may have had an unsettling short-term effect on regimental morale, but apparently no long-range repercussions.

By late May the war news from other theaters had a cheering effect. In the West, on the very day Fort Macon fell, a combined army-navy force had captured and occupied New Orleans, the South's largest city and a point from which to begin operations aimed at denying the enemy the strategic Mississippi River. On the Virginia Peninsula, Maj. Gen. George B. McClellan, who had succeeded to the command of the Army of the Potomac following the debacle at Bull Run, was moving steadily north from Fort Monroe, isolating a Confederate force at Yorktown and forcing its evacuation. Meanwhile, a small naval force ventured up the James River to trade shells with a fort at Drewry's Bluff, a few miles below Richmond, retreating when their guns could not be elevated enough to inflict significant damage. Writing to his cousin in Jersey, Pvt. William Amerman of Company E spoke glowingly of "the recent victories won by the Army of the Potomac and we soon expect to hear that Richmond is taken." A comrade, in a letter published in the pages of his hometown paper, spoke hopefully of the "present phases of the rebellion . . . Yorktown taken—the enemy routed—Norfolk occupied— our gunboats before Richmond—the rebel rout on the Potomac, and New Orleans in our possession, combined with the decided Union sentiment in North Carolina, impress all here most emphatically with the belief that the Union cause is as sure as the returning day."[32]

Other members of the Ninth, Symmes Stillwell among them, were equally certain that the contest was turning in the Union's favor, especially along the North Carolina coast. The newly promoted sergeant proclaimed that the Rebels were being steadily forced out of the Old North State "to the Gulf States. As soon as we get Ralah [Raleigh, the state capital] and Wilmington we will have all the main places in the State." Stillwell's claim was debatable, but for supporting evidence he could point to the arrival at New Bern of the state's newly appointed military governor, Edward D. Stanly, an occasion the occupants of Fort Macon honored with a multigun salute on May 27. Stanly's primary task, according to the new secretary of war, Edwin M. Stanton, was "to reestablish the authority of the Federal government" in the Tar Heel State. Considering that nearly 50,000 North Carolinians had taken up arms against that government, and that Ambrose Burnside himself had begun to doubt reports of the state's continuing pacification, Stanly had his job cut out for him.[33]

The local Confederates refused to be cowed by portents of defeat. They continued to be active in the Ninth's bailiwick through the spring and well into the summer, trying the regiment's patience and endurance and, by inflicting casualties and prompting retaliation, eroding its strength. On June 11—the day the U.S. Military Railroad began regular service from New Bern to points south—guerrillas kidnapped a local Baptist clergyman, the Reverend Thomas Mann, a vocal Unionist who lived around five miles from Newport Barracks. The minister had been preaching to the Ninth in the absence of Chaplain Drumm, and "the boys all liked him well." The next day, "filled with indignation and burn[ing] for revenge," Companies A, B, and H went looking for the perpetrators with hopes of freeing the prisoner. They accomplished neither, but on the evening of the thirteenth Companies I and M under Captain Hufty joined a forty-man detachment of the Third New York Cavalry, just arrived from New Bern, on a "long and tiresome march" in the direction of Swansborough, the supposed location of the guerrillas' camp.[34]

Unable to cross a creek whose bridge had been burned and failing to find a convenient ford, on the fourteenth the horsemen returned to Newport Barracks. Hufty's men were unwilling to give up so easily. Slowly and carefully they made their way across the stream on the few remaining bridge beams. After trudging another four miles on the White Oak Road they reached a Confederate cavalry barracks, several buildings strong, adjacent to the manor house of one Mr. Sanders, a devout secessionist. Hufty carefully aligned his ranks, pointed detachments toward both objectives, then shouted: "Forward march—double-quick—charge!" Sergeant Stillwell reported that "away we went, [one] squad for the house and the rest of us for the barracks."[35]

The main objective proved unworthy of the valiant effort: the Rebel cavalry had evacuated the barracks a short time earlier. "We soon built a fire," wrote Stillwell, "and it was not many minutes" before the captured building was a smoldering ruin. Meanwhile, the detachment that rushed the plantation house found Sanders and two companions at breakfast. They bolted but were pursued and rounded up. Finding "the table all spread nicely," their captors finished the half-consumed meal before turning back to the starting point of their twenty-five-mile march. They returned greatly fatigued but well-fed and "all satisfied with what we have done" despite having failed to recapture the "regular hard shell Baptist" who had preached the word of the Lord to the Ninth.[36]

Enemy provocations continued. Two weeks after Reverend Mann's seizure a band of mounted guerrillas attacked Captain Curlis's post at Havelock Station, driving in his pickets. When word reached Newport Barracks a train happened to be waiting there; Colonel Heckman loaded it with detachments of Companies E, H, and I . Two of the companies disembarked at Havelock, from which the Rebels had departed hours earlier. They reconnoitered toward the home of a planter named Lewis where a large force of cavalry had been reported the night before, but, as with the pursuit of the Rebels on the White Oak Road, the enemy withdrew upon the Ninth's approach. Retiring glumly to Havelock, the men of Company I lingered there to assist the laborers of Company F in erecting the local blockhouse. The rest of the ad hoc expeditionary force—including a dozen reinforcements rushed to Lewis's plantation by handcar under Major Zabriskie—returned to their camps by train.[37]

The following day, June 25, yet another scouting party, four companies strong, accompanied by a 175-trooper squadron of the Third New York, all under Heckman, returned to the White Oak Road in search of yet another force of irregulars accused of "committing depredations" against local "tories" and contrabands. A "toilsome march" of twelve miles, consuming two days and nights, tried the strength and patience of the party. Sergeant Goldsmith reported that "in some places in the road the mud was knee deep, and the night being very dark we could not see to pick our way, but waded right through it." Again, the regiment's ordeal went for naught; failing to overtake the plunderers, the men endured a "wet, cold and hungry" march homeward. The

Ninth's contingent resumed picket duty on the railroad; their cavalry comrades trotted back to their camp near New Bern.[38]

Two days later, Company E was moved by train to within three miles of New Bern. There it relieved a Pennsylvania infantry company in picketing Evans's Mills, the 6,000-acre estate of Capt. John Nathaniel Whitford, local planter and leading light of the First North Carolina Artillery. The change of scenery was an eye-opener for 2nd Lt. Albert Beach, who, writing in the August 9 edition of the *New Jersey Herald and Sussex County Democrat*, described his unit's new venue as "a splendid place," in fact, "the only property I have seen in the whole State that looks anything like living." The plantation included beautifully manicured lawns, apple and peach orchards, two grist mills, a saw mill, two cotton gins, and more than a dozen slave cabins, "which make quite a little town of themselves."

These attractions aside, Evans's Mills was no Eden. Hard labor was required of its occupiers, Company E having been ordered to erect a blockhouse adjacent to the plantation, one of four such defenses the Ninth would construct across the length and breadth of its area of operations. Beach described his situation as "anything but pleasant. We are obliged to quarter down in the hollow at the mills, and our bed-room is a very open one, it being . . . among the mosquitoes, fleas, and all kinds of insects, with the mill-dam right under us making such a roaring that sometimes upon awakening I imagine myself at Niagara Falls."[39]

While acquainting the newspaper-reading public of Sussex County with the tribulations of Company E, Lieutenant Beach explained that "when Gen. Burnside advanced to aid McClellan it was done in a hurry. He expressed a desire to have the 9th N. Jersey with him, but could not spare the time to exchange a regiment for us: thus we were ordered to remain and guard the railroad from New Bern to Beaufort." The hasty move Beach referenced had come about in part because by the advent of summer Burnside lacked manpower sufficient to carry out his long-deferred invasion of the North Carolina interior. Thousands of troops had been siphoned from his command to garrison New Bern and the dozens of other positions wrested from the enemy; meanwhile, McClellan claimed to be in dire need of reinforcements on the Virginia Peninsula.

This state of affairs had become manifest to the Ninth New Jersey on Independence Day, which the regiment observed with patriotic activities at its several duty stations. During the festivities the men were read glowing reports of McClellan's success and a rumor that Richmond had fallen to his mighty host. The latter left the men of the Ninth, as Sergeant Goldsmith wrote, "of course overjoyed." He added, however, that "almost before the cheering died away," more accurate bulletins announced the defeat of the Army of the Potomac a few miles outside the Confederate capital and McClellan's withdrawal to the banks of the James River.[40]

McClellan's shocking demise had come about through the desperate, heroic efforts of a much smaller Confederate force during a weeklong series of battles ending on July 1. The outcome dramatically altered the course of the war in the main theater of operations and called into doubt the strategic assumptions under which the Federals were operating. One result was the hasty transfer to Virginia of Burnside accompanied by Reno's brigade and a couple of Parke's regiments. Left behind to hold the Department of North Carolina was a force of less than 10,000 under General Foster (now promoted to major general), and while Lieutenant Beach's explanation for the regiment's retention seems simplistic, Burnside did not see fit to take the Ninth New Jersey with him.

Following Burnside's departure no major operations would take place in North Carolina for some time, not only due to the reductions in the occupation force but because most of the state's defenders had already gone north to reinforce Gen. Robert E. Lee's Army of Northern Virginia. Even so, one could understand why the men of the Ninth might feel suddenly vulnerable in their present situation. Confederate forces, both regular troops and guerrillas, continued to prowl its lines and attack its picket posts as if hopeful that the accumulated effect would drive at least one more Yankee regiment from the state.

One result was that work on the four blockhouses the Ninth was building, especially those at Gayles Creek and on Bogue Sound, was expedited. The former, erected about four miles west of Newport Barracks on the Cedar Point Road, was home to a boat landing and a network of roads that ran northwest toward Swansborough and Pollocksville and east to Carolina City and Morehead City. The wooden structure in that location was protected by earthworks; a local church and meeting house had been turned into a headquarters and barracks for the garrison.[41]

The Gayles Creek stronghold was of standard dimensions and lacked heavy armament, but the blockhouse under construction on a Bogue Sound estate known as Oglesby's Plantation was a minor masterpiece of military engineering. The main defensive work of "Camp Boudinot" (named for Company K's commander), it was built of twelve-inch pine logs, twenty feet square and two stories high. The upper story, which served as company quarters, had been set diagonally upon the lower so that any point for hundreds of yards around was within view and firing range. The roof contained an observation platform from which a sentry kept watch twenty-four hours a day. The blockhouse was protected in front by a six-foot-high parapet and surrounded by a moat and a ditch sixteen feet wide. It was defended not only by the rifles of the company but also by a brass six-pounder cannon that the Ninth had captured at New Bern and been permitted to retain, in the service of which a gun crew drilled daily. With understandable pride, a member of the unit, Pvt. George Teates, claimed that the work "presents quite a formidable appearance and with Company K inside, I think the Rebels will find a stronghold not easily taken."[42]

Teates's boast may have come from the heart but had a hollow ring to it. In February 1864—by which time the Ninth New Jersey was long gone from North Carolina, preparing for a campaign against

Richmond—Confederate forces under Maj. Gen. George E. Pickett attacked toward New Bern in hopes of recapturing the long-occupied city. While the overall operation would fail, local troops under Brig. Gen. James Green Martin would capture and burn not only Newport Barracks but both the Gayles Creek and Bogue Sound blockhouses. Upon the enemy's approach short-term volunteers who had replaced the Ninth on railroad duty fled in panic and disorder, permitting Martin to carry all three objectives, which he emptied of arms and stores valuable to his command. Then, as he noted in his report of the operation, his men "burnt or destroyed" everything that remained "except one valuable piece of artillery"—presumably the six-pounder that had guarded the approaches to Camp Boudinot.[43]

Frustrated by its failure to overtake and chastise enemy raiders, the Ninth hoped to salvage a sense of accomplishment when in late July it started out on its first operation under the overall direction of General Foster. On the twenty-fifth the new department commander set in motion no fewer than four scouting missions. The first, a mix of infantry, cavalry, and artillery, succeeded in surprising a Rebel picket post at the fork of the roads to the city of Kinston and the village of Trenton, but the Rebels beat a successful retreat. The second expedition, consisting of six companies of infantry and one of cavalry, intended to burn bridges in the vicinity of Pollocksville only to be attacked by bushwhackers who severely cut up the command. A frustrated Foster complained that "the perfect knowledge of all the by-paths, serpentine roads, &c. possessed by these small parties of the enemy, renders pursuit almost hopeless." His third reconnaissance was more successful. Another combined-arms force managed to surround a "picket headquarters" on the Neuse River road five miles from Batchelder's Creek, killing one defender, wounding three, and capturing ten members of the Second North Carolina Cavalry as well as twenty horses.[44]

The fourth reconnaissance was led by Colonel Heckman, the first occasion on which he had charge of more than his own regiment. On the mission, designed to support another of Foster's scouting parties, he led Companies B, C, D, H, I, and M under Major Zabriskie, three companies of the Third New York Cavalry, and a two-gun section of the so-called New York Rocket Battalion. This unique unit, which had been sharing garrison duties with the Ninth at Newport Barracks since early in the month, fired not artillery shells but twelve- to twenty-inch rotary rockets launched from tubes attached to wrought iron carriages. Supposedly rocket batteries had done good work during the Mexican War, but because they had proven inaccurate at long distances the degree of support they would provide Heckman was uncertain.

Starting from the barracks before light on the twenty-sixth, the force moved along the railroad toward Young's Cross Roads, on the road between Pollocksville and Wilmington, a distance of twenty-five miles. The sun made its presence felt, "the men suffering a good deal from its piercing rays." That night heat was replaced by fluid as the skies opened, soaking everyone to the skin. By noon the following day the head of the column had reached Young's Cross Roads. Pushing on along the road to Onslow, the vanguard came to an abrupt halt when struck by gunfire from a creekside woods. The ambush hit home: Heckman, who was riding in advance with a company of cavalry, had his pistol and holster shot off his hip in much the same manner as his wounding at New Bern. Also struck was Surgeon Woodhull, who had been trotting incautiously at the colonel's side. Two shots grazed his side and forearm while a third perforated his hat. A fourth missile struck his horse, unceremoniously dismounting the good doctor.

Once the cavalry returned fire, their assailants mounted, fled across the creek, and from the far bank set the bridge afire. This failed to stymie Captain Hufty and the men of Company I, who crossed on the span's still-intact stringers and gave pursuit, eventually bagging upward of twenty prisoners. By then Heckman had brought up one of the rocket launchers. Apparently it served him well, for he learned from local civilians that the enemy force—estimated at between 200 and 300 troops of all arms—carried off two wagonloads of wounded.

The number of dead could not be determined, as they too were hauled off. In his after-action report Heckman claimed the Rebels left behind numerous weapons including sabers and shotguns. Six of his own men had been wounded, one mortally.[45]

Under instructions to push on and if possible communicate with the expeditionary force it was supporting, on the twenty-eighth Heckman started for New Bern via Pollocksville, but upon arriving at the designated rendezvous he learned that the other column had come and gone. Now closer to New Bern than Newport Barracks, on the thirtieth Heckman directed his command toward the former. On the way some of his men set fire to the plantation home of a Confederate colonel. The prevailing attitude was that if Heckman had not ordered the destruction neither had he forbidden it. As one Jerseyman wrote, "our colonel understand how to treat secesh. . . . He is a terror to the foe." By the time they reached New Bern the men were "completely fagged out." After a short respite they were returned to Newport by train that evening.[46]

Although General Foster appeared pleased with the results of Heckman's mission, the reaction of most of the participants was less than positive. The operation, which had covered almost seventy miles, had been unusually grueling. When it ended, as one Jerseyman complained, "a large number were without boots or shoes; most of us [were] covered with mud and dripping with sweat. Those who were not shoeless, walked lame." At such a cost, "our errand has been an almost fruitless one, on account of the misunderstanding as to where our two forces were to meet to pursue the enemy." For this outcome "who was to blame? Quien sabe?"[47]

Given the army's consistently inadequate efforts to punish an enemy capable of coming and going much as he pleased, able to inflict damage virtually at will on the hard-pressed occupiers of his state, that question would remain unanswered indefinitely.

6   Failed Raids and Futile Pursuits

Attacks and rumors of attacks on the Ninth's lines continued through the summer months. The raiders struck without warning and drew off almost every time. On August 31, 1862, an alarm was sounded at an outpost manned by a detachment of Company B two miles from Havelock Station; it had been attacked by a force estimated at several hundred strong. The rest of the company, augmented by men from Company E, rushed to the threatened area and the enemy withdrew. Over the next two months numerous false alarms alerted the regiment needlessly, to the great provocation of both officers and men. In most instances the sentinels heard someone or something in the darkness and fired into the night. The entire company was called out, nearby woods were searched, but no interlopers were found. Company K's camp on Bogue Sound was a favorite target of regular and irregular Confederates, who caused the defenders to rush to their now-completed blockhouse, take up firing positions, and return to camp on those occasions when no enemy appeared. Late in October twenty-year-old Edmund J. Cleveland, a recent recruit from Elizabeth, noted a "furor in camp," the result of rifle fire at a picket post that had been set up near a schoolhouse. The entire company filed inside the blockhouse till the all-clear was sounded. It turned out that a sentry had fired on a black bear thrashing in the underbrush.[1]

More than a few of the alarms were in response to the activities of bushwhackers—civilians by day, many professing loyalty to the Stars and Stripes, and terrorists by night. Symmes Stillwell, for one, had had enough of them. Writing to his family in Cranbury in early August, he mentioned an attack on a Company B station during which one of its corporals was wounded in the hand: "It is supposed he was shot by a citizen that lives not far of[f] but we could not prove it against him. . . . Such men have the advantage. They take the oath and claim to be good Union men and then we have to protect them and at the same time they shoot our pickets which they can easly do by sneaking up through the bushes with a doublebarrel gun loaded with buck shot and lay [low] until they see a man and then shoot him and run home and jump in the bed." Here was a war within a war—without rules, without mercy—and by late 1862 every member of the Ninth New Jersey felt as if a bull's-eye had been painted on his back.[2]

Making the regiment's burden even heavier was the fact that its companies were frequently on the move, trading one precarious outpost for another. Early in September Companies B and E, formerly posted to the "wilderness at Havelock," were moved down the railroad to Morehead City. At about the same time Companies C and L were transferred to occupied Beaufort, where regimental headquarters had been established, while Company M left for Carolina City after being relieved by a detachment of a Massachusetts regiment. Soon afterward Companies F, H, and I joined their comrades at Beaufort; A and G relocated to Morehead City; and Company D moved in with M at Carolina City. Company K, tied to its blockhouse, held the regiment's only permanent post.[3]

Most of the new stations received praise for their livability and healthfulness. David Hankins considered Company D's setup at Carolina City "the nicest camp we have had since we have bin in the servis. Our camp is right along the river, as we have got new tents so we live firstrate." He added that Company M was quartered "in an old store rite by the side of us, and we two companies gets along firstrate together. . . . But I think we have got to[o] good a camp to stay long." Sergeant Stillwell gushed over Carolina City, "a beautiful" and "very healthy place," where the primary duty was to "guard the sound [and] to hail every boat that passes and a[s]certain their business and so forth." In this work the company was supported by a small cannon that Stillwell described as "a baby" that spoke "with a very harsh voice."[4]

The units now at Morehead City and Beaufort were quartered in houses, which the men much preferred to tents. Those men stationed at the latter were lulled to sleep at night by the gentle thud of waves on sand only a few yards away. Company K's quarters on the sound were perhaps less restful, being invaded by so many "obnoxious quadrupeds" that the men could, as one wrote, "easily distinguish a hog from a secessionist on the darkest night, although there is little difference between the two." To brighten the prevailing mood, a photographic "artist" visited Camp Boudinot to take several views of the surroundings including the blockhouse in which Company K had invested so much time, labor, and pride. Many men purchased copies of these views, which they sent home to their families. "They are pictures of much interest," Private Cleveland declared, "and, without a doubt, will attract much not disinterested attention on their arrival at Elizabeth."[5]

Despite the several references to healthful living, the frequent shuffling of picket posts seems to have had a pernicious effect on the physical condition of the regiment, which by the advent of autumn was perceived to be declining. Members of every company and officers including Captain Stewart and the new adjutant, Lieutenant William H. Abel, were forced to take medical leave; most were lost to the Ninth for weeks at a time. By mid-September Andrew J. Gafney was describing the overall health of the regiment as "very bad," nearly half of the regiment, in his estimation, being unfit for duty. Pvt. Andrew W. Little, another recent recruit (a former militia officer as well as the editor and publisher of a Hunterdon County newspaper) wrote that while Company H's camp at Beaufort was caressed by "a healthy sea breeze all the time," other companies "have been in poor health situations." Sergeant Stillwell affirmed that by early October "some of the Company boys are quite sick with the chills and fever," though at least a few were recovering. Hankins attributed the high sick rate to the weather and outdoor living. As he informed his sister early in November, "when our Company first come here [Morehead City] we [were] quartered in tents but there was so much wet weather that the whole Company came prety near getting sick. The Doctor ordered us to move in a vacant house that was here." At the time Stillwell and Hankins wrote, a rumor was making the rounds that every man in the regiment too ill to do duty would be discharged and sent home, a situation that would surely undercut regimental performance.[6]

Testimony to the unhealthy conditions was the death of several officers and men to weather-influenced maladies including typhoid and intermittent fevers. One victim, Lieutenant Springer, died suddenly at the end of July of "bilious fever." He was mourned by the men of Company I as "an efficient, brave and faithful officer . . . beloved by all the officers and privates with whom he formed an acquaintance." By this time seventeen members of the Ninth had been buried in New Bern's Cedar Grove Cemetery, the great majority having succumbed not to bullets but to disease. These interments, the first in the local area, presaged the burials of more than fifty Jerseymen over the next three years, all of whom rest in the national cemetery established there in 1867.[7]

To a large degree, the health of the Ninth rested in the hands of its surgeons. Dr. Woodhull appears to have been regarded highly by his superiors; early in October he was placed in charge of the general hospital at Beaufort, which ministered to every duty station south of New Bern. Two and a half months later Woodhull was appointed chief surgeon of the brigade that included the Ninth. Later he was assigned to direct construction of a new hospital at Morehead City. The rank and file, however, had mixed opinions of his skill and care. One anonymous enlisted man, writing in the *Newark Daily Journal*, criticized the chief surgeon's return to the regiment following a furlough in Jersey: "We were in hopes that he would have remained there, for his presence is not as welcome to us as his absence would be—this is the sentiment of the whole regiment." The basis of the man's discontent is unknown; one of his comrades lauded "the skill and attention paid our men" by Dr. Woodhull.[8]

Assistant Surgeon Davies, who transferred to the medical department early in 1862 after a stint as first sergeant of Company M, ministered to the regiment almost as long as Woodhull. He appears to have served competently although often detached from the regiment, assigned to the department's several hospitals. Davies's service went largely unrecorded, his principal distinction being his March 1864 marriage to a New Bern woman.[9]

More notable was the other assistant surgeon, New York-born and South Jersey-raised Dr. Fidelio B. Gillette, who joined the Ninth at Beaufort early in September. According to one admirer, he "instantly became popular with officers and men." One reason may have been an unassuming nature. When applying for a position with the army, the twenty-eight-year-old graduate of the medical school of the University of Pennsylvania informed Governor Olden that he was not qualified to assume the position of chief surgeon. Olden was taken aback: "Why, every applicant wants to be a full surgeon, with a double row of buttons on his coat." Gillette assured his host that "a single row is all I ask at this time," though he hoped to prove himself worthy of promotion—strictly on merit. J. Madison Drake would claim that no medical officer "was more beloved" than Assistant Surgeon Gillette, whose genial personality and capacity for hard work "endeared him to all—his kind greeting and wonderful fund of wit restoring many to health and strength."[10]

With the regiment's effective strength decreasing, Colonel Heckman and his staff began to consider ways of securing replacements. In late summer a select few soldiers were sent home to drum up recruits. Other Jersey regiments sought the same remedy for the same problem. In mid-August Sgt. Valentine Eckert of Company B, himself a recent enlistee, set up a recruiting office in Trenton in coordination with an officer of the Eighth New Jersey Volunteers, then serving in Virginia under General McClellan.

Their efforts to fill up the state's "old regiments" bore some fruit, aided as they were by monetary incentives: the thirteen dollars a month paid to a private; a state bounty; and an additional bonus, a gift of some "patriotic citizens" of Trenton. Another lure was the support that soldiers' aid societies provided to a recruit's family. The generally poor economic climate and veiled threats by both federal and state authorities to resort to a draft to fill up the field units were additional spurs to recruiting. By the end of summer results were being felt. In August sixty recruits came down from Jersey; the following month another large detachment arrived from Trenton. A majority of the newcomers appear to have been assigned to Company K. Over the next two years that unit would receive the most recruits—128 all told—of any company in the regiment.[11]

Buoyed by this modest success, the Ninth redoubled its attempts to gain new blood. In October Lt. Joseph B. Lawrence opened a recruiting office for Company H in Belvidere; an advertisement he placed in the pages of the *Intelligencer* offered a "chance to those who wish to join the army, to do so on good terms." In late November Capt. Boudinot went home to Newark to publicize a need for "a few more able bodied men" for the Ninth. His pitch: "If you wish to fight side by side with old veterans, now is your chance."[12]

It may be surmised that Boudinot was happy to be back in Jersey—in fact, happy to be anywhere at all. Some weeks earlier Company K's commander, whom one of his men described as a "hale hearty fellow," popular with his men but a military neophyte prone to getting "tight," had been aboard a small boat capsized by a squall in Bogue Sound more than a mile from shore. At first it was feared the captain had been swept away and drowned; later reports had him devoured by a large shark seen in the area. Against all odds, Boudinot survived. Throwing off his clothes to shed excess weight, he managed to stay afloat, then swam ashore and walked fifteen miles in the nude "through the burning sand" to Fort Macon. An observer reported that "when he presented himself to the pickets his *uniform* was red, white and blue—*least* of [all] *white*."[13]

The additions that Boudinot and other recruiters secured would not bring the regiment anywhere close to its original (and excessive) strength of 1,159 officers and men. The Ninth would not gain a hefty increase of manpower until the last two years of the war. During that period more vigorous and better-coordinated efforts at the state level to supply reinforcements for existing regiments, added to the effectiveness of a federally supervised draft that began in March 1863 and operated through the remainder of the war, brought more than 1,000 men into the ranks of the Ninth. At the same time improvements in regimental health would return ill and wounded veterans to the parade ground and the battlefield, helping ensure that the Ninth would complete its service term in strength sufficient to maintain the honorable record it had forged in the earlier campaigning.

The limited success of the recruiting program in 1862, however, played a part in the Ninth's reduction from twelve to ten companies in conformance with the organizational norms of the War Department. According to most accounts, this was done because of the difficulty of recruiting for so large a regiment. Rumors about the reorganization had been making the rounds well before the details began to trickle in around early October when Pvt. Jonathan R. Reading of Company F learned that two other companies—L and M—were going to be broken up. Only enlisted men would be involved; as he informed Judge Thompson of Hunterdon County, "the commissioned officers are going home, and they are going to fill up the ten [remaining] companies. I don't know how they will do with the corporals and sergeants," though he supposed the latter would be reduced to private soldiers.[14]

Reading had some of his facts straight, but although Companies L and M disappeared from the rolls as of November 18, 1862, in fact it was A and L that were emptied of personnel, their men being assimilated into the ranks of four other units. Concurrently, Company M was designated Company A. Thus the two units that contained the largest number of German immigrants and first-generation German Americans effectively lost their ethnic distinction. No evidence supports the suggestion that the consolidation was a deliberate attempt to weaken the influence of those members of the Ninth derided by non-German comrades as "damned Dutchmen," but such was the result.

Private Reading was correct to assume that upon the reorganization the officers of Companies A and L would be classified as supernumerary and subsequently mustered out. Gone from Company A as of late November were Capt. Charles Hayes and Lts. Frederick Felger and George Muller. They were replaced, respectively, by Captain McChesney and Lts. Thomas B. Appleget and Charles W. Grover. When Company L went out of existence Captain Erb and Lts. Edward Wilborn and Anton Moll were discharged and sent home. And although Reading did not "think it right" that the noncommissioned officers of A and L should be reduced to the ranks, that is what happened. Most of those who lost their stripes to the consolidation never regained them, being forced to accept lesser pay and authority.[15]

Disruptions caused by poor regimental health and organizational changes had little or no effect on the regiment's operational commitments. Search and disperse missions continued to be its primary duty. On the evening of August 14, Colonel Heckman, with 100 men of Companies B, H, and M and two companies of New York cavalry, set out from Newport Barracks to reconnoiter enemy-held Swansborough via the White Oak Road and the bridge over Pettigrew's Creek. Next morning the mixed-arms force reached the left bank of the White Oak River opposite the village that was Heckman's objective. It was an unusually taxing journey even by the standards of the Ninth, almost thirty miles covered in nine hours. A Jersey City reporter called it "the quickest march of the kind that has been made in this department since its organization."[16]

The mouth of the river could not be crossed except by boat, a contingency supposedly taken into consideration. But two gunboats towing cannons on barges, assigned to meet Heckman at this point, failed to appear, having run afoul of treacherous Bogue Sound. "Determined not to be foiled," the colonel dispatched parties to search the riverbank for craft capable of crossing his entire force. They found an old yawl and a single canoe, with a combined capacity of sixteen persons. At Heckman's order, Captain McChesney (at this point still in command of Company M) filled the boats with fifteen of his men and shoved off for the far shore.

McChesney had nearly reached the wharf at the lower end of Swansborough when Confederates broke from nearby woods. According to one participant, "in a few minutes several hundred armed men rose up and delivered volley after volley." This was a much larger force than McChesney had expected to encounter.

According to Private Gafney, "a few well directed volleys" from Company M dispersed a portion of the enemy force, "and they left in double quick time." But when three boatloads of Confederates came down the river in hopes of cutting off his retreat, McChesney hustled back to the water, safely crossed the river, and rejoined the main body. Heckman, unable to pit his entire force against the enemy, ordered a return march to camp, which ended in a driving rain at 10 p.m. on the fifteenth. On the way back, according to Gafney, Heckman reinforced his reputation as a "terror to the foe" by ordering the burning of a dozen or more houses belonging to known secessionists while confiscating at least 100 firearms, mostly single- and double-barreled shotguns. Gafney noted proudly that the operation resulted in no casualties to the Ninth.[17]

Few such expeditions occupied the Ninth over the next several weeks. One exception was a march in mid-September by Company E from Morehead City and Companies C and H from Beaufort, to Adams Creek, a settlement along a Neuse River tributary about a dozen miles east of Havelock Station. A fugitive slave who had entered the Ninth's lines brought word that an enemy cavalry force was encamped near the place and that recruiting was underway to form an infantry company. Acting on the intelligence, Colonel Heckman secured permission to locate and disperse the Rebels and burn their rendezvous.

The result was one of the most debilitating and frustrating outings in the peripatetic history of the Ninth New Jersey. It began after long and careful preparation. Sergeant Goldsmith wrote of the "bustle and excitement" in camp when the news of the mission was received, the men cleaning their rifles and the cooks hustling about to ready provisions. At 6 a.m. on the sixteenth Goldsmith's unit started for Beaufort, where it joined the other participants. By 9 a.m. all three companies were heading north on the New Bern road. After proceeding about five miles they were joined by two companies of a familiar support source, the Third New York Cavalry. The next leg of the journey covered five miles. When Heckman called a halt for the night it was found that the New Yorkers' commissary train had failed to keep up. Goldsmith reported that "our men generously divided what they had with them, and we were well repaid, for the next morning when their wagons came up they divided their coffee and meat with us."

Foot soldiers and horsemen spent the dark hours in "a miserable place," a woods thick with brush and briars. The men had neither overcoats nor blankets. A heavy dew settled on the earth overnight, and by morning "a more shivery, shaky, used up set of men, I never saw," wrote Goldsmith, "except just before the battles of Roanoke and Newbern." Some little warmth was provided by a few fires, around which the soldiers huddled like refugees from the Frozen North.

In accordance with Colonel Heckman's plan, before dawn on the seventeenth the cavalry started for Adams Creek, now only a few miles off—the Jerseymen were to join them at a prearranged time. Well before that hour, however, the New Yorkers returned empty-handed except for some firearms confiscated from the homes of local "secesh." They had found not a single Confederate, either regular or guerrilla, anywhere near the place that the slave had brought to Heckman's attention, "and so," as Goldsmith observed ruefully, "we had our trouble for our pains." After an hour of uncertainty, the entire force turned about and started back to Beaufort, arriving long after dark. Writing of the fiasco years later, J. Madison Drake recalled that "many of the men, although footsore and weary, [were] incensed enough to have cowhided the aforesaid contraband," who by then had prudently disappeared.[18]

Through the balance of the year racial and political issues caught the attention of, and prompted strong responses from, the men of the regiment. Some of these issues were directly or indirectly related to the ever-vacillating fortunes of the Union armies in various theaters. On the day that Companies C, E, and H returned from their discouraging outing to Adams Creek, the Army of the Potomac clashed with Robert E. Lee's Confederates in western Maryland. The Army of Northern Virginia had invaded the Old Line State two weeks earlier with the intention of bringing the war closer to the doorsteps and breakfast tables of the Northern public. The encounter along Antietam Creek and near the village of Sharpsburg—the deadliest day in American history—ended in a strategic draw although by forcing Lee's return to Virginia two days later it could be described as a strategic victory for the Union.

Antietam was notable for a number of reasons, not the least of which was the stop it put to a series of lopsided defeats by the Union armies in the East, the most recent being the drubbing of Maj. Gen. John Pope's army by Lee near the old Bull Run battlefield on August 29–30. Thereafter Union fortunes in the western theater were very much in flux, with Confederate forces driving into strategic portions of Mississippi, Tennessee, and Kentucky. Eventually each of these offensives would be blunted and turned back, but the Southern forces remained strong and cohesive, qualities they would retain for months to come. Consequently, the news from various parts of the war-torn country that reached the eyes and ears of the Ninth New Jersey had the potential to play hob with regimental morale.[19]

The same was true of an executive order issued by Abraham Lincoln in the aftermath of the imperfect victory at Antietam. Although at first glance the effects of the preliminary Emancipation Proclamation appeared modest—the liberation of slaves in those areas of the South not yet under Federal control—its implications were far-reaching. By declaring slaves in the eleven states currently in rebellion "henceforward, and forever free" and by ordering the military forces of the Union to "recognize and maintain" the freedom of former chattels, the document, which would go into effect on the first day of 1863, added a moral dimension to the conflict. It would also open a wider variety of government-sanctioned roles to African Americans in support of the Union armies. Those roles would no longer be limited to laborers, teamsters, pioneers, and officers' servants. Henceforth black men would be armed, equipped, and trained as soldiers—and not merely to do rear-guard duty but to take their rightful place on the firing lines.[20]

The initial reaction of the Ninth to Lincoln's sweeping decree appeared to be positive. Private Cleveland, writing in the *New Jersey Journal* under the pseudonym "Vidi," called it "one of the most judicious acts during this rebellion," though the basis of his opinion was a bit vague. The well-educated private appeared to believe that the very existence of the proclamation would stiffen the resolve of the army to succeed while at the same time persuading the Confederacy to cease military operations before the decree was enforced. A like-minded member of Company K informed the readers of Newark's *Sentinel of Freedom* that the proclamation "will serve as quite an effectual anodyne to our national troubles. If the rebels 'can't see the point' in that document, we think it is quite time they were made to feel the points of some Minie musket balls and bayonets." Despite its foreseeable effects, Lincoln's gesture did not appear to upset greatly those North Carolinians the regiment had contact with. A soldier calling himself "Censor" informed the readers of the *Newark Daily Journal* that "the slave holders and men of property . . . say it is only what they expected" of the administration— further evidence of Lincoln's capacity for tyranny.[21]

These and other, similar reactions did not mean that the ranks of the Ninth were suddenly free of race prejudice. A recent spur to anti-African American sentiment was the arrival in the department, beginning in late October, of some 6,000 reinforcements, most of them nine-months' volunteers from Massachusetts. The neophyte soldiers were poorly disciplined, inadequately trained, and indifferently armed, and the veterans did not welcome them with open arms. The fact that they had received high bounties (the Ninth dubbed them "two hundred dollar men") did not expedite their acceptance. Nor did the fact that they hailed from a hotbed of abolition, a political credo many Jerseymen considered almost as despicable as secession.[22]

Sergeant Stillwell declared himself "disgusted and supprised" that General Foster should welcome the new troops: "The abolitionists of Massachusetts . . . have no honor about them." Overlooking the repeated efforts of his regiment to make Southern civilians feel the hard hand of war, Stillwell compared the Bay Staters to "the savages of some far Country" in their well-publicized desire to destroy North Carolinians' homes and confiscate their property including their slaves. Private Hankins proclaimed that "Id rather be with any other states troops than" the nine-months' men, who "like a Negro better than a white man. They will fight for a blame Nigger any time before they would fight for a man out of their company. . . . This going to war to fight for Nigers hant what it is cracked up to be." Other Jerseymen supposedly asserted that "sooner than fire another shot at the rebels to free negro[e]s, they would blow their arm off."[23]

Hankins's comrade Private Reading agreed that undue favoritism was being shown toward liberated slaves. He accused officers who sheltered and fed contrabands of attempting to curry favor with the administration, claiming that many had gained their commissions through influence rather than ability. In a letter to Judge Thompson, Reading repeated a comment he had recently read in a newspaper, "that Niggers were kings and white men are slaves unless they have straps upon their shoulders, that money bought straps and straps bought money. That comes the nearest of being the truth of any thing I have heard lately."[24]

Two large-scale expeditions with major objectives closed out the year in the Department of North Carolina, and the Ninth New Jersey, now a part of a provisional brigade under Col. Horace C. Lee, played prominent and highly commended roles in both. The first, launched in early November, was aimed at the vicinity of Tarboro, a village in a bend of the Tar River about sixty miles northwest of New Bern. In that area three Confederate regiments were reported to be scouring the countryside for rations and forage to support not only their local operations but also those of General Lee in Virginia.

The result would be the first major Union thrust into the eastern part of North Carolina since the capture of Fort Macon. Until now General Foster had considered his command too small to handle anything more than strengthening the works at New Bern and elsewhere and conducting small-scale expeditions of the sort the Ninth New Jersey had been involved in over the past six months. Bolstered by those short-term reinforcements, the department commander felt able to move inland, not only to halt the enemy's foraging but to retaliate for the small but nettlesome hit-and-run strikes the enemy had recently staged against his coastal garrisons including Washington (known locally as "Little Washington"), on the north bank of the Pamlico River, and Plymouth, on the Roanoke. As if to emphasize the importance of the operation, Foster would lead it in person.[25]

On the evening of October 29, the move got under way. Members of every portion of the Ninth except Company K—each man carrying three days' cooked rations and sixty rounds of ammunition—left their point of concentration at Morehead City and took the railroad to New Bern. Next morning they were being carried down the Neuse and later up the Pamlico via a transport and a gunboat, accompanied by the rest of Colonel Lee's command and a second brigade of infantry and cavalry. Arriving at Little Washington ("one of the prettiest villages in the State," thought one visitor), the Ninth lay over until the morning of November 2, when the last one-third of Foster's 5,000-man force of infantry, cavalry, and artillery finally closed up on the village—a delay, Colonel Heckman wrote, that "jeopardized the success of the enterprise." When the march began, the Ninth was third in line among the regiments that composed Foster's main column.[26]

Within an hour of departing Washington, heading northwest, the Federals began skirmishing with an enemy who became "more active and aggressive as the day wore on." By late afternoon, the march having covered almost twenty miles, the Rebels brought the head of the column—occupied by one of the nine-months' outfits—to a sudden halt along a creek with a swamp in front, two miles from Rowell's Mill. Unwilling to wade through the swamp under fire, the short-termers fell back precipitately, thereby showing, as one onlooker put it, "the most consummate cowardice." Foster quickly sent forward the veteran Twenty-fourth Massachusetts, only to see it reel backward after taking numerous casualties.

Frustrated and angry, the general looked about for the "one regiment here that can cross that swamp" and then shouted: "Bring up the Muskrats!" Having anticipated the call, Colonel Heckman was already hastening his men to the front. He deployed Companies B and I as skirmishers, then called to the balance of his command: "Forward, double-quick, march!" Moments later the men were rushing through the disordered ranks of the regiments that had preceded them, before sloshing through the morass with the same insouciance they had displayed at Roanoke and New Bern. Despite drawing volleys of rifle fire, they gained the other side and shoved the Rebels across the creek.

Getting at the enemy in their new locale promised to be tricky. At Heckman's order, Adjutant Abel went forward on a daring reconnaissance and discovered that the only accessible bridge had been set afire by the now-retreating Rebels. Abel opined that the span could still be crossed, and Heckman agreed. He stationed a body of sharpshooters from Company G as well as a battery of the Third New York Light

Artillery to cover the rest of his force, then directed the others to charge. According to Sergeant Drake, "in an instant Company I sprang upon the smoking structure, and despite a well-directed fire, succeeded in gaining the opposite side, when it again extended itself, and hurrying forward, drove the Confederates half a mile."[27]

Companies B and L soon joined the chase, "screaming and hollooing like a set of wild Indians." One attacker wrote, "we fell and tumbled and crowded over in double quick time [and] succeeded in gaining the opposite side." The flabbergasted enemy cleared out too quickly to be overtaken; a half-hearted pursuit was soon halted. The Confederates' celerity and the approach of darkness curbed Foster's urge to damage them further, and so Heckman set up a picket line and placed the Ninth in bivouac.[28]

Not everyone got to sleep right away—burial details were kept busy for some hours. "Our men buried 33 of the rebels," wrote a member of Company L, "some of them all cut to pieces by the cannister shot. We found 46 wounded." Many others had been evacuated from blood-stained houses. In turn, the Ninth had lost four men killed and ten wounded. The grisly chore completed, the Ninth spent the night on the ground it had taken, basking in the praise of all who had observed its dash across the flaming bridge. As Sergeant Drake boasted, every Jerseyman "was esteemed a hero."[29]

Although the regiment comported itself with equal panache during the balance of the expedition, what followed the skirmish at Rowell's Mill smacked of anticlimax. On the morning of November 3 the regiment, now leading the column, reached the Roanoke River village of Williamston. It had covered the nine miles from Rowell's Mills so rapidly it was forced to wait for the rest of the command to catch up before resuming the march toward Tarboro. No sizable body of Confederates offered resistance this day or the next when the Ninth passed through the deserted village of Hamilton. Without provocation, members of some of the other outfits in Foster's command broke ranks to burn local houses, barns, and outbuildings. Spread by a northwesterly wind, the flames draped the countryside, as Drake wrote, in "a blood-tinged pall."

The Ninth maintained its position in the lead on the fifth, bivouacking that night four miles from Tarboro. Seemingly so near, the main objective of the expedition was suddenly beyond reach of the Federals. By now Rebel prisoners had persuaded Foster that the town was so heavily defended that attacking it "so far from his base of supplies" would be a fatal mistake, especially with a nasty-looking storm about to strike the area. Shaken by what he heard, the following day the general turned the column about and marched homeward—a decision that, as Colonel Heckman wrote, had a "thoroughly dampening effect" on his troops' spirits. The only cheering note was the compliment Foster gave Heckman on the return route: "You have the best regiment in my command." From now on, he added, "you are an independent command; you shall report direct to my headquarters and receive your orders thence."[30]

The Ninth, now playing the role of a rear guard, shared the many hardships of the retreat including a snowstorm on the seventh that produced several cases of frostbite. As one man remarked afterward, the regiment's new position was "the post of honor—for although we marched on the average 20 miles a day, not one of our men fell out of ranks," even to forage briefly. Great restraint was shown throughout even though, as one soldier put it, everyone "would have been much pleased, could they have brought home with them the cotton, cattle, corn and other property of value, instead of a long train of niggers which followed in our rear."[31]

On the tenth the regiment reached Plymouth, where it boarded a gunboat on the Roanoke and "amid the cheers of the assembled troops" steamed up the river and, seven miles farther on, Albemarle Sound. By midnight the vessel had anchored off Roanoke Island, some of the men "not being able to sleep owing to hunger." Others were kept awake by aches and pains including "very tired and blistered" feet so swollen that any man who removed his brogans could not get them back on.[32]

At 10 a.m. on the eleventh the ship hove to in the Neuse River seven miles from New Bern. Reports had the city under threat of attack, and so the weary, hungry men were landed at midnight and marched to one of the city's forts, where they remained under arms until morning. The reports proved untrue—no enemy appeared—but the men were held outside Fort Totten (where, presumably, they were finally fed) till early evening, when they took the cars to their old station at Newport Barracks.

By then, Company K had joined them, having been rushed to the defense of New Bern on the heels of a forty-mile scout to Swansborough and Peltier's Mills in a blinding rain—thus becoming, as a member of the unit wrote, "as tired a set of mortals as the bleak clouds of Heaven ever emptied their contents upon." From Swansborough Captain Boudinot's men made a four-mile march to the railroad in little more than a half hour. Although spared the debilitating, disappointing trek to and from Tarboro, Company K thus experienced at least a degree of the discomfort and hardship its comrades had suffered, although perhaps not the crowning misery: the undergarments of many of those under Foster had become infested with "graybacks"—body lice. As Sergeant Drake drily observed, "a two weeks' tramp, without change of clothing, is apt to make a man of cleanly habits feel wretched."[33]

Although the official line was that the "object of the [Tarboro] mission had been accomplished," most of the participants were not fooled. Some, like now-Corporal Little, took a cautious view of events, remarking that "what we have accomplished remains to be seen." Sergeant Stillwell, who had caught a bad cold by sleeping on hard and icy ground for nights at a time, was more blunt, claiming that the expedition "did not amount to much," leaving him and his comrades "disgusted and surprised" by its meager accomplishments.[34]

At Newport Barracks the Ninth reoccupied familiar quarters where they rested dead-tired bodies and aching feet and hoped for a long respite from drilling, fighting, and, especially, marching. But their rest would be brief and unsatisfying; before November ended reports of another major expedition were already circulating. Men groaned and cursed the news, but there was no hope for it. As if they had not endured enough physical punishment, an even more demanding round of campaigning lay just ahead.

The interval between operations was marked by a few notable events. On November 17 Lieutenant Colonel Wilson left the regiment, having resigned his commission "by request," as Sergeant Drake reported without providing details. According to "Censor," Wilson's departure was "much regretted" by most of the men, "for he was an officer of whom we were proud." Rumor identified the cause as "a disagreement among our officers"—a comment suggesting that infighting at the command level remained a problem. Those sorry to see Wilson go, however, were buoyed up by the promotion of the estimable Major Zabriskie to succeed him. On the eighteenth the dissolution of Companies L and M was officially consummated, prompting an exodus not only of those units' officers but of others as well, including Capt. Uriah DeHart of Company E. According to one "P. L. S.," writing in the *Register and Times* of Rahway, unlike Wilson's leave-taking, "there were not many tears shed" when DeHart left the regiment. It appears that Governor Stanly had sworn out a warrant for his arrest (the grounds for which remain unknown) and that the captain fled by boat shortly before he could be detained.[35]

Thanksgiving, November 27, came and went without much notice and little celebration, the only events worthy of mention being the capture of a couple of beeves on Bogue Sound and the winterizing of tents and cabins at the Ninth's various outposts. Transported to Newport Barracks, the cattle made for a "very palatable supper" for members of the Ninth. But the erection of winter camp was scarcely underway when definitive word of the next major movement reached regimental headquarters.[36]

This time General Foster was after bigger game. His new objective was the destruction of a resource of great importance to the enemy, the railroad bridge over the Neuse River at Goldsboro. Thanks to its strategic location, that city was the main communications center of Confederate forces. It was seated at the junction of the state's two leading railroads, the Atlantic and North Carolina and the Wilmington and Weldon, both of which carried rations, forage, and materiel to Lee's forces in Virginia. Foster also intended to damage as much track on both roads as he could get his hands on. To reach these goals he collected at New Bern a force composed of 10,000 infantry, 640 cavalry, and 40 pieces of artillery. This was the largest field force assembled in the department since Burnside had left it to take a bigger and more difficult job: command of the Army of the Potomac following Lincoln's firing of McClellan in early November.[37]

Foster would never embark on such a critical operation without his "Muskrats." And so on December 4 the various pieces of the regiment were transferred by rail to New Bern. When its most distant element, Company K, reached the city the following day the outfit was intact for the first time since early April. The consolidation made the Ninth feel mighty enough to take on its present mission regardless of past failures and disappointments and chancy weather.

Not till the eleventh were all of Foster's people on hand and sufficiently supplied with rations and ammunition to support a lengthy outing. On that "splendid wintry morning" the march began. The Ninth was now under the immediate command of Major Zabriskie (his promotion to lieutenant colonel was eleven days away). Colonel Heckman, himself only a few days from being promoted, now led that "independent command" Foster had promised him, consisting of the Ninth, a battalion of the Third New York Cavalry, and Capt. James Belger's Battery F, First Rhode Island Light Artillery. As many as eight regiments would be temporarily assigned to Heckman at various times during the coming operation, most frequently the Seventeenth Massachusetts. To reward his performance at Rowell's Mill and afterward, Heckman's force was given the "post of danger" at the head of Foster's gigantic column. The Ninth would lead the way almost daily while protecting the rear on the return to home base.

The regiment did not have to wait long to prove worthy of Foster's and Heckman's confidence in it. Only fourteen miles outside New Bern, it encountered enemy skirmishers behind fallen-tree defenses. Its own skirmishers, "leaping from tree to tree," drove the Rebels out, pursued briefly, and then, per orders, bivouacked for the night. It camped in quiet isolation, having made such good time on the road that Foster's main body lay miles behind.[38]

The next day began before dawn in raw weather. Shaken awake by his sergeant, Private Cleveland "scraped the frost from my eyes and nose." Other tribulations soon arose. Throughout the morning a variety of obstructions barred the way and those who had created them sniped spitefully at the regiment. To help the Ninth surmount the barriers Colonel Heckman sent forward the New York cavalry, and the combined force eventually cleared the way. The rest of Foster's troops having caught up, the command spent the night fourteen miles from the Neuse River town of Kinston. By now several Jerseymen were hurting, the result not of Rebel bullets but of angry bees. In a farmyard near the Ninth's bivouac stood a row of bee hives. "As soon as they stacked arms," Private Cleveland wrote, "they boys made a charge on the hives, eager to rob the industrious insects of their food. But the bees were ready for them, and drove them back in disorder . . . the boys, nursing their wounds."[39]

The first major encounter of the expedition occurred next day, the thirteenth, along Southwest Creek. The Confederates had destroyed the local bridges, but, as at Rowell's Mill six weeks earlier, this stratagem failed to stymie the Ninth even though no point on the stream was fordable. When Foster came up and ordered him to cross the stream and outflank the Rebel position, Heckman saluted smartly and moved out. Deploying Companies C, G, and H to guard the right, he led the rest of the Ninth, supported by the Eighty-fifth Pennsylvania of Brig.

Gen. Henry W. Wessells's brigade, to cross farther to the left on the dam at Hines's sawmill.[40]

The result was further proof that the men of the Ninth could keep their heads above water and at the same time shoot straight. As historian John G. Barrett writes, "with the aid of felled trees, some fragments of the bridge, an old mill dam, and a bit of swimming, the two regiments crossed the stream and dislodged the enemy." Left with no other course, the enemy commander, Brig. Gen. Nathan G. Evans, swiftly withdrew his 2,000 troops to prepared defenses along the river south of Kinston. Most of his rear guard, however, did not get that far. Pursuing Jerseymen and Pennsylvanians overtook it, shot it up, took numerous prisoners, seized a blood-spattered cannon, and propelled the few survivors into even hastier flight.[41]

On December 14, having downed their all-too-familiar breakfast of hardtack and coffee, the men of the Ninth took to the road and soon encountered the obligatory phalanx of enemy skirmishers. Major Zabriskie countered with skirmishers of his own. Picked men of Companies C, D, E, and I moved ahead slowly but with accumulating momentum. A few miles short of the Neuse, the Rebels halted, took up a new position, and held it with greater determination. Zabriskie accordingly maneuvered in an effort to turn the enemy's left—fittingly enough, by way of a knee-high swamp, "the meanest one I ever saw," in the words of one Muskrat. Private Cleveland described the ordeal that resulted: "Here we lay for three hours while the enemy shelled us . . . cutting the branches of trees and wounding several men."[42]

When the fire finally slackened and the regiment cleared the morass, it discovered that a Confederate regiment was trying to return the Ninth's favor by curving around its right. The outfit was momentarily staggered when the Southerners rose as a body from behind a tree-sheltered fence and poured a volley "into our very faces," as Sergeant Drake put it. A comrade wrote that "it seemed as if the fires of hell were all around us. I did not believe one of us would come out alive." Yet not only did the Ninth survive the barrage, at Zabriskie's order it delivered a charge at bayonet point that drove its opponents across the only standing bridge to the far bank of the river, where they dug in yet again.

By the time the regiment reached the bridge it was on fire, a desperate attempt by the enemy to relieve the pressure it had been under all day. The structure had been torched so hastily that it imperiled the lives of several of Evans's men, who had been caught on the left bank when the fire was set. In a desperate attempt to reach safety some leapt into the water and swam for their lives. At least three or four others, who had been wounded and disabled while lighting the turpentine-soaked span, perished in the flames.[43]

A burning bridge was an unmanageable handicap to some pursuers, but a temporary deterrent to the Ninth New Jersey. Assisted by artillerymen who filled their battery's sponge buckets with water from a nearby well, the regiment doused the fire sufficiently to permit it to cross what remained of the structure and gain the far bank. Most accounts have the Ninth being the first to cross, but Private Cleveland, a careful chronicler of events, claimed that the Tenth Connecticut reached the objective first. He added, however, that the Ninth was the first to plant its colors on the bank in front of the bridge. This occurred, said Cleveland, because Sgt. George Meyers, while hastening to the bridge, grabbed the collar of the Connecticut color bearer who was running beside him and yanked him off his feet.[44]

Led by Captain Curlis and the men of Company F and followed closely by Company K, the Ninth sprinted across the smoldering bridge and on the far side overtook the Rebel rear. In his official report Heckman noted the capture of four cannons and "several hundred" prisoners as well as the battle flag of a South Carolina regiment, snatched up by Lieutenant Townley. One Jerseyman wrote that "it took the rebs five days to bury their dead and [that we] mowed them down like grass before the [s]cythe." Private Reading gloated that the Confederates "allowed that one of them could whip [several] Yanks but it was not long before they came back [with] their coat-tails standing strait out behind."[45]

The Rebel prisoners included a major who had "taken to his heels in a very undignified manner" but was apprehended by fleet-footed Charley Geary of Company F. Before handing over his prisoner, Geary relieved him not only of his side arms but of a gold watch and chain, which he considered legitimate spoils of war. When the major was presented to Captain Curlis, he complained loudly of the theft, adding that "I didn't know that Yankees stole!" Made to feel guilty, Geary returned the man's possessions. Later in the day he was heard to mutter: "The next rebel I capture who has a good watch, *I will bring him in dead*, so he can't make any complaint!"[46]

Prisoners and prizes of war had come at the cost of two members of the Ninth killed, thirty-two wounded, and one missing and presumed captured. The casualty total had a sobering effect; as one survivor lamented, "many a poor fellow was left in that miserable swamp." Some of the wounded came close to being struck a second time when Dr. Gillette set up the regimental field hospital inside a house too close to the front. Warned to move farther to the rear, the assistant surgeon demurred, believing that a nearby artillery unit would shield him and his charges. Instead, the battery drew the enemy's fire and the house was struck repeatedly by shot and shell, forcing a chaotic evacuation. A stretcher-bearer, racing to the rear, halted long enough to vent his spleen at Gillette: "You are a hell of a doctor to put the hospital in front of a battle!" It was noted that the assistant surgeon never made that mistake again.[47]

By 2 p.m., with the enemy on the run, the Ninth entered nearly deserted Kinston, which later-arriving troops secured. They came too late to prevent foragers from helping themselves to "all manner of booty" including the contents of a barber shop whose every razor and bar of soap was appropriated by an unnamed member of Company E who evidently placed a premium on personal grooming. The capture of the town failed to offset the mood of soldiers reeling from heavy fighting and relatively heavy losses. As Corporal Little wrote afterward, "it was an awful day."[48]

By daylight on the fifteenth the Ninth was countermarching through the "handsome little town." It tried but apparently failed to deceive its enemy by initially moving toward Goldsboro on a road other than the one General Foster had selected for his main body. This day the men marched rather than fought while feasting on chickens, pigs, and other delicacies offered up by an especially hospitable countryside.

On the sixteenth and again the next day the Ninth was under fire from Rebels desperate to prevent the capture of their operations center. The first clash occurred outside the village of Whitehall, where a bridge crossed the Neuse and an ironclad ram that would be named for the river was under construction. Opposed in freezing weather by Confederates occupying heavy breastworks, long lines of rifle pits, buildings on both sides of the stream, and wooded sanctuaries, the combat-weary Ninth, its energy and ammunition running low, spent upward of two hours trying to clear a path to Goldsboro before being forced to give way to fresher outfits. By then musketry and shelling had taken a grievous toll: three of its men killed, forty-two wounded, and one man missing.[49]

The enemy's superior position on a thirty-foot bluff had contributed much to this outcome. An unidentified Jerseyman described Rebel sharpshooters "in the trees . . . picking off our officers; some of them were swinging from ropes in the large pines. We tried to get at them, but could not reach them." Under the intense fire "our colors were completely riddled." It was reported that the Ninth's national standard was pierced twenty times while its state colors were shredded by a piece of shell. The hours-long engagement ended inconclusively, with the Federals again suffering relatively heavy casualties. Thanks to their artillery they damaged the unfinished ironclad, which would never see active service. If any humor could be found in the day's proceedings it came from an overheard conversation between a New York chaplain and an artilleryman who had been slightly wounded. The man of God asked the youngster: "Are you supported in this your hour of pain and need by Divine Providence?" "No, sir," was the reply, "this battery is supported by the Ninth New Jersey."[50]

At the close of the fighting a member of one of the short-term Massachusetts regiments encountered "a little runty, oldish-appearing soldier of the Ninth New Jersey. He was one of those tough, wiry men, made of steel." This fellow, whose name the writer never learned, held out his gun, "smutty from firing," and remarked: "I *know* that I have killed three rebels with this to-day." The writer noted that "these words were uttered with an earnestness and intensity of feeling which would have done credit to John Brown. There was nothing, however, of malignity in them, nothing any way ferocious. There was a patriotic fervor about the man that made it apparent to me that it was not individual hate which actuated him, but a whole-hearted devotion of soul to his calling as a defender of the Union."[51]

The seventeenth marked the final day of major combat on the expedition. Having replenished its cartridge boxes, the Ninth, still leading the column, resumed its westward march. Before the morning was over its skirmishers drew near a covered railroad bridge over the Neuse just outside Goldsboro. In a reversal of the normal order of things, the enemy wished to keep Thompson's Bridge intact while General Foster desired its destruction. To do the hard work Colonel Heckman called for volunteers from the Ninth and the Seventeenth Massachusetts. According to Sergeant Drake, "nearly every member of the Ninth within hearing of the Colonel's voice, begged to be selected for the duty." Heckman chose five volunteers: Lieutenant Carrell, along with a Massachusetts lieutenant serving as one of the colonel's aides, and three enlisted men of the Ninth, Corp. James W. Green and Pvts. Elias Winans and William Lemons.

Armed with artillery fuses, the little party moved stealthily down the embankment toward the 220-yard-long bridge, braving a "terrible fury" of enemy fire from the other side of the river. Through some miracle all five reached the span but were unable to use the fuses, which lacked an accelerant. Undeterred, Winans dashed into the woods and scooped up an armful of twigs and leaves. Covered by his comrades' rifles, he piled the combustibles on the bridge abutment, managed to ignite them, "and in another minute the interior was enveloped in flames." While the fire raged other regiments destroyed three miles of track on the Wilmington and Weldon Railroad.[52]

Despite the damage thus inflicted, and with Goldsboro apparently within his grasp, Foster suddenly decided to advance no farther. As he had on the outskirts of Tarboro, he reacted badly to reports that his objective had been strongly reinforced. He also gave credence to newspaper accounts, relayed by Confederate prisoners, that four days earlier the Army of the Potomac had been decisively defeated outside Fredericksburg, Virginia, and forced into retreat. Burnside's plans had been known to Foster; one of the latter's aims had been to prevent North Carolinians from reinforcing Fredericksburg. This opportunity lost, Foster ordered a return march to New Bern.[53]

The result was a three-day, seventy-two-mile nightmare. Abused by the weather, the killing pace, and the realization that another well-mounted and costly operation had been aborted at the eleventh hour, the Federals plodded homeward. By day they warded off freezing temperatures and bone-numbing winds through marching, and by night by tearing down farm fences to fuel their camp fires. "We burnt [more] fence rails," wrote Private Knapp of Company K, "than Old Abe every split in his whole life."[54]

On the afternoon of the twentieth the men of the Ninth finally felt the welcoming embrace of New Bern's defenses, having covered the last thirty-two miles in a near-record twelve hours. A "considerably used up" Andrew W. Little considered the feat a fitting end to two weeks "of the hardest marching and fighting that this regiment has ever endured." He was "a pitiable sight, my feet all in blisters, shoes cut to pieces and clothes nearly torn off my body."

Once he regained the strength and desire to write home, Little offered a vivid summary of the hardships he and his comrades had managed to survive: "We had a hard time every day wading through swamps through mud and bushes, when chasing the rebels hallowing and shouting [with] all our might. I became so hoarse as to be almost unable to speak. We was kept up by the excitement and feared nothing." He added that he "saw men's heads shot off with cannon balls as slick as if cut off with an axe." He had also seen wounded men burned to cinders on a ruined bridge. These memories may have preyed on his mind for although Little would survive the war, less than three months after returning home he would take his own life.[55]

Having suffered almost 100 casualties on the recent mission, the regiment was utterly exhausted physically and mentally. As one man put it in a letter home, over the past ten days "I have been in four battles, and God knows, I have seen enough." The Ninth desperately needed time to recuperate. This it got, at least to a certain extent. Over the next month the men rested in their old camp south of New Bern, treating aches and pains and clearing combat-befogged minds. In this way the most hectic and physically demanding year in the life of the Ninth New Jersey Volunteers came to a quiet close.[56]

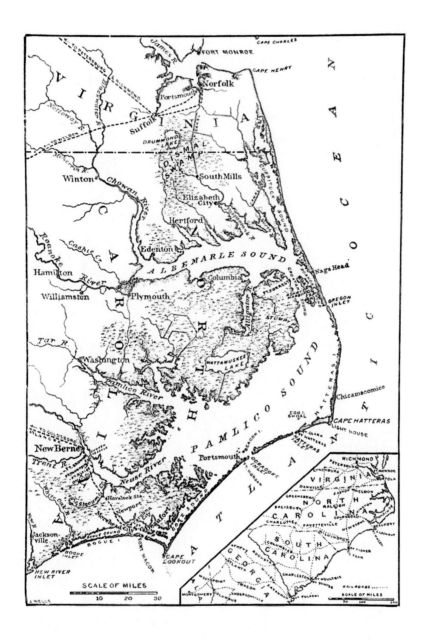

1. Map of Coastal North Carolina. (Robert Underwood Johnson and Clarence C. Buel, *Battles and Leaders of the Civil War* [New York: Century Company, 1887].)

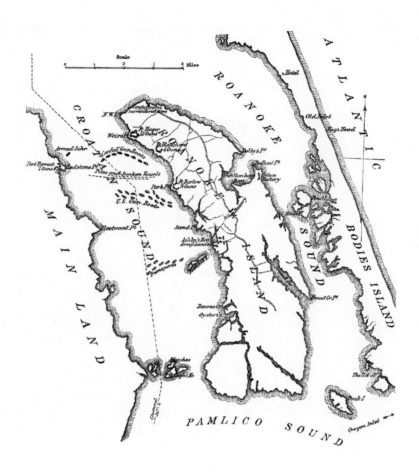

2. (*above*) Map of Battle of Roanoke Island. (Robert Underwood Johnson and Clarence C. Buel, *Battles and Leaders of the Civil War* [New York: Century Company, 1887].)

3. (*opposite page*) Map of South Carolina Coast including St. Helena Island. (Robert Underwood Johnson and Clarence C. Buel, *Battles and Leaders of the Civil War* [New York: Century Company, 1887].)

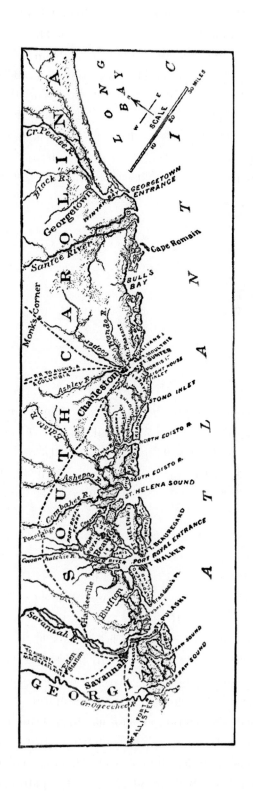

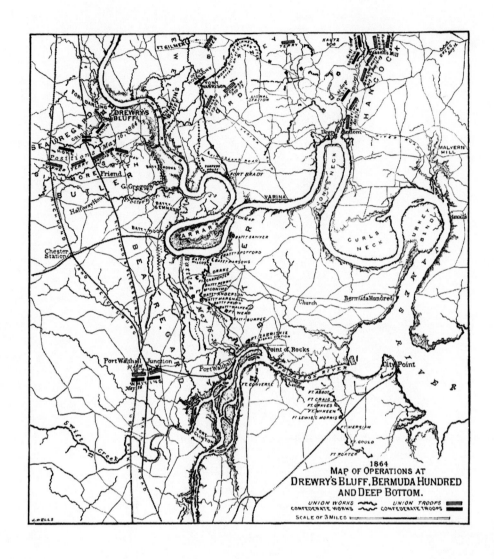

4. Map of Bermuda Hundred Campaign. (Robert Underwood Johnson and Clarence C. Buel, *Battles and Leaders of the Civil War* [New York: Century Company, 1887].)

5. Drawing of Battle of Roanoke Island. (Drake, *Ninth New Jersey*, 1889.)

6. Drawing of Breastworks at Bermuda Hundred. (Drake, *Ninth New Jersey*, 1889.)

7. Regimental Monument in New Bern (NC) National Cemetery. (Author's collection.)

8. (*above*) Drawing of Trenches at Cold Harbor. (Robert Underwood Johnson and Clarence C. Buel, *Battles and Leaders of the Civil War* [New York: Century, 1887].)

9. (*bottom, opposite page*) Gen. Ambrose E. Burnside. (Courtesy Library of Congress.)

10. Gen. Benjamin F. Butler (*fifth from left*) and staff. (Courtesy Library of Congress.)

11. (*left*) Gen. John G. Foster. (Courtesy Library of Congress.)

12. (*right*) Gen. Jesse L. Reno. (Courtesy Library of Congress.)

13. (*left*) Gen. William F. Smith. (Courtesy Library of Congress.)

14. (*right*) Capt. William H. Abel. (Courtesy of the John Kuhl collection.)

15. Col. Joseph Allen. (Drake, *Ninth New Jersey*, 1889.)

16. (*left*) Pvt. William P. Amerman. (Courtesy of the John Kuhl collection.)

17. (*right*) Capt. A. Benson Brown. (Courtesy of the John Kuhl collection.)

18. (*left*) Chaplain John J. Carrell. (Drake, *Ninth New Jersey*, 1889.)

19. (*right*) Capt. Edward S. Carrell. (Drake, *Ninth New Jersey*, 1889.)

20. Pvt. Edmund J. Cleveland. (Courtesy of the John Kuhl collection.)

21. (*left*) Lt. Col. William B. Curlis. (Courtesy of the John Kuhl collection.)

22. (*right*) Lt. J. Madison Drake. (Courtesy of the John Kuhl collection.)

23. (*left*) Surgeon Fidelio B. Gillette. (Drake, *Ninth New Jersey*, 1889.)

24. (*right*) Capt. Edwin S. Harris. (Drake, *Ninth New Jersey*, 1889.)

25. (*left*) Col. Charles A. Heckman. (Courtesy of the John Kuhl collection.)

26. (*right*) Capt. Joseph J. Henry. (Drake, *Ninth New Jersey*, 1889.)

27. Capt. Charles Hufty. (Courtesy of the John Kuhl collection.)

28. Quartermaster Samuel Keys. (Drake, *Ninth New Jersey*, 1889.)

29. Capt. Edgar Kissam. (Courtesy of the John Kuhl collection.)

30. Capt. Joseph B. Lawrence. (Courtesy of the John Kuhl collection.)

31. Capt. Joseph M. McChesney. (Courtesy New Jersey State Archives.)

32. Lt. Joseph A. Schnetzer. (Courtesy of the John Kuhl collection.)

33. Col. James Stewart, Jr. (Courtesy of the John Kuhl collection.)

34. (*left*) Sgt. Symmes H. Stillwell. (Drake, *Ninth New Jersey*, 1889.)

35. (*right*) Capt. Jonathan Townley. (Courtesy of the John Kuhl collection.)

36. (*left*) Surgeon Addison W. Woodhull. (Courtesy New Jersey State Archives.)

37. (*right*) Col. Abram Zabriskie. (Courtesy of the John Kuhl collection.)

7 Southern Excursion

The new year brought both change and a return to familiar routine. As the Ninth recuperated from its labors on the grounds of what was still called Camp Reno in honor of its former brigade commander, who had been killed in action during the Antietam Campaign, it reinstated company and battalion drill, pulled guard duty, trained an increasing influx of recruits (deemed essential since casualties and sickness had reduced the regiment to fewer than 400 effectives), held dress parades, and turned out for an occasional review by General Foster or his subordinates. On the surface, the ebb and flow of camp life was much as it had been ever since the Ninth left New Bern to picket the Atlantic and North Carolina Railroad.

As the men alternately rested and labored, the war around them underwent dramatic change. The Emancipation Proclamation had refocused the Union war effort, and by the start of its third year the tenor of the conflict was hardening, becoming more violent, and extending its reach ever closer to the civilian population, thus becoming what Lincoln, in his first annual report to Congress, had feared: "A violent and remorseless revolutionary struggle." The Ninth had contributed to the new order during both of the recent expeditions, plundering the enemy's country and, deliberately or not, terrorizing the Confederacy's civilian base.[1]

Efforts to expedite this fundamental shift in objectives and procedures were afoot in various theaters. They were particularly visible in the West where Ulysses S. Grant's foremost subordinate, William T. Sherman, was honing long-contemplated theories of total war. The previous autumn the red-haired Ohioan had put these to the test throughout the military district he commanded in West Tennessee, burning out citizens who had aided or abetted guerrilla attacks on his lines while sending other enemy supporters into exile or to prison. As he wrote to Grant in October: "We cannot change the hearts and minds of the South, but we can make war so terrible that they realize the fact that, however brave and gallant and devoted to their country, still they are mortal and should exhaust all peaceful remedies before they fly to war." In time Sherman's viewpoint would be adopted and acted upon by other commanders.[2]

One reason for this shift toward "hard war" was the sudden lack of progress the Union armies were making across the chessboard of war. The previous autumn the picture had seemed bright with the repulse of Rebel incursions into Maryland, Kentucky, and Tennessee. By January 1863 that picture had clouded over with the overwhelming defeat of Burnside's army at Fredericksburg, where 13,000 Federal soldiers had become casualties in a single day, and the abrupt end to Burnside's subsequent attempt to regain momentum by a stealthy envelopment of Lee's position, a weather-plagued debacle that would become known as the "Mud March." Within a week of the disaster, an overland effort by Grant's Army of the Tennessee to seize strategic Vicksburg had been aborted by crippling attacks on its supply lines in northern Mississippi. Immediately following Grant's setback, a 32,000-man expedition under Sherman had suffered a bloody repulse at Chickasaw Bayou. The only Union success at this time came in Middle Tennessee, where Maj. Gen. William S. Rosecrans's Army of the Cumberland eked out a victory against Braxton Bragg's Confederates at Murfreesboro. With this exception, the war to preserve the Union appeared to have bogged down, and prospects for reviving it looked bleak.[3]

The military situation was being felt on the political front. During the fall 1862 elections Democrats, including antiwar Copperheads, had made significant gains in states including Ohio, Indiana, and Pennsylvania, suggesting that public support for the administration's handling of the war was weakening. The apparently growing disaffection among Northern voters was suddenly as much a problem for the warlords of Washington as the incapacity of McClellan, Burnside, Pope, and Foster and the apparent brilliance of their opponents.

New Jersey, given its strong Democratic base, was another locus of political change although, perhaps unexpectedly, not to a marked degree. On November 4 Democrat Joel Parker, a former state assemblyman from Monmouth County, had won the governor's chair by routing the Opposition Party's candidate, Marcus L. Ward. Though a staunch opponent of Abraham Lincoln's political and social programs, the "War Democrat" (a title Parker shared with the majority of those in the Ninth New Jersey) pledged, and with few exceptions maintained, his support of the military effort.[4]

The men of the Ninth reportedly gave "hearty cheers" when the results of the canvas became known in North Carolina. Writing in the columns of the *Newark Daily Journal*, the soldier who signed himself "Censor" regarded Parker's victory as a well-merited rebuke to Lincoln's racial policies. He rejoiced that "our State has done her duty to herself and the whole country by throwing overboard the 'abolition fanatics,' by whom he have been so long ruled." Even those more favorably disposed toward the administration welcomed the news from Trenton. A member of Company K, writing to the editor of the *Plainfield Union* shortly before the Goldsboro Raid, had lamented the "general depression of spirit among the three years' troops of this department, concerning the progress of the war, and the wranglings of political parties at the North." It had reached the point that almost any change could be construed as an improvement.[5]

And yet, rather than despair, the Ninth New Jersey had ample reasons to celebrate its current situation. Its highly visible achievements on the road to Goldsboro had won it respect and praise. On several occasions during the expedition other outfits had saluted its bravery, energy, and skill. The day after the regiment's return, an enlisted man remarked that "as I walk along [the streets of] Newbern every one compliments me on the conduct of the Ninth. 'The Ninth' is the subject of conversation for the town and the army."[6]

In later weeks those officers considered responsible for much of the regiment's success were honored in ways that bolstered unit pride. The highest tribute went to Colonel Heckman, who was promoted brigadier general of volunteers for "signal ability and meritorious services." His appointment, which dated from November 29, created a domino effect that included the elevation of Abram Zabriskie to colonel, James Stewart to lieutenant colonel, and William B. Curlis, the regiment's senior captain, to major. Zabriskie and Stewart had barely adjusted to their late-December promotions to lieutenant colonel and major, respectively, before assuming the duties of their higher rank.

The regiment welcomed the ascension of all four officers, but Heckman's appointment generated the greatest measure of approval. "He was almost idolized," wrote one Jerseyman. "No officer ever behaved more bravely." Another remarked that "you cannot imagine how he has endeared himself to all of us, always anxious for our comfort and sparing no labor to advance the welfare of the humblest private." These qualities, added to Heckman's record as a combat commander, ensured that "his name belongs to history."[7]

Another event that promoted regimental pride was the receipt at New Bern of a new stand of colors, costing two hundred dollars, the gift of state officials "in remembrance of Roanoke and Newbern." Along with the flags, which would replace the shot-torn banners the Ninth had carried from Trenton to Goldsboro, came a copy of the resolutions of appreciation the legislature had passed the previous March. The gifts were presented to the assembled regiment at New Bern by the state's representative to the army (and its future adjutant general), 2nd Lt. William F. Stryker. An onlooker reported that "the colors were then paraded through the streets, behind a band." They were taken, first, to General Heckman's headquarters at Morehead City, where, along with the old flags, they were inspected by General Foster and his staff. It was said that Foster studied the standards "with admiration for the beauty of the new colors, and respect for the honorable scars, the bullet holes and shell marks in the old ones."[8]

As J. Madison Drake explained, nothing pleased the regiment more "than to be assured that their patriotic services were fully appreciated by the authorities and people at home." The men were likewise cheered by another well-received gesture extended at this same time: the belated receipt of two months' pay, with the promise of more soon to come. Drake believed these several occurrences placed the Ninth in a frame of mind quite different from the one that beset it upon its return from its long, arduous, and highly disappointing excursion to the Neuse River.[9]

As of December 24 the Ninth New Jersey, along with every other unit in the Department of North Carolina, became part of the XVIII Corps. This organization, commanded by General Foster, consisted of the remaining units of Burnside's Coast Division as well as Maj. Gen. John J. Peck's division (formerly a member of the IV Corps, Army of the Potomac) and the garrisons of New Bern, Beaufort, and Plymouth. Upon ascending to star rank, General Heckman took charge of one of the corps' three "unattached" brigades of infantry. His command, soon to be designated as the First Brigade, Second Division, and known throughout the corps as the "Star Brigade," consisted of, in addition to the Ninth, the Third, Eighth, and Twenty-third Massachusetts Volunteers, some of whose men had served under Heckman during the Goldsboro raid. According to historians Joseph G. Bilby and William C. Goble, "unlike the brigades of the Army of the Potomac, the Star Brigade's units were constantly shuffled and transferred during the final two years of the war and the unit was often broken up for detached service. It always contained the Ninth New Jersey and several Massachusetts regiments, however."[10]

If the War Department had its way, the Star Brigade and the rest of the XVIII Corps would soon see campaigning in a sector of North

Carolina not previously touched by invasion. Early in January rumors of an attack on the Rebel stronghold of Wilmington were making the rounds of Camp Reno and, after January 13, the Ninth's new camp at Carolina City. General Foster had been called to Washington for consultations, and when he returned it was expected that the corps would be shipped down the coast to attack that haven for the blockade runners who helped keep the Confederacy in business. By early 1863 so many Southern ports had been closed to shipping that Wilmington on the Cape Fear River had become the logical target of an army-navy expedition like the one that seized Roanoke Island.

Foster had long favored such an operation, but the naval support he considered critical to its success suffered a major blow when the first Union ironclad, the USS *Monitor*, sank in a storm off Cape Hatteras on December 31 while en route to Wilmington. The loss of the celebrated vessel—the only ironclad with the recognized ability to cross the bar into the Cape Fear inlet that gave access to the city—scuttled the expedition, and when Foster returned to North Carolina he was acting under orders that would send his command, instead, to South Carolina. The Navy Department had turned its attention to a target more popular with the Northern public: Charleston, where the war had begun and where Foster, then a captain of engineers, had weathered the bombardment of Fort Sumter, his initial wartime station.[11]

At Charleston Foster's command would cooperate with the local forces, members of Maj. Gen. David Hunter's X Corps. Hunter's vast bailiwick, which he had occupied for the past ten months, was the Department of the South, headquartered on Hilton Head Island. Hunter, a Virginia-born abolitionist, was one of the earliest supporters of African Americans in arms, having formed the all-black First South Carolina Volunteers in the spring of 1862. Even more controversially, he had announced the emancipation of every slave in his department.

Although "Black Dave" was a friend and confidant of Lincoln, the president—then unready to promote a cause he now embraced, fearful that it would antagonize conservative Northerners including slave-owning Unionists—had repudiated Hunter's decree and then disbanded the First South Carolina. Yet Hunter retained Lincoln's support, which explained why he wore two stars on his shoulder straps. By no one's imagination could he be considered a great captain. His achievements in command, other than in the realm of social engineering, had been few, and his successes in the field even fewer. In his dealings with colleagues and subordinates he could be autocratic, overbearing, even duplicitous. But his commission dated from the earliest months of the war, granting him considerable seniority, and he was the undisputed authority in his realm.[12]

The conservative soldier Foster was unsure of his ability to get along with such a man, but he was certain of one thing: he was not about to head for a new field of operations without his sharpshooting Muskrats. He saw to it that the Ninth and the rest of Heckman's brigade were included in the two divisions he would lead to South Carolina, under Brig. Gens. Henry M. Naglee and Orris S. Ferry. On January 20 the Ninth left its latest habitation for Morehead City, where officers and men boarded two of the six troopships assigned to Heckman's brigade, the *Key West* (Companies A, B, C, E, F, and I), with the rest of the regiment on a smaller steamer, the *Curlew*. Accommodations were extremely cramped. "We are piled on like hogs not like men," wrote Quartermaster Sgt. John Bamford, and they would get only one meal per day.[13]

All expected to be off soon—for somewhere. Most of the speculation centered on Wilmington, although Charleston, Savannah, and Mobile were other possibilities. It soon became apparent, however, that, as had been the case when boarding the transports at Annapolis twelve months ago, no one was going anywhere any time soon. The Ninth remained aboard ship for more than a week, buffeted throughout by storms. Not till the afternoon of the twenty-ninth did the transports weigh anchor and breast the breakers of the Atlantic. They had a rough time clearing the harbor, perhaps a harbinger of things to come. The *Key West* struck the bar three times, almost grounding, before reaching deep water. "The vessels would plunge under every time," wrote Corp. Richard J. Berdan of Company E, "completely washing the decks" and causing much seasickness." Sgt. Symmes H. Stillwell agreed that "a sick time it was. . . . Sometimes our vessel would seem to stand on on[e] end pitching and tossing us from one side of our bunks to another." The following day the seas calmed, "although many were still weak from the severe vomiting, etc."[14]

Some passengers were especially glad to have left North Carolina and not merely because they wished to get on with the business of fighting Rebels. Their quarters had become cramped upon the arrival of new inhabitants whom they viewed as undesirables. On the recent raids hundreds of runaway slaves had attached themselves to Foster's column in hopes of being led out of bondage. Some had won the commendation of the soldiers by serving in a variety of support roles. Two hundred or more had been formed into a pioneer battalion that on numerous occasions went to work with axes and poles to remove obstructions from the routes of march.[15]

Runaways less useful to the army, especially women and children, were regarded in a much different light. Two weeks before boarding the *Curlew*, David C. Hankins had protested that "the Nigers is so thick do[w]n here that we can hardly stuir. There is a [civilian] Camp . . . on each side of us. There is about six hundred in one Camp and about three [hundred] in the other." Their inhabitants, he added, "have got so sassey" and were so well supported by the government as to be unwilling to work for the army. A comrade remarked that "it is a common saying here, 'fresh bread for the nigger and hard tack for the soldier.' The fact is, the cursed 'nigga' is the only one who has any liberties at all. They come and go as they please, and are protected by their abolition hirelings." But if those who voiced such opinions believed they were heading for a place where they would not have to associate with former slaves they would soon be disabused of the notion.[16]

On the thirty-first, following a voyage marked not only by rough seas and cramped quarters but also by the intervention of a blockading crew that somehow mistook *Curlew* for a Confederate commerce raider, the ships bearing the men of the Ninth entered Port Royal Harbor. Under "delightful weather" they anchored off the Sea Island known as St. Helena, almost forty miles southwest of Charleston. By now almost everyone on board had surmised the general outline of future operations but none of the specifics.[17]

As before, the passengers expected a speedy return to service on land; again, they hoped in vain. As if Foster's coming was unexpected, the men were confined to the ships for ten days. "As no signs of a forward movement were visible," wrote Sergeant Drake, "and as the Department of South Carolina was not noted for push or daring, the men began to grumble at their continuance on shipboard, especially as there was ample room on the lovely island upon which we could almost throw a line from the deck of our vessel."

From those decks the men squinted disapprovingly at a row of Negro shanties that wandered along the edge of the inland. Drake related that the "cozy homes" sheltered "thousands of fat, well-dressed and indolent negroes . . . [who] come down to the shore daily, gather pails full of oysters, and after taunting us retrace their steps homeward. Is it, then, any wonder that some uncomplimentary things are said by our men."[18]

Another target of unflattering commentary was the reported proximity of Negro troops, a species the Ninth had never before laid eyes on. In late 1862 the Department of North Carolina had authorized the arming and training of about 250 blacks, but they had been restricted to service in and around Elizabeth City where the Ninth had not ventured. The presence of a large number of colored troops in this new area of operations was an unappreciated novelty. Edmund J. Cleveland, who hailed from a family that espoused liberal social views, noted in his diary: "It is said that a negro brigade is quartered at Port Royal. The boys do not seem to like the idea of fighting along side of the colored gentlemen." Yet not everyone felt this way, at least not at this juncture. In a letter to his mother on February 1 Sergeant Stillwell appeared to welcome the Negro troops: "It is rough but any thing to whip the rebs and end the war."[19]

On St. Helena the Ninth would be introduced to another class of humanity with whom it was wholly unfamiliar. Long before the outbreak of war the blacks on the Sea Islands had forged full-scale communities of their own, gaining thereby a certain amount of autonomy. To escape outbreaks of malaria and other lowland diseases, every summer slave owners and their families fled to the mainland, leaving their property in the hands of their chattels. Upon Port Royal's capture in November 1861 by a fleet of warships under Flag Off. Samuel F. Du Pont, the planters had left the island for good. Thus, long before they were officially relieved of servitude by the invading forces, the remaining inhabitants had acquired the trappings, and the mind-set, of independence.[20]

On February 9 the *Curlew*'s passengers were finally put ashore, no explanation given for their extended confinement to shipboard. The following day the rest of the Star Brigade including the remainder of the Ninth came ashore. Though it was said that the regiment embarked "in the best of humor," trouble was brewing. Reportedly, Generals Foster and Hunter were already at loggerheads, the former having been "illy treated" by the latter. According to the most recent rumors, Foster had left the department in a huff, returning to Washington to air his grievances before Gen.-in-Chief Henry W. Halleck and perhaps President Lincoln as well.[21]

The rumor mill had it pretty much correct. Whether or not badly treated (Hunter claimed to have offered only "cordiality and kindness"), ten days after reaching South Carolina Foster departed for Virginia, an action Hunter characterized as "tending to excite mutiny and insubordination among the troops ordered to re-enforce this department." Upon reaching Fort Monroe, Foster bombarded Halleck with a litany of complaints. The principal allegation was that he had been given to understand that while in South Carolina his troops would serve as a separate and distinct force under his command; yet Hunter had declared them adjunct to his department and thus subject to his authority.

Hunter would respond that his action was temporary, in force only until the army's operations got under way. "Serious injuries" sustained by one of the ironclads en route from Hampton Roads to Port Royal and the failure of two other warships to arrive on schedule meant that Du Pont (now a rear admiral) would not be ready to attack Charleston for three or four weeks. Hunter also claimed that Foster, upon hearing the news, had intended to return his troops to North Carolina, something Hunter would not allow.[22]

With support from the equally irate General Naglee, Foster complained loudly, but futilely, to Halleck. In the end the general-in-chief upheld Hunter's authority to place Foster's troops "subject to your orders" but rescinded the order that formally integrated them with the X Corps. To further placate Foster, Halleck permitted him to return to North Carolina where the Rebels under their new commander, Maj. Gen. Daniel Harvey Hill, were, according to reports, "becoming aggressive." By early March Foster was back at New Bern, where he established XVIII Corps headquarters and reassumed command of the three divisions he had left behind when heading south. By now his well-publicized clash with Hunter had placed a cloud over an operation that had attracted the interest of the entire North. In the end, however, the acrimonious affair would be seen as a fitting prelude to the events that followed.[23]

It took not four weeks but two months for Du Pont to gather the ships, and the resolve, to strike an extremely well defended objective. Gen. G. T. Beauregard, the feisty Creole who commanded in the city, had so thoroughly buoyed Charleston Harbor that the gunners in Fort Sumter and on the surrounding islands could determine the exact range of any attacking vessel. Booms had been strung across the channel and floating mines (known as "torpedoes"), theoretically able to be detonated from shore, had been placed where the ships had to pass. A second line of defense consisted of inner fortifications such as Fort Ripley, Castle Pinckney, and the batteries on James Island. Attackers surmounting these obstacles would face concentrated artillery fire from guns mounted in the city, whose defenders were prepared to engage any landing party in street-to-street fighting.[24]

While the navy dithered and Hunter, who claimed his soldiers were "ready to embark at six hours' notice," fumed over the delay, the Ninth New Jersey settled uneasily into its semitropical environment. For some of the companies, which encamped under "fragrant orange trees," life seemed pleasant. Other units were less comfortably bivouacked; they included Company K, which bedded down on the grounds of a cemetery adjacent to an abandoned plantation, an act Ed Cleveland considered a desecration. Seeking more appropriate housing, the private discovered a Negro hut, charmingly built of oyster shells mixed with lime, whose owners, an elderly couple named Robert and Lucretia, put the youngster and one of his comrades up for the night. One night's lodging was all that was needed; on the eleventh the regiment's tents were carried ashore and set up in neat rows across the length of the plantation.[25]

Later interaction between the regiment and the local people did not end as happily. Less than twenty-four hours after debarking, a group of Jerseymen attempted to procure drinking water from a well on a contraband's property. Accustomed to slaves who readily assented to their needs and wants, the men were furious when the homeowner, as Sergeant Drake explained, "objected to this, and forcibly resisted. . . . This was more than some of the men who had left pleasant homes to fight for the country would submit to." Those denied water reported the incident to comrades as well as to the men of neighboring regiments. Several listeners decided that the blacks of the vicinity should be taught a lesson in civility. Some had predicted that something of this sort would come to pass. As Corporal Little put it, the islanders "are quite independent and saucy, but . . . they will be tamed."[26]

Shortly after dark some of those who had been barred from the well, along with members of at least two infantry regiments and an artillery battery from New York, revisited the obstreperous owner carrying improvised torches and quite possibly reeking of alcohol. In a matter of minutes, despite loud protests and wails of anguish from the inhabitants, not only the principal target of the mob's wrath had been burned out but also fifty of his neighbors including women and children, Robert and Lucretia among them. By dawn fifteen or twenty shanties had been reduced to smoldering embers and the perpetrators were nowhere to be found.[27]

Reaction to the tragedy included Little's comment that "I was sorry to see the poor niggers abused, but . . . there are too many here for our" peace of mind. Private Cleveland was incensed by the vandalism but believed it the work of "the rascals from the New York regiments." Other members of the Ninth blamed the victims, some of whom were said to have publicly insulted the soldiers, while one anonymous contraband was accused of firing a shot at them (though the source of the claim admitted that "this story is not authenticated"). Yet another provocation—the final straw, perhaps, for those disturbed by the sight of black men in uniform—was the observed visit of two members of the United States Colored Troops (USCT) to the village a few hours before the attack.[28]

Given General Hunter's well-known sympathy for African Americans in and out of uniform, the regiments reported to have been involved in the attack were not surprised when subsequently punished by official order. Because the vandals were never positively identified, the Ninth New Jersey as a whole—and apparently several other XVIII Corps regiments—suffered for the crimes of a few. According to Pvt. Hermann Everts, the Ninth was denied fresh bread and beef for an entire month "and other rations only in small quantities during that time." This may have been the source of Private Cleveland's February 17 complaint that "we had coffee minus sugar for supper this evening. The boys were loud in their denunciation of it."[29]

Extra drill and multiple roll calls ("every two hours, from reveille to taps") were also imposed on the supposed vandals. According to Sergeant Drake, Black Dave also ordered drums to be beaten at night in the camp of every regiment in Naglee's command to deprive the inhabitants of sleep. Finally, any officer or enlisted man absent from camp would be reported to department headquarters. These penalties appear extreme, and the extent to which they were implemented cannot be determined. Although newspaper reports had the entire regiment arrested for the attack on the shanties, a member of the Ninth, writing almost two weeks later, insisted that "not an officer or soldier of our regiment was put under arrest for it." But another Jerseyman declared that Hunter treated the regiment "not [as] Union volunteers, but Union prisoners."[30]

Not surprisingly, the men did not appreciate their treatment at the hands of a general more kindly disposed toward Negro civilians than white soldiers. An anonymous member of the Ninth considered himself confined to duty in "a regular Negro Department." Sergeant Stillwell called Hunter "a black hearted abolition fiend & fanatic that never has accomplished anything nor gained a victory in his department and I fear never will." A comrade agreed that "Hunter and his 10th Army Corps have never known anything but defeat. . . . The 18th Corps have always seen the Rebels' *backs*, and never knew anything but victory."[31]

Another source of the Ninth's antipathy was Hunter's sponsorship of black soldiers, several regiments of whom were serving outside Charleston. Many of these took part in the parades and reviews Hunter staged in February and March (during the first of which, one Jerseyman claimed, the regiment was "much surprised to notice the light complexion of 'Massa Hunter'"). Some who criticized the USCT used the same epithets frequently directed at black civilians. An unidentified officer called them "saucy and impudent. I think it is high time the Government dropped the negro [soldier] and went to work" to defeat the Rebels. Originally in favor of using Negroes to advance the war effort, Stillwell now considered "the arming of negroes a confession of weakness, a folly, an insult to the brave Soldier, and a crime against humanity and civilization. . . . I hope the time will come when the President will have to recall his proclamation." Even so, as always, there were dissenting views on the subject of African American troops. In mid-February a member of Company K noted that "near Beaufort, S. C. (about six miles from us,) a negro regiment is encamped. . . . We do not see why some of them should not make good soldiers." This division of opinion would characterize the Ninth during the remainder of the war. Some soldiers would always express a deep-seated antipathy to people of color and their brothers in the ranks, while others would continue to commend black civilians and soldiers for the unselfish and dedicated service they rendered to the army.[32]

For weeks the navy continued to dawdle, adding ships to the flotilla, stocking ammunition, shifting personnel, and revamping plans for the attack that everyone in Charleston knew to be coming. The delay had a dispiriting effect on the army. Results included lassitude, fatigue, and boredom, which affected the soldiers both mentally and physically. In early March an enlisted man described the Ninth as reduced by sickness, "its members broken down and exhausted" by constant drill and duty for no evident purpose. Sergeant Stillwell believed that any move on Charleston would have to await heavy reinforcements of both soldiers and seamen: "The rebs are very strongly fortified there, and we have to make great preparations before we attack it." Suddenly homesick for North Carolina, where the weather was cooler and the high command appeared more willing to engage the enemy, the men felt the days limp past. "I wish they would do what they are a going to do pretty soon," wrote Private Hankins, "and settle this question for I think this war has been carried on prety near long enough." Meeting a boyhood friend who served on a navy schooner, Hankins began to dream of home, which only fed his increasing desperation to get off St. Helena Island.[33]

Restive and surly, the men began to take out their frustration on themselves, their officers, even noncombatants. Shouting matches and fistfights broke out in camp, filling up the regimental guardhouse. One night Private Cleveland and some comrades in Company K, unable to sleep, spent the night "hallooing to one another." A passing officer, Captain Edwin S. Harris of Company C, "being disturbed by the noise, very authoritatively told us to 'shut up' with a threat to report us to the officer of the day. Some of the boys not recognizing his right to order us around 'sassed him back.'" An irate Harris reported them, instead, to Colonel Zabriskie, who punished them with hours of extra drill. Even the revered General Heckman attracted some offensive language when he decreed that every member of the brigade had to appear at guard mounting "with shoes shined, and our clothes, equipment and guns in 'an extra polished condition.'" Virtually every man in the Ninth protested, arguing that "Uncle Sam does not furnish shoe blacking and they [the soldiers] have no money to buy any, and some, through no fault of theirs, have shabby uniforms." Because shabby uniforms usually drew some form of penalty, grumbling and cursing became the daily routine.[34]

Vocalizing one's dissatisfaction with the current situation was one thing; acting it out was a more serious matter. By early March, according to the *Newton Register*, the regiment had begun to display "a spirit of rowdyism and insubordination" never before observed. A growing number of incidents appeared to validate this claim. When punished for "sassing" Captain Harris, the stay-awakes of Company K showed their resentment by deliberately underperforming on the drill field. Ennui and apathy appear to have affected the regiment's well-earned reputation for sharpshooting. One careless round of target practice by the regiment's fifty-man sharpshooter unit produced worrisome results. An onlooking surgeon remarked that although hundreds of shots had been fired, "not more than a dozen would have taken effect." Unwilling to overlook this lapse, Capt. Charles H. Sofield, commander of the unit, drilled the riflemen relentlessly for more than a week. By mid-month results were acceptable: out of 200 shots fired at a range of 230 yards at a target resembling a Confederate soldier, 140 struck the target and nearly a dozen hit the Rebel squarely in the eye.[35]

One of the most serious episodes of rowdiness during this period was an assault by several soldiers on an unnamed sutler who had erected a stand on the St. Helena wharf. The "stampede," as Private Cleveland described it, took place while the man was transferring additional goods from ship to shore. Because he lacked an employee to guard his merchandise, the barrels of food and bottles of spirits he had offloaded were ripe for the taking. All the hungry, thirsty, and irritable soldiers needed was an excuse to raid his stock. That took the form of a rumor that the "wealth-begetting" merchant was charging a 300 percent markup. The result: dozens of containers broken into and their contents—chiefly fruit but undoubtedly also something with a higher alcoholic content—carried off, secreted in the soldiers' pants and blouses. As had been the case with those who destroyed the contraband village, the sutler's attackers were never identified. Had they been brought to justice they probably would have been incarcerated. After March 11, however, this was no longer possible, for that night a suspicious fire razed the Ninth's guardhouse. No one was charged in that incident, either.[36]

Six weeks after reaching South Carolina the army was still playing the waiting game. "We are expecting to leave here every day and go aboard boats for Charleston," wrote Sergeant Stillwell on March 13, but delays continued to dog the assembled forces, with unpleasant results. Squabbling among the high command led to the relief, by request, of General Naglee, who returned to North Carolina to rejoin his old superior. In his absence General Ferry assumed commanded of all of the troops from North Carolina and General Heckman temporarily took over Naglee's division. The Ninth did not endorse Ferry's promotion. He was accused of showing disrespect by "refusing to sign any passes" for members of the regiment and by posting punishments for certain offenses that "would do very well for a State Prison keeper to enforce."[37]

These irritants notwithstanding, some men had settled down to a more or less cozy existence. "We have just got our camp fixed up nice," wrote Private Hankins, "with green trees around the tents and plenty of them, which makes the camp nice and cool." Andrew Little (newly promoted to sergeant) agreed that "we are living better now than we have before on the island." The visit of the paymaster with four months' back pay was a morale booster for everyone. Others drew strength from the fact that the Ninth was now brigaded with veteran and well-regarded regiments including the Twenty-third Massachusetts and Eighty-first and Ninety-eighth New York, all under Brig. Gen. Thomas G. Stevenson, who as a colonel had led the Ninth's brigade during the Swansborough expedition. "Censor" considered the organization "the finest Brigade in the corps," though he would have preferred it had remained in General Heckman's capable hands. Even so, like everyone else in the regiment, the writer was proud that Heckman had moved up to lead Naglee's erstwhile division. Testimony to Heckman's standing in his present position was the size of his command, which was considerably larger than the other XVIII Corps division serving in South Carolina.[38]

Before March was over, however, those benefits and improvements had lost the ability to prop up morale. Sergeant Little complained that "we are lying idle much longer than anticipated and from appearances we will still be inactive for some time." Another enlisted man wailed: "We do little else than turn out for reviews and inspections. When will something toward ending the war be done in this department?"[39]

That something finally took shape in the first days of April when Du Pont made final preparations for his attack and in consultation with General Hunter ironed out the services' respective roles. At 4 p.m. on the second, the Ninth, along with every XVIII unit outside Charleston, was ordered to strike tents and stand ready to board transports. "The men received the order to embark with cheers," Sergeant Drake recalled, "preferring any service to the confinement and continual drill which they had undergone" over the past two months.[40]

Early that evening, under a sudden shower, seven companies of the Ninth returned to the hold of the transport *Key West*, which had brought them to St. Helena Island. A last-minute snag kept the remainder of the outfit—Companies C, D, and G—waiting for twenty-four hours before being permitted to board the schooner *Tillie*. The ships cast off early on April 5, heading north. That evening they came to anchor in the North Edisto River eighteen miles from Charleston. At that distance the men lacked a view of a scene that would have stirred their senses: the nine ironclads that made up Du Pont's striking force lying at anchor just off the bar of the main ship channel, their 11- and 14-inch guns and 8-inch Parrott rifles leveled at a city that appeared to be at their mercy. Once they steamed forth in line of battle, what could possibly prevent them from seizing the harbor in which the war had begun?[41]

The next day brought a rumor that the city's defenders were planning to set fire to ships and rafts off Edisto Island, forty-some miles southwest of Charleston, then aim them at the army's transports and send them downriver. At General Heckman's direction Colonel Zabriskie unloaded Companies I and K and sent them, under Capt. Samuel Hufty and Lt. Jonathan Townley, to determine the truth of the rumor. Once ashore the companies were joined by Generals Heckman and Stevenson, who ordered that picket posts be set up on Edisto. It was all for naught; a thorough search located neither ships, rafts, nor enemy troops.[42]

When the navy launched its long-awaited attack on the morning of the seventh, the men of the Ninth could hear clearly the combined roar of the guns of the fleet and those of the forts and land batteries encircling the harbor. Through morning and afternoon the bombardment, which Sergeant Drake believed "never had a parallel in history," gave testimony to the desperate nature of the attack and defense. At first it offered hope to the passengers aboard the transports that a path into the city had been opened, whereupon the army would go into action ashore. Instead, by midday it had become apparent that the attack was verging on failure.[43]

The trouble had begun when Du Pont's leading warship, the monitor *Weehawken*, absorbed numerous shots from Beauregard's shore batteries and then struck a mine that disabled her. The next gunboat in line, the *Passaic*—named for the river and county in northern New Jersey—became a slow-moving target. In a little over a half hour she was hit thirty-five times; her gun carriage having been displaced and her pilot house crushed, she had to drop out of the fight. The two gunboats next in line took "a frightful pounding," while the third ship, the *New Ironsides*, Du Pont's flagship, became unmanageable in the shoal water of the inlet, collided with other vessels, and, to avoid running aground, anchored within a few feet of a mine that, had it not failed to detonate, would have blown the ship, and her high-ranking passenger, to glory.

Of the four monitors following the *New Ironsides*, one, the *Keokuk*, got to within 900 yards of Fort Sumter whereupon shot after shot pierced her at and near the water line. Eventually riddled by almost ninety shells, *Keokuk* somehow managed to withdraw beyond artillery range, only to sink and be abandoned outside the harbor. The other warships committed to the attack fared almost as badly; none got within close range of the inner harbor.

By five-thirty, having sustained unacceptable losses while repeatedly striking Forts Sumter and Moultrie without inflicting critical damage, Du Pont ordered his fleet to retire. That night he conferred with his captains; upon learning of the condition of their ships, he decided not to renew the attack the next day. Given the accuracy of Beauregard's guns—they had struck Du Pont's ships more than 500 times—his decision was probably a wise one. It would, however, cost him the goodwill of both General Hunter and Secretary of the Navy Gideon Welles—in the end it would also cost him his command. Though Morris Island, south of the city, would fall to Union troops the following September,

Charleston itself, and her famous forts, would remain in Confederate hands until two months before war's end.[44]

The soldiers kept waiting on their transports were disgusted with the navy's defeat. And yet the initial reaction of the Ninth New Jersey was muted and even hopeful. Sergeant Little struck the prevailing note when writing home on the twelfth: "The results of the past weeks work has not been as encouraging as we had hoped it might be. . . . I think that Charleston can and will be taken, [but] it may take time to do it." For benefit of the readers of the Toms River *Ocean Emblem*, Sergeant Drake predicted that "the ironclad 'monitors' will yet be successful—they only suffered a temporary check. . . . Charleston's proud battlements shall yet be hurled to the earth in ruins."[45]

Not until the tenth did the regiment's ships head back to Port Royal. That night they anchored off Hilton Head, and two days later they reached Port Royal Harbor. By then the men had come to consider the operation an embarrassing failure and to assume, correctly, that they would soon be returned to North Carolina. Even so there was "no enthusiasm among the troops" for quitting an uncompleted job. As a member of Company I put it, he and his comrades "did not like having to leave this place without seeing a gun fired."[46]

Upon reaching Port Royal Harbor, the regiment learned from the captain of a steamship out of Morehead City that a large body of Confederates had attacked Little Washington, where General Foster had assumed command, and had besieged the outnumbered garrison. Because General Heckman "felt solicitous concerning the safety of his old chief," he hastened to Hunter's headquarters and applied to be returned to North Carolina as quickly as possible. The department commander took his time considering the request, but the next morning Heckman received a copy of a special order releasing him and his brigade to New Bern, "where he will report to the general in command for service in relieving Major General Foster." The next sentence, however, must have given Heckman pause: "This duty executed, or it being found that Major General Foster has been already relieved, Brigadier General Heckman will forthwith return with his command to this department."[47]

In grandiloquent prose Sergeant Drake described the reaction of the Star Brigade to the news: "A wild scene took place among the men, especially in the Ninth. Cheer after cheer—the first they had ever given in the department—rent the summer-like air, and were wafted by zephyrs across the broad bay to the lazy-looking headquarters on the other side." A few hours later the command was again aboard its two transports. A delay ensued while water and coal were loaded, which gave rise to fears that before the brigade cast anchor Hunter would countermand the order releasing it. Either this did not happen or, if it did, nothing came of it. According to Sergeant Drake, Hunter sent an officer in a dispatch boat to order the brigade to return, but "General Heckman did not find it convenient to officially recognize the signals displayed, and continued on his course."

Almost as soon as it put to sea the Ninth encountered the kind of weather that seemed to bedevil any ship it ever boarded. During the night of the fourteenth a gale arose, causing both transports to be "tossed about on the angry waves like a cockle shell." One result was that the *Key West* almost collided with an unseen ship heading in the opposite direction. Once again, however, the men survived through the mercy of "that kind Providence which had preserved the Ninth from many sea perils in the past."[48]

In addition to being life-threatening, the Ninth's departure from Charleston left a foul taste in everyone's mouth. Had nature taken its usual course, the men would be returning north savoring the memory of an important task well and successfully performed. And yet, for many in the Ninth it was enough to escape a department where they had never felt comfortable, forced as they were to serve alongside soldiers they neither respected nor trusted. As one unidentified enlisted man put it, "we left the 'Nigger Department' with tears in our eyes, but they were tears of joy."

They were equally happy to be out from under the thumb of a commander they had come to despise. George Teates summed up the prevailing reaction: "Our trip to South Carolina did not amount to anything beyond a pleasure excursion, at Uncle Sam's expense, and a few weeks under Gen. Hunter. I need not tell you the boys were dissatisfied with his Department, and he did not like us any better than we liked him. He never gave the 9th a chance to do anything."[49]

8 Sweet Home North Carolina

Two months after the Battle of Fredericksburg, the War Department ordered the IX Corps transferred from the Army of the Potomac to the western theater. In late February 1863 its vanguard reached the extensive landing at Newport News on the James River about twelve miles west of Fort Monroe. Since Hampton Roads had been the staging area for the earlier operations against the Carolinas, the authorities in Richmond feared another such attempt, this time aimed at Wilmington or Goldsboro. To meet the threat, Robert E. Lee detached his senior subordinate, Lt. Gen. James Longstreet, to Petersburg to command a department that encompassed sections of Virginia and North Carolina.

Longstreet's acquired subordinates included D. H. Hill, newly installed at Goldsboro as head of the Department of North Carolina. When Longstreet decided to operate against the strategic outpost at Suffolk, he urged Hill to support him by attempting to reclaim New Bern for the Confederacy. Hill did so on March 8 but when he failed to receive promised reinforcements his attack proved inadequate; he ended it and retreated after eight days of inconclusive fighting. On the thirtieth, at Longstreet's suggestion, Hill headed for Little Washington with a beefed-up force 9,000 strong. Failing to gain anything by direct attack, Hill invested the 1,200-man garrison and parried two attempts to relieve it by subordinates of General Foster. By now more substantial help was on the way. Hill's siege lines had become the next objective of the XVIII Corps troops who had happily bid farewell to General Hunter.[1]

Early on April 16, the *Key West*, having weathered the treacherous storm, entered the harbor of Beaufort and deposited the bulk of the Ninth New Jersey on dry ground. The men were joined the next day by Major Curlis, with the other three companies. That day the reunited outfit, along with other just-arrived regiments, was marched at the double-quick to its old camp at Morehead City. Curlis's soldiers "thought this hard, having just come ashore" and still on their sea legs. At Morehead everyone was packed aboard railroad cars and shuttled up the tracks to New Bern. Arriving about midnight, they witnessed a "most cordial" reunion of Generals Foster and Heckman. The former, in hopes of leading a third relief expedition, had returned to the city after running the blockade that Hill had set up on both banks of the Pamlico. During the daring escape Foster's vessel had been fired on more than 100 times; one six-pounder shell had penetrated his stateroom minutes after he vacated it.[2]

The men of the Ninth were "jubilant and eager" to be back in the venue they had come to think of as home. As Symmes Stillwell put it, they were equally glad to be out of "that abolition town [Hilton Head] inhabited by the black snakes of the North." Sergeant Little considered his old bailiwick "the best place to be posted . . . in the whole United States."[3]

The move to Little Washington was made by overland march on "execrable" roads but at a furious pace: fifteen miles covered on April 18, ten miles during a six-hour period the next day. Just before noon on the nineteenth the troops reached the river bluff overlooking the trapped garrison only to learn that Hill had lifted his siege and retreated. At 2 p.m. the regiment went by schooner to the beleaguered outpost, arriving three hours later. Frustrated by the late arrival, Heckman sent cavalry and horse artillery to smite the rear of Hill's column. Entering the town, one Jerseyman was told that over the past three weeks the garrison had endured "at least one hundred tons of shot and shell."[4]

The regiment did not lay over but quickly returned to New Bern, part of the way by steamship, the remainder by shank's mare, arriving around 8 a.m. on the the twenty-first. Some men expressed disappointment that "nary [a] Reb" had been found at Washington, but not everyone felt that way. "For my part," wrote Corp. Robert B. Vanderhoef of Company B, "I was not sorry that they left for I have seen enough of them."[5]

By the twenty-fifth the Ninth was back in the campground at Carolina City that some of its companies had occupied before leaving for South Carolina. Here the bulk of the regiment, in company with the rest of the Star Brigade, guarded the countryside west of the railroad in the direction of Wilmington. Soon afterward Company B under now-Lt. Thomas W. Burnett was dispatched to Bogue Island to put a halt to blockade runners operating between Beaufort and Swansborough. "Barring the alligators and mosquitoes which infested the island," it was a pleasant enough spot, though the only enemy soldiers the company found were some pickets bathing in the ocean opposite Swansborough. Though brief—three weeks—Company B's move emphasized the Ninth's peripatetic existence. "If there is any regiment in the service which is on the move as we are," one man commented, "we pity them."[6]

Supposedly the return to familiar scenes "invigorated" the men. "We will have some rest now," Sergeant Little predicted. "Here, too," wrote Corporal Vanderhoef, "we can get all kinds of fish and clams and the sea breeze from the ocean." A return to General Hunter's department appeared a dead letter, at least in the minds of the Ninth's officers. As if to make clear that the majority of the outfit would remain at Carolina City, on the twenty-sixth Colonel Zabriskie had the men level the campgrounds to provide a new drill field while stockading and enlarging their Sibley tents so that each would accommodate more than a dozen inhabitants, who would "spoon together" at night. Hours of hammering and sawing made the camp "as noisy as a carpenter's shop." Another indicator of a lengthy stay was the construction of permanent fortifications (including "Fort Heckman") and a general hospital at Morehead City. Work on the latter was superintended by Surgeon Woodhull, now the medical director of Heckman's newly acquired command, the District of Beaufort.[7]

These labors notwithstanding, the duty demanded of the Ninth was generally light. The raiders who had so frequently attacked the regiment's picket posts the previous year were less active now in the shadow of a much larger Union presence. The relative inactivity enabled some of the officers including Colonel Zabriskie and Adjutant Carrell to go home on leave. Early in May Lieutenant Colonel Stewart, commanding in Zabriskie's absence, began to grant thirty-day furloughs to the enlisted force, one noncommissioned officer and two privates from each company traveling north at the same time.[8]

The easy-living soldiers agreed that the Ninth's current stations were "pleasant and healthy" places. David Hankins attributed this to their location "rite along the sea shore." Though not as hot or as humid as Charleston, the North Carolina weather was sometimes oppressive; to cool their tents some of the men gathered cedar boughs to create a "scalloped hedge" finished with a clamshell border. The result was so impressive that almost every company street was soon sheltered in this way. Other improvements followed. Company K celebrated May Day by erecting a birdhouse. Later that month several German Americans fashioned an exercise bar from pine poles to facilitate gymnastics. The regiment was mustered for pay and issued new clothing including dress coats for the noncommissioned officers. According to rumor, the attire had been furnished not by the government but by civilian benefactors from Jersey. Rations had improved since the Ninth's last stint in this district. "I am now having good times, and get plenty to eat," wrote William P. Amerman. Seafood of all varieties was abundant including a seemingly inexhaustible supply of clams and oysters.[9]

According to the army grapevine, not only the Ninth but the entire XVIII Corps had been assigned a single major duty, one familiar to many men: to guard New Bern, Beaufort, and the railroad between.

The rumor appeared accurate, for the Ninth's camp settled down to low-intensity routine, set forth in orders published early in May. They fixed reveille at 5:30 a.m., breakfast call at 6, surgeon's call at 6:30, guard mounting an hour later, followed by company drill at 8:30, dinner call at noon, battalion drill beginning at 3 p.m., dress parade at 5:30, tattoo (a roll-call ceremony) at 8:30, and light's out at 9.[10]

Life may have appeared cushy, but there were discomforts, physical and emotional. One day swarms of gnats descended on the regiment during the afternoon parade, sending the officer in charge "into all kinds of contortions, causing many men to laugh" until they too were assailed by the tiny flies. The attackers did not let up; eventually the men were allowed to break ranks and hasten to their tents. An observer found the scene ludicrous in the extreme: "The Ninth regiment, that never quailed when the air about them was freighted with the music of bullets, driven in from dress parade by gnats."

Equally unwelcome was the news, received in mid-May, that Burnside's successor in command of the Army of the Potomac, "Fighting Joe" Hooker, had been outwitted and throttled by Lee west of Fredericksburg near a wilderness crossroads known as Chancellorsville. The report elicited "very sorrowful feelings" in the men of the Ninth, especially as it included word that several New Jersey regiments had suffered grievous losses. The only favorable news was the wounding of Lee's trusted subordinate "Stonewall" Jackson, who died on the tenth from complications of his injury. Hooker's defeat at the hands of a much smaller enemy made at least one member of the Ninth fear that the Union effort was faltering. As this man wrote, "that we will soon founder, if the war is conducted in the same manner as it has been we have not the least doubt."[11]

Another troubling aspect of service in the Ninth's operational area was the growing acceptance of total war, a concept not every member of the regiment was comfortable with. Months earlier Symmes Stillwell had condemned the extension of the conflict to the civilian population. Having witnessed the results of multiple foraging expeditions in the enemy's country, the sergeant knew "war is war but this is a civilized nation. I believe in harasing the enemy and dislodging them evry way we can, but poor innocent women of the South cannot do us any harm, their husbands are taken away from them . . . in droves in the Southern army and they are left to starve to death." Yet Stillwell cautioned his family in Cranbury not to "make public of what I have said for fear harm may grow from it."[12]

Stillwell admitted that "hard war" was becoming government policy, but he was not alone in condemning its pernicious effects. In mid-May about thirty local families were forcibly removed from the Union lines south of New Bern, some for refusing to take the oath of allegiance to the U.S. government, others for "uttering Secesh sentiments after taking the oath." Company F's Jonathan Reading believed that this treatment "hurts them [the civilians] worst of anything we can do to them." In a letter to Judge Thompson, Reading opined that had the practice been adopted a year earlier, fewer attacks on the Ninth's lines would have occurred. Even so, he sympathized with the plight of the refugees, especially those families that lacked a father gone off to war.

Reading had observed that few men of military age were to be found anywhere the Ninth operated, only "old men that are teetering on the verge of the grave almost—they are not able to earn their living and are almost starving to death." Not all the absent men were diehard Rebels; many had been "forced into the service by the conscript acts." Since the spring of 1862 the South had been drafting all able-bodied white men between the ages of eighteen and thirty-five. At the time Reading wrote, those laws were being tightened by the Confederate Congress to eliminate the few exemptions permitted under earlier legislation.[13]

Another sign of a changing war was the accelerating formation of African American regiments. While many in the Ninth saw the practice as a confession of weakness or an expression of Lincoln's malice, a growing number of Jerseymen, by mid-1863, were accepting of the need for reinforcements regardless of skin color. By late May Brig. Gen. Edward A. Wild, a zealous abolitionist and an avid supporter of

African Americans in arms, had arrived in North Carolina to raise and command an entire brigade of United States Colored Troops. When the news was read to the Ninth on dress parade, it "excited much talk among the boys."

There were of course dissenting voices ("Censor," true to form, complained that "this is a white man's government, and we're bound to keep it so . . . no matter what Abraham Lincoln or any other man may say to the contrary"). Yet the overall reaction was not entirely negative. Private Reading, for one, called Wild's undertaking "a fine thing." Writing in the pages of the *New Jersey Journal*, Private Cleveland applauded the idea of a "contraband brigade" and described Wild as "a gallant soldier and accomplished gentleman." He added that "several companies of colored troops have been recruited and drilled in Newbern" to the satisfaction of all who observed them. To his diary Cleveland confided the hope that "the negroes prove good soldiers and do honor to the flag which flies over their camp."[14]

It seemed logical that the recruiting of black men would produce at least a grudging acceptance by the army. Self-interest alone made the policy viable. The Union's well-publicized series of setbacks, defeats, and narrow victories, especially in Virginia, cried out not only for abler commanders but for more men—men capable of being transformed as quickly as possible into capable fighters. For this reason many soldiers were eagerly anticipating implementation of the first national conscription law in American history. Affecting most civilians between twenty and forty-five, the so-called Enrollment Act had passed Congress in February. Although riven with inequities including several classes of exemptions and a provision that permitted the wealthy to buy their way out of the draft or hire a substitute to take their place in the army, the law would eventually furnish nearly 170,000 replacements for soldiers lost to wounds, sickness, and other causes. When put into operation, however, the law would foment opposition and protest, spawning riots in some of the larger cities of the North. Those that broke out in New York City in July, lasting four days, would remain,

150 years later, the largest and most destructive civil disturbance in American history.[15]

By early June, men of the Ninth were at hard labor for the first time in months. More than 100 had been detailed to help construct the fortifications surrounding Morehead City and Carolina City, including trenches and artillery revetments. These were going up under the direction of one of General Foster's brigadiers, Francis B. Spinola. Like many of the district commanders in Foster's department, Spinola was a relatively inexperienced soldier, his prewar career being steeped in Democratic Party politics and his prior military service being mainly in the militia. The men of the Ninth did not take kindly to his style of leadership, which was heavy on discipline and ceremonial show and light on ability. As one Jerseyman put it, "we think the Administration was 'hard up' for Generals when this New York politician was appointed to the position he now fills." Yet the Ninth did its best to make the defenses, and by association, Spinola, look good. On June 1 Ed Cleveland wrote that he and his comrades in Company K "procured 50 shovels from Gen Heckman's headquarters. I worked on the entrenchment. It was good hard labour." By mid-month, according to Sergeant Little, "we will [soon] be secure against any attack the rebs may see fit to make."[16]

There were compensations for the energy and sweat expended. The hours were not long: Private Cleveland and some buddies enjoyed a two-hour dinner break and quit work before the summer heat became intolerable. Even when harder work was required, conditions could have been worse. Sergeant Stillwell, in charge of a detail from Company A erecting a six-gun battery at Morehead City, reminded himself that he was "3 miles away from swamps." While the forts went up, regimental drill and other onerous duties were suspended. This pleased the men a great deal. Private Hankins, just returned from a furlough in Jersey, wrote that the regiment "hasent drilled any since I left and I don't want to see them drill any until cool weather comes on." Then, too, the work did not go unrecognized. Inspecting the defenses at Morehead City on June 5, General Foster applauded not only the progress being made but the men making it. As he rode past the camp of the Ninth, he remarked to General Spinola: "There is my right arm."[17]

A sudden slight improvement in the war news helped brighten the mood, if not lighten the burden, of the fortifiers. Throughout June, Ulysses S. Grant's renewed campaign to seize Vicksburg was bearing fruit, his troops taking one enemy position after another on the way to the Mississippi River stronghold. In Middle Tennessee, the army of William Rosecrans was making inroads against Braxton Bragg's Confederates, whom it would eventually drive from the state through expert maneuvering rather than pitched battle. Reports from the Virginia front were less promising. On June 3 Lee's army had begun its second invasion of the North, ranging through the Shenandoah Valley en route to south-central Pennsylvania. Ahead lay an epic encounter with the Army of the Potomac under Maj. Gen. George Gordon Meade, successor to the hapless Joe Hooker.

Weeks later the outlook in the eastern theater remained uncertain. Lee's ability to catch his opponent unawares and capitalize on his mistakes had assumed nearly legendary proportions, even among the Union forces in North Carolina. Still, there was room for optimism. According to Private Cleveland ("Vidi"), writing in the *New Jersey Journal*, by ranging so far from his base of support in Virginia Lee was offering his adversary a golden opportunity: "This invasion, instead of being a disaster to us, will prove one of the most effectual 'final strokes' to rebellion, for if Lee does not keep wide awake he will find he has entered a keystone trap." The private from Elizabeth was no seer, but on this subject he knew what he was talking about.[18]

At daybreak on June 26 almost every member of the Ninth left camp and marched to the nearest railroad depot where, two hours later, they were being shuttled back to New Bern. As Ed Cleveland noted, rumors as to their ultimate destination were many and varied: "It is said that we are soon to go to Virginia. Others say that we are headed for Washington, North Carolina, Bachelder's [*sic*] Creek, Fortress Monroe, Va., or to do provost duty at New Bern." A few days later other potential destinations—Kinston and the line of the Blackwater River, in southeastern Virginia—had been added to the gleanings of the grapevine. Sergeant Stillwell had no theory as to the destination but believed the movement was aimed at destroying some salt works and fortifications recently evacuated by the enemy. He did not expect a major engagement because "there is no [large] rebel force in this state at present, the most of them have gone to Virginia."[19]

Upon reaching departmental headquarters the men were herded into the barracks at Fort Totten. Their habitation withstood a cyclone that struck the city that evening, but an adjacent building was blown apart and a sentry was buried under debris from which several members of the Ninth extricated him. On July 3 the men were still quartered in the city, whose defenses were under temporary command of General Heckman in the absence of John Foster. That day several squadrons of cavalry set forth to wreck sections of the railroad between Goldsboro and Wilmington in the vicinity of Kenansville, forty-five miles southwest of New Bern. Hours after the horsemen started out, infantry support was ordered up, and so the Ninth spent Independence Day marching in the same direction along with portions of three Massachusetts and two New York regiments and two artillery batteries, a total of perhaps 2,500, all under Heckman. Each man had been issued five days' cooked rations and 100 rounds of ammunition. He toted two days' worth of victuals and forty cartridges; the rest were hauled by the supply wagons that brought up the rear of the column.[20]

The infantry made its way south via the Island Creek Road to Pollocksville, a village of deserted and windowless houses twelve miles from New Bern. A short distance beyond, around noon, the column came to a halt. Because the heat was rising steadily, the men were permitted to rest until 6 p.m., during which they "ate our Fourth of July dinner of coffee, cold ham, and hard tack." They then spent four hours on the march before bivouacking for the night on an abandoned plantation. Thus far no enemy had been sighted. The next morning the march resumed, the column trudging through the "pretty little village" of Trenton, nine miles from Pollocksville. "We passed many fine houses this morning," wrote Private Cleveland, who described the area as "the best part of North Carolina I have seen." Late in the afternoon came another halt, during which Companies B and F of the Ninth disassembled, plank by plank, the 125-foot-long Wilcox Bridge over the Trent River. Still no opposition materialized, though "the Confederates were known to be but a short distance away."[21]

Early the next day, the sixth, the foot soldiers failed to link, as planned, with the railroad-destroying cavalry, but when the horsemen finally appeared around noon so did the enemy. The Rebels, who, though not in overwhelming force had at least two cannons, were discovered to be guarding another Trent River span, Free Bridge, first from the near side and later from the opposite bank. According to plan the cavalry would cross Free Bridge when returning from their mission, so the structure had to be secured. At Colonel Heckman's order, four companies of the Twenty-third Massachusetts under Lt. Col. John G. Chambers advanced on the bridge but reeled when hit with a heavy shelling that severely wounded their leader.

At this point Col. James Jourdan, Heckman's senior subordinate on the expedition, sent forward Companies E and G of the Ninth, who deployed as skirmishers. Two men fell wounded including a bugler shot in the face, but the skirmishers held their ground until Belger's Rhode Island battery unlimbered in their rear. The gunners speedily cleared the approaches to the bridge, enabling the cavalry to cross it around 1 p.m. The troopers were received with "enthusiastic cheering," for they had carried out their orders, tearing up the railroad for five miles. They had also destroyed powder mills and a foundry that manufactured sabers and pistols; had captured a mail train whose cargo included sixty thousand dollars in specie and paper currency; had confiscated from the countryside 400 horses and mules; had seized forty or more prisoners; and had liberated 200 slaves, some of whom would be recruited into the ranks of the USCT drilling at New Bern. The endurance displayed by the contrabands, many of whom had walked fifty miles a day in order to keep up with the cavalry, was extraordinary, but worth it. As one member of the Ninth put it, "they roll freedom like a sweet morsel under their tongues."[22]

Mission accomplished, infantry and cavalry returned to New Bern on the seventh, the Ninth covering the rear of the column. Under a torrid sun, then a soaking rain, the regiment reached its barracks that evening. Many men were now shoeless; others were suffering from blistered feet, having marched almost seventy miles in what one man called "the hottest [day] of the season, many of our men being prostrated from the effects of the heat." Although the liberated slaves had weathered at least as much adversity without collapsing, Sergeant Little observed that on the way home "the roads was lined with men that had given out and obliged to fall to the rear." Even so, "the expedition was a success and will do very well for a 'Fourth of July Excursion.'"[23]

Joyous news greeted their return. For weeks the soldiers had been following newspaper accounts of Grant's operations against Vicksburg, which as of May 18 had morphed into a full-fledged siege. In late June Sergeant Stillwell had written that "Grant has chosen a slow but shure way of getting Vicksburg. He has taken up the spad[e] and gone to work a digging the rebs out." The citadel finally succumbed on July 4, though the men of the Ninth did not receive definitive news for more than a week. Simultaneously "good news from Maryland" reached New Bern: Lee was in full retreat from Gettysburg, where his army had suffered a critical defeat at the hands of Meade's Federals. Later in the month the New Bern garrison received confirmation of yet another victory, this at Port Hudson, Louisiana, where the last important outpost on the Mississippi fell to another siege. With Port Hudson's capture the entire extent of the war's most important waterway fell into Union hands. The Confederacy effectively had been split in two.[24]

The men of the Ninth and their comrades throughout the war zone rejoiced that after two years of spoiled hopes and deferred dreams a possible turning point in the struggle had been achieved. Although months of struggle and disappointment lay ahead, the soldiers of the Union could now dare to believe that the cause for which they had endured so much hardship and experienced so much heartbreak would be crowned with final victory, however long it took. "Perhaps we will have another years hard fighting," wrote Sergeant Stillwell in mid-September, "but the tide of the war is turned."[25]

There was no rest for the weary, or for the footsore or the heat-struck. July closed out with two more expeditions against enemy enclaves southwest of New Bern. The first, which was aborted in mid-career, was mercifully brief, but the second proved to be a lengthier and more debilitating affair. On the thirteenth, one day after Confederate raiders captured an outpost across the Neuse from New Bern, the Ninth rode the cars to its old station at Newport Barracks. There it rendezvoused with the rest of the expedition: nine companies of the Twenty-third Massachusetts, one company of the Twelfth New York Cavalry, and a two-gun section of a New York battery. By 10 a.m., with General Heckman at its head, the multi-arms column was wending its way along the road to a suspected enemy assembly area at Cedar Point on the White Oak River.

The march was made under the usual conditions, heavy rain and knee-deep mud. The route led across Broad Creek, which was being picketed by New York infantry who had constructed a corduroy bridge (built of pine planks laid side by side) on which the column crossed. The cavalry ranged ahead of the main force; near Smith's Mills it encountered the only body of the enemy seen on the trip, which it routed in "fine style."

At daybreak on the fourteenth, the column left its evening bivouac on Saunders's Plantation, twelve miles from its starting point, and marched to the banks of the White Oak River. Travel had been an ordeal given the tropical-like heat that had replaced the rain. J. Madison Drake—recently promoted to second lieutenant of Company D—ever recalled "the burning condition of the sand in the roadway—almost hot enough to roast an egg in four minutes." The weather and the marching pace—nine miles covered this day in three hours—cost the column a number of men who, unable to endure another long trek so soon after the last, were carried back to New Bern for medical treatment.

They suffered in vain. At Cedar Point the expedition came to a frustrating conclusion when a steamer that was to have enabled the column to cross the river failed to appear, having run hard aground on the shoals of Bogue Sound, ten miles away. With the vessel held fast and lacking an accessible ford on that stretch of the river, a disgusted Heckman saw no profit in extending the expedition and called it off. Infantry, cavalry, and artillery returned to Newport just before noon on the sixteenth. The next morning Heckman and his troops were back at New Bern to report their mission unaccomplished. The only memorable feature of the three-day ordeal was the liberal foraging the men conducted in a rich farming area of the state ("we lived well," wrote Sergeant Little, "on water melon and boiled corn"). Another reward of sorts was a dispatch received on the way back and which Heckman disseminated among the column, announcing that Lee's army—then crossing the Potomac back to Virginia after its drubbing in Pennsylvania—was "completely demoralized."[26]

But unpleasant news quickly followed. When they reached home the troops read the first definitive accounts of the rioting in New York City in opposition to the Enrollment Act. Millions of dollars' worth of municipal and private property had been destroyed and more than 100 civilians—mainly the rioters' victims, which included numerous African Americans—had lost their lives. In the ranks of the Ninth, reaction to the news was mixed, although a majority favored harsh punishment for the rioters. According to Private Cleveland, "some are in favor of the insurrectionists and some are of the opposite opinion. Mobism,

I think, should always be punished." A comrade of his—an Irish American like a majority of the rioters—shared Cleveland's opinion: "The only way to deal with those who interfere with the government in the prosecution of the war is to shoot them down, show them no mercy." Although an adherent of the Democratic Party, this man saw in the rioting the hand of the peace factions of the North, whose adherents he considered "secessionists at heart."[27]

By early August rumors were rife that several regiments would be ordered north to enforce the draft and that "every influence is being used to have the Ninth selected for provost duty in good old Jersey." While disturbances on a smaller scale had broken out across the Hudson River in Jersey City, this possibility would not come about. In the end, a few units of Regulars and volunteers were detached from the Army of the Potomac to assist local police, militia, and naval forces in suppressing the rioters. By July 17, the burning, killing, and looting had effectively subsided, though sporadic outbreaks of violence continued to ripple across the North in cities such as Boston, Albany, Brooklyn (then an independent municipality), and Troy, New York.[28]

The rioting suspended but did not shut down the enrollment process even in New York, where it resumed the following month and continued to operate through the remainder of the war. Its first effects were felt in North Carolina as early as mid-August, when several hundred conscripts were delivered at New Bern. The Ninth was among those units that received an infusion of new blood. The experience was considered beneficial, but in the end the draft would supply less than 6 percent of the Union's total manpower.

Recruiting remained the most effective way to gain replacements. Before August ended Capt. Edgar Kissam left for Jersey to escort south a second group of conscripts. At this same time, a nine-man recruiting party including 1st Sgt. Edward S. Pullen of Company H returned home to seek men who did not have to be coerced into taking up arms in defense of their country. Others who signed on did so from a realization that, if drafted, their options would suddenly disappear. Here, perhaps, was the most powerful effect of the Enrollment Act.[29]

The second July expedition got under way on the twenty-fifth, three days after Lieutenant Drake reported "considerable excitement" in reaction to rumors of a pending attack on New Bern. Twice during the next two days the Ninth was called out to defend Fort Totten, but each time it was returned to its barracks. Finally, at General Heckman's order the regiment formed for the march along with some long-time associates, members of the Seventeenth, Twenty-third, and Twenty-fifth Massachusetts, the Eighty-first New York, and Belger's Battery. The first leg of this expedition was by water—aboard the steamer *Convoy* up the Neuse River and then through Pamlico and Albemarle Sounds to the mouth of the Chowan. For part of the way the men were escorted by gunboats and accompanied by General Foster. But neither Foster nor Heckman were forthcoming about the objective of the mission. Pvt. Hermann Everts, however, was at least partially correct when he surmised that it was aimed at the destruction of the strategic expanse of railroad track around Weldon.[30]

The journey had begun agreeably enough—Drake called the run to the Chowan "a delightful sail"—but it deteriorated as soon as the men disembarked at Winton around 2 p.m. on the twenty-sixth. Winton, on the right bank of the Chowan some seventy miles north of New Bern, had been at one time a pretty little village, but gunboats firing on local defenders had rendered it "a collection of houseless chimneys." Even less charming was the local geography: the deserted hamlet straddled the southwestern edge of a vast plague zone known as the Great Dismal Swamp. A breeding ground for diseases including what was known as "the regular North Carolina chills," it was especially unhealthy in midsummer. The Ninth would pay a price for campaigning here.[31]

To make things worse, the men did much extra marching, going a mile out of their way on a wrong road while the rest of the expeditionary force went ahead without them. The Ninth had been leading the column; when it went awry the next regiment in line, the Seventeenth Massachusetts, did not realize that it was now in the vanguard. The inattentive outfit fell into an ambush, struck simultaneously in front and flank by Confederates hidden from view in heavy woods. The Seventeenth formed line and returned fire as best it could until the Ninth, having countermarched, hustled to its support. The forward companies of the Ninth, "perfectly used to the work," charged straight ahead and cleared the road, "driving the enemy in confusion before them."

For a mile or more they chased the Rebels, who seemed unwilling to turn around until, crossing Pollacasty Creek over the partially dismantled Hill's Bridge, they took cover behind a 100-yard-long line of earthworks. By Lieutenant Drake's purplish account, the Ninth hesitated only briefly before forging ahead under a blistering fire: "With a shot which struck terror to the hearts of the foe, [we] dashed forward across the structure and into the works, capturing some thirty Confederates who were unable to make their escape." Several Jerseymen including Drake himself fell wounded, but the result appeared to justify the casualty count.

The next day the regiment remained in place. Authorized to forage off the land including the grounds of more than one plantation, the men had a field day. "We took and helped ourselves to anything we wanted to eat," wrote Symmes Stillwell. "We trimmed out a cornfield & 5 acre potato patch." But not everyone wandered about in search of food or plunder. Pvt. Charles Muller of Company A, having traded his Springfield for a walking stick, was exploring a patch of woods when he happened upon three Confederates, their arms stacked nearby. It was said that Muller "terrorized" his enemy "with a yell" that paralyzed them. Snatching up one of their rifles, he marched the hapless trio to the Ninth's bivouac to the accompaniment of cheers from his amazed comrades. Colonel Zabriskie, to whom the private presented his prisoners for interrogation, was so pleased he promised Muller a free pass from camp every day "if he would promise to do as well each time."[32]

The men had learned that a mounted force out of Suffolk, Virginia—two cavalry regiments and a horse artillery battery—would attend to the destruction of the railroad near Weldon. The troopers and gunners rendezvoused with Heckman's force later that day; ferried across the Chowan, they galloped off toward their objective. Upon their departure the expedition, now reduced to a covering force, continued to hold its position. Over the next two days its men were alternately assailed by intense heat and heavy rain. As a consequence several came down with fever, chills, and that debilitating upper respiratory condition known as the ague. Drake found himself unable to "adequately describe [the] many cases of suffering" that occurred over the new few days. Given the supposed medicinal properties of alcohol, the sick men perked up when, on the afternoon of the twenty-eighth, someone discovered two barrels of whiskey. Unfortunately, as Private Cleveland reported, the liquor "was immediately taken in charge of by the officers, much to the chagrin of the captors."

By the thirtieth, when the raiding force returned from its mission, everyone was anxious to vacate the area, especially once it became clear that the expedition had come to naught. Due to an unexpected buildup of troops in the Weldon area the cavalry had given up the idea of striking the railroad. And so the entire force turned about and headed home. Around midnight, after a slog through "slippery, clayey mud," the weary, ill, and disheartened soldiers reached the steamboat landing where they reembarked for the return run to New Bern. By now about 300 officers and men of the Ninth had been prostrated with one malady or another including symptoms of malaria.[33]

The expeditions of the past several weeks proved valuable in clearing the enemy from areas they had previously controlled. Sergeant Stillwell informed his mother that "some time ago our piquets was attacked every day or night by guerilas, but our late raids and scouts have cleaned the woods and swamps of them entirely for many miles around." On the debit side of the ledger, those operations had exerted a devastating effect on the readiness of many of Heckman's regiments, especially the Ninth.[34]

Over the months the health of the regiment had waxed and waned, but it had never been as precarious as it was during midsummer 1863. It had been for "sanitary reasons" that drill had ceased weeks earlier. In June Dr. Woodhull had called the attention of his departmental superior to the "extremely unhealthy" posts the regiment had occupied over the past several months, especially Havelock Station and Newport Barracks. According to the surgeon more than 90 percent of the troops who had occupied Havelock for any length of time had contracted intermittent or remittent fever; for this reason he had laid in an extra supply of quinine.[35]

The regiment's condition remained fragile over the next two months. Early in August Sergeant Little, himself unwell, reported that "the weather is very warm and we do not feel like doing much." He blamed the "hard months work in July . . . in the swamps and woods," during which the regiment traveled more than 650 miles by land and water. As of the day Little wrote, 139 members of the outfit were on sick leave, including every officer in his company.[36]

The sick list grew appreciably in the first two weeks of August, when the afternoon heat rose to 100 and even 110 degrees. Later that month Private Hankins wrote that "about half of the Regiment goes to the Doctor every morning. . . . There isent about ten officers fit for duty in the whole Regiment and less yet of privates in proportion." Well into September only a few hundred men out of a paper strength of 1,000 (including 300 recruits added in the past year) were healthy enough to attend regimental inspection. Larger affairs such as reviews and parades were simply out of the question. "Many of those who are ill," wrote a concerned Private Cleveland, "are the most rugged men."[37]

At length the regiment's condition came to the attention of the high command, which had been shuffled in mid-July upon the merger of the Departments of Virginia—basically the VII Corps, which garrisoned Hampton Roads—and North Carolina. On August 25 Maj. Gen. John J. Peck, commanding the newly created District of North Carolina (a post Charles Heckman had been filling for the past month), wrote to his immediate superior, Foster. Peck informed the commander of the Department of Virginia and North Carolina that "there is a large amount of sickness in the Ninth New Jersey, and in some of the Massachusetts regiments, which is attributed to the raid or raids by them. After consultation, I have decided to send the New Jersey regiment down to the sea-shore for a few weeks."[38]

When General Foster voiced no objection, at 10 a.m. on the twenty-seventh the Ninth left New Bern for its old haunts around Carolina City and Morehead City. The transfer would prove a godsend, but it began badly. An all-day rain, which soaked to the skin men riding on open platform cars, worsened the condition of those laid low by chills and fever. Sergeant Stillwell reported that "I have almost lived on whiskey & quinine for the last week, the afternoon temperature at New Bern having risen to "130 degrees *in the shade*." By now only around 150 men were fit to do duty out of 600 men present for duty: "If we had stayed at Newberne two weeks longer we would not have had 10 men in the regt fit for duty."[39]

Upon reaching Carolina City the regiment found its old camp in "sad condition." Bunks had been removed from the barracks and the tents still standing were so badly perforated they provided no shelter from the continuing rain. Even so, men healthy enough to do the work set about erecting the regiment's Sibley tents upon the pine-plank stockading that remained standing. The commodious Sibleys offered considerable protection from the local weather, but for a few weeks the regiment's health remained fragile. Although at least one soldier wrote that by month's end "the healthful effects of the bracing breezes from Bogue Sound are already noticeable," Sergeant Stillwell noted that the regiment "continues very sickly." Four days later Colonel Zabriskie procured leave to "recruit his shattered health" at his family's home in Jersey City. In later weeks other officers who desired to escape a disease-plagued environment—an opportunity unavailable to most of their men—followed Zabriskie north.[40]

Though few men appeared healthy enough to turn out for inspection or roll call, those who fared better had enough energy and malice in their systems to "have some fun" at the expense of a neighboring civilian. On the last day of August Pvt. Steve Crane of Company K, known among his comrades as something of a jokester, played a costly trick on an unnamed sutler whose supply tent stood only a few feet from the railroad. Without attracting the merchant's attention Crane fastened the guy ropes of the tent to the last of a long line of box and flat cars. When the train started moving the tent was heaved from its moorings and dragged down the track. Its contents—boxes, barrels, and bottles of food and drink—spilled out with a thunderous crash. Numerous soldiers, attracted by the noise, rushed to scoop up the goods in the absence of the sutler, who, terrified by the crash, had fled the scene "as if pursued by a thousand fiends." Lieutenant Drake wrote that the men "helped themselves to the tobacco, sweetmeats, etc., lying promiscuously about. The thefts cost the sutler several hundred dollars." High-priced businessmen who sold to the soldiers being fair game for such antics, neither Private Crane nor his light-fingered comrades were brought to account for their theft.[41]

The health of the Ninth finally began to stabilize in the latter half of September. By then "most of the men," as Sergeant Little wrote, had "returned from the Hospitals and are doing duty." The change was at least partially attributable to the exertions of Surgeon Woodhull, himself recently recovered from an unspecified illness. In company with Assistant Surgeons Gillette and Davies, each morning the dutiful doctor inspected every tent in camp for its sanitary properties. Most of those habitations—"our houses of canvas on the banks of the deep blue sea," Little called them—were secure from both disease and the elements. Not so other areas of the camp. Under Woodhull's direction, deeper pits were dug in which kitchen and hospital refuse was dumped, while the camp "sinks" (latrines), which had been "filled to overflowing," were covered up with dirt and new ones were dug.

Camp rubbish, which had been left standing uncovered, was loaded into wagons to be buried a safe distance from camp.[42]

Daily drill, now regarded as a beneficial exercise, was cautiously reinstated, eventually for an hour and a half each day, but camp duty remained light. No taxing chores were required of anyone. As "Censor" wrote on the twenty-sixth, "we are now enjoying ourselves to our hearts' content." Rations were especially abundant and tasty: "Our boys never lived better than they do now. . . . 'Hard tack' is no longer our only food. Sweet potatoes, corn, tomatoes, onions, hoecake, &c., is the food which the Ninth lives on." The prevailing problem was a lack of rain. As Sergeant Stillwell noted in the second week in October, "it is very dry and dusty. The sand is ankle deep, and while we are drilling the dust arises in clouds so thick we can scarcely see each other."[43]

The Confederates in the area were keeping a low profile to such a degree that it seemed as if the war in eastern North Carolina had gone into hiatus. The Ninth's area of operations was considered so pacified that the wives of General Heckman and other officers arrived for an extended stay in quarters erected by the enlisted men. Suddenly, with no enemy to stir them into meaningful activity, the men "began to express their discontent, and long for something more exciting."[44]

Those who desired a change of scenery got their wish when orders came to prepare three days' rations and be ready to turn out for a long march. Rumors of a move had been filling the air around Carolina City for days; potential destinations included Hampton Roads locales such as Fort Monroe and Norfolk. Speculation had heated up following an October 13 review of the regiment by General Heckman. The men were aware that reviews often presaged a major movement, and this one was obviously special, attended as it was by a civilian photographer who captured the parade-ground activities. Following the performance, the men were released to their tents while the officers and their ladies enjoyed a round of merrymaking. A resentful Private Cleveland complained about the "holiday for the officers who have been imbibing rather freely. Dared we do likewise we would be severely punished."[45]

Reportedly, General Heckman was well pleased with the appearance of the Ninth on parade. This offered compelling evidence that the men had survived their recent tribulations—which had included a late-September gale that nearly blew apart the regiment's camp, sending tents and tree limbs, as one inhabitant wrote, "down upon our poor devoted heads." It appeared that the regiment was fit for a new round of active service—somewhere.[46]

"Somewhere" turned out to be Newport News, more than 150 miles north of Carolina City. On October 9 General Foster had ordered General Peck to send all five of Heckman's regiments to that landing on the James River via Fort Monroe. In so doing Foster was acting against his better judgment, and Peck thought it a bad idea. As the latter cautioned in an October 12 letter to his superior, "the active force is very small in North Carolina from sickness and other causes. The regiments named in the order [a total of 2,700 men] . . . are the flower of the command."[47]

Peck's argument fell on deaf ears, for the transfer had been mandated by General-in-Chief Halleck as a means of providing contingency support to the Army of the Potomac. On September 19–20 Union fortunes in the West had suffered a major setback. Along Chickamauga Creek in northwest Georgia, Rosecrans's army had been routed by a Confederate force under Bragg that included railroad-borne reinforcements from Lee. The War Department had ordered Grant to hasten to Chattanooga, to which Rosecrans had retreated and where he was now under siege. After consulting with his civilian overlords Halleck had decided that two corps from Virginia would augment the relief force. Meade's loss must be made good by forces drawn from other theaters including the District of North Carolina. Rosecrans's defeat was a case of unfortunate timing. As Halleck told Foster, it prevented him from reinforcing Foster's command rather than Meade's, as originally intended.[48]

On October 18 a resigned Peck informed Foster that the transports *Albany* and *Jersey Blue* were being readied to carry the Ninth New Jersey up the coast. Late that afternoon the regiment was assembled and sent by rail to New Bern. Alighting from the cars, the men boarded the waiting steamers; within two hours, followed by vessels carrying the rest of Heckman's command, they were sailing down the Neuse, although not comfortably. "Such a crowded ride I never had before," Private Cleveland complained. "No one had room to lie down and we sat on our knapsacks." The *Albany*, that "dirty tub," had recently transported livestock and "the atmosphere below decks, filled with cattle smells, was stifling." When the ship's captain was asked about the accommodations, he replied that he had heard the Ninth New Jersey could survive any conditions, and "if they could stand this he would believe it." As usual when the Ninth went to sea, the surf was rough and the winds were strong. A bugler of Company B who ventured out on the deck of the *Albany* lost his footing and drowned.[49]

The regiment—minus Companies A and K, bringing up the rear aboard the *John Rice*, accompanied by General and Mrs. Heckman and the brigade staff—reached Fort Monroe at 8 a.m. on the twentieth. Continuing up the James, the main body landed at Newport News that afternoon. Rumor said that the Ninth would make camp near where General McClellan began the famous march on Richmond that had ended so badly for all involved. Even to those who had desired a change of scenery, the portents were worrisome.[50]

Other men openly expressed their discontent at having to trade a relatively quiet existence in North Carolina for an uncertain future in the theater where Union forces had mostly experienced disappointment and defeat. But their fate had been sealed: for the next eleven months, for good or ill, southeastern Virginia—the jumping-off point of the critical 1864 campaign—would be the regiment's home base.

9   Veteran Volunteers

From the day the regiment set foot in Virginia, it was dogged by speculation as to whether it was in for a long stay at Newport News or would soon take the field. Enough rumors flitted about to give credence to either prospect. Although the various regimental encampments had every appearance of transitioning to winter quarters, the almost daily arrival of fresh troops led some members of the Ninth to suspect an early campaign up the James toward Richmond. Writing to his family in Cranbury, Symmes Stillwell doubted that "we will have any more active service to perform here than we had in North Carolina," but added "you must not be surprised to hear of our brigade in Richmond before spring."[1]

David Hankins reported that the new arrivals included regiments not previously or recently part of Heckman's command such as the Twenty-fourth and Twenty-seventh Massachusetts Infantry. This seemed to suggest that a new campaign was in the offing—how long before it commenced was anyone's guess. Two weeks after reaching Virginia "Censor," the otherwise unidentified enlisted man from Newark, opined that "from present appearances we are soon to see active service, for the old fighting troops of North Carolina are continually arriving, and in a week, at the farthest, they will all be here." On three separate occasions in October and November, orders came down apparently presaging a general movement, only to be canceled at the last minute.[2]

There were equally strong reasons to expect an extended stay along the James, one of the most basic being the local weather. As Ambrose Burnside had learned during his Mud March, with few exceptions the cold season was not conducive to active campaigning. (Even so, by late November Meade's army would be on the march, seeking to penetrate the right flank of Lee's depleted command along the Rapidan River before snow, freezing rain, and cutting winds rendered field operations impossible.) Another sign that Newport News was a semipermanent station was the number of civilians permitted to visit camp throughout late autumn and winter. From day one, sutlers and hucksters descended on the Ninth, hawking "all kinds of eatables" at "very high prices—but the men would buy, were the prices double what they are." Another indication of a lengthy stay was the presence of "many fair ladies"—those officers' wives who had visited the Ninth at Carolina City and had made the trip to Virginia, where they were joined by other army spouses. Still another sign was the regular appearance of the army paymaster—heretofore, given the regiment's well-traveled existence, his coming had been erratic and unpredictable.[3]

Then there was the reinstitution of daily drill and rifle exercise, an occurrence that suggested an effort to keep the troops busy rather than prepared to break camp at a moment's notice. To the men's general discontent, they drilled by company from 10 a.m. to 11:30 a.m. each day and by battalion from 2 p.m. to 4 p.m. The simultaneous renewal of target practice validated the Ninth's cherished reputation for sharpshooting. Typical were the shooters of Company K, each of whom, as Edmund J. Cleveland reported, expended seven rounds at a target at least 100 yards away and "so riddled it [that it] hardly held together." A few days later the ten best marksmen in the regiment squared off, firing at a much more distant target. The competition established Corp. William J. Parker of Company F as the most proficient shooter in the Ninth. For this distinction Parker was awarded a sterling silver medal, a token of merit he surely cherished through the rest of his war service, and probably throughout his life.[4]

The opinion of an unnamed private from Gloucester County was typical of those who believed the Ninth was in for an extended encampment. "We have but little excitement," he informed the readers of his hometown newspaper. "Occasionally an order is issued to cook two or three days rations, and be ready to move at any moment, but so far they have all been countermanded." This man quoted a recent editorial in the *New York Herald* proclaiming that now was the time for an advance on Richmond. "Certainly it is," the private wrote, "but [our] armies are too small for such an undertaking at present." He attributed this to thousands of young, able Northerners who preferred "sitting in their easy chairs by the fire-side, to shouldering a rifle and marching to the rescue of their fellow-sufferers, and their Country's defense."[5]

The premise of this man's argument was dubious but he was correct to surmise that the Ninth New Jersey was not going to leave Hampton Roads for some time—as it happened, not until midway through the spring of 1864. The only hostile action the regiment saw during that period was a "spirited engagement with an army of rodents, which had occupied the grounds since the time McClellan's force was encamped there in idleness." It was said that the contest "afforded considerable exercise for the men and rich amusement" for the civilian onlookers. These included the ladies of the regiment, who, rather than repulsed by the sight of the rampaging rats, responded with shrieks of laughter to the ludicrous gyrations of the combatants.[6]

Not since the regiment's first weeks of war on Meridian Hill had it entered upon camp life not only as an intact organization but as a component of a body of troops several-thousand strong. Within hours of its arrival at Newport News the Ninth began to erect a "beautiful encamping ground" on a ridge overlooking the warship-filled river. The location greatly impressed the youngest member of the outfit, fourteen-year-old Pvt. Henry F. Keenan, who had lied about his age in order to enlist in Company H. Looking back years later, the New York native, since early youth a devotee of tales of martial glory, described the first camp of his military career: "No site more charming for a military bivouac could be imagined than the camp of the Ninth on the Newport News table-land. Flanked on the south by the wide, misty waters of the James—beyond which, on clear days, we could see the rebel shores to the south and east almost to Norfolk, there was a perpetual panorama of nature's most varied pageantry. By day, the monitors with their many colored fabrics, their nimble seamen, their portentous and mysterious power, were under our eyes. At night their bells, ringing out musically, gave reassurance of guardianship from the waters. Then to the east the dim gray walls of Fortress Monroe and the hazy glimpse of the ocean. West and north were encircled by thick, clustering, swamp-like groves—made solemn and awful by clumps of pine and the plain laurel which holds its dark, dead green all the year round."[7]

The landing was a sprawling place, but long before Private Keenan's arrival it was filling up fast. An assortment of units had occupied the surrounding area for months but with the addition of Heckman's command and other units, the campgrounds expanded exponentially. Soon it was home to perhaps 10,000 men, with more expected over the next several weeks. Simultaneously a few of the older outfits left for other venues. The Star Brigade, however, would not be departing with them.

The day after the regiment reached its new station, Colonel Zabriskie, his health restored by his furlough in Hudson County, rejoined it. The following day General Heckman was duly installed as commander of the post and assumed authority over every operational and support unit at Newport News. Under his supervision, everyone kept busy, mainly at some form of hard labor—for Private Hankins and his comrades in Company D, "cleaning off camping grounds and stockading our tents. The weather is a good bit cooler here than it was in North Carolina. It has made us keep the fire going prety steady here the last two or three days."[8]

Writing to the editor of the *Ocean Emblem* of Toms River, J. Madison Drake described the intricate process of "winterizing" the men's canvas habitations: "In the first place, we cut timber in lengths varying from six to ten feet—these pieces are hewn smoothly with axes, and then placed upright in a trench dug around the circumference of the tent for that purpose. After these pieces are planted firmly in the ground, the tent is raised up on a long pole, and the bottom fastened to the top of the timbers. By doing this we have more room, and besides it is more convenient. In each tent, board 'bunks' have been put up—thus you see the men are not compelled to sleep on the cold, damp ground. Most of the boys have ticks—not sand ticks—which they fill with dry grass, or leaves, or hay, as it happens, and in sleeping with a comrade, they divide four heavy woolen blankets, besides sundry overcoats, &c., between them. Each tent is provided with a stove and pipe, and with plenty of fresh bread, good fuel, roast beef, baked beans, and many other little luxuries, how can we help being happy and content."[9]

Lest Drake's description of the Ninth's home life sound too rosy to be credible, Sergeant Stillwell corroborated most of the lieutenant's claims. Like many of his comrades, Stillwell occupied a rough-hewn but sturdy cabin in lieu of a tent and thus fared even better than the average defender of Hampton Roads. He informed his mother and sister that "the rain and hail is coming down on my roof in torrents, but it does not disturb me in the least. My log cabin is well built, not the least drop of water can penetrate through anywhere. It is all sod[d]ed over inside and out witch is very warm, and I have a nice log fireplace, one of the old-fashioned kind with a beautiful blazeing fire all the time, witch makes my cabin very pleasant. I could not wish to live more comfortable than what I am at present."

The sergeant did not have to buy or even chop wood for fuel, since there was plenty available, "all hauled and cut for me at the woodpile, so I have nothing to do but carry it in." When weather permitted, he and his comrades bathed in a pond formed by the James. Their dirty clothes were washed by the wife of one of the enlisted men for a small fee. Especially when the day was too cold and raw for extended outdoor activity, the men enjoyed leisure time in their tents and cabins. "While I am writing this," Stillwell added, "some of the boys have come in and are laying back, enjoying a delicious pipe by my comfortable fire. Some are looking over the [news]papers, and others are getting interested in some of Sir Walter Scott's literary works. We get plenty of reading matter here, religious papers, books and tracts furnished by the Christian [and] Sanitary Commission[s], and what we get are well read."[10]

Stillwell also revealed that "we have a variety of amusements to cheer up the soldier" and make his time in camp pass swiftly. As was true of far-flung military stations in any war, a majority of the entertainments available to the units in Hampton Roads were produced and performed by the men themselves. At Newport News the center of group activity was a large wooden building most frequently used as a chapel. Private Cleveland called it "quite a curiosity. It is made of hewn logs placed endwise in the ground, forming a wall 10 feet high. The roof is made of split pine slabs. Logs, levelled off on top and supported by rough legs form the seats. The pulpit has been constructed with cracker box boards."

When not housing religious services, the building was available for secular functions including songfests, political debates, and skits and plays. Occasionally a group of singers made up of members of the various regiments would entertain their comrades. Cleveland joined the group but bowed out when he realized that "others are better singers than myself." He singled out a lieutenant and the drum major of the Twenty-seventh Massachusetts, the sergeant major of the Twenty-fifth Massachusetts, and someone he knew only as "a big fellow with a black moustache, famous not only for his deep bass voice but also for his gay antics." Sometimes the regiment's newly reconstituted band would accompany the choir as it belted out "America," "Land of Our Fathers," and other patriotic and popular numbers.[11]

The first major occasion hosted by the chapel after the Ninth's arrival took place on a national holiday—Thursday, November 26, the first official Thanksgiving Day in American history. The observance had come about by proclamation of President Lincoln as a time to show gratitude for the blessings of the past year and "in humble penitence for our national perverseness and disobedience." Services conducted by two regimental chaplains, including Chaplain Carrell of the Ninth, were attended by a huge congregation thanks to an order from General Heckman compelling the presence of every able-bodied, off-duty officer and enlisted man in the brigade.

When the service concluded, the attendees found themselves freed from all unnecessary duty. As one Jerseyman put it, "from noon until tattoo, liberty was given us to roam from camp wherever our fancy might direct." The Ninth's camp quickly emptied out as the men visited other sites where games and sporting events were being held. The regiment made a good showing in several competitions, members of the outfit winning the day's 200- and 400-yard footraces as well as a trial of strength and speed with axes known as "woodchuck."

At the height of the activities a letter from General Heckman was read in every camp, announcing Ulysses S. Grant's smashing victory over the former besiegers of Chattanooga. It was said that "cheer upon cheer greeted the glorious news, and for the time being all were as happy as happy could be." Lieutenant Drake added that "you cannot imagine how much real good the cheering news has done us good fellows. I never felt happier; I never was happier."[12]

Although heartened by the report, Sergeant Stillwell saw political meddling afoot in Tennessee. He revealed that "I was almost certain that the War Department would not allow Gen Grant to follow up Bragg, and annihilate the rebel army . . . for if he did it would end the war, and then of course Grant would be the peoples man for the next President and the [office] seekers in Washington would stand a poor chance." In fact, neither prospect came to pass: Bragg's overwhelming defeat did not end the war and Grant did not succeed Lincoln. The magnitude of his success, however, muted some of the general disappointment stemming from later word that Meade's advance on the Rapidan had come to naught, forcing his army to retreat and go into winter camp.[13]

Assuredly, at some point in the not-distant future the war in southeastern Virginia would again be at full volume and the thousands of troops gathered there would march forth in hopes of storming the Confederate capital and quashing rebellion and treason. The man who would lead them thither was as yet unknown. One would suppose that it would be a commander of considerable experience and demonstrated strategic and tactical ability. Although General Foster, now ensconced at Fort Monroe, occasionally visited Newport News and on November 2 reviewed the Star Brigade, many soldiers doubted that he had the reputation or the cachet to gain command of an effort against the enemy's capital.

Apparently the War Department shared these doubts; nine days after the gala review Foster was relieved of command of the Department of Virginia and North Carolina and dispatched, first, to Washington and then westward to replace his old boss Burnside as head of the Army of the Ohio. Foster's demise owed to his inconsistent and generally ineffectual efforts to extend the footholds Burnside had gained along the Carolina coast in 1862, as exemplified by the many failed expeditions in which the Ninth New Jersey had participated over the past several months. The situation was summed up by a *New York Tribune* correspondent based at Fort Monroe who wrote in early November: "What has been accomplished in this command during General Foster's administration, in a military view, is not of much importance."[14]

If not Foster, then who would guide the XVIII Corps in the forthcoming campaign? The answer would stun many of the troops in Hampton Roads as well as those in other theaters and also military and political analysts throughout North and South. On October 28 President Lincoln announced Maj. Gen. Benjamin Franklin Butler as Foster's successor at Fort Monroe, and the war in Virginia took a sudden and sharp turn.

By late 1863 Ben Butler—prominent lawyer, state legislator, militia general, and one of the conflict's earliest and most unlikely heroes—was well on his way to becoming the most notorious political general in American history. It was true that he had made a name for himself in military or quasi-military positions. In 1861 he had seized pro-secessionist Baltimore for the Union and had captured (with a large dose of help from the navy) the Rebel defenses at Hatteras Inlet. Sent west in the spring of 1862, again with the navy's assistance he had occupied New Orleans, the Confederacy's largest city. Yet he had left his mark mainly in the political and social realms as promulgator of the "contraband" theory by which freed slaves were put to work for the Union armies; as staunch supporter of African American soldiery; and as such a persistent thorn in the side of the Confederacy that he had been declared a war criminal, liable to summary execution if captured.

Butler had worked hard to gain notoriety. During his seven-month rule in New Orleans, he antagonized foreign governments by riding herd on consular officials who clandestinely supported the Confederate cause. He publicly executed a local man who dared deface the U.S. flag. And he shocked Southern sensibilities by threatening to treat as a prostitute any woman who harassed or assaulted his troops. These and other controversial actions had led to his relief in December 1862; since then he had remained more or less quietly at his home in Lowell, while political supporters and hard-war Unionists pressured Lincoln to reinstate him. This effort was successful primarily because the president felt he needed the support of prominent War Democrats such as Butler if he were to win reelection in November 1864. Thus he took a calculated risk by offering the man Foster's old job, acutely aware that the shrewd and ambitious New Englander might become a presidential rival, especially if he made a well-publicized success of his new command.[15]

The formal announcement of Butler's ascension to lead all XVIII Corps units in Virginia and North Carolina was read to the troops at Newport News on November 13. Not surprisingly, reaction was mixed.

The soldiers knew relatively little about their new commander but they regretted the loss of his predecessor, in whom they reposed a certain amount of confidence. Sgt. Andrew Little's feelings were typical of the regiment: "We part with our old General reluctantly, but hope it may be for the benefit of our Country, as his services it appears is required at Washington."[16]

The Ninth got its first close look at the new leader on the morning of December 8, when Butler held a gala review of the occupants of Newport News. Private Cleveland described him as "a rather good-looking man." Either the private needed glasses or his standards of male beauty were remarkably low, for Butler was anything but handsome. A bald head, bulging eyes (one marred by a cast), and a corpulent body atop unnaturally short legs made him a comical sight, especially in the saddle. He did, however, have a sense of humor about himself. In the aftermath of the review, while riding through the Ninth's camp accompanied by his staff, Butler suddenly reined to a halt, dismounted, drew a pistol from his belt, and pointed it at the head of Pvt. Joel Hulse of Company D. Hulse's nonplussed comrades clustered about the couple, asking "General, what's the matter?" Butler replied: "I once swore that if I ever saw a man uglier than myself, I would shoot him on the spot, and there stands the man who has haunted me!" As Lieutenant Drake wrote, "the boys now understanding the matter, burst out into a hearty peal of laughter, and the general . . . rode off amid cheers." In the days following the mock confrontation, Hulse, known throughout the regiment for "his amiable traits of character," was the butt of much good-natured ribbing.[17]

At Newport News the remainder of the year passed quietly, with a single exception. In mid-December a smallpox epidemic broke out in the neighboring camp of the Twenty-first Connecticut. Over the next three days Drs. Woodhull, Gillette, and Davies vaccinated every member of the Ninth against the contagion. Though inoculations were in their infancy and their effectiveness was unestablished, no member of the regiment is reported to have contracted the dreaded malady. A cold snap at this same time, which caused the regiment's bathing pond to gain a layer of ice half an inch thick, may have served to limit transmission by keeping most of the men under canvas instead of in close contact with one another.[18]

A happier time came with the advent of Christmas, which the men recalled as "one of the few bright spots that illumed our rugged path," a merry occasion for "those who had been spared through all the vicissitudes of the past to enjoy it." Like Thanksgiving, the day was given over to both religious and secular festivities. The former included a holiday service conducted by Chaplain Carrell, prior to which he made the rounds of the camp, wishing every man Merry Christmas and presenting him with a copy of Oliver Wendell Holmes's "Army Hymn." The latter encompassed not only athletic and marksmanship competitions but also "burlesque parades in which some of the officers saw their peculiarities cleverly mimicked." Imbued with the spirit of the season, the targets of these parodies took no offense, or at least voiced none.[19]

Many men received presents including holiday edibles sent from Jersey by families, friends, and soldiers' aid societies. Other gifts were self-provided, such as a quantity of alcohol stuffed inside a "fine fat turkey" and smuggled past the camp sentries by some thirsty Jerseymen. Lieutenant Drake noted that "well-filled boxes from home had arrived a day or two previous, and so the happy recipients had invited their particular friends to enjoy the good things." Perhaps the best-stocked of these gift boxes was sent via express to Ed Cleveland by his loving family in Elizabeth. The private gladly shared with his tentmates the contents, which included not only reading material and personal articles but also "doughnuts, crullers, cakes, hickory nuts, head cheese, pickles, preserves, jellies, fruit cake, pound cake, cup cakes and two pies. Everything was in excellent condition. We had a first-rate supper. The pie was the best I have eaten since leaving Jersey."[20]

Officially, the service term of the Ninth New Jersey would end in September 1864. Determined not to lose the support of such a well-regarded veteran outfit and unwilling to wait until that deadline approached, federal and state officials made strenuous efforts to persuade a majority of the men to reenlist. These efforts began only two weeks after the Ninth reached Hampton Roads. On November 6 an order read on dress parade announced that if certain conditions were met soldiers reenlisting for three years or the duration of the conflict would receive, over that period, more than four hundred dollars in government bounty money. Since many states, counties, and municipalities added bonuses of their own, a reenlisting private or noncommissioned officer could pocket a thousand dollars or more over time.

Army regulations mandated that when "three-fourths of a company or regiment reenlist, the volunteers so enlisted may be furloughed in a body, for at least 30 days, to go home with their officers to their respective States and to organize and recruit, and the individuals of the companies or regiments who do not reenlist, shall be assigned to duty in other companies or regiments until the expiration of their term of service." Furthermore, officers in reenlisting regiments "shall have their commissions continued so as to preserve their date of rank as fixed by their original muster into United States service." Two other provisions served as lures to re-upping. Regiments with the requisite number of reenlistees would be awarded the honored title of "Veteran Volunteers." To highlight this distinction, each veteran would be issued a "service chevron" of white edged with red. The stripe was expected to engender great pride in those who wore it.[21]

The reenlistment program was well conceived and reasonably well implemented, but not everyone considered the rules of the game fair or just. Private Cleveland, who like many later recruits had initially signed for only seventeen months rather than three years, disliked the fact that the "anti-veterans" would be denied leave. As he wrote in his diary, "the boys, generally, think this unfair. It is too much like forcing men into service." In a later entry he added: "Those who had faithfully served for more than two years will be deprived of long-expected furloughs because they will not volunteer for three years longer. It may be that this will be more of a detriment than an incentive to re-enlistment."[22]

It did not turn out that way. When state agents visited the Ninth's camp on December 4, reportedly offering hundreds of dollars to any soldier who would take advantage of the opportunity, at least 100 men signed up on the spot. Another 100 signed the reenlistment forms before December was out, and it appeared certain that the required quota would be met early in the new year.[23]

Not every member of the regiment could be tempted to sign on for "three years or the war." The soldier-correspondent "Censor" remarked that "how men like those of the 9th could sell themselves for a paltry sum and thirty days furlough, is more than I can see." Another who was determined to serve out his original enlistment was Sergeant Stillwell, whose eyes "cannot see enough money to induce me to [re]enlist. . . . If they should offer me the office of the highest rank in the army I would not take it." Stillwell believed that a majority of the regiment felt as he did, resentful of the limitations placed on their rights as civilians only temporarily under arms and disgusted by the leadership material to which they had long been exposed. In mid-November the sergeant opined that "I do not think there is one in our Company that will reenlist now. They all seem to want to get out of the present bondage and be free once more from tyrannical upstarts."[24]

Stillwell misread the corporate mood. By early January enough Jerseymen had agreed to extend their service that the first group—110 enlisted men including a majority of those in Company A—left Newport News, along with six officers as escorts, on the propeller steamer *City of Richmond* for Jersey City via the port of New York. Members of other regiments in Heckman's brigade shared deck and hold space with the veterans of the Ninth. The passengers reached Trenton on the sixteenth.[25]

Over the next few weeks additional Trenton-based "patriots" arrived in the Ninth's camp to promote the bounty program. At their urging and with the cooperation of the officers, although ultimately unnecessary, the regiment's reenlistment period was extended through February. Colonel Zabriskie was a major factor in persuading men to sign on for the duration. According to Lieutenant Drake, virtually the entire enlisted force had expressed a desire to reenlist if Zabriskie, who had suffered from several health problems over the past two years, "would stand by them." When apprised of the men's sentiments, the colonel at first declined to respond, raising concern that he might resign his commission on the verge of a new round of active service. But in a January 21 address to the assembled regiment Zabriskie announced that "I cheerfully give it [my answer]—yes, we will continue to serve our country together." The men cheered his pledge "until they were hoarse," after which the band "performed several National airs."[26]

By the end of January, almost 500 members of the regiment had signed the reenlistment forms, ensuring the Ninth of veteran volunteer status—the only regiment from New Jersey to attain this distinction. That day another 258 members, accompanied by Zabriskie and several other officers, sailed to Fort Monroe and then for home. Their ship reached New York harbor on the evening of February 3 and next day unloaded its passengers at Jersey City. There the detachment was gathered together and treated to speeches of welcome by the mayor and other officials. That evening, after being fed as a body by the ladies of the city, the men reached Trenton by rail and reported at Camp Perrine, on the east bank of the Delaware and Raritan Canal.

At Trenton the returning soldiers were joined by a large enough group of recruits to raise the strength of the Ninth to almost 550 officers and men. All were addressed by the newly installed governor, who lauded their patriotism and sacrifice. Following another bountiful supper they were put up at the camp for the night. While they slept, their colonel joined a circle of friends for an evening of dining and entertainment at a local hotel, "the occasion of much pleasure" for the assembled group. In later days Zabriskie was showered with gifts including a "magnificent" sword presented by leading residents of Jersey City. He accepted the sword "with the proud boast that I am one of a band of volunteers that have never, on any occasion, dishonored themselves, their state, the uniform they wear, or the flag under whose folds they fight."[27]

The next day, the soldiers were released from Camp Perrine and dispersed by rail, boat, and stage for their homes. A small number, however, remained in Trenton long enough to get drunk, involve themselves in various altercations, and lose an estimated aggregate of four thousand dollars to an assortment of pickpockets, prostitutes, and professional gamblers.[28]

By all indications, the men enjoyed their three weeks in the bosom of their families, but for the majority the blessed respite from combat, hard labor, and military regulations ended far too soon. The first group of furloughed men, having left Newport News on January 13, reported to Trenton for the return trip to Virginia on February 12. Bedeviled by travel delays, they rejoined the army on the twenty-second. On March 2 the second detachment, their leaves expired, assembled in the state capital. These men, slowed by a lack of transportation via Philadelphia and Baltimore, did not reach Newport News until mid-month.[29]

Edmund Cleveland, who had been granted a furlough even though he had not yet served three years, was among the second group of returnees. The private had reached his hometown of Elizabeth on February 5. He spent the next thirty-two days in "Betsyville" among family, friends, and state officials—the latter in an effort to secure a commission that failed despite recommendations from several of his superiors. On February 8 Cleveland glumly packed his knapsack, said his goodbyes, and walked to the house of his tent-mate and best fried Tunis Peer, where he "witnessed the affecting separation of him and his wife." From there the two boarded the train for Trenton. Cleveland never forgot how badly he felt when his all-too brief reunion with loved ones and long-time companions came to an end, nor did he forget the sad parting at his friend's home. Private Tunis Peer never saw his wife again; six months later he died of starvation at the notorious prison camp in Georgia known as Andersonville.[30]

The returning soldiers were transported not to Newport News but to a new camp outside Portsmouth on the south side of Hampton Roads. Here on Julian's Creek the 231 members of the Ninth who were unwilling to reenlist had been sent on January 22. Their transfer coincided with a general breaking-up of the camp on the banks of the James. The following day the last inhabitants, the ladies of the regiment, left for home "in the joyous expectation of an early meeting with their [furloughed] husbands in New Jersey."

At Portsmouth the "anti-veterans," under the command of Maj. William B. Curlis, occupied the tents of a Connecticut regiment that had recently vacated the area. The men were delighted to learn that in their new surroundings they were again under command of General Heckman. On the twelfth, Heckman had been sent to relieve Brig. Gen. George W. Getty in command of a full division of troops occupying Portsmouth and vicinity. When departing Newport News he issued an order bidding an "affectionate farewell" to the Ninth, for whom he had ever entertained a feeling of "affection and pride." Although it is not known if Heckman sought his old outfit's transfer to his new post, it can be assumed that the reunion pleased him every bit as much as it did the men who so highly respected him.[31]

The principal duty of Major Curlis's detachment was to hold the left flank of the twenty-mile-long picket line that protected the military railroad from Portsmouth to Suffolk. This cordon was the repeated target of raiders reminiscent of those that had bedeviled the Ninth in North Carolina. To facilitate operational flexibility the men were divided into three provisional companies commanded by five line officers. Sergeant Stillwell, the senior noncommissioned officer in one of these units, declared that he and his compatriots "have seceded from the 9th." The companies lacked visible signs of regimental affiliation including the Ninth's tattered, shell-torn colors, which were due to be exchanged for pristine banners during Sgt. George Meyers's furlough in Trenton. For a time rumors had it that the men at Portsmouth would be transferred to the Army of the Potomac, to be distributed to regiments of complete strangers. Fortunately the scare stories were devoid of fact; once this became evident, many minds were relieved. In time Curlis's detachment, and the Ninth in its entirety, would be assigned to Col. W. H. P. Steere's brigade of Heckman's division, XVIII Corps.[32]

At first the upheaval that accompanied their transfer from Newport News left the men feeling, as Stillwell put it, like "lost babes." The majority must have felt, as he did, that "it is hard to see the main part of the regt go home and take those colors away from us, that we have stood by and fought under in many a hard contested battle field, untill they have become riddled to pieces with bullets. It is almost like parting with some near relative for life. . . . I must say it is hard, very hard." Gradually, however, the detachment acclimated to its new location and to the workload there, which, as had been the case at Newport News, was relatively light. With the veterans gone, military routine virtually came to a halt. Occasionally there was some excitement such as on February 6, when orders were received to stand ready to repulse a rumored attack on the railroad near Julian's Creek. Expectations were not met, however, and the men returned to normal duty, which included training the raw recruits that had joined the Ninth at Newport News.[33]

The only spate of combat was a skirmish on March 1 with Confederate cavalry along the southward-running road to the Dismal Swamp Canal. The fighting occurred during a reconnaissance mission ordered by Lt. Col. Martin R. Smith of the Eighth Connecticut, commanding the post at Deep Creek, seven miles south of Portsmouth. Reacting to reports of an attack on one of his picket stations, Smith sent 100 members of the Ninth to that point, only to find the Rebels gone. A brief pursuit turned up a body of dismounted horsemen lying in wait along the Bear Quarter Road. Before the enemy could strike Smith detached Lt. Thomas W. Burnett with twenty-five men and sent them forward as skirmishers.

A mile and a half up the road, the little band was fired on by a force variously reported as 150 to 500 strong. First to draw Rebel bullets was a three-man advance guard under Corp. Thomas MacQuaide. By throwing himself to the ground and playing dead, the corporal avoided being hit or captured, but his companions—Pvts. Albert S. Nutt and Joel Hulse— were struck several times. Before succumbing to his wounds, Nutt got off a shot that killed one of his assailants. Apparently this infuriated the Rebels, for his abandoned body was found next day stripped and, according to some reports, mutilated, lying in a ditch where it had been thrown. Private Hulse, the target of General Butler's self-deprecating humor, though wounded in the right arm and side not only managed to elude capture but returned under his own power to the camp at Julian's Creek. He was evacuated to the Balfour Military Hospital at Portsmouth, where, despite intensive medical care, he died on March 8.[34]

Discovering that his many opponents were maneuvering to take his twenty-two men in flank and rear, Burnett fell back to more defensible ground near a crossroads where supports dispatched by both Colonel Smith and General Heckman reached him two hours later. By good fortune the few Jerseymen had held on against repeated attacks without taking additional casualties.

The main body of reinforcements—950 infantry and cavalry and two guns—evicted the Confederates and pursued them southward. The three-day operation, conducted under extreme conditions, ended with the enemy thrust across the North Carolina line, whereupon the pursuers halted and marched back to their former stations. "We was gone four day and nights," David Hankins wrote his sister, "and I tell you we had a pretty rough time of it for it rained and snowed pretty near the whole time we was gone."[35]

Although Rebel forces attacked the railroad from Portsmouth several times throughout March and early April, most of the action took place along sectors of the picket line beyond the Ninth's reach. Consequently, "time hung heavy" on the men of the outfit. They spent a good portion of their many off-duty hours keeping track of the military and political news. It was during this time that the forces of George Pickett assaulted New Bern, Beaufort, Newport Barracks, and other sites familiar to the Ninth, destroying millions of dollars of property including the blockhouses at Gayles Creek and Bogue Sound. Three weeks after the raid a column of cavalry under Brig. Gen. H. Judson Kilpatrick entered the Ninth's lines en route to a raid on Richmond. The troops at Portsmouth had high hopes for the expedition, aimed at destroying military facilities and freeing Union prisoners including, possibly, some from the Ninth. Hopes were dashed three days later when the raiders were beaten back on the city's doorstep and their coleader, Col. Ulric Dahlgren, was killed.[36]

The news from the political home front was no less disheartening. The Democrat-controlled legislature in Trenton quietly decided that absentee voting violated New Jersey's constitution; thus it denied the franchise to the state's soldiers during the fall elections. Reaction to the move ran mainly along party lines. A Republican writing in the Trenton *State Gazette* under the pseudonym "Nosidam" railed that "the army demand the re-election of 'Honest Abe'—but what have the soldiers to say in this little matter? Have we lost the prerogative of freemen, in going forth to defend the Government? Yes! disfranchised of our dearest privilege." More conservative members of the Ninth, of whom there were many, applauded the action of the legislature, believing that a soldier's duties lay outside the political realm.[37]

Jerseymen of all political faiths united in responding positively to the news that on March 10 Ulysses S. Grant, the most successful of the Union's field commanders, had been appointed general-in-chief of its forces. Reports had Grant making his headquarters with Meade's army in Virginia, leaving command in the West to his most trusted lieutenant, Sherman. This strongly suggested that a major, perhaps the climactic, campaign in the eastern theater lay only weeks away. Lieutenant Drake expressed the prevailing opinion that "with Lieut. General United States Grant at the head of our grand armies you may soon expect to hear of stirring news from all quarters of rebeldom." Another member of the Ninth had "no doubt there will be a move made from this Department, and if the Army of the Potomac and Gen. Butler move at the same time, we will be very apt to give the rebs a pretty hard rub for Richmond."[38]

Military activities and political controversy could stoke emotions and raise hopes and fears almost to a fever pitch, but many soldiers wished for a calmer existence. Seeking respite from the burdens and tribulations of their adopted profession, the soldiers on the south side of Hampton Roads took their relaxation where and when they found it. One outlet was the entertainment occasionally available at the main camp outside Portsmouth. There "an immense rough building" akin to the one at Newport News, housing church services and other events, provided a stage for soldier-theatricals.[39]

The major production of that winter was a most ambitious project indeed, a three-act grand opera entitled *Maritana*, performed by members of the Ninth and the other regiments in Heckman's command. Because he was the youngest soldier for miles around "and as I hadn't the faintest appearance of beard," Private Keenan was induced to take the title role, that of a gypsy singer from Madrid who becomes the love object of King Charles II of Spain. The work of a British composer, *Maritana* combined romance, intrigue, and deception in a thoroughly European setting. It had been a favorite with American audiences since its premiere in Philadelphia in 1848.[40]

As the female lead recalled, "never was a play cast under more difficulty, or mounted with such exertions." Not only did young Keenan essay a difficult part, he was compelled to purchase material for his own costumes, which cost him the princely sum of sixty dollars. In doing so "I exhausted all the finery in the Norfolk and Portsmouth shops . . . and I think to this day that the audience got more for their money than they ever did before or since."

By the time Keenan and the other actors took the stage, the theater was crammed with civilians, officers, and enlisted men including the entire detachment of the Ninth New Jersey, everyone hooting, whistling, and stamping his feet. An orchestra was in place but it had arrived too late for a rehearsal. When the youngster appeared in his corsets, skirts, and powdered wig, the audience erupted, "the men rising in their seats to cheer, while you may be sure there was no end of facetious remarks on the comeliness of the heroine's arms, legs, and bust!"

Keenan believed the evening went well, everything considered, although his voice, which had just begun to change, went through "unexpected gradations from a piping treble to a shrill voice." The effect produced constant guffaws, "but the uproar of the evening came, when between acts, I was presented as Senorita somebody from Havana—and danced a Castilian minuet with castanets. . . . The result was simply ludicrous. In the dance I would be caught on one toe—just preparing for a spring and clash of the castanets when the music would halt, stop dead, a few pipes would sound from the horn and of course my pirouet was ruined. The men roared, they got up and stamped and danced and shouted with delight. I think they kept me an hour repeating that infernal dance, until my tarletan skirts and pink tights were wet with perspiration as a towel after a bath."

Because Keenan took the miscues good-naturedly, when the opera ended members of the audience presented him with "profusions of bouquets." A colonel and several of his officers came to the players' dressing room and offered them "an engagement at Butler's headquarters." The cast politely refused, but "the young officers carried us off to their quarters and gave us a regal supper, the actors all the time in our stage toggery!"[41]

When Colonel Zabriskie and the second group of furloughed men reached the camp at Julian's Creek on March 17, they were serenaded with "Auld Lang Syne" by their comrades under Major Curlis. The newcomers appreciated the cordial greeting as well as the new tents waiting for them in rows of fourteen, those of every two companies facing each other. They were not especially happy, however, to reimmerse themselves in a life of drudgery and hardship. Many must have shared the feelings of Private Hankins, a member of the first detachment to go north, who upon returning from a long and difficult voyage had to shoulder his knapsack and march five miles through the mud to reach camp: "I tell you that did not set very good on me after being in Jersey thirty days."[42]

It is not known whether any tension or discord arose between the reenlisted men and those who had refused to sign on for another hitch, but it cannot be ruled out. There may have been cause for resentment on both sides, the reenlistees skeptical of the patriotism and fidelity of the "anti-veterans," the latter upset at the former's ability to enjoy hearth and home in the midst of war. Symmes Stillwell, for one, was privately critical of the moral core of the returning veterans, "some few [of whom] have followed the dissipated habits of vice while away, which begins to tell upon their persons quite plain." The stories the returnees told made the non-com regret, as he told his brother Daniel, "that so many of the fair sex belonging to the State of New Jersey have lost their virtue. I hear there is representatives from our village of nativity [Cranbury], residing in Trenton following the occupation of vice." After castigating those "that wish to satisfy their anamel propensities in that kind of way," he assured his mother that he was a stranger to sins of the flesh: "I must say, the Ladeys hasent troubled me any for the last two years."[43]

One doubts that the sergeant informed his family that less than a month later he developed a case of syphilis. The next several months—up to the end of his enlistment term—Stillwell spent in a military hospital, either as patient or part-time attendant, while his regiment fought the war without him. Ironically, by failing to measure up to what his country expected of its soldiers, the sergeant was spared from the bloodletting the Ninth underwent as a participant in Grant's 1864 campaign in Virginia.[44]

Once the regiment became whole again, life at Julian's Creek speeded up with the reinstitution of full-scale camp routine including guard duty, unit inspections, dress parade, and, until weather interfered, squad, company, and battalion drill totaling four hours every day—mainly for the benefit of the regiment's recently acquired recruits, conscripts, and substitutes. Winter came to a grudging close: howling storms on March 22 and 28 produced two feet of snow as well as interregimental snowball battles that contained aspects of actual combat. "The right wing, making several terrific charges," wrote one observer, "finally drove the left wing to their shanties and marched around the camp yelling and cheering."[45]

When spring finally dawned, the men turned their thoughts to coming events. They cleaned their Springfields, overhauled their clothing, and wrote what some feared would be their last letters home. The newcomers appeared to be learning fast, solidifying confidence that the Ninth would acquit itself honorably in the campaigning ahead. "They are getting along with drill firstrate," wrote Private Hankins of the recent recruits. "Our old regiment begins to look something like it used to when we left Camp Olden." On April 8 Sergeant Stillwell, only days away from leaving the regiment, considered the future course of the conflict: "I think this year will either end it or lengthen it. I hope the former, but I fear the latter."[46]

In mid-April the Ninth took the field for the first time in six months. Many suspected the operation that began on the fourteenth heralded the commencement of the long-anticipated campaign under its new general-in-chief. "We were going to march up the south side of the James," Henry Keenan was told, "and cut off Lee's communications, while Grant came down from the Rapidan." The man could not have been more wrong, for the expedition proved to be merely a brief and indecisive prelude.[47]

That morning several regiments including elements of the Star Brigade under overall command of Brig. Gen. Charles K. Graham were shipped up the James and Chuckatuck Rivers toward the supposedly enemy-held village of Smithfield. The Ninth, leading the column, disembarked at Cherry Grove Landing near the grounds of an abandoned plantation. Followed by the 118th New York (the rest of the brigade was en route to Smithfield via other directions), the regiment moved forward for a mile or more, Companies A, C, and D advancing as skirmishers. When the vanguard located a force of the enemy inside a thick woods on the edge of the plantation, Pvt. Jesse Wilkins of Company D took careful aim and knocked a Rebel officer off his all-too-conspicuous white horse. Thereupon the officer's troops—100 or more members of a North Carolina infantry regiment—retreated, leaving Smithfield open to occupation.

The Ninth found "comfortable quarters for the night" in some vacated houses. These included an old habitation on the main street near the steamboat landing, which the men assiduously looted of everything of value. The plunder included a cache of books later found to be the property of Leopold C. P. Cowper, the recently installed lieutenant governor of the Restored Government of Virginia. By order of Lieutenant Colonel Stewart, who led the regiment on the expedition, the purloined volumes were recovered, boxed up, and returned to their owner.[48]

Here was a most unfortunate way to begin the campaign of 1864, especially as a member of the Ninth had been wounded in the skirmish at the woods. By the time it returned via water to Portsmouth on the afternoon of the fifteenth, the regiment was hankering for a more meaningful opportunity to test its savvy, strength, and endurance. This it would get, in spades, little more than a fortnight later.

10 The Killing Fields

Benjamin F. Butler's command, unofficially but consistently known as the Army of the James, was assigned a major objective for the coming campaigning. On April 2 when Ulysses S. Grant visited Butler's head-quarters at Fort Monroe, he adopted a suggestion by the Massachusetts general. While Grant, traveling with Meade's army, engaged Lee's Army of Northern Virginia fifty miles above Richmond, Butler's troops would sail up their namesake river to strike the lightly guarded Confederate capital from below. If unable to take Richmond by storm Butler would invest the city until the Army of the Potomac, driving Lee before it, came down from the north to join in the siege. Even if unable to break through the city's multiple lines of defense, by methodically cutting off its links to areas of reinforcement and supply the combined armies would starve the Rebels into submission, probably within a few months. Grant had achieved as much at Vicksburg without great difficulty; no one doubted he could do it again in the main theater of operations.[1]

It took a month for the Virginia roads to dry and for Grant to iron out his overall strategy, which included simultaneous operations by three armies under Sherman in the West with the manufacturing and supply center of Atlanta as their common objective, and by other forces in the Shenandoah Valley. All was ready as of the first week in May. By then erroneous reports that the Ninth New Jersey would fail to take part in the coming operation, being withheld to garrison Portsmouth, had been dispelled. Days before the armies rumbled into motion, Andrew

Little wrote that thanks to the "beautiful" weather, preparations were nearly complete for the job ahead: "We have always been allowed to have plenty of clothes but will be cut down and will appear much like working men hereafter." The regiment would accomplish the task with Colonel Zabriskie at its head, he having completed a several-week stint in charge of a general court-martial at Portsmouth.[2]

The work appeared to get underway around midnight on April 26–27 when the Ninth departed Julian's Creek by ship for Fort Monroe and then up the river—not the James but the York, on the eastern side of the Virginia Peninsula—to the wharves of Yorktown. Moving inland, the regiment camped on what Henry F. Keenan described as "a sandy waste . . . in a vale of infection. The water for cooking ran through the putrefying debris made during McClellan's siege. By day the sun beat down upon us, and at night the exhalations of the noisome soil shut us in like the vapory density of the English fog."[3]

On the twenty-ninth the Star Brigade abruptly marched up the peninsula toward Williamsburg as if intending to take Richmond all by itself. Later that day, without explanation—having accomplished nothing of visible importance—the command departed Virginia's colonial capital on a return march to Yorktown made in an almost impenetrable cloud of dust. There on the thirtieth, one day before a violent rainstorm turned the area into a sea of mud, Butler reviewed the Ninth and numerous other regiments accompanied by his newly appointed XVIII Corps commander, Maj. Gen. William Farrar "Baldy" Smith.[4]

The generals' attendance was considered final proof that the great movement was imminent. But the seemingly aimless march in the direction of Williamsburg had left the men in what Private Keenan called "an irritable state of conjecture" as to their role in the proceedings. Symmes Stillwell believed the troops at Yorktown were intended "to act independent of Grants and Burnsides [i.e., Meade's] armeys." Sergeant Little mistakenly supposed that the Ninth—now a part of Heckman's First Brigade of Brig. Gen. Godfrey Weitzel's Second Division, XVIII Corps—had joined the Army of the Potomac, but he clung to the prevalent rumor that the men were "moving on Richmond. We have a large army here, and troops are being landed constantly. . . . We leave our knapsacks and blankets, and take our own little shelter tents on our backs and our grub in our haversacks." Nine days' rations had been issued to each man, enough for an extensive movement. Private Ed Cleveland took note that the York River was "full of vessels, mostly transports," ready to be boarded by Butler's soldiers.[5]

H-hour finally arrived on the morning of May 5 with the Ninth aboard a transport near the head of Butler's gunboat-escorted flotilla. At 6 a.m. anchors were weighed and the *Nellie Penz* steamed down the York into Hampton Roads and then up the James River, the direct route to Richmond. With her passengers "keeping a keen watch on either side for any lurking enemy," the troopship passed Newport News, and later Harrison's Landing where McClellan's defeated army had regrouped after being shooed from the doorstep of Richmond. "All that soft delicious May day," wrote Private Keenan, the young romantic, "we swept up the splendid river, the air balmy and fragrant, the shores an endless succession of exquisite lines and colors." To add a touch of hard reality to Keenan's reverie, while on board the men were drawn up and ordered to load their rifles.[6]

At 3:30 p.m. the Ninth's troopship deposited her passengers—as a few earlier-arriving transports had done—on the swampy shore of Bermuda Hundred, a peninsula formed by loops of the James and Appomattox Rivers about fifteen miles south of Richmond. An advance echelon consisting of United States Colored Troops from the division of Brig. Gen. Edward W. Hinks had already secured City Point, a landing at the confluence of the two rivers. At both places the Federals debarked unopposed, which told them that the movement had come as a complete surprise to the defenders of the capital. This was also the dominant emotion of the invaders. As Keenan put it, "for once General Butler surprised the enemy instead of himself."[7]

Butler may have been adept at maintaining operational secrecy, but many a soldier doubted his ability to do the right thing once field campaigning began. Reflecting years later on the movement up the James, Keenan complained that "in competent hands, our army, ten thousand or more, would have been before, even in, Richmond by noon the next day. . . . Butler, however, for heaven only knows what reason, sent us into camp on the hot open heaths between the two rivers [and] dawdled there." The teenager was not privy to the orders the army commander was operating under. The broad outlines of the prevailing strategy, including landing troops at and east of Bermuda Hundred, had been Butler's idea but Grant had directed him, immediately upon disembarking, to fortify his base of operations and supply. This Butler took pains to do; when his engineers laid out a position for a line of heavy works across the three-mile neck of land between the James and Appomattox it became the western flank of his enclave. Keenan was likewise unaware that the force pouring onto the strategic peninsula consisted not only of Smith's corps, some 18,000 strong, but also 10,000 members of the X Army Corps, just arrived from South Carolina and asssigned to Butler. The newcomers were led by Maj. Gen. Quincy Adams Gillmore, who had seized Morris Island the previous summer but whose subsequent efforts to capture Charleston had been no more successful than Admiral Du Pont's.[8]

The commander of the Army of the James had sufficient manpower to mount a strong advance on Richmond, but he had other responsibilities to attend to first. One was to break the railroad between Richmond and Petersburg, the capital's main supply center twenty-one miles to the south. Only after he destroyed enough track and telegraph cable to prevent reinforcements from coming to Richmond's defense from the Carolinas would Butler be free to attack the city's southern works at Drewry's Bluff, a heavily defended position on the right bank of the James known to the Confederates as Fort Darling.[9]

Grant expected Butler to assign these preliminary tasks to his ranking subordinates. Aware that the army leader was a novice at warfare but obliged to work with him in order to placate Lincoln, Grant had bracketed Butler with professional soldiers—West Point graduates with years of tactical experience—to keep him from making a botch of his role in the campaign. The only problem was that Grant, so recently arrived from the western theater, lacked a personal knowledge of either general's abilities as a field commander. In fact, neither Smith nor Gillmore was anything close to a military genius; in some respects they were less capable than their common superior. Both were slow-moving, prone to shy from contact with the enemy unless conditions were perfect, and unwilling or unable to cooperate when their troops fought side by side. Gillmore, at least, usually was willing to take orders from Butler, whom he quietly disparaged, but Smith, who considered himself a mental giant and almost everyone else a pigmy, was always critical, and sometimes openly contemptuous, of Butler's leadership.[10]

After debarking, the men of the Ninth were marched about two miles inland. They camped for the night near an elevation known as Cobb's Hill on the extreme left of the army's embryonic defensive line. The remainder of Heckman's brigade, 2,700 strong, bivouacked on adjacent ground. The command passed a quiet night, although Rebel units, some of whom had already come up by railroad from points south, were known to be occupying territory just beyond the line Butler was constructing across Bermuda Hundred neck.

It seemed as if no one was in a hurry to confront those defenders. At around 4 p.m. on the sixth the division commander, General Weitzel, finally ordered Heckman's infantrymen, accompanied by two guns of Battery L, Fourth United States Artillery, to advance to the railroad in the vicinity of Port Walthall Junction, almost three miles out, to ascertain the enemy's positions and to estimate their strength. Heckman was cautioned to develop the opposition without bringing on a general engagement. As the brigade moved west in the slowly fading sunlight, Colonel Zabriskie and the Ninth New Jersey proudly leading the advance, Heckman saw a force of several hundred Rebels holding a sunken road about 300 yards in front of the railroad. These were elements of the Twenty-first and Twenty-fifth South Carolina Infantry, the former recently arrived from Drewry's Bluff, the latter from Petersburg.

The combined force was small—about 600 officers and men—but it occupied a strong position and was supported by cannons. Between the two bodies, as Lieutenant Colonel Stewart observed, "was a clear field, almost without an obstruction, while on our left and the enemy's right, was a strip of timber."[11]

Unable to determine how many soldiers he was facing—they were well hidden by the sunken road as well as by the woods—Heckman used his three Massachusetts regiments to form his center and left flank while placing the Ninth in column on his right to guard against an attack from the north. As the regiment moved into position, Sgt. Jesse R. Hulsart of Company D, who had traversed this area in prewar life, pointed out to his comrades the spires of Petersburg, visible above the trees to the south. Eventually the Ninth halted on the edge of "the beautiful plantation" of Dr. Walthall, namesake of the junction where the Richmond and Petersburg met a short line running east to the banks of the Appomattox (according to some sources, the main edifice was also known as the Mary Dunn house).[12]

By 5 p.m. the advancing Federals were driving in the Rebel pickets. Then the main Confederate force opened fire from its partially hidden position, stunning its opponents and forcing many of them to scatter for cover. Seeing his advance halted, Heckman ordered up the Ninth and personally led it across open ground toward the center of the Rebel defense line. When close enough to cover the distance with a rush, Heckman turned to Colonel Zabriskie and called on the Ninth to charge. His exact words were less dramatic—"From right to left, forward"—and not everyone heard them, but each man had a pretty clear idea of what lay ahead. "Whether or not an order to 'charge' was given I cannot say," wrote Private Cleveland that night. "But as soon as we fixed bayonets we dashed forward pell mell and received a volley from the enemy."[13]

Lacking both clear targets and good cover, the regiment pressed ahead against a torrent of musketry and shell. The air soon became filled with the "sulphurous stench" of cannon fire, which proved to be brutally effective. Within minutes thirty-four Jerseymen fell dead or wounded—the greatest battle loss the outfit had ever suffered. The result rid Private Keenan, who was experiencing his first dose of combat, of his rose-colored notions of war: "In the twinkling of an eye my ardor for battle came to an icy pause! The blood-curdling, venomous whiz-zip of the bullets as they hit or passed stunned my reasoning faculty. But most horrible of all, was the vicious, almost human malignity of the impact, as the lead penetrated the flesh of my comrades near me. The man at my right—Callahan, I think his name was—a gentle, amiable fellow, was struck square in the breast, pitching headlong under my feet with the exclamation, 'My God!'" The expectations of Private Cleveland, also experiencing a full-fledged battle for the first time, were more realistic. Like a seasoned veteran he wrote in his diary that "the field was covered with the usual horrors" and he calmly enumerated the many casualties in Company K. Those killed included Pvt. John Weder, "shot through the head. I saw him with the blood flowing from his mouth."[14]

At the height of the action General Heckman took a wound in his hand and was unseated when at least a dozen rifle balls struck his steed, "Mustang." Mounting the horse of an aide, he continued to try to direct the escalating fighting. Mindful of his orders and the lateness of the hour, he soon directed the Ninth to retire from the advanced position it had assumed near a swale in front of the sunken road—then he ordered a general retreat to Bermuda Hundred. Some sources suggest that the Ninth's withdrawal was conducted "in less than perfect order," and that Heckman, fooled into believing he had been facing two brigades instead of a force smaller than a single regiment, made a critical error by disengaging before reaching the railroad. The criticism of the Ninth's departure is not upheld by extant sources, while in postwar years Heckman lodged a vigorous denial that he had been cozened by his enemy.

Whatever the state of the regiment's fallback, one of its components did not return to base with the rest of the brigade. Its skirmishers, under command of Lieutenant Drake, not only covered the advance of the regiment that afternoon but remained in place long after the shooting ceased. For holding "his position all day and during the night," Drake would become, years after the war, the only member of the Ninth New Jersey to be awarded the Congressional Medal of Honor.[15]

When he learned the results of the day's fighting, Baldy Smith was critical of Heckman's tactics as well as angry that some X Corps troops who had been ordered to support the Star Brigade had not advanced from their camps. From this time forward, the relationship between Butler's corps leaders was fraught with distrust and discord. Smith persuaded Butler to order another advance to the railroad on the seventh, this one conducted by another of his division commanders, Brig. Gen. William T. H. Brooks, but with the assistance of three of Gillmore's brigades. Heckman's troops would provide support to the left rear of Brooks's command by returning to the same location they had fought from on the sixth. By now some 2,700 Confederates had arrived to hold Port Walthall Junction and vicinity; even so Brooks would outnumber them almost three to one.

The fighting on May 7 achieved little more than Heckman had gained the day before. Through indecision, delay, and inexpert maneuvering only a handful of Brooks's nineteen regiments got into action, and they failed to dislodge the few defenders under Brig. Gens. Bushrod R. Johnson and Johnson Hagood. They did, however, tear up a few hundred feet of track above the junction and, by angling southward, made the Confederates believe they intended to attack Petersburg rather than Richmond, an impression Butler and Smith wished to implant in their minds.[16]

The Ninth New Jersey saw relatively little action throughout this day of sweltering heat that cost it more casualties to sunstroke than to bullets. As Lieutenant Colonel Stewart noted in his after-action report, the men "did not get into a general engagement at this time; [our] position being an exposed one we were ordered to hold it awaiting the result of the movement of our troops on the right." The proximity of the Walthall/Dunn plantation enabled the outfit's advance units, Companies D and I under Capt. Samuel Hufty, to enter the manor house and help themselves "to such valuables as could be carried along without impediment." By pulling rank Lieutenant Drake relieved one of his men of a "handsome Marseilles counterpane," which took the place of the blanket he had donated to an enlisted member of Company D, wounded on the sixth.

Shortly afterward, while the fighting between Brooks and the Rebels flared to the north and west, Heckman massed his brigade behind a slight rise in an open field near the Walthall house. There, according to Drake, the command "remained inactive throughout the entire day." Latter-day historians would agree that the brigade remained "quiescent" on the seventh and "did not advance" at any point that day. They fail to note, however, that the Ninth, along with other elements of the Star Brigade, endured a heavy and sometimes devastating artillery barrage. Edmund Cleveland reported one of its effects: "A spherical case shot landed in the centre of Co. K, striking [Pvt. John G.] Klotz in the head, decapitating him and scattering his brains over those near him. . . . The rebs had a fearfully accurate range of us and dropped shells just where they chose."[17]

Once again, the Federals broke contact and withdrew. According to some sources Brooks ordered the movement; other participants claimed that one of Gillmore's brigade leaders retired without authorization. Whatever the cause, the day's work fell far short of Butler's and Smith's expectations. Although briefly engaged, the Ninth had suffered eleven casualties, most of them while making a demonstration in favor of Brooks's troops.[18]

The heavier casualties the Ninth had sustained the previous day had been very much on the minds of the survivors throughout the seventh. That afternoon, when advancing in front of the main body, Drake's skirmishers found themselves crossing the earlier battlefield. Upon the sun-baked ground lay what the lieutenant called "the mute, mutilated and terribly decomposed bodies" of the Ninth's dead; in their midst lay the bullet-riddled carcass of Heckman's warhorse. Private Keenan, for one, never forgot the sights and smells he experienced on this occasion: "Bodies were lying about the cleared ground denuded of all garments except the shirts. They were in every instance black as negroes and swollen beyond human semblance. . . . It was a ghastly, repulsive sight, one that prudent commanders would have spared men advancing under fire."[19]

Little was required of the Ninth, or any considerable portion of Smith's and Gillmore's forces, on Sunday, May 8. The day was given over to strengthening the army's works, repositioning the units that held them, and interrogating prisoners. The respite permitted some men, including several members of the Ninth, to enjoy a "skin bath" in the Appomattox. It also afforded time for second-guessing and grumbling by the soldiers involved in the fighting of the past two days. One XVIII Corps officer called the army's recent performances "possibly the nearest answer ever made to the question: 'How to fight without winning?'" Another question quickly gained currency among Butler's troops: "How long will it take to get to Richmond if you advance two miles every day and come back to your starting point every night?"[20]

Hoping to dispel such doubts and concerns, on May 9 Butler advanced the army again, this time in the direction of Petersburg. He did not intend to attack the "Cockade City," merely to feint toward it, holding its defenders in place, before turning north toward Richmond. Since an advance against the enemy's capital was to be a cooperative effort, Butler awaited word by courier or telegraph from Grant before committing himself to the movement.

Butler's latest foray accomplished mixed results. This day the army laid hands—and picks and crowbars—on the railroad near Chester Station as well as Port Walthall Junction. A large section of track was torn up, three miles' worth by labor teams from the Ninth. But the shift toward Petersburg came to an abrupt halt along Swift Creek, three and a half miles north of the city. A steep riverbank and well-guarded bridges prevented the Federals—large elements of both army corps—from getting close enough to seriously threaten Richmond's support center. Even so, the movement greatly concerned Petersburg's commander, General Pickett, and his meager garrison.

For the Ninth New Jersey, the day featured another clash with the staunch fighters of Johnson Hagood's brigade, this time in a wooded area near Arrowfield Church, astride the Richmond-Petersburg Turnpike west of the railroad and a quarter mile north of Swift Creek. In mid-afternoon General Heckman, holding the approximate center of the army's position, formed his brigade in two lines, two regiments east of, and two west of, the pike. The engagement that ensued raged at an uneven pace for no less than seven hours. Several times Hagood's men advanced "with their long-practiced and peculiar yell from the cover of the woods," only to be driven back by "a pitiless storm of leaden hail." At other times the Rebels seemed content to hug their sheltering defenses—with good reason. During that extended period each side held, then relinquished, the advantage until a final charge by the Confederates near midnight was beaten back with heavy loss. By then the pine boards of a long fence behind which Colonel Zabriskie sheltered a portion of the Ninth had been reduced to "strips of sieve." Hagood's repulse left the field strewn with his dead, but the Federals had become all too familiar with such sights.[21]

Day's close did not bring an end to its horrors. Because Company F pulled picket duty, it was never far from the field of battle. "We lay all night on the ground we had won foot by foot," Private Keenan recalled. "As night deepened, there arose in front of us long, low moans. These, as the dew fell and the air grew chilly, swelled into a bedlam of shrieks and pleadings. I begged permission to go out and relieve the poor fellows, but the officer in command sternly forbade such a thing. The cries came from wounded rebels, left between the lines when the enemy were driven back. Had we gone to their aid we should have been slaughtered from ambush; he even hinted that the cries were a ruse to lure us within range of the rebel pickets. But to this day I can hear those wretched cries, those inarticulate prayers for drink or food.

Toward morning the cries grew fainter, I could even fancy I heard the final gurgle and I felt like a murderer."[22]

Two days after his latest fight, General Heckman issued an address, read to every unit in his brigade, praising its conduct in the recent fighting. His final sentence nicely summarized the author's sentiments: "The fatigues and privations which you have suffered without a murmur are but characteristic of your previous conduct, and the punishment inflicted upon the rebels is one of the many lessons you have taught them, that will cause them to ever remember and fear the Star brigade." Such praise had a heartening effect on its audience. Writing to his family that same day, Sergeant Little proclaimed that although the Ninth had seen hard fighting over the past several days, suffering upward of sixty casualties, "all feel confident that we ar[e] able to wipe out all the rebels before us."[23]

Heckman left unstated an impression that had worked its way into the minds of his men. Throughout May 9 the Star Brigade had fought without close support from other elements of the XVIII Corps. This fueled a deepening suspicion that General Smith had deliberately withheld assistance, having determined, as Lieutenant Drake contended, "that General Butler should not win the battle, and many precious lives were sacrificed in preventing it." The claim would have been dismissed as farfetched had not Smith and Gillmore met for the first time following the close of the day's action. Initially they conferred on the field with Butler, who had committed himself to a more aggressive movement against Petersburg on the tenth by General Hinks's division. Butler asked his subordinates to comment on the plan, but neither had anything to say. After Butler left them to return to Bermuda Hundred, Smith and Gillmore suddenly came up with some ideas. They decided that their superior, who was still fixated on the enemy capital, was going about things all wrong, that Petersburg, not Richmond, was the proper objective. That evening they composed a memorandum they sent to Butler's field headquarters recommending that the army return to Bermuda Hundred. There Butler should throw a pontoon bridge across the Appomattox east of Petersburg and cross it to seize the city from that direction.

Not surprisingly, the joint communiqué did not meet with Butler's approval. He penned a scathing reply in which he regretted his generals' "infirmity of purpose which did not permit you to state to me, when I was personally present, the suggestion which you made in your written note, but left me to go to my headquarters under the impression that another and far different purpose was advised by you. I shall [not] yield to the written suggestions which imply a change of plan made within thirty minutes after I left you. Military affairs cannot be carried on, in my judgment, with this sort of vacillation." His subordinates bristled at the retort, and the divide between them and Butler became a yawning abyss.[24]

The breach occurred at a critical time for the Army of the James, but neither Smith nor Gillmore were privy to the details of its situation. Shortly before his subordinates' memo arrived Butler had received by the military telegraph messages from Secretary of War Stanton covering the recent operations of the Army of the Potomac. Grant and Meade had made contact with Lee on the fifth in the Virginia Wilderness, the same area where Joe Hooker had lost a battle, his confidence, and his reputation almost exactly one year earlier. The two days of fighting in that tangled woodland had ended in stalemate, but the road to Richmond had been blocked. An unfazed Grant decided to press on, sending Meade's army on a southeastward detour toward Spotsylvania Court House.

Although Grant's progress had been negligible thus far, Stanton gave Butler the impression that Meade's command was on the fast track, driving Lee's veterans before it. This being so, Butler could not spare additional time operating against Petersburg—the Army of the James must get moving northward. Thus he canceled the plan involving Hinks's troops and issued orders for an advance on Drewry's Bluff. It would not begin, however, till the morning of the twelfth; the army would spend the eleventh reorganizing for the job ahead, gathering supplies and wagons, and distributing marching rations.[25]

Already Butler's delays had given his enemy time to prepare a defense of the capital's southern reaches; the two-day hiatus on May 10–11 further improved their advantage. The Confederate war office had relieved G. T. Beauregard at Charleston and had assigned him command of the Department of North Carolina and Southern Virginia. Beauregard would have charge of the troops defending Richmond as well as thousands of others from the Carolinas and Petersburg. The additions had been permitted to move north thanks to the inadequate destruction of the railroad.

When Beauregard reached Drewry's Bluff in the small hours of May 14, he had at his disposal 16,000 troops of all arms, including the Richmond garrison under Maj. Gen. Robert Ransom, Jr. He divided the force into three divisions, with a fourth, under Maj. Gen. William H. C. Whiting, held north of Petersburg. Expecting Butler to target Fort Darling, Beauregard hastily drew up a plan to counterattack in front while Whiting struck simultaneously from Port Walthall Junction, cutting off the Federal rear and blocking any retreat to Bermuda Hundred. The Louisiana Creole had a well-established reputation for grandiose planning divorced from hard reality such as an insufficiency of manpower. On this occasion, however, he commanded almost as many troops as his enemy—about 19,000 Federals would oppose him south of the capital—and he knew how to use them to good effect. Another advantage was that he was not burdened with subordinates of the caliber of Baldy Smith and Quincy Gillmore.[26]

The march from Bermuda Hundred to Drewry's Bluff, a distance of seven miles, took three days, testimony to the caution of Butler's subordinates and to the sturdiness of the several lines of works in advance of Beauregard's main position. Before sunrise on the twelfth Heckman's brigade—the Ninth New Jersey leading the advance as usual—moved up the plank-road turnpike. Around 9 a.m., the regiment detected the not-unexpected presence of Rebel skirmishers. When pressed, they fell back upon a substantial force of infantry and artillery, ensconced in a woods that they held "with wonderful tenacity." When the enemy's guns started in, Union batteries came up to oppose them. The artilleries monopolized the fighting until after dark.

On May 13 Butler's advance resumed its now-customary glacial pace. "The Confederates contested every foot of the ground," Lieutenant Drake recalled, "but the superiority of our forces enabled us to dislodge them from every position." The fighting this day was instructive: "The Ninth had seen desperate fighting in the Carolinas, but had never witnessed such dogged persistency and stubborn bravery. It was a fine sight, however, to see General Heckman leading his brigade hither and thither, oftentimes passing through a wall of fire while endeavoring to find a vulnerable spot in the enemy's lines."[27]

Another stirring sight, witnessed by the skirmishers of Companies D and G late in the afternoon, was the firepower displayed by the riflemen of the Thirteenth Indiana Infantry of Col. Jeremiah C. Drake's X Corps brigade. The Hoosiers, having moved across the skirmishers' path either by accident or design, drew up facing an enemy-infested woodlot that the Ninth had been ordered to clean out. Armed with Spencer repeating rifles, the Westerners unleashed a veritable blizzard of cartridges at the trees in their front. Then, having emptied their magazines, they turned about and continued up the road to retake their assigned place in General Gillmore's column. When the Ninth's companies entered the woods to evict any remaining defenders, they found none. "From the wide berth which the Confederates gave us that night," wrote J. Madison Drake, "they must have been under the impression that nothing less than an army corps was firing at that moment."[28]

Early on May 14 the Ninth's skirmishers reached the first line of enemy works south of a sluggish stream named Kingsland Creek, and drew fire. General Heckman came forward and personally reconnoitered the position, which consisted of a line of breastworks and entrenchments protected in front by an abatis and stretching "as far as the eye could reach." When Heckman withdrew, his mission completed, the Ninth edged forward to a line of trees from which a portion of the abatis might be reached. At great risk, Companies D and G climbed over, and in places under, the felled trunks. From vantage points on the other side they were able to fire inside the Rebel works while well protected by the abatis.

Until relieved late in the afternoon, the sharpshooters of the Ninth "had things pretty much their own way. . . . There was considerable sport in picking off 'Johnnies' who had the temerity to expose any part of their persons over the breastworks, and it was impossible for the enemy to discharge their artillery" given their proximity to the main line of works. One of the few casualties was Captain Townley, whose Company K was one of the relief forces. Shot through the wrist as he brandished his sword, the much-admired officer had to go to the rear for medical treatment. He always regretted having to leave his men at such a critical point in the campaign.

The following day, May 15, was relatively quiet. This appeared ominous to many of the officers and men of Butler's precariously positioned command, which now extended for nearly three miles, from an old stagecoach road near the banks of the James westward to the Richmond-Petersburg Railroad. For the Ninth New Jersey the day passed, as Lieutenant Drake wrote, "without any exciting event" except a curiously timed mail call. Several men received letters from home addressed to them "care of the Ninth New Jersey Volunteers, Richmond, Virginia." Here was wishful thinking carried to extremes—no one in the Army of the James would reach the enemy capital on this occasion except as prisoners of war.[29]

Throughout the day mounting signs and sounds suggested that the Rebels were moving troops and guns into position to attack every sector of Butler's line. This was enough to raise the concerns of Colonel Zabriskie and his officers, but the corporate anxiety experienced a sharp uptick when, near dusk, the regiment was shifted from its initial position, which the men had fortified to the best of their ability, to a cleared stretch of ground east of the stage road. The sudden move was made necessary by the interposition of two regiments from another brigade, temporarily assigned to Heckman.

The dispossessed Jerseymen now found themselves on the extreme right of the army's line a little more than a mile from its namesake river. A small stream and pond ran through the cavernous gap, whose only defensive characteristic was a thick woods that would also serve as a cover for any attackers. Supposedly the ground was picketed by a regiment of United States Colored Cavalry—a force too small and, in the minds of the Ninth, too undependable to provide peace of mind. Other sectors of General Smith's line were protected by lengths of downed telegraph wire strung from tree to tree at such a height as to trip any attackers, but the hastily improvised entanglements did not extend far enough to offer protection to Heckman's men.

In its new position the Ninth was ordered to entrench. As one historian of the campaign notes, "this was a difficult task in the gathering darkness, without proper tools, and with muscles aching from the previous set of works constructed and left behind." Lieutenant Drake recalled that the brigade's only shield was a "rude" breastwork "improvised from decayed trunks of trees, limbs, stumps, etc. It was all the men could do, but how gladly they would have hailed picks and shovels."[30]

They did have a semblance of an early-warning system. Lieutenant Colonel Stewart, in charge of deploying the brigade's pickets, placed three companies drawn from various outfits about 100 yards in front of Heckman's main line. He had them spread out until they connected on the left with the pickets of Brig. Gen. Isaac J. Wistar's brigade—a link that came apart during the night and, despite strenuous efforts, was not restored. On the far right Stewart ordered the fifty men of Company H under Joseph Lawrence to occupy the house and grounds of one R. A. Willis, atop a slight rise 400 yards in advance of the main body of the Ninth. Mr. Willis's domicile thus became the most vulnerable point on a vulnerable line, but its location gave Company H a commanding view for miles around. It was believed that it would enable Captain Lawrence to detect any attempt by Beauregard to turn the army's flank. Still, no one at the Willis house, tired as they were, slept that night. As an officer in another company recalled, "how slowly passed the hours, as the night wore on—sleep and rest being impossible owing to the unremitting fire of the enemy, and the wretchedness of our situation."[31]

General Heckman fully appreciated his old outfit's predicament. More than once he brought it to the attention of General Smith. In so many words Heckman pointed out that "this was the most important point in the whole line, as it covered the shortest route to our base of supplies, and on its retention depended the safety of the Union army. Our false position invited attack. Beauregard's advance, if not unexpected, was totally unprovided for." The corps commander promised to reinforce the flank, but the only supports the Ninth received—sections of two light batteries—moved well down the turnpike soon after reporting to the exposed sector. They remained beyond the Ninth's reach through the rest of the night.[32]

The effect of this egregious lack of high-command attention was first felt about 10 p.m. on the fifteenth when the outpost at the Willis house came under attack by dismounted cavalry. For hours Henry Keenan and Pvt. John McCausland, posted behind a picket fence about twenty yards in front of the house, had been alert to suspicious shapes and noises in the night. On a few nerve-wracking occasions, dimly seen groups of men made a dash on the position, screaming the rebel yell. Every attempt had been checked until the horsemen unleashed a volley of carbine fire in response to a shot from the rifle of young Keenan. Dashing back to the house, Keenan and McCausland, who through some miracle had escaped being wounded, joined the rest of their company in returning fire.

They continued to exchange shots with a nigh-invisible enemy until around 5 a.m. on the fog-shrouded morning of the sixteenth, when a body of infantry, having replaced the dismounted cavalry, rushed the house. "Volleys now came from the house itself," Keenan recalled. "It was plain we could do nothing. I don't know who gave the order to retreat, but by a common impulse, as the mass of rebels became clearly defined by the flashes of their own guns, we turned and ran toward the main line, a third of a mile behind us."[33]

Upon reaching Heckman's main body, Jerseymen who had been routed from their picket posts hunkered down against what proved to be an onslaught of infantry and artillery. Hurtling out of the fog were members of Ransom's division, whose job was to assault and if possible uproot the Union right. Sergeant Little was one of many blinded by the mist until almost too late, surviving the onslaught after "many narrow escapes. . . . We could not tell our men from the rebels until we got close to them." Only when the enemy was a few feet away, a comrade wrote, could the Ninth see "their grey and motley dress and emaciated features . . . and we could deliver our fire with telling effect."[34]

The vanguard of Ransom's force was a brigade of Alabamians led by Brig. Gen. Archibald Gracie, Jr., a New York native who had spent his boyhood in Elizabeth, New Jersey. In time Gracie's four and a half regiments of foot soldiers would break the Ninth's flank near the place where Colonel Zabriskie was trying to establish a new defensive perimeter, but it was Ransom's field guns that opened the fight on that part of the field. At first, wrote Private Keenan, "the shells passed far over us to the rear and fell among the colored cavalry, routing them. . . . Then for hours the battle raged, face to face, almost hand to hand, for I could see the men I was firing at, within twenty feet of our line. I could hear every word said by the rebel officers as distinctly, indeed a good deal more distinctly, than I could hear our own." All around him, men went down with wounds. Keenan's rifle became so foul from repeated use that he seized another, then a third, from two of the fallen along with additional rounds from their cartridge boxes.

Already in precarious shape, the regiment began to shed leadership. Looking about, Keenan was shocked to see Colonel Zabriskie clutch his throat and topple against a tree. A bullet had penetrated his windpipe, lodging near his spine. Before being borne to the rear, Zabriskie, bleeding profusely, contacted Lieutenant Colonel Stewart and informed him that he was now in command of the regiment. Not long afterward, Stewart was disabled by a minie ball through his left thigh. His loss hit the Ninth especially hard because he had been working strenuously to prevent the regiment's right flank from breaking. Twice Stewart had re-fused the three companies on that end of the line, temporarily checking Gracie's attack. Because Major Curlis was in the hospital, having suffered severe injuries four days earlier when his horse fell on him, the Ninth was suddenly bereft of field-grade officers. Eventually command passed to Sam Hufty, the senior company commander. This "gallant and efficient officer" led the Ninth through the rest of the fight and out of it when ammunition ran low and everyone was ordered to retreat.[35]

Soon after Zabriskie and Stewart were hit, Private Keenan was felled by a bullet that struck him in the head just below the right temple. His first thought was: "Now I shall know the mystery that has baffled human reason. Now I shall know what death is." But he was not dead, and although when taken to the rear a surgeon pronounced his difficult-to-treat wound mortal, the teenager recovered sufficiently to be evacuated to one of the hospitals in Hampton Roads, and eventually to a general hospital in New York Harbor. There, eighteen days after he was shot, a large round of buckshot was "pried backward out of the skull bone." Despite being threatened with gangrene, Keenan not only survived the operation but five months later was pronounced healthy enough to rejoin his regiment, which he did.[36]

Minutes after Keenan's wounding, almost the entire extent of the line held by the Ninth gave way. At first fired on only in front, by late in the morning the regiment was being struck from the right and rear as well. Though attackers farther to the left were stymied briefly by the telegraph-wire entanglements, Gracie's men and the other brigades charging close behind them had no difficulty slipping around the unanchored right of the XVIII Corps. Unable to fight effectively in three directions at the same time, a few minutes after twelve noon the Jerseymen obeyed General Heckman's frantic order to retreat.

Before doing so, Sergeant Meyers and another member of the color guard, fearing the capture of the national and state flags, ripped them from their staffs and stuffed them inside their shirts before heading for the rear. When a group of almost 100 men of the regiment under command of the Ninth's recently appointed adjutant, 1st Lt. Frederick Coyte, rallied and made a stand, Meyers joined them. Removing the Stars and Stripes from around his waist, he attached it to the end of a stick, which he waved defiantly aloft. In this way the colors, though torn and grimy, escaped the ignominy of falling into enemy hands. Coyte's hundred were not the only Jerseymen to rally. Twenty others, separated from the balance of the regiment, halted their retreat to join a Maine outfit that had rushed up in a belated effort to plug the gap through which the enemy had poured. According to a Maine officer, the men of the Ninth "began popping away at the rebels as though they were duck hunting."[37]

These exceptions notwithstanding, the Ninth's retreat was a chaotic and in many respects a fruitless exercise. This was especially true of the men of Companies D and G on the far left of the regimental line, who somehow failed to get the order to withdraw. By holding their ground west of the stage road to the last minute they found themselves nearly surrounded by Rebels who made "a rude and ill-mannered request" for Capt. Edgar Kissam, Lieutenant Drake, and Company G's 2nd Lt. George Peters to surrender. Instead, the officers turned and joined their men in a frantic dash to the rear. They did not get far, however, before a Confederate battle line burst out of a woods to take most of them prisoner. Only a handful, including Pvt. Benjamin W. Reidinger of Peters's company, managed to escape.[38]

By late morning the troops who had circumvented the Ninth's flank were not only rolling up the length of General Smith's line but threatening Gillmore's, farther west. Like Smith, Gillmore considered his position sufficiently threatened to prompt him, at about 10 a.m., to order a full withdrawal. Soon afterward the morning fog burned off and Butler's subordinates finally had a clear view of the battlefield. They were surprised to find that Beauregard's once-unstoppable assault had effectively stalled. But by then an irreversible retreat was underway, the army falling back in groups large and small toward the turnpike, seeking the safety of the works they had evacuated three days before. They were permitted to reach their fortified peninsula through the almost inexplicable failure of General Whiting to strike as ordered and cut off their retreat. By early evening most of the defeated army, including the remnants of the Ninth New Jersey, were back inside their line of defense, beyond reach of their nearly exhausted but ecstatic enemy.[39]

Like many another regiment in Butler's command, the Ninth had suffered grievously. At least 150 of its men had been killed or wounded this day. The dead included Captains Edward Carrell, the newly appointed commander of Company G, and Edwin S. Harris of Company C. In addition to Zabriskie and Stewart, eight officers had been wounded in the battle or in the days leading up to it: Captains Townley, Lawrence, Burnett, and Benjamin W. Hopper of Company E; 1st Lts. Lewis D. Sheppard of Company B, A. Benson Brown of Company C, and Frederick Hobart of Company G; and 2nd Lt. Jacob Hawk of Company H. Not all would survive their wounds. Despite the expert care he received from Surgeon Woodhull and his assistants, Colonel Zabriskie would succumb on May 24 at the Chesapeake Army Hospital at Fort Monroe, muttering in his delirium: "*Poor boys, poor boys, they are in a bad scrape!*" Captain Lawrence, whose leg was amputated on the field of battle, would die in the same hospital a week later.[40]

As if these losses were not sufficient to cripple the regiment, almost eighty of its people had been captured, corralled, and readied for shipment to the military prisons in Richmond. Many would later be transferred to prison camps in the Deep South including the hell hole of Andersonville. Among the number were the trio of officers cut off when Companies D and G failed to get the word to retreat.[41]

On the boat carrying them from the wharf at Drewry's Bluff to Richmond, the prisoners of war of the Ninth were joined by hundreds of other unfortunate Yankees. Lieutenant Drake was surprised to find General Heckman among them, he having been captured early in the battle. Trying to keep up his courage, the future historian confided to his fellow prisoner that "the greatest object of my ambition has ever been to be able to follow you into Richmond." Heckman replied with a wan smile: "Well, Drake, you are now in a very fair way of having your wish gratified."[42]

11   Decline and Revival

The Ninth New Jersey Veteran Volunteers presented a sorry sight when they returned from Drewry's Bluff, tattered, exhausted, and bloody, throughout May 16. Since daybreak Ed Cleveland, who had missed the battle due to illness, had been hearing the "booming of cannon and the crackling of musketry," and around 10 a.m. wounded men had begun to limp back from the front. By early afternoon the trickle of casualties had become a steady stream. This troubled Cleveland, but he was not prepared for the sight of the woefully small body of men who made their way inside the defenses of Bermuda Hundred a few hours later.

The bedraggled remnant almost made him believe the rumor then making the rounds, that the Star Brigade had been cut to pieces and captured virtually en masse. He was especially upset to learn that those killed, wounded, or captured included close friends in Company K such as Tunis Peer, John Simmonds, and Fred Kneller. Cleveland spent much of the following day writing to their families to impart as much information as was available about his comrades' fate. In common with many another Jerseyman, the recruit from Elizabeth also mourned the mortal wounding of Abram Zabriskie, "a brave officer and a good soldier. We will never have another Colonel like him."[1]

The returnees spent the night after the battle in a temporary camp near the works along Bermuda Hundred neck. The following evening Captain Hufty led them to an open field near the Appomattox River not far from the old campsite at Cobb's Hill—future site of a large earthwork officially christened Fort Zabriskie in honor of their fallen leader. There the men rested and tried to recruit their strength while familiarizing noncombatants including Cleveland with the details of their ordeal. They did not have to strive to convince their listeners that the Ninth had upheld its long-held reputation as a fighting regiment; the gaps in the ranks made the point clearly and concisely. Even so, many who had heard of the regiment's exploits sang its praises. On May 23 the medical inspector of the XVIII Corps, writing to the editor of the *Freehold Democrat*, reported that the Ninth had "fought splendidly" before and at Drewry's Bluff and "suffered severely," adding that "New Jersey should be proud of its officers & men."[2]

Many were angry, some very much so, at having been, as they thought, led to the slaughter by incompetent commanders. Sgt. Amos H. Evans of Company F sharply asked the question that was on the minds of many comrades: "Why did he [Butler] not fortify in the position he held and if such was not his intention I cant see any possible use of his marching us up there to sacrifice so many useful lives." Evans did not know, and possibly never did, that Butler did not entrench because he had intended to attack out of his position late on May 15, only to be talked out of it by Baldy Smith. At the Chesapeake Hospital in Hampton the disabled Symmes Stillwell learned from some of the wounded at Drewry's Bluff that "if our Brigade had been supported in time they would have been in Richmond in two hours, but no, there must be [a] blunder made somewhere. . . . Now they have lost the best Brigade in the war and the brave Heckman . . . is wounded and a prisoner. It is hard to think so many brave men should loose their lives through the neglect of some drunken General."[3]

Other veterans of the battle tried to focus not on an opportunity so flagrantly wasted but on the job ahead and the need to see it through. Sergeant Little wrote the editor of his hometown newspaper that Petersburg and Richmond were both within the reach of the Army of the James from its strong position between the two cities. The former "we can demolish . . . at any time." Although Richmond was "a hard[er] road to haul," it could be taken "if we can hold this place, which we can as all hands has worked night and day fortifying" it.[4]

In time the regiment also took comfort from the replacement of General Heckman by Brig. Gen. George Jerrison Stannard, who assumed command of the Star Brigade on May 18. Stannard, a flinty New Englander whose capable service dated from First Bull Run, had especially distinguished himself on the third day at Gettysburg, when his Vermont brigade shredded the right flank of the attacking Confederates, helping ensure the failure of Pickett's Charge. The wound he received that day from a shell fragment had kept Stannard out of action ever since. Healthy again, he was one of the few highly competent officers to make the transfer from Meade's army to Butler's. Aware of his reputation, the Ninth, along with the other soldiers Heckman had left behind, welcomed their new commander—even after he issued an order putting an end to the too-frequent purchase of whiskey from the brigade commissary, a practice initiated not by Heckman but by General Smith, ostensibly as a stimulant to soldier health.[5]

Not content to chase Butler's troops from the environs of Richmond, G. T. Beauregard determined to evict them from Bermuda Hundred. Though he pursued the defeated Federals at a deliberate pace, beginning on the eighteenth the Creole launched a series of attacks on various sectors of the line between the James and Appomattox. Each was repulsed, including two especially determined assaults before daylight on the twentieth. The outcome validated Sergeant Little's belief that the army's works were impregnable, while highlighting the unwillingness of Butler's subordinates to cooperate against their common enemy. When one attack struck heavily at a X Corps's position and its commander called on his colleague for help, Baldy Smith is supposed to have replied: "Damn Gillmore—he got himself into a scrape, now let him get out of it!"[6]

The Ninth New Jersey, whose camp had been moved a quarter mile south of Cobb's Hill, had thrown up a strong breastwork in its new position. From behind this barrier the regiment threw back the nearest attackers without loss to itself. During one of the assaults on the twentieth it captured several Confederates, while a neighboring outfit made a prisoner of Brig. Gen. William S. Walker, a Pennsylvania native who had served under Beauregard in South Carolina before following him to Richmond. The next day Butler raised the hopes of every man in the Star Brigade by offering Beauregard an exchange of captives, Walker for General Heckman, but the Confederate authorities, probably suspecting they would come out second best in any such deal, summarily rejected the proposal. Their action found favor with the editor of the *Richmond Examiner*, who expressed "a lively satisfaction at the destruction of Heckman's Brigade, and the capture of its daring commander. His celebrated New Jersey Rifle Regiment has been completely destroyed—thus ridding, although at a late day, the bleeding Carolinas of a terrible scourge."[7]

Not only had the Ninth New Jersey escaped destruction, eventually it would be made whole, or almost so, by the return of sick men to the ranks along with soldiers who had gone missing in battle but had avoided capture. The regiment would also benefit from the continual receipt of recruits, conscripts, and substitutes from the draft rendezvous at Trenton. It would take time and effort to bring the new men up to the level of proficiency attained by the veterans, and not all would reach it—some of those forced into the service would not try to reach it. Over time, however, the Ninth would experience a revival of strength and durability. In the meantime, it would have to draw heavily on the savvy and tenacity it had acquired through two and a half years of service in camp, field, and battle.

Even in its reduced condition, the regiment was considered fit for active campaigning including special duty of a hazardous nature. On May 22, Beauregard's attacks having apparently run their course, General Smith called on the regiment for volunteers to sneak inside the enemy's lines and gain information on what they were up to; those returning with the desired intelligence would be paid five hundred dollars from the corps's treasury. Smith got four takers: Corp. Robert H. White and Pvt. James Van Buskirk of Company B and Pvts. Marshall Howell and David S. Johnson of Company H. That evening the quartet set out with four days' rations in their haversacks. Van Buskirk and White headed south toward Port Walthall Junction, Howell and Johnson northward toward the known location of some Rebel picket posts.

White and Van Buskirk managed to penetrate deeply inside the enemy's lines, where they gleaned much information of value. On their return, however, they were captured by a regiment of North Carolina cavalry and nearly hanged as spies. Escorted to General Beauregard's headquarters, the two were treated to their host's Gallic temper. As Van Buskirk put it, the Creole "called us liars rogues and northern scum and quite a number of hot names in unbroken french not mentioned in webster's." Unable to coerce his captives into confessing what they had learned, Beauregard had them escorted under guard to Petersburg but only after ordering "us stripped of every thing but our pants knit shirts and blouses." Eventually the two privates ended up at Andersonville where they suffered "the tortures of the damned." Both managed to survive the abominable conditions but at the cost of permanently shattered health.

Howell and Johnson fared better than their comrades though only one of them completed his mission. After stumbling into a picket line in the darkness, the two became separated when fired on. No longer willing to risk his neck, Johnson returned to camp empty-handed but in one piece. His companion forged on, eventually gaining a vantage point from which to observe labor crews repairing the railroad the Federals had broken two weeks earlier. This and other intelligence he carried back to General Smith, who saw to it that his informant received the promised bounty. Howell, five hundred dollars richer, thereby became "the most envied man in the regiment."[8]

By May 27 Grant's and Meade's attempts to circumvent Lee's right flank had bogged down at frightful cost. More than 33,000 soldiers of the

Army of the Potomac had been killed or wounded in the Wilderness (May 5–6), near Spotsylvania Court House (May 7–20), and along the North Anna River (May 23–26). Now Grant was again swinging east and south, this time across the Pamunkey River toward Hanovertown in what amounted to a last-ditch attempt to envelop his enemy before he ran out of maneuvering room at the banks of the James.

As he moved toward the Pamunkey, Grant, concerned by reports that many of Beauregard's troops had joined Lee's army, called on Washington for reinforcements from the Army of the James. War Department emissaries including army Quartermaster Gen. M. C. Meigs, sent to Butler's headquarters at Grant's request, would liken Butler's troops inside the defenses of Bermuda Hundred to the contents of a "bottle, strongly corked." They could not be driven from their heavily fortified position but neither could they operate freely outside of it. Meigs estimated that 10,000 of them could secure Butler's enclave, freeing up 20,000 others for transfer to a more active front.[9]

Only about half of the transferees Meigs envisioned—six brigades of infantry and some artillery—made the movement Grant desired. Not all would be on hand for the opening round of his next clash with Lee, an especially sanguinary one near Cold Harbor, a strangely named hamlet about ten miles northeast of Richmond. The movement began on the twenty-eighth as a sizable portion of the XVIII Corps and a small slice of the X Corps, under overall command of Baldy Smith, folded up their shelter tents, filed out of their field works and entrenchments, and stood ready to leave the peninsula by boat and overland march. Upon the Ninth's departure, its breastworks were taken over by dismounted troopers of the Second United States Colored Cavalry. Given the regiment's well-documented disdain for black troops, especially for those who had failed to secure its exposed flank at Drewry's Bluff, Private Cleveland's diary entry for this day is not surprising: "Some of the boys thought it was hard on them to build breastworks for darkeys to fight behind."[10]

Crossing the Appomattox on a pontoon bridge, Stannard's brigade, now part of the division of Brig. Gen. John H. Martindale, marched to

City Point early on the twenty-ninth. After the usual delays the Ninth boarded two ships that steamed down the James toward Fort Monroe. Opposite Jamestown, several miles short of her destination, one of the vessels ran aground about 8 p.m. Not until the last day of the month was the regiment afloat again, having been transferred, along with two other regiments of the brigade, to a large ferryboat that, thanks to overloading, threatened to sink at any moment. By now the men were out of both rations and good humor, especially after the ferry grounded off Fort Monroe, forcing another ship transfer. Corp. Bill Knapp of Company K, whom his comrades described as always hungry, loudly complained that "I had just as leave remained where I was and drowned as to be here and starve."[11]

The travel delays prevented the regiment and other components of Smith's command from reaching Cold Harbor, via the York and Pamunkey Rivers, until the forenoon on June 3. They arrived upon a field of slaughter. Two days earlier Meade's army, along with the majority of those transferred from Bermuda Hundred, had launched a series of disjointed and uncoordinated assaults west of the little village against Confederates dug in behind well constructed works and supported by banks of artillery. Some 2,650 Federals had become casualties. The bodies of many of the dead lay rotting under a merciless sun, while dozens of wounded men, trapped between the lines, struggled to stay alive though denied food and water.

The renewed fighting on the morning of the third was even more horrific. In less than an hour 7,000 Federals fell dead or wounded along Meade's and Smith's lines. On the Army of the James's front, Martindale's division delivered the main attack, supported on both flanks by the balance of Smith's command. Martindale's units—which did not include the late-arriving Ninth New Jersey—were partially sheltered by a deep ravine, enabling them to penetrate the outer layer of the enemy's right-center, though unable to prevent the Confederates from enveloping their flanks. After halting to regroup, Martindale resumed his advance, throwing forward Stannard's depleted brigade. The Vermonter's troops delivered three determined attacks, all of which foundered against the virtually impregnable Rebel defenses. "We carried their works," Jon Reading wrote of the brigade, "but they shelled us out of them." In early afternoon Meade finally called off the offensive and the survivors of the forlorn effort pulled back to their original positions.[12]

The Ninth did not reach the scene of battle until shortly before 12 p.m.; thus it missed the largest share of the day's butchery. Even so, it quickly found itself in "a perfect hornet's nest," targeted by almost continuous rounds of sharpshooter bullets and artillery shells. "We were immediately formed in line," wrote Sergeant Evans, "and ordered to lie down for we were exposed to a severe fire . . . with no protection but such as we could throw up with cups, plates, & hands." The men would agree that the regiment "had been in tight places before, but never had it been subjected to so ruthless a fire." Private Cleveland believed that "this is the place where one should be prepared to meet the Dark Angel." The small breastwork the men threw up and the trenches they dug with their inadequate substitutes for picks and spades enabled the Ninth to escape destruction, but for a time it was a near thing.[13]

Revolted by the extreme carnage and convinced of the futility of further attacks, Grant and Meade ordered no more of them, but the armies remained in close contact—Cleveland estimated the distance between some of the opposing forces at twenty yards. One result was that the corpses trapped between the lines were allowed to remain amid baking heat, feasted upon by carrion, until they produced a ghastly stench. At first rejected by the Rebels, a proposal for a cease-fire finally went into effect on the seventh. Burial teams from both armies dumped the rotting bodies into mass trenches, while medical crews succored the few who had fallen on the first and third and somehow clung to life. On the Ninth's part of the line, it was "nauseating to those who handled the disfigured corpses," and scarcely less so to those who removed the wounded: "In many instances maggots swarmed upon the wounds of those who had been maimed, presenting a revolting sight—one that no man, made however callous-hearted by war, would ever again wish to look upon." Since its arrival on the third, the regiment had added thirty-five of its men to this grisly total including five killed or mortally wounded.[14]

His path to Richmond blocked yet again, Grant was forced to revamp his strategy and choose another objective. Fully attuned to the critical importance of the lifeline between Richmond and Petersburg, he decided to operate against the latter, whose garrison, now under Beauregard, remained small and unprepossessing. Grant's move began on the evening of June 12 with Smith's command pulling out of the front lines and reassembling well to the rear. By midnight the Ninth New Jersey was marching east on "a dusty road strewn with dead horses, emitting a most offensive odor." Eight hours and eighteen miles later the regiment reached the wharf at White House. There Captain Hufty placed the men aboard waiting transports; soon they were sailing down the Pamunkey, then the York along the eastern side of the Virginia Peninsula, and finally up the James to their old camping grounds.[15]

Since Smith's troops were known to be reinforcements for Meade and their movement might be construed as a return to Bermuda Hundred, the Confederates were not suspicious that an army-wide evacuation had begun. Over the next two days the Army of the Potomac would evacuate its lines to follow Smith, some by boat, others by an overland march to the James, which it would cross on a 2,000-foot-long pontoon bridge. Until then Meade kept up the deception: bands played loudly, troops moved conspicuously along the picket lines, and artillery pounded away in hopes of convincing Lee that his enemy was going nowhere. The ruse worked to perfection, and the road to Petersburg lay tantalizingly open.

The men of the Ninth New Jersey were overjoyed to be breaking contact with an enemy that had kept them huddling behind defenses of one kind or another for what seemed forever. As Private Reading wrote just before evacuating, "this is 5 weeks we have been fighting and dyeing and during this time we have scarcely had any thing but the broad canvas of heaven to cover us and the boys bear it like martyrs. . . . We are I think the dirtiest set of men I ever saw in my life. We have not had a change of clothes for 5 weeks and all that time lying in ditches and marching through the mud."[16]

By late in the evening of June 14, nine of the regiment's companies had returned to their old haunts at Bermuda Hundred, Company I belatedly following in a second steamer. Marched four miles to a bivouac in an open field, exhausted men collapsed as soon as the column halted. The following day they were moved back to the camping ground they last occupied on May 28. Private Cleveland noted that thanks to new and intricate fortifications Butler's base of operations "looks very different from what it did when we first landed here." Conspicuously absent were many of the troops yet to return from Cold Harbor; so too was Quincy Gillmore, whom Butler had fired following a botched raid on Petersburg during the Ninth's absence.[17]

Gillmore's was not the only failed effort to take the Cockade City in this hectic and disconcerting month of June. Even as the Ninth and the rest of its brigade reached Bermuda Hundred, Butler, per Grant's orders, was moving against Petersburg with 15,000 men whom he had placed under Baldy Smith, including Hinks's Negro division. Despite Smith's overly cautious leadership, early that evening the United States Colored Troops attacked and captured more than a mile's worth of defenses northeast of the city, including several cannons. Despite their conspicuous success, some white soldiers withheld praise and offered criticism. At the hospital in Hampton Sergeant Stillwell heard "from men that was there"—but erroneously—that while "the negroes charged the rebel earth works and drove them out," they "would not stop when ordered to . . . [so] that the white soldiers had to shoot and knock down three hundred of them before they could be made to stop."[18]

Although he outnumbered Petersburg's defenders by more than five to one, Smith suspended his offensive until the vanguard of the Army of the Potomac, Maj. Gen. Winfield Scott Hancock's II Corps, reached him some hours after dark. Through a massive breakdown in staff work, Hancock had not been informed that an attack on the city was in progress; he would contend that had he known, he would have reached Smith in time to join him in entering and occupying Petersburg. Communications foul-ups would continue to dog the Federals over the next three days. The result was a series of uncoordinated attacks by Meade's army that failed to enlarge on the gains of June 15 and that gave the desperate Beauregard time to draw reinforcements from Bermuda Hundred and, finally, from Cold Harbor. These should have arrived too late to prevent the city's fall. The fact that they got there in time meant ten arduous, frustrating, and deadly months of siege operations by the armies of Meade and Butler.[19]

As at Cold Harbor, the Ninth New Jersey's delayed arrival on the field of conflict spared it from the heaviest fighting. Instead of moving directly to Petersburg under Smith's command, the regiment was assigned to General Gillmore's temporary successor, Brig. Gen. Alfred Howe Terry, then commanding near Ware Bottom Church, a picket post in advance of the X Corps' entrenchments at Bermuda Hundred. Early on the sixteenth Terry pulled four regiments including the Ninth out of their rifle pits and sent them on a march to the railroad to Petersburg, along which reinforcements were hurrying on foot to Beauregard's assistance. The forces clashed near Port Walthall Junction, generating all-day skirmishing. During the afternoon Union forces peeled off to tear up a mile or more of track that had been destroyed early in May and afterward repaired by the Confederates. At sundown, having suffered minimal casualties, the Ninth and its comrades broke contact and returned to Bermuda Hundred under a spiteful skirmish fire.[20]

For a time, life inside Butler's triangular enclave was tolerable, even pleasant. By the eighteenth, with a "terrible" cannonade to the south signaling the final, failed attacks on Petersburg, the men of the Ninth were fraternizing with their enemy across the way. David Hankins wrote that "our breast works are about a hundred yards from the Rebels. We talk with them every day and also exchange [news]papers with them."

When off-duty the entire regiment was marched down to the Appomattox where it bathed en masse for the first time in many weeks. But the good times did not last. By June 20 rumors were afloat that because of its sharpshooting prowess the regiment was going to be shifted to "a more dangerous part of the line."[21]

Within hours, the speculation was borne out. Shortly after midnight, the regiment trod the pontoons to the south side of the river, crossed the tracks of the Petersburg and City Point Railroad, and took up a position on the right flank of the combined Federal armies at Petersburg. Placed behind the first layer of a triple line of breastworks, it found itself reunited with the rest of Heckman's old brigade, expanded now by the addition of regiments from Maryland, New York, and Pennsylvania. Due to the casualties each outfit had absorbed over the past six and a half weeks, the supposedly enlarged command was smaller than it had been at the outset of the year's campaigning. This was in keeping with the depletion of both of the Federal armies in eastern Virginia dating from the day Grant and Meade had entered the Virginia Wilderness and Butler had sailed up the James to Bermuda Hundred.[22]

Initially the Ninth considered its situation an improvement over Cold Harbor, where cannonading and musketry had been interrupted only "by the darkness of the night" and that "to put ones head up [above the breastworks] was a sure mark for the rebel sharpshooters." Soon enough, however, the regiment saw its transfer as an example of fire-to-frying-pan. Less than twenty-four hours after it assumed its assigned place, the enemy attacked it under a heavy barrage. Though beaten back at the cost of only one casualty, the attack was repeated, in greater force, two days later. This time two members of the Ninth were wounded before the enemy was repulsed. "At one moment," however, "it seemed as if nothing could withstand the onslaught."[23]

Again the next day, the twenty-fifth, the Ninth's left flank came under attack. Likewise repulsed, the Rebels renewed the effort one hour later, but by then the regiment had been withdraw to the third line of works where it had to deal principally with artillery fire. Only a few sharpshooters targeted the regiment, but one put a bullet through the heart of Pvt. Hiram Gray of Company E, who had just wolfed down a midday meal. Minutes earlier Gray had told his captain that "if I die now I will die with a full belly."[24]

Late that day the regiment was shifted once again, this time to the intermediate line of defenses in its sector. It bivouacked on the grounds of a once-luxurious plantation on a hilltop overlooking Petersburg, two miles away; from there the men could study the effect of the almost incessant shelling of the city. The Ninth was still atop the hill on the twenty-sixth, when the enemy launched a series of attacks, each of which fell short of dislodging the XVIII Corps but produced numerous casualties. The following afternoon, the Ninth returned to the first line of breastworks, relieving the Twenty-fifth Massachusetts.

This pattern—moving from one line of breastworks and rifle pits to another so that every component of the brigade shared, more or less equally, the hazards of frontline duty—continued day after day, week after week, through this fourth summer of the war. Sometimes the Ninth enjoyed two or even three days in the relative safety of a deep ravine in the rear. Days would pass without an attack, even an aborted one; at other times cannon would thunder away at every sector of the lines, showering earth and woodwork upon those it did not kill or maim outright. Occasionally defective shells or poor gunnery by Union batteries mistakenly caused as much havoc and destruction as the Rebels worked hard to achieve. One midsummer's day a railroad-mounted seacoast mortar in the Union rear, dubbed by its crew the "Petersburg Express," dropped a round in the midst of a group of Jerseymen engaged in a game of poker. "It came thundering down between us," recalled Corp. Francis A. Kenyon of Company B, "within six inches of our heads, tearing up a hole as deep as a sugar bowl in the very spot where we played our cards. . . . We all *passed* immediately out of that game."[25]

It did not take long for the stress of siege warfare to affect the physical and mental stamina of the men in the trenches and behind the earthworks. More than a few members of other regiments of the Ninth's brigade shot off their own trigger fingers in order to be rendered unfit for active duty. In an effort to improve the corporate health and also reward the men for their fortitude and perseverance, a brigade whiskey ration, issued at night, was reinstated. Almost equally well received were the various items distributed behind the front lines by members of the Sanitary Commission, including tobacco, canned milk, vegetables including pickled onions, and lemons.[26]

While enjoying these luxuries the men caught up on regimental and army activities derived from newspapers and the ubiquitous fruit of the military grapevine. Especially welcome was the news, received in mid-July, of the recent promotions of James Stewart to colonel, William B. Curlis to lieutenant colonel, and Samuel Hufty to major. The wounded Stewart returned to the regiment a few weeks later, but the injured Curlis did not reappear until late September, and then on crutches. In a case of poor timing, as soon as Curlis returned, Hufty went on sick leave in New Jersey. Upon his return to the Petersburg trenches three weeks later the newly minted major was shot in the arm, which required another convalescent leave. Hufty would not be back with the Ninth until the end of October.[27]

The debilitating and often deadly monotony of siege warfare continued throughout one of the hottest seasons to plague eastern Virginia in many years. A morning sun capable of striking down dozens of men at a time often gave way to heavy and sometimes torrential afternoon rains, turning pathways of choking, blinding dust into mud-soaked quagmires. Rats, body lice, and winged insects infested the siege lines and ravaged the bodies of their inhabitants. The stench of corpses beyond recovery, rotting under the summer sun, added to the noxious vapors arising from the vermin-ridden trenches, rekindling the worst memories of Cold Harbor. Even noncombatants could no longer tolerate the conditions. Sutlers, who usually longed to be as close to their prospective customers as possible, packed up their wares and bade the firing lines goodbye. Newspaper reporters covering the XVIII Corps begged their editors for reassignment to Fort Monroe, if not to the front office in New York or Boston. A *New York Times* correspondent traveling with Butler's army poured out his misery in one plaintive dispatch: "Suffocating heat! Blinding dust! Torturing flies!"[28]

By late July men confined to the rifle pits under fire of sharpshooters just across the way began to despair that their hellish life would ever end. Then came rumors—piecemeal at first and plainly incredible, then more and more persistent and believable—that Grant and Meade were striving for a dramatic end to the stalemate. Before month's end the men of the Ninth New Jersey were hearing that a mine shaft had been dug under a Rebel salient northeast of Petersburg; blasting powder was to be placed inside the shaft and detonated, blowing a hole in the enemy lines and creating a path into the city. The reports placed the Ninth in a better frame of mind than it had experienced for months, especially since, if ordered to attack the defenses across from it in the wake of the blast, it would be led by Colonel Stewart, who had returned to the Ninth from the hospital on the twenty-third. By virtue of seniority, however, Stewart was immediately assigned to lead the Star Brigade, General Stannard having moved up to division command. In the absence of Major Hufty, Capt. Augustus Thompson left Company F to command the regiment.[29]

The rumors of a mine proved true. The work of a regiment of Pennsylvania coal miners in the IX Corps, a command now led by the Ninth's old patron Ambrose Burnside, the 411-yard-long tunnel and two shorter lateral shafts, which had taken a month to construct, had been filled with 320 kegs of powder connected by multiple fuses. Banking on the operation's success, a division of the USCT in Meade's army had been trained and was prepared to attack through the gap created by the explosion. At the last minute, however, election-year politics dictated a switch to untutored white troops. The result was disaster. When the mine was detonated just before dawn on July 30 it succeeded spectacularly. With a tremendous roar it obliterated the enemy salient, throwing men, guns, caissons, and wagons into the air and creating a smoking crater almost 200 feet long, fifty feet wide, and twenty-five feet deep. But when the white troops attacked, they did so in small groups under clueless officers. Instead of skirting the crater and charging through the suddenly vacant works beyond, many men piled into the hole where the Rebels, once recovered from the shock of the blast, shot them down like fish in a barrel.

Units of the XVIII Corps had been assigned a supporting role in the assault, but the Ninth New Jersey was not one of them. Although advanced slightly forward of its most recent camp, the outfit watched from a safe distance as their comrades faltered, then shook their heads when, too late to redeem the day, the black soldiers were thrown into the maelstrom. They fought admirably despite lacking close support, most of the white attackers having fallen or retreated, until overwhelmed and decimated. Recoiling from the carnage, survivors ran for their lives, en route plowing through Burnside's rear guard. In so doing the blacks gained a reputation for instability and cowardice. With their withdrawal Meade conceded defeat and put an end to the botched offensive. The debacle would have long-lasting effects. Ulysses S. Grant would forever consider the loss of "so fair a chance" to end the stalemate at Petersburg and perhaps the war one of the most heartbreaking episodes of his military career.[30]

The criticism leveled at the black troops who fought in the crater, most of it unmerited and unfair, found its way into the letters and diaries of some members of the Ninth, who based their conclusions on second- and thirdhand accounts. Sergeant Stillwell called African Americans, especially those in uniform, "a very excitable race of people. What they do, they do with a rush headlong with no judgement. They will fight well enough as long as they have the best of the enemy and can keep them agoing so when they get the enemy retreating, when they are not meeting with much resistance, but when it comes to an equal contest and hardy steady fighting to do . . . they will not stand but get excited and like a mob run through their supports and cause a stampeding. . . . Such troops do more harm than good on the battle field."[31]

Other Jerseymen came to the blacks' defense. Private Cleveland, who entertained a much more favorable view of the USCT, at first decried their "disgraceful skedaddle" but came to blame their failure on "the cowardice of their officers." He strongly rejected the opinion of the *New York Herald* editor who castigated Meade for "placing raw troops in front" and declared that "niggers are miserable material for the army." In a letter carried in his hometown paper, Cleveland wrote that "some unjustly blame the negroes for their conduct, but it is about the same as blaming Heckman's brigade for falling back at Drury's Bluff when assailed by three times their number on as many sides." An anonymous comrade, quoted in the *Newark Daily Advertiser*, opined that "the negroes charged boldly up to their [the enemy's] works, showing a courage that would do credit to white troops."[32]

The pluck and energy the black soldiers had displayed until overwhelmed appears to have had a therapeutic effect on their white neighbors, for in later weeks the races began to fraternize for perhaps the first time in the Virginia theater. Suddenly the USCT were welcome in the Ninth's camp, where one illiterate soldier sought out Cleveland and asked him to "write a letter for him to his true love. I willingly penned a letter for him—an affectionate one—adding a note to his 'Uncle Sandy.' He was much pleased."[33]

Comments and incidents such as these suggest that the Ninth's attitudes toward Negro troops and African Americans as a race were changing. Under the influences and pressures of a war in which they fought side-by-side in pursuit of a shared cause white and black men slowly but surely were coming to think of each other as comrades if not as brothers.

The strategic deadlock had not been broken, and the siege of Petersburg resumed as before. The day after the mine blew, the Ninth marched back to its bivouac two miles from the city prior to returning to the stinking, sweltering trenches where death constantly beckoned. For the soldiers of the Army of the Potomac there seemed little chance that the situation would improve, even incrementally. For the Ninth and some of its comrades in the Army of the James, however, a two-tiered respite from the horrors of the front lines suddenly materialized. On August 11, six days after the Confederates exploded a counter-mine in front of the XVIII Corps's position that "made a great dust only," Colonel Stewart secured an audience with General Butler during which the latter promised that as soon as the Ninth finished building two sets of fortifications in its sector it would be permitted to take the place of some units in North Carolina "who have done nothing except draw rations and pay."[34]

Butler's words came sweetly to the colonel's ears, and to those of the rank and file to whom he relayed them. Some men including Ed Cleveland refused to credit the report, but two weeks after his meeting with Stewart Butler's headquarters published Special Orders No. 233, which, among other things, directed the Ninth and three other regiments of the Star Brigade to report to Brig. Gen. Innis N. Palmer, commanding the District of North Carolina. The transfer, contingent on sufficient transportation, would take place in two stages, two regiments going south at the same time. The Ninth would depart with the second group, one month hence.[35]

During that month the Ninth was subjected to the same dangers and hardships as before, plus some new ones. Its work on the twin fortifications provoked the Confederates across the way, whose ill will took the form of a four-hour cannonade. The bombardment inflicted few casualties, one being Pvt. Ernest Biehl of Company D, who had his arm severed above the elbow by a shell fragment. Biehl's comrade, now-Corporal Hankins, noted that "we loos two or three men every time we go in the rifle pits. I would like to know how much longer we hav got to stay in this critical position. For my part, I would like to move pretty soon." One day after Hankins wrote, Colonel Stewart answered his plea, announcing that since the new forts were nearly complete the Ninth would be relieved at the front "in a few days."[36]

Stewart spoke the truth but the move did not come soon enough to spare the regiment from a murderous flash flood—the result of days of torrential rain—that surged through the trenches of the Army of the James on August 15. The raging waters, nine feet deep in places, swept everything from their path including breastworks, tents, wagons, stacked rifles—in short, "everything moveable." Fortunately, the Ninth was in the rear this day, encamped on a hill that kept the men above water even as nearby streams overflowed. Private Cleveland wrote that "in an hour's time the brook was one sheet of water. As the storm increased, tents which were up floated by. I saw some bunks with their occupants going down stream. . . . At first men scrambled for their knapsacks but soon they were glad to escape with their lives." More than twenty men were not as lucky; unable to climb out of their pits, they were swept away and drowned in the mud-stained waters.[37]

This was one calamity the XVIII Corps had not bargained for; thus its people were supremely glad when within a week afterward they were shifted closer to the Appomattox and then back to Bermuda Hundred. On the twenty-fifth the Ninth crossed the river and returned to its old bailiwick near Cobb's Hill and the newly christened Fort Zabriskie. Upon their arrival the men were made even happier by the sudden appearance of Charles Heckman, who had been released from confinement in Charleston following a prisoner exchange. It was said that "cheer after cheer rent the air as he reined up in front of the Ninth to address it." The cheering grew deafening when Heckman announced that the Ninth would in fact be heading back to North Carolina as soon as logistical issues could be worked out. He would not be accompanying it, however; his assignment to the Petersburg front would effectively sever his ties to his old outfit.[38]

The safe return of their commander was not the only rewarding feature of the regiment's new station. After sixty-four days before Petersburg, forty of them in the trenches, the men could afford to raise their heads above the breastworks without fear of falling back dead or wounded.

"Affairs are very quiet along this line," wrote Private Cleveland in the pages of the *New Jersey Journal* under his pseudonym "Vidi." He heard comrades "who came in off picket say it is fine to picket here. The picket lines are fifty yards apart and no firing on either side."

The opposing sentinels were open to fraternizing, sharing tobacco, coffee beans, and newspaper coverage of military and political affairs. Cleveland noted that "the Confederates seem to base all their hope on the Chicago convention." In that city on August 31 the regular Democrats nominated George B. McClellan to oppose Lincoln in the fall election. Bowing to the antiwar sentiment that infused his party, the controversial general had tacitly endorsed the view that the war to save the Union was a failure, thereby holding out hope of a negotiated peace. Even before Little Mac was nominated, Lincoln had despaired of reelection, but his prospects had improved dramatically with the news, recently received, that Sherman's armies had captured and occupied strategically important Atlanta.[39]

Even given the relatively cushy environment of Bermuda Hundred, the men of the Ninth and their comrades in the Star Brigade longed for shipment to the state in which they had served the longest. They had had enough of the war in Virginia, and of the men behind it. When General Grant and some of his subordinates passed through the Ninth's camp on September 6, he received a subdued greeting. "Some of the boys above us cheered him," wrote Cleveland, "but our boys never uttered a sound."[40]

The day of deliverance finally dawned on the morning of the seventeenth when, having prepared two days' rations, the Ninth partook of coffee and hardtack, then formed line and marched to the local wharf. There Companies A, C, E, G, H, and K boarded a familiar vessel, the steamer *Convoy*, the balance of the regiment embarking on the *Utica*. By 5 p.m. they were at Portsmouth, where they welcomed the return of comrades recently released from the local hospitals. Sergeant Stillwell, then completing duty as a clerical assistant at the Balfour and awaiting a return to New Jersey with the others who had declined to reenlist, observed that "the army is getting reinforced from the hospitals. All the men able to do duty have been sent to the front of late. There is hardly enough left here to nurse the sick." The additional manpower, coupled with a wave of recruits and draftees expected to join the regiment over the new few weeks, ensured that when the Ninth reached North Carolina it would be at close to peak strength.[41]

The Ninth's steamers left Portsmouth late on the eighteenth for Fort Monroe where the men were transferred to the propeller steamers *United States* and *Dudley Buck* for the ocean voyage to their once and future destination. The ships arrived off Fort Macon on the evening of the twentieth and the next morning headed for the giant steamboat wharf at Morehead City. On none of its sea voyages had the Ninth traveled first class and the present journey was no exception. Private Cleveland complained that no man had "stretching-out room" on any of the four transports: "On our deck it was awful. I had the pleasure of bearing the weight of two or more men all night." While the officers enjoyed spacious interior quarters, "I was never so cramped in my life." He complained of the situation in a letter to his hometown paper which, when published, brought him a sharp reprimand from Colonel Stewart.[42]

Homecoming occurred around noon on September 20. As soon as they set foot on dry ground, the two boatloads of men were grouped and led up the railroad on foot to Carolina City. Upon arriving they occupied the tidy camp of the departing 158th New York, which abounded in such amenities as a well and a log cookhouse for each company. Before their tents arrived, however, the newcomers spent three days out in the open on top of the highest eminence outside the town—drenched by rain each day.[43]

Inhospitable as the greeting was, the soldiers of the Ninth were vastly pleased to be back in the Old North State, where active operations appeared to be at an all-time low. "We feel much at home here," wrote Sergeant Little, "and we are glad to get out from the thundering of cannon, and rest in peace and quietness. I think we will spend the winter here and if we do, it will be a greater relief than was anticipated." Even when at Bermuda Hundred the regiment was frequently on picket in sight of the enemy, but "here no enemy is within approach of us."[44]

The new venue was not free of irritants, afflictions, or dangers. These ranged from swarms of sand fleas—which not only disrupted drill-plain evolutions but, by penetrating tents, kept the men awake at night—to a yellow fever outbreak in New Bern that raged for several weeks and took a severe toll of soldiers and civilians alike. Although the disease did not spread to the outlying camps, it killed at least two members of the Ninth stationed in the city on detached duty, Sgt. Pulaski Hinds of Company G and Corp. John S. Parkhurst of Company K. The men were also threatened by a smallpox outbreak in a neighboring USCT regiment, but again their own camp was spared from the dreaded scourge. Sergeant Little believed the Ninth inhabited a healthy section of the state: "We live good here. There is plenty of fish, clams, oysters, and sweet potatoes. This is making up for what we suffered last summer." Another effort to make amends for past mistreatment and neglect occurred on October 11, when ten months' worth of back pay was distributed to the regiment.[45]

Although no large body of the enemy lurked in the Ninth's sphere of operations, Confederate forces in other parts of the state occasionally invaded it, and their ability to do damage was plain to see. Pickett's February offensive had resulted in the destruction of several sites the Ninth had once called home. On September 27 Private Cleveland visited Bogue Sound to find that "Camp Boudinot is no more. The block house and surrounding buildings have also disappeared." Two weeks later, when Companies I and K were hastened to Newport to guard against an attack that never came, the men found their old barracks reduced to charred timber.[46]

Almost as welcome as back pay was the arrival at Carolina City on October 11 of 150 recruits and men returned from furlough and sick leave. The latter included Henry Keenan, fully recuperated from his near-fatal wound at Drewry's Bluff and who upon reporting was presented with a corporal's chevron. The youngster was shocked at the condition of his old unit: "Company H was no longer the hundred stalwart fellows I had known. There were some recruits, but the roll call rarely was answered by more than fifty men." Later additions made up the difference, though Keenan's best friends in the regiment were dead of wounds or disease or had been invalided out of the army, and he missed them terribly. Other companies fared better; Company K, thanks to the recent receipt of "a very passable set" of recruits, now boasted a strength of eighty-one.[47]

The new arrivals helped make up for an almost equal loss to the regiment. On October 21, two weeks after their enlistments had officially expired, more than 200 enlisted men, escorted by 1st Lt. Robert D. Swain of Company I, left Carolina City for home and muster-out. Before departing for New Jersey the group picked up Sergeant Stillwell and others who had not reenlisted and were now on detached service in Virginia and elsewhere in North Carolina. Accompanying the departing men was Sgt. George Meyers, once again carrying the shot-torn colors of the Ninth to Trenton for "honorable retirement" and replacement. Rather than excoriate or embarrass those who were leaving, Colonel Stewart paid them "a high tribute for the faithful services rendered by them on many fields of battle." It was noted that "as they moved away towards the waiting train hearty cheers were given by both parties—by those who were going home, as well as by those who remained to see the war ended."[48]

In the months leading up to the presidential election of 1864, political affairs were much on the minds of the soldiers of the Ninth. A majority of the regiment, including its numerous Democrats, favored the president's reelection as a means of bringing the conflict to its proper conclusion—one gained on the battlefield, not through negotiations with the enemy. Those who supported Lincoln made fervent pleas, through their local newspapers, to turn out the vote in favor of the Union Party, a coalition of Republicans and War Democrats. "Never was there a time when the American people were called upon to act in a manner of so great import," an anonymous soldier from Gloucester County informed the readers of the *Woodbury Constitution* late in September. "Not only are our armies to destroy the armed hosts now in rebellion against our government, but the masses at home are to uphold and support that army and vindicate its acts and its honor; and in what way can they as well do so as by the re-election of the present Chief Magistrate?" Private Cleveland, writing to his hometown paper in a spirit of bipartisanship, declared that "by the re-election of Mr. Lincoln, we will show to the world our determination to maintain and uphold those who[m] we place in power, no matter which party they are from."[49]

The soldiers were still seething over being denied a voice in determining the outcome of the election. "J. W." of the Ninth wrote the editor of the *Trenton Daily Monitor* that "you may be assured that if the Ninth had a vote in the coming contest it would strike a blow at traitors at home as bravely and with as much effect as it ever struck at traitors in arms. . . . We have a right to, and do demand that the State we represent shall not repudiate all our deeds of heroism, our suffering and fatigue for the good cause by giving her suffrages to its opponent"—not only McClellan but the entire Confederacy.[50]

It was expected that the great majority of those soldiers whose states permitted absentee balloting would vote for Lincoln by a large enough margin to assure his victory. As Sergeant Little observed, "Uncle Abe will be re-elected. There is no show for McClellan, his friends have too much sympathy for the rebels. The Army is all for Uncle Abe [al]most unanimous." The sergeant's assumption that no one in his regiment favored Little Mac was, of course, wrong. Writing under the nom de plume "Equal Rights," a comrade informed the reading public of Newark that "no good, honest Democrat (and I believe there are many yet) will ever desert McClellan, or is anxious that the scenes of the past four years should be re-enacted." He claimed that "the nigger worshippers have no hopes of keeping up the nuisance longer, except by unfair means. . . .

But, my good friends, we do not anticipate a defeat for McClellan—not by any means."[51]

The expectations of "Equal Rights" were not met and his rant against the administration proved futile. On November 8 Lincoln swept to reelection, winning 55 percent of the popular vote including a four-to-one margin among soldiers voting in the field. The outcome effectively ended the hopes of Confederates everywhere that they might gain at the bargaining table a victory denied them elsewhere. Interestingly, McClellan's paltry gain of twenty-one electoral votes included seven from New Jersey, whose popular vote he won by a margin of 7,300. Even in the midst of wartime, the "northernmost border state" refused to reelect the man most capable of ending the bloodshed and repairing a broken nation.[52]

12 War's End, and After

Henry F. Keenan recalled that after he rejoined the regiment from convalescent leave "we passed an eventless winter on a high plateau overlooking Bogue Sound. The dull season was diversified with one famous expedition, to a neighboring island—the most miserable, muddy, purposeless escapade a sane body of men ever undertook." Keenan was referring to a fruitless search for guerrillas by a detachment of the Ninth in February of 1865. Yet his scathing critique was equally applicable to an ill-considered expedition launched two months earlier. Conducted during one of the coldest seasons in local memory, the mission heaped on its participants greater hardships and privations than most had ever experienced. This was a rare distinction for a regiment that had endured more than its share of suffering over the past three years while trying to subdue a crafty, deceptive, and elusive enemy.[1]

The strategy that underlay the combined army-navy operation was head-scratching, to say the least, and the selection of its leaders defied rational explanation. Ostensibly it was aimed at reducing Confederate defenses on the right bank of Rainbow Bluff (or Rainbow Bend), on the Roanoke River just upriver from the village of Hamilton. These consisted of ten guns, four of them bearing on the river and six on land, as well as the 1,500-man garrison of neighboring Fort Branch. By some accounts the expedition was designed to assist at long range General Butler's simultaneous attempt to capture Wilmington, the last operating seaport of any value to the Confederacy. Corporal Keenan supposed it was intended to "help Grant's left flank operations at Petersburg." The naval officer in charge of the operation wrote that it was launched to prevent Rebel forces in North Carolina from reinforcing Savannah, Georgia, General Sherman's next objective on his march from Atlanta. Given the great distances between Hamilton and the cities Butler, Grant, and Sherman were moving against, none of these claims sounds credible.[2]

Rainbow Bluff began as a project of the Navy Department, and its principal leader was Cdr. W. H. Macomb, a North Atlantic Blockading Squadron district commander. Macomb was an old salt, albeit a slow-moving and unimaginative one, but he stood head and shoulders above the leader of his supporting force, which included substantial portions of the Ninth New Jersey, the Twenty-seventh Massachusetts of the Star Brigade, detachments of five other infantry outfits, plus some cavalry and cannons. This was Col. Jones Frankle of the Second Massachusetts Heavy Artillery, who had much experience in neither infantry nor naval operations. Col. James Stewart would serve under him because Frankle was his senior by date of commission. Frankle was not, however, the commander of the brigade to which the Ninth was now attached, the military arm of the so-called Sub-District of Beaufort. That position was held by Col. Joseph M. McChesney, erstwhile commander of Company A of the Ninth but since February 1863 colonel of the First North Carolina (Union) Volunteers. McChesney, who considered his continued presence at his headquarters at Beaufort mandatory, would not accompany the expedition.[3]

For the Ninth, the advance unit on the expedition, things got underway on the morning of December 5 in response to orders to head north with three days' prepared rations and full cartridge boxes. Two hours later it was back at its old camping ground across the river from New Bern. That night the regiment boarded two transports for yet another water journey, this up the Neuse into Pamlico Sound and past Roanoke Island. It was noted that the Ninth's many recruits "evinced much interest in the scene before them" and listened intently to stories of the battle fought there by the old-timers who had taken part in it.

Before daylight on the seventh the transports reached Plymouth, where, as Keenan related, "there was an attack threatened on the town and we manned the fortifications determinedly." The attack never materialized, and the next day saw a new issuance of rations. On the ninth the regiment marched outside the town to unite with the other components of the expeditionary force, just then arriving.[4]

Later that day the column finally lurched forward along the riverbank, the Ninth in the advance per the usual order of affairs. That same day Commander Macomb's fleet of gunboats and tugs sailed out of Plymouth, expecting to meet Frankle's troops at Jamesville, twenty-four miles southeast of Hamilton. Just short of Jamesville, however, two of Macomb's ships were sunk by floating mines in the Roanoke. Unwilling to move upstream until he could locate and disarm other such weapons, Macomb failed to make contact with his army supports.

Unaware of the navy's troubles, Frankle had pushed on beyond Jamesville until encountering Rebel forces two miles farther north at Gardner's Bridge. When the enemy threatened to cut off a company of cavalry that had forged ahead of the Ninth, Colonel Stewart, ably supported by Major Hufty (recently returned to the regiment after recuperating from his Petersburg wound) led the men in a charge that dispersed a much larger force of enemy horsemen "like chaff before the wind." Calling on their long experience with such operations, the Jerseymen swarmed over the turpentine-soaked bridge before the Rebels could set it aflame. The foe subdued, the attackers could devote their attention to the discomforts of the day—one "colder than any they had experienced since leaving New Jersey"—including a heavy snowfall from which the men suffered greatly.[5]

Having yet to establish contact with the slow-moving ships to the rear, at 9 a.m. on the tenth the landlubbers reached another and better defended span on the Roanoke. Unable to forge a safe path to Foster's Bridge, Stewart had his sharpshooters pop away at Confederate infantry on the north bank. The storied marksmanship of the Ninth had its effect, and against steadily declining resistance the colonel led the way in a charge up the "wet and soggy roadway . . . and in a moment was in possession of the coveted structure," at the cost of only two men wounded.

Crossing the river, the regiment halted to eat, not only partaking of its assigned rations but feasting on the sheep, pigs, and poultry found on the grounds of neighboring Foster's Mill. Three miles farther on, a small force was discovered near Williamston (a village the Ninth recalled from the Tarboro Raid of November 1862) and was made to retreat by musketry and shells from a couple of field pieces that had been attached to the Ninth. The troops then turned in for the night on a plantation owned by a Mr. Biggs, fitfully grasping at sleep under freezing temperatures.[6]

December 11, the third consecutive day of heavy skirmishing, marked the nadir of the operation. After a several-hour halt at Williamston, Frankle's command drew within striking distance of Rainbow Bluff. There, about noon, it came into contact with Rebel horsemen. Although the Ninth and the Twenty-seventh Massachusetts, which shared the advance, "had no difficulty in forcing back the daring Confederate horsemen," the latter retreated stubbornly, delaying Frankle's efforts to secure his next objective, Butler's Bridge. That structure, according to a local informant, a black man named "Mose," was defended by a strong force of infantry and cavalry with several pieces of artillery. By early evening, with the bridge still some distance away, Commander Macomb's ships nowhere in sight, and the temperature dropping rapidly, Frankle conferred with his subordinates. It was decided that Colonel Stewart, with his own men, the Massachusetts outfit, and a battery of New Jersey light artillery serving as infantry, would cross the Roanoke and take a road that would put them in rear of the enemy at the bridge. According to the plan, Stewart would attack from that direction, rout the Rebels, and chase them toward Frankle's main force, which by securing a key crossroads would cut off their retreat and bag the entire force.

Stewart and his men did their job. Starting out at 10 p.m. with Mose leading the way, they crossed Butler's Creek on a mill dam consisting mainly of logs floating about in the water near the stream's point of confluence with the Roanoke. Once the undetected crossing—by now a specialty of Stewart's outfit—was complete the next step was to gain the road to the well-defended bridge, a quarter mile away. To do so involved passing inside the outer line of works of Fort Branch, "whose frowning guns could be plainly seen a short distance away, and within easy rifle range." The darkness and the unpropitious weather added to the stealth of the command, which, after some nerve-wracking minutes, cleared the fort full of inattentive defenders.

Once his men reached the main road, far enough from Fort Branch to breathe easier, Stewart sent toward the bridge Companies A and I of the Ninth under, respectively, Capts. Thomas B. Appleget and Charles Hufty, the younger brother of Major Hufty. The advance units "had lots of sport," gobbling up squads of the enemy passing between bridge and fort. Larger prey included the camp of the Sixty-eighth North Carolina Infantry, whose sleeping men, along with their colonel, were captured without a shot being fired.

Gathering up their prisoners, Stewart started for the bridge, only to have his cover blown by a party of Rebel cavalry, whose leader detected the presence of "Blue bellies, by God!" Hearing his shout, the horsemen turned and raced off, A and I in pursuit. The fugitives alerted the defenders of the bridge, who promptly evacuated their post and rushed toward the point where Frankle's main body was supposed to be. They retreated too swiftly for the attackers, now encumbered by prisoners, to overtake them. When the Rebels reached the key crossroads unmolested and escaped via the road to Tarboro, Stewart realized to his chagrin and disgust that Frankle had failed to block their passage, thereby defeating a major objective of the operation.[7]

Anxious to reestablish contact with the expeditionary leader and threatened by the arrival of troops from Fort Branch, who, opening fire on the Ninth, killed his horse, Stewart turned back toward the starting point of his journey to Butler's Bridge. When he linked up with Frankle, the movement toward Rainbow Bluff resumed but with extreme deliberation due to the deteriorating health of men long exposed to the savage weather and the grueling marching pace. That morning Major Hufty, leading the Ninth while Stewart commanded the larger force that had been assigned to him, discovered an enemy force of indeterminate strength blocking the road ahead and "acting in a strange manner." Suspecting it was composed of would-be desert-ers, Hufty held a parlay with its leader under a truce flag, only to learn that the Rebels wished to fight it out. To punctuate their bellicosity they threatened their opponents with capture en masse by a large cooperative force under Gen. James Longstreet.

The patently false information constituted a poor attempt at a ruse de guerre, but according to some sources it so frightened Colonel Frankle that he called off the expedition and had the entire command countermarch, the Ninth covering the rear and keeping back the enemy through spirited skirmishing. Another reason for Frankle's action was supplied by his naval cohort, whose ships had been "struggling up the river, dragging night and day to clear out the torpedoes."[8]

On December 15, when Frankle and Macomb finally met at Cedar Landing on the Roanoke, the colonel proposed a new plan of action by which the army would cross to the north side of the river, defeating some enemy forces known to be in that area. The soldiers would also destroy a four-gun ironclad known to be under construction at Edwards Ferry, birthplace of the celebrated ram *Albemarle*, before rejoining the navy at one of two proposed locations. Macomb thought the plan had merit, but, as he later wrote, "when Frankle returned to Jamesville to prepare for crossing his troops over the river, he was informed by his surgeon that most of the men were sick or frost-bitten, they having started without proper shoes, etc., and it was thought necessary that they should return to Plymouth to recruit [their health], which they did."

At this point the Rainbow Bluff expedition effectively collapsed, although Macomb's gunboats would try to reach their objective for another two weeks. Bedeviled by innumerable torpedoes and continually fired on by land forces that Frankle's troops were not available to disperse, Macomb finally turned downriver, reaching Plymouth shortly after Christmas. There the harried seaman reported to his superiors. Citing the "greatest difficulties" he had ever labored under, he insisted that despite the navy's inability to accomplish its assigned tasks, "the failure can not be attributed to any fault of ours."[9]

Quite clearly, he was shifting blame to Frankle, who surely deserved a large share. In fact, Macomb was going easy on the colonel by implying that he had aborted his revised plan on humanitarian grounds. In fact, when Frankle broached it to his subordinates on the fourteenth, "one and all plainly told him that nothing could now be accomplished" owing to the severe weather and terrible condition of the roads, and the fact that 600 members of the expedition had been incapacitated by wounds or disabled by sore and diseased feet. Back at Carolina City, David Hankins, who had not joined the expedition, reported that Colonel Stewart had sent some fifty participants back to camp, "the most of them with their feet frozen all blue."[10]

In addition to being treated badly, when Frankle's main body returned to Plymouth on the fifteenth some of its members found themselves in official disfavor. A few days later several houses in the city suddenly caught fire, "and as the veterans of the Ninth New Jersey and Twenty-seventh Massachusetts were suspected of being dissatisfied with matters, and somewhat hostile to the commandant, the latter did not hesitate to declare that members in these commands were guilty of destroying the property." By Christmas Day, when Colonel Frankle visited the various camps to dispense holiday greetings, the men of the Ninth responded with a song "in which," Pvt. Hermann Everts related, "the history of the late expedition was rendered in verse, in language more elegant than complimentary to its commander."[11]

By the ninth day of 1865 the regiment had returned to Carolina City via New Bern, happy to be back in its old bailiwick and equally glad to "escape from the command of a man totally unfit for the position assigned him." There the Ninth resumed drill and dress parades and slowly regained the strength drained from it by "the recent profitless expedition." Dozens of men, their health shattered by the rigors of the operation, had been sent to the hospitals at New Bern and Beaufort but their loss was made good to some extent by an influx of as many of 300 conscripts and substitutes. Though at first the regiment put only about 200 men on the parade ground, Brig. Gen. Innis N. Palmer, the local commander, was said to be highly impressed by the Ninth's appearance. According to one account, upon reviewing the regiment on January 29 Palmer pronounced it "the best equipped and finest-looking regiment in the army."[12]

Two weeks earlier the many new faces at Carolina City had been joined by a familiar one, though his once-youthful features had been replaced by an aged, haggard, and sickly look. Following his capture at Drewry's Bluff, Lt. J. Madison Drake had spent five months of confinement and near-starvation at Richmond and Danville, Virginia; Macon and Savannah, Georgia; and Charleston, South Carolina. On October 6 Drake was among a group of 600 prisoners placed aboard a train bound for Columbia, South Carolina. That night, just after crossing the Congaree River, Drake, along with three other officers, leapt from the train to what appeared to be only temporary safety. Thus began an improbable six-week odyssey that took him and his companions through woods and swamps and over the snow-covered foothills of the Blue Ridge, circling around Rebel encampments and picket posts. Assisted by free blacks and Southern Unionists who concealed them from Confederate regulars and guerrillas, on November 16 the worn, torn, and blood-spattered officers reached the Union lines at Knoxville, Tennessee. The 650-mile trek, part of which Drake made barefoot, would be described as "the greatest [escape] made by any prisoners during the war."[13]

Even after the lieutenant was returned to the eastern theater following a lengthy stay in military hospitals and a furlough to his home in Elizabeth, he was not free of life-threatening hazards. On January 9, the steamboat conveying him to North Carolina collided in the Rappahannock River with a schooner hauling oysters. Eight people were killed and more than a dozen injured. Drake and the other passengers, who included Gen. George Meade and members of his staff, escaped unharmed.[14]

Upon being welcomed back, Drake was offered a promotion to captain, which he had to decline on account of "frozen feet, hemorrhoids, and general debility." His name, however, would remain on the rolls of the Ninth for another three months. The War Department would not grant his request for a medical discharge until two weeks before the war in North Carolina ended.[15]

Changes in personnel assignments defined the Ninth as it endured its last winter of the war and prepared for the resumption of active campaigning. By the close of January Colonel Stewart was commanding the Sub-District of Beaufort, having succeeded Colonel McChesney. A week earlier the latter had been mortally wounded while leading his First North Carolina Unionists on an expedition against guerilla bands near Little Washington. Meanwhile, Lt. Col. William B. Curlis had been placed in charge of a second regiment of North Carolina infantry stationed at Beaufort, but the lingering effects of his riding accident eight months earlier would force him to accept a disability discharge early in February. In the absence of his superiors, Major (later Lieutenant Colonel) Hufty commanded the Ninth as he had during a portion of the Rainbow Bluff expedition.[16]

Another field and staff change was the departure for home of Surgeon Woodhull, whose three-year enlistment ended on February 8. He was replaced by Dr. Gillette, who rejoined the regiment after being relieved of his directorship of the general hospital at Morehead City. Upon leaving the regiment Woodhull released a report on the state of health of the Ninth throughout his term with it. The statistics he cited were impressive and even startling: during three years of service 3,000 cases of sickness had been reported in the ranks of the Ninth, but only three men had died of disease. Nineteen officers and 279 enlisted men had been wounded in action; only four officers and twenty-six men had died as a result. Four hundred forty-seven officers and men, in need of a level of care not available in the regiment's camp, had been evacuated to the general military hospitals in the war zone and in the North. Seventy-seven men, too badly wounded or injured to continue with the regiment in an active-duty capacity, had been transferred to the Veteran Reserve Corps, composed of health-impaired soldiers assigned mainly to noncombat and garrison duty.

Though Woodhull had his critics, some of whom considered his bedside manner lacking, he had many more supporters. One of the latter, noting the regiment's remarkably low death rate, doubted "whether any other Surgeon can show a similar record."[17]

Throughout January and February, the war news received in the camps of the Ninth was uniformly positive and encouraging. Ben Butler's December expedition against Fort Fisher, guarding the approaches to Wilmington, had failed spectacularly, resulting in the politician-general's relief from command. Three weeks later, however, a second expedition by forces from Butler's erstwhile command under Alfred Terry, ably supported by the warships of Adm. David Dixon Porter, took the fort by storm despite the desperate resistance of its garrison.

In preparation for an offensive against Wilmington itself, Terry's command was joined by the larger portion of Maj. Gen. John McAllister Schofield's XXIII Corps. Schofield, with the divisions of Maj. Gens. Jacob D. Cox and Darius N. Couch and Brevet Maj. Gen. Thomas H. Ruger, had been sent from Tennessee by Grant to help establish a base of operations for the armies of Sherman, then marching from Savannah through South Carolina. Schofield, who was assigned to head the reconstituted Department of North Carolina, was in overall command when his and Terry's troops combined to enter and occupy Wilmington on February 22.[18]

The success gained at Wilmington and Sherman's relentless push toward North Carolina told the men of the Ninth that they would soon be on the march—along with the rest of the occupation forces between New Bern and Beaufort—to stamp out points of enemy resistance such as Kinston and Goldsboro. To achieve this they would have to overcome opposition from the troops who had evacuated Wilmington under Gen. Braxton Bragg and a larger combination of forces drawn from disparate parts of the Confederacy including the remnants of the once-formidable Army of Tennessee under Bragg's superior and Sherman's longtime "special antagonist," Gen. Joseph Eggleston Johnston.[19]

The weather appeared to mesh with the timetable of operations set by Grant, Sherman, and Schofield. Through February it gyrated between raw and mild, from winds that Andrew Little at month's start called "as piercing as I ever experienced in N. J.," to weather he described two weeks later as "genial." Good weather meant roads capable of supporting a long march, and by late February the earlier "most vague rumors" of a movement had solidified into a general belief that an offensive was days away.[20]

That thought did not disturb the majority of the troops at Carolina City. According to an enlisted man from Gloucester County, an advance would relieve "the dull monotony of camp life [that] holds us in its inexorable sway." The men had gone to some lengths to relieve the boredom. Several of the Ninth's officers attended a Washington's birthday ball held at one of the hospitals in Beaufort. At the same venue three days later a minstrel troupe composed of former bandsmen from the Ninth joined with local musicians to present a "grand variety entertainment" for any soldiers and civilians willing to pay the admission price of fifty cents. But these were temporary expedients; only orders to begin a new campaign would quell the oppressive tedium and an associative disorder, nervous anticipation.[21]

Those orders arrived on March 3, one week before Sherman's legions entered the Tar Heel State. That morning, with knapsacks and baggage packed and ready to be sent to Beaufort for storage, the Ninth vacated

Carolina City, "the stockades alone standing, reminding one of ruin and desolation." Aware that they would not be living under canvas any time soon, the men "burned their tents," as Ed Cleveland reported, "and tore up things in general." Then it was off to New Bern by rail, next to Batchelder's Creek, where the 516 officers and men of the Ninth were welcomed by earlier-arriving elements of Palmer's division, part of a provisional corps that General Schofield had placed under his senior subordinate, Jacob Cox.[22]

On the fifth the assembled force took to northwest-leading roads in the direction of Kinston, which the Ninth had last visited during the December 1862 raid on Goldsboro. En route the Ninth learned that it was now part of a brigade under Brig. Gen. Edward Harland, a veteran of the North Carolina campaigns, which also included the Twenty-third Massachusetts, the Eighty-fifth New York, a six-gun battery of the Third New York Light Artillery, and four companies of Colonel Frankle's heavy artillery regiment, serving as infantry.[23]

On the sixth the march continued along the line of the Atlantic and North Carolina Railroad, the Ninth in its customary position at the head of its brigade. The Rebels had torn up large sections of track, but repair crews would accompany the Federal advance toward Goldsboro to permit the road to serve as the principal line of supply for Sherman's army group. The Federal advance was monitored by the forces that had evacuated Wilmington under Bragg. One hundred miles from New Bern, in the countryside south of Raleigh, the state capital, the larger but more disorganized forces of Joe Johnston were assembling. Johnston was preparing his die-hard veterans to contest Sherman, though he doubted that he had the manpower to do more than slow his opponent's march. This he hoped to do while some sort of armistice was worked out by the warring governments.[24]

Contact between Cox and Bragg occurred early on March 7 when, after a slow start due to errant wagon trains, Harland's brigade penetrated to within five miles of a familiar landmark, Southwest Creek. Discovering strongly held entrenchments along the west bank and noting that each of the many bridges over the stream had been destroyed or dismantled, Cox moved his two divisions up to the edge of a swamp near a crossroads known as Wise's Forks. He spread them out, placing Palmer's troops along his right flank, covering the railroad, while the division of Brig. Gen. Samuel P. Carter, on the left, guarded the Dover Road, one of the forks of the strategic crossroads.

Throughout the seventh, as Bragg made plans to attack the invaders to delay and perhaps halt their advance, the opposing artilleries carried on the fight. At the head of its brigade, however, the Ninth New Jersey saw a considerable amount of action. Ordered to press forward along the railroad, Colonel Stewart moved up four companies of skirmishers. For several hours they engaged the troops of Maj. Gen. Robert F. Hoke, an erstwhile stalwart of the Amy of Northern Virginia. Experts at making the best use of even the slightest cover, the men of the Ninth suffered few losses but these included Captain Hufty, who, while leaning upon a fence in advance of his company's skirmish line, became the target of a sharpshooter. Despite the utmost efforts of Dr. Gillette, the well-respected company commander would die of his wound a week later. An admiring comrade stated that "death in 'Charlie' Hufty got a shining mark, to the intense grief of the regiment."[25]

On the morning of the eighth Bragg, reinforced by a combination of veterans and North Carolina Junior Reserves under D. H. Hill, ordered Hoke's division to cross Southwest Creek and attack the left of Cox's elongated line. The assault drove off two of Carter's regiments along the Dover Road and for a time threatened the stability of the entire flank. Around noon, Hill's recently arrived force attempted to turn the opposite flank. Upon crossing the creek, his troops gained some ground, but once they came in contact with the seasoned Federals of Palmer's division, the Junior Reserves either broke and fled or went to earth, refusing to advance.[26]

On the Union right, the Ninth New Jersey, anticipating an attack come dawn, had fallen back from its position of the previous day and had improvised entrenchments with "knives, bayonets, tin-cups, and bare hands." Despite the lack of proper tools, the defenses were not tested during the day, which ended in confusion and defeat for the Confederates. A misperception by Bragg that his enemy was retreating under Hoke's pounding resulted in Hill's remaining troops making a five-mile detour, only to find no fleeing Yankees. Late in the afternoon Hill, at Bragg's suggestion, returned to his position behind the creek, having contributed little to Hoke's partial success against the Union left.[27]

The Federals had suffered fairly heavily on the eighth, but that night reinforcements arrived in the form of Ruger's division, which Cox placed between Carter and Palmer. The next morning Bragg sent Hoke to envelop the Union right, but the entrenchments thrown up by the Ninth and other regiments in that sector defied seizure. As on the eighth, the strongest attacks came against the left flank, where the Ninth, shortly after noon, moved "on a lively run" under orders to shore up the position. Upon arriving, the regiment slid behind a sturdy line of breastworks that put its own defenses to shame. Unaccustomed to such luxurious accommodations, at one point Colonel Stewart shouted to Captain Ben Hopper of Company E: "This is real fun!" Hopper agreed: "The Ninth never had a softer thing than this!" For the rest of the day the Ninth and the troops it was supporting absorbed a heavy fire but kept the enemy at arm's length.

After dusk, when the fighting died down, Captain Hopper established several picket posts in an area of "extreme danger" three-quarters of a mile toward the enemy's lines. It was a bold but imprudent move. Some time before dawn Amos H. Evans, now the first lieutenant of Company E, vanished along with sixteen of his men, who had been manning an outpost near an abandoned schoolhouse. At the risk of his own life Hopper spent several hours in the dark trying to locate the squad, but finally admitted that everyone had been taken prisoner. Evans would make good his escape and rejoin the Ninth within a month, but the men taken with him would not secure their freedom until war's end.[28]

The third day of battle near Wise's Forks began with another early-morning advance against the Union left, this time via a sweeping movement by Hoke. The native North Carolinian made inroads against Carter's works—members of the Ninth counted a dozen attacks that struck farther to their left—but rifle and cannon fire eventually drained the momentum from his effort. As Private Everts wrote, "they fought like devils, but it was all of no avail, they could not break our lines; our men stood firm, repulsing every charge."

Per orders, Hill's troops moved out upon hearing the sounds of Hoke's attack. The hodgepodge command captured an entrenched skirmish line before being threatened with envelopment by Federals farther to the rear. Learning that Hoke's movement had lost momentum, Hill suspended his advance until receiving word from Bragg to pull back once again. "These bloody attacks," wrote Everts, "were followed at evening by a remarkable stillness, indicating either that the enemy was preparing a ruse, or evacuating his strongholds." Either way the quiet was welcomed by the bleary-eyed men of the Ninth, who had gotten little sleep over the past several nights.[29]

In fact, Bragg was falling back toward Kinston en route to joining Johnston. He would arrive in time to help his superior land an unexpectedly heavy blow on Sherman's advance echelon at Bentonville on March 19, which the stunned Federals eventually repulsed. Following this, the final major clash between the combatants in North Carolina, Sherman had an open road to Goldsboro, where he would link with the forces of Schofield and Terry.

The three-day fight near Wise's Forks had taken a toll of both armies. When the Confederates withdrew on the eleventh, "800 dead lay on the field besides many wounded," according to Sergeant Little. Casualty figures for the attackers were never fully tabulated but their three-day losses were considerable. So too were Cox's: 1,337 killed, wounded, or missing, thirty of them in the ranks of the Ninth including the wounding of 1st Lt. Joseph Wright of Company F.[30]

The victors anticipated a quick and close pursuit. "We will soon move forward after the retreating rebels," Sergeant Little told his sister on the eleventh, adding that "they will not make a stand this side of Goldsboro: where we expect to meet Gen. Shermans Army and then we will fleece them out if they make a stand." Little's supposition that Bragg would not fight short of Goldsboro was correct, but the latter was permitted to clear the area before the Federals resumed the effort to unite with Sherman. Supposedly Colonel Stewart asked permission to follow the Confederates but Cox's headquarters denied the request. Thus for a time after the fight the Ninth held its most recent position, on the Tilghman farm. Mr. Tilghman, a fervent secessionist, had fled his estate but his pro-Union brother remained, and he urged the men of the Ninth to help themselves to "whatever they could find." Without hesitation, the Jerseymen obliged. Corporal Keenan allowed that this was to be expected of soldiers on the march, whose rations had a habit of giving out: "Then the men kept an eye out for the casual pig, the chance cow, or delight of delights, an unconscious brood of poultry." All this and more they enjoyed as the unexpected (but not uninvited) guests of Farmer Tilghman. The tidbit of recreation helped relieve the somber feelings of those who spent the next few days helping bury the hundreds of dead lying about in uniforms of blue, gray, and butternut.[31]

On the morning of March 14 the Ninth was again in motion, crossing Southwest Creek and passing a formidable-looking set of enemy field works. By noon the regiment's column had reached the Neuse outside Kinston. During a brief halt the Ninth found itself within sight of the bridge it had captured and burned in December 1862. There, according to Private Everts, the men discovered "bones of human bodies and pieces of clothing laying all over the ground." Moving on, the column took a road leading to another venue familiar to the regiment, Whitehall.[32]

The next morning under a steady rain the regiment accompanied its corps across the Neuse on a pontoon span. The continuing storm kept the Ninth and the other members of its brigade in place about a half mile southwest of Kinston. On the seventeenth they dug entrenchments against an anticipated attack from Confederates holding the town. When none materialized, the march was taken up again on the nineteenth.

The movement disappointed many Jerseymen, who had heard rumors that they would remain behind to garrison Kinston. Instead, before dawn the Ninth filed inside a section of the local defenses, where it halted while three days' rations and sixty rounds of cartridges were doled out to each man, strongly suggesting that further marching lay ahead. The distribution was overseen by Colonel Stewart, who had been placed in charge of a provisional brigade that also included the three Massachusetts regiments of the old Star Brigade and the Eighty-fifth New York.[33]

Before noon on the twentieth the Ninth went into bivouac near Whitehall, having marched sixteen miles since daybreak. This was not an unusual feat by any means; as Corporal Keenan remarked, "the Ninth was noted all through the department as being 'hell on foot,' that is, it could cover more ground in a given time than any infantry regiment that ever marched with it." Its motive prowess enabled the Ninth to be one of the first units to reach Goldsboro on the twenty-first, although it was said that on this day the regiment "marched slowly, to accommodate the troops following." In the village of Webbtown, on the outskirts of the city, a few defenders appeared and offered resistance. At first it was a cavalry-versus-cavalry affair, but when an infantry force challenged the Union horsemen, the Ninth "rushed forward with a yell, and the place was ours."[34]

Opposition surmounted, the Ninth, the vanguard of Cox's corps, entered the streets of Goldsboro where it was "received by the citizens with warm demonstrations of enthusiasm, many ladies waving their handkerchiefs from the doors and windows of the houses." In the heart of the city the regiment was met by the mayor and chief constable. According to one source, "the mayor, in surrendering the place to Colonel Stewart, said it gratified him to perform that duty to New Jerseymen, whom, he knew, would protect the citizens, and save their property from pillage." Pledging to do just that, the colonel led his men to the county courthouse, atop which the national standard of the regiment was soon waving.

According to military custom, the first body of troops to occupy an enemy city would perform provost duty there. The first ranking officer to reach Goldsboro, General Carter, formally assigned that task to Lieutenant Colonel Hufty and his men. Hufty placed provost details in various sections of the city while quartering the regiment at the courthouse and in several adjacent buildings. Within half an hour, the Ninth was "patrolling the streets as quietly and naturally as if it had been doing provost duty there for a month." At the same time, Surgeon Gillette and his staff got to work transforming hotels, houses, and a female academy into hospitals for the care of the many wounded of the corps. These facilities were in operation by the time the main body of Cox's command trooped in "with flags flying, bands playing, and drums beating." It was said that "cheer followed cheer and huzzah after huzzah, to the Union flag of the Ninth, waving from the Court-house."[35]

Within two days large elements of Sherman's forces—veterans of the Armies of the Tennessee and of the Cumberland—had reached the countryside around Goldsboro. To Sergeant Little the command presented a "lively appearance." Private Everts wrote that "I have seen larger armies in Europe, but there can be no competition between them and these Western troops." These lean, wiry, dangerous-looking men had traveled light since leaving Atlanta four months earlier: "They have only received seven days' rations from the Government, living [for] over two months on the country." The great majority of Sherman's "bummers" were poorly clothed, their uniforms dirtied and torn from extended campaigning across rough and broken territory.

When their leader entered Goldsboro to clasp hands with General Schofield, it was noticed that he too "wore a shabby uniform, and as he put on no airs, he took with the 'boys,' as he familiarly called them." Corporal Keenan sized up the great captain as "red haired, grim, with quick, searching eyes and the most careless disregard of state which we had ever seen in an officer of rank." But if the veterans of North Carolina admired Sherman, they had a much more critical opinion of the conduct of his men, who at every opportunity attempted to run wild.

Their antics were quickly controlled by the provost guards of the Ninth, whom the tattered and dirty newcomers derided as "white-gloved soldiers." Private Cleveland reported that "these fellows of the 15th and 17th Corps entertain a perfect hatred of the 9th N.J." On more than a few occasions they set upon the Jerseymen and tried to beat them into submission but found the majority proficient with fists and rifle butts.

For the duration of its stay in Goldsboro, the Ninth was kept extremely busy. It policed the city, protected the citizenry from looting and vandalism, and arrested lawbreakers. On April 4 two companies under Captain Hopper took into custody fifty "dissolute men and women" from a brothel in Webbtown. It was said that "the procession attracted much attention and created great merriment as it marched through Goldsboro to the lock-up."[36]

The outfit also oversaw local commerce, keeping tabs on scores of sutlers and other businessmen who had followed the troops from New Bern. It helped secure housing and other services for those crewmen working to repair the railroad. Every day it corralled groups of Confederates who, perceiving imminent defeat, had deserted their units; many expressed a willingness to take the oath of allegiance to the U.S. government. The Ninth did its best to succor the civilians forced from their homes by the movements of the armies. Sergeant Little marveled at "the sight that is presented at the rail road depot every afternoon when the refugees collect for transportation to Newbern. A train is loaded every day with these people; men, women and children and in every state of poverty. It is a hard sight. Many of these people have been very wealthy but are now stripped of everything and are dependent on the Government for support."[37]

When not on police duty, the regiment worked hard to keep soldiers and civilians posted on the latest military and political news. Corp. Charles Hinton of Company K, a would-be newspaper editor who had been one of the first skirmishers to enter Goldsboro, took it upon himself to transform a local printing office into the home of the *Loyal State Journal*, of which he became proprietor and publisher. With the assistance of a comrade who had worked as a compositor for the *New York Tribune*, Hinton published his paper using three abandoned presses; newsprint being scarce, he printed copies on the underside of wallpaper stripped from houses in the neighborhood. His first issue, released the day after the city was occupied, included an editorial by now-Major Appleget singing the praises of the Ninth New Jersey. Copies sold "like hot cakes."[38]

Its eager readership, especially the soldier portion thereof, kept the paper in circulation long after the Ninth was relieved from police duty on April 10—to the chagrin of the local people, who had petitioned General Schofield to keep the regiment in place. During its early run the *Journal* broke several stories of lasting significance. On April 6 it printed a War Department bulletin announcing the evacuation of Richmond and Petersburg. Both strongholds had fallen to Ulysses S. Grant's patient but effective strategy of stretching their elongated defenses to the breaking point. Now the race was on to overtake Lee's fleeing troops before their commander could devise an escape stratagem.[39]

Equally momentous news, capable of bringing great cheer to the soldiers and plunging them into gloom and grief, followed the Federals out of Goldsboro at the outset of the last fortnight of their wartime service. On the day the Ninth was relieved at Goldsboro, it marched "twelve long North Carolina miles" on the roads toward Raleigh, in which direction Joe Johnston's little army had moved after waylaying Sherman at Bentonville. The regiment was now a member of a brand-new XXIII Corps brigade commanded by Brevet Brig. Gen. John S. Casement and which also included three regiments that had served under Sherman, Schofield, and Terry: the Sixty-fifth Illinois, Sixty-fifth Indiana, and 177th Ohio.[40]

On the eleventh Casement's command marched all day in a torrential rain, a common meteorological event in this part of the state at this time of year. When the sodden troops bivouacked for the night on a large farm, various and contradictory rumors were circulating through the ranks. Some had Johnston's troops beaten down, exhausted, and on the verge of surrender. Considering that cavalry in advance of Sherman's columns had recently encountered a force of Rebels who appeared as hardy and combative as ever, "it began to look as if more bloody work had yet to be done ere our 'erring brethren' would lay down their arms."

Then, suddenly, the picture became clearer and rosier. On the morning of the twelfth General Sherman, trailed by a queue of subordinates and staff officers, came galloping through the ranks, shouting for all to hear: "*Lee has surrendered to Grant!*" The news set off a wild chorus of cheers and prompted music from dozens of regimental bands. Soldiers threw their caps in the air; some broke ranks to dance a merry jig; many unabashedly wept for joy, "embracing each other again and again." No longer could there be a doubt that the war was in its final days. With Lee's army laying down its arms, Johnston's would be forced to follow suit.[41]

But first the North Carolina Rebels, being few, feisty, and used to hard marching, had to be overtaken. That task took a week, and by then, with Raleigh evacuated by Johnston and occupied by Sherman, tears of joy had been replaced by tears of bitter grief in the eyes of Johnston's pursuers. On the eighteenth, the soldiers in and around Raleigh learned of the assassination of President Lincoln at Ford's Theatre three nights earlier.

Most of the Jerseymen took the news hard and responded to it angrily. Sergeant Little called it "the most painful news that we have rec'd in a long time. . . . It has shocked every body and every soldier feels like revenging his death on any Southern citizen that dares to express any endorsement of the fiendish act. The soldiers threatened to burn this city last night, and it was only saved by the utmost vigilance of armed patrols. I could see it go down without regret." Private Cleveland fervently hoped that the dastard who struck at Lincoln and those who tried to kill other members of the government "are caught and meet their due reward. A general feeling of sorrow pervades the army." Corporal Keenan recalled that the news was met by "but one cry, rage, and then revenge. Every man asked to be led forward at Johnston's army, then a few miles to the westward of us at Durham's station." Keenan cited a general feeling that Lincoln, "alone of all the politicians, meant well, that he had a tender, compassionate nature. The men loved him, and they mourned him at Raleigh."[42]

On the day that details of the president's murder reached Raleigh Sergeant Little noted that "the citizens are very mute and express regret in hearing such news. It will not result to the benefit of the South or the Copperheads of the North. . . . Many of the leading men of the South is coming in here and want to settle the war immediately. Meetings are being held, and some thing must surely result from them." He was correct to assume that negotiations were under way to end the bloodshed in North Carolina. On the seventeenth and eighteenth Sherman and Johnston met at a private home at Durham Station to discuss terms for surrendering the latter's army.[43]

Having conferred with Lincoln and Grant at City Point, Virginia, in the last days of March, Sherman believed that the president favored the granting of lenient peace terms to Johnston. At Durham Station, therefore, he and his opponent forged beyond local military issues to propose a general armistice by all armies still in the field, including those operating west of the Mississippi. Sherman's terms, which included the recognition of existing state governments in the South and a guarantee of rights of person and property to ex-Confederates, ran counter to the attitudes of Congress and the War Department. On April 24 Grant was sent to North Carolina to notify his subordinate that the government had rejected the agreement he had made with Johnston.

Since the eighteenth the opposing forces had been standing down, but now Johnston was given notice that hostilities would resume in forty-eight hours if he refused to surrender. The army leader carefully considered his course and two days later—April 26, the day on which pursuing cavalry overtook and mortally wounded Lincoln's assassin, John Wilkes Booth—the generals met again at Durham. This time they signed terms of surrender matching those Grant had offered Lee at

Appomattox Court House. With a final stroke of a pen, the war in the eastern theater of operations came to a long-overdue end.[44]

With the coming of peace the Federals expected, or at least hoped, to be discharged and sent home sooner rather than later. For most of the men of the Ninth, however, this would not happen for almost three months. The upshot, as Corporal Keenan put it, was "weeks of tedious waiting." By early May rumor had the Ninth on the verge of being mustered out, but at least as much speculation concerned the prospect that the regiment, along with most of Sherman's troops, would be sent to the Rio Grande to overawe the French forces that had invaded Mexico three years earlier. Neither report proved accurate, but in the first week of the month nine companies of the Ninth were sent by rail to the countryside around Greensboro. In that vicinity some of Sherman's soldiers were "raising the devil" by applying the foraging tactics they had honed in Georgia and South Carolina. One of Cox's subordinates stationed there asked for two regiments to help him restore order. Because it had done such a good job of keeping the peace in Goldsboro, Cox immediately replied: "Send up the Ninth New Jersey." A second regiment would not be needed.[45]

The Ninth's arrival at Greensboro was heralded by the local people, whose lives and possessions had been threatened by guerrillas and bushwhackers as well as by Yankee thieves. The regiment pitched camp on a plantation a mile west of the town. While Colonel Stewart set up guard posts and added staff to the local prisons, he assigned several subordinates to special duty. Company G under Capt. Morris C. Runyan and 1st Lt. David Kille's Company I traveled, respectively, to Charlotte and Salisbury to confiscate ordnance, ammunition, and other supplies abandoned by Johnston's troops. Capt. Lucius C. Bonham and Company A made a fifty-mile trek to Yanceyville, where they helped organize a company of Union men to suppress lawlessness in that part of the state. And Capt. Jonathan Townley's men of Company K took possession of rolling stock, supplemental trackage, and other railroad materials stored at the repair facility known as Company Shops, midway between Goldsboro and Charlotte. There on the night of May 5 Private Cleveland, assigned to guard the home of a local Unionist, "tumbled into the only feather bed I have occupied for a year."[46]

Each of these missions constituted a necessary step toward the pacification of western North Carolina, but at Charlotte Captain Runyan and his men rendered a service of inestimable value to generations of historians. In that town, where President Jefferson Davis and members of his staff had stayed briefly after fleeing Richmond, Company G found not only military assets including dozens of national and regimental colors captured in battle but also a warehouse full of archival material. The latter comprised eighty-four boxes of records documenting the operations of the Confederate States government. Runyan immediately appreciated "the great importance of these documents, especially to the historian and scholar for their correct understanding of this great conflict, containing the official history on their side of the greatest of rebellions." A large portion of the material the captain collected and safeguarded would make its way into the pages of the *Official Records of the Union and Confederate Armies* when that incomparable compendium was published over the next thirty-six years.[47]

For the troops remaining in and around Greensboro, duty was light. Lawlessness declined rapidly upon the regiment's arrival; thereafter its time was largely devoted to supporting indigent civilians and paroled Confederates who required medical care. Sergeant Little found the town "filled with their sick and wounded and so was all the villages and churches in the neighborhood." Because Greensboro had been spared the hard hand of war and, until recently, enemy soldiers had been scarce, Little and his comrades were "a great curiosity to the country people. Many has come 20 miles to see us, believing that they would see some monstrous human beings. I had to laugh at a remark made by an old lady after she had looked around at the Yankees. Her opinion was that we was not as bad looking or as desperate men as she had supposed us to be."[48]

Little had hopes of imminent discharge. When Colonel Stewart went north on May 21 the rumor was that "he has gone to prepare the way for the return of the regiment to Jersey." Until his return, the men made the most of peacetime pursuits. Private Cleveland spent the afternoon of May 25 "strawberrying up the [Richmond and] Danville R. R. It had been a long time since I had been on such an expedition and partaken of the delicious fruit." Three weeks later he went picking in the same vicinity, returning to camp with a quart-size pail filled with blackberries to share with his comrades. Other Jerseymen spent their free time seeking souvenirs to carry home as mementoes of their war service, including boxes of Confederate currency that Henry Keenan found "scattered in the streets. Every man in the command became a 'millionaire,' if he chose."[49]

On June 5 an order of General Schofield's, read on dress parade, announced that all soldiers whose service time would expire by October 1 would be discharged. It was understood that the order would be carried out immediately but when the days dragged by Private Cleveland, one of those who qualified for early release, groused that "the prospects of getting mustered out are daily growing more dismal." To his surprise and joy, on the twelfth the preparation of muster rolls began and two days later, per General Orders No. 72, Headquarters Army of North Carolina, they were ceremoniously signed by Cleveland and 215 other members of the Ninth. It was noted that the longer-term men looked on "somewhat sadly."[50]

The next day, immediately after roll call, those about to depart turned in the Model 1861 Springfield rifle-muskets that had helped give the Ninth New Jersey its enduring reputation as marksmen. On the afternoon of June 16 the short-termers boarded a train for the first leg of a long-anticipated homeward journey by land and water. Before starting out, they were visited by some of their officers. Ed Cleveland noted that Capt. Thomas Burnett came into the cars to bid farewell to "his boys" of Company B: "He was a little 'up' and could not refrain from tears at parting from those who had been with him for four years. It was an affecting scene."

The journey north via Goldsboro, Kinston, New Bern, Cape Hatteras, Fort Monroe, Baltimore, Wilmington, and Philadelphia was a much-interrupted ordeal. The travel delays only added to the soldiers' anxious anticipation of reuniting with loved ones they had not seen for many months and in some cases for two or even three years. Not till the evening of the twenty-first, when his train was ferried across the Delaware River to Camden prior to conveyance to Trenton for final pay and discharge, could Cleveland exult: "Glory! I am on Jersey soil!"[51]

The comrades he left behind did not languish in North Carolina for long. On July 5 "unbounded satisfaction" greeted their receipt of a telegram announcing that the balance of the regiment would be mustered out by Capt. A. B. Smith of the 100th Ohio Volunteers. It took a week, but on the twelfth the remaining officers and men took part in the muster-out process at Greensboro, to which all detachments had returned. The following evening, surplus ordnance and camp and garrison equipage having been handed over to the departmental quartermasters, the happy members of the Ninth were carried north on what Corporal Keenan called "the most rickety cars I ever saw and, at the rate of not more than five miles an hour."[52]

The journey may have had its vexations, but the men traveled with a glorious tribute to their three and a half years of service singing in their ears. Having returned from leave to learn that he had been brevetted a brigadier general of volunteers to rank from March 13, James Stewart received letters of thanks and appreciation from several ranking officers of the XXIII Corps. The one he and his men valued most came directly from General Carter, the local district commander, who wrote that "I cannot have you leave for home without joining my testimony to those of others, as to the discipline, drill, gallant conduct, soldierly bearing, and efficiency of your noble regiment. On the march, in camp, under fire, and in the performance of all the duties of a soldier, the example of the 9th N. J. V. V. Inf'y has been worthy of imitation, and entitles it to all praise and commendation."[53]

The men who preceded the bulk of the regiment on its homeward course may not have known of this tribute before their departure, though they assuredly learned of it at a later date. Even so, they returned to warm greetings and expressions of appreciation. For Private Cleveland, homecoming consisted not only of a return to the bosom of his loving family but of being feted and applauded at a series of local events suffused with patriotic fervor. The centerpiece of these activities was a Fourth of July celebration that served as a grand welcome home to Elizabeth's veterans. "At daybreak," he noted in the last page of his diary, "the cannon fired, the bells rang and the fire crackers exploded by the thousands." At 7 a.m. he and the other returnees—some seventy-five in number, all in uniform—assembled at the Union League hall, where they were grouped into three "platoons." The first platoon, composed mainly of Ninth New Jersey men, was commanded by Lieutenant Drake, whose prison-escape exploits had made him a local hero beyond compare.

Escorted by the militia units of the town and accompanied by horse-drawn floats conveying patriotic tableaux (as well as "veterans unable to walk"), the ex-soldiers were paraded through the streets to the constant applause of the citizenry. The procession ended at the Presbyterian Church, whose pulpit had been converted into a platform on which the pastor, the mayor, and other political and religious officials spent hours praising the soldierly contributions of the veterans and thanking God for their safe return. When the orations ceased, Drake, Cleveland, and their comrades were marched to Library Hall, where, seated at tables piled high with victuals, they were treated to a "repast which would have graced a king's table," the handiwork of the ladies of the local Union Aid Society.

The gala day concluded with everyone adjourning to the Union County Courthouse for an evening of fireworks. Cleveland wrote that "the streets were filled with people. It seemed as though the whole town had turned out. The final piece—'Washington, Union Forever' surmounted by 'Victory' was especially fine. The exhibition closed at 10:00 p.m. . . . Little did I think when I commenced this diary that I would finish it on the most memorable Fourth of July our country has ever seen. To Thee, O God, would I render my thanks with the providence with which Thou has blessed our nation and myself in particular." Then Edmund J. Cleveland added a final thought to his wartime journal, one he undoubtedly shared with every member of the Ninth New Jersey Veteran Volunteers:

"Tomorrow I begin again to live the life of a civilian."[54]

APPENDIX

Regimental Roster

* = Killed or mortally wounded in action
** = Missing in action
*** = Died of Disease or Non-combat Injury

D = Draftee
R = Recruit
S = Substitute
T = Transferee (from Another Regiment)

Field and Staff

ORIGINAL ENLISTEES

Colonel
    Allen, Joseph W.***
Lieutenant Colonel
Major
    Heckman, Charles A.
Adjutant
    Zabriskie, Abram*
Quartermaster
    Keys, Samuel
Chief Surgeon
    Weller, Frederick S.***
Assistant Surgeon
    Braun, Lewis
Hospital Steward
    Lewis, John W.
Chaplain
    Drumm, Thomas

LATER ADDITIONS

Chief Surgeons
    Gillette, Fidelio B.
    Woodhull, Addison W.
Assistant Surgeon
    Davies, John M.
Chaplains
    Carrell, John J.
    Lane, Gilbert

Noncommissioned Staff

Company A

[Disbanded; enlisted men transferred to other companies, November 18, 1862]

Frank, George
Fricke, Henry
Fricke, William
Fuchs, Martin
Gaessler, Valentine
Gasser, Peter
Geist, William
Giles, Enoch
Goss, Charles
Graeber, Jacob
Grienich, Adam***
Hans, Joseph
Harris, William
Heck, Joseph***
Heller, John
Helmer, Francis
Hermes, Peter
Heydecker, Henry
Hilde, Charles
Hockenjoss, Gottlieb
Hoff, John
Hoffman, John
Hopp, John
Hoyer, Gottleib
Hubner, Charles
Hunt, William A.
Jordan, Conrad
Jung, Valentine
Jurgens, Martin
Kirmick, Anton
Klotz, John G.*
Knobel, Matthias
Koenig, John M.
Kraster, Frederick
Krauss, Herman
Kuhn, William
Kulin, William
Kunder, Adam***
Kuntz, Joseph
Kurtze, William
Lamps, Albrecht

Lautenbach, Christian
Mathes, Henry
McGintay, Michael
Meiss, Albert***
Muller, Franz*
Muller, John
Muller, William*
Nittinger, Benjamin
Pelar, John
Perrine, George
Quigley, Daniel A.
Rappe, William
Reidmuller, Louis
Rolfe, George N.
Rudolph, Augustus
Scheible, John
Scheidemantel, Andrew***
Schill, Martin
Schultz, Andrew
Schweitzer, Philip***
Schwinghammer, Anthony
Shcleicher, Henry
Spitznagel, Felix
Stand, Sebastian
Stussy, Jacob
Their, Peter
Thiele, John
Trautwein, John
Turschman, Charles*
Ulrich, Martin***
Weitzel, John G.*
Westerman, Ferdinand
Yeager, Benjamin
Zimmerlin, John

LATER ADDITIONS

Privates
Anderson, John (R)
Bader, John (R)***
Baird, John (R)
Baker, John (S)

Ball, Henry J. (R)
Barnbury, Patrick (S)
Bauer, Jacob (S)
Beaver, John (S)
Bechler, Knox (R)
Beckett, Hiram D. (R)
Biehl, Ernest (R)
Black, George (R)
Bowman, Edgar A. (R)
Breckman, John (S)
Bright, Frank (S)
Broughton, John (S)
Brown, David (S)
Brown, George (S)
Brown, Henry (S)
Carman, Luke K. (R)
Clark, William (S)
Compton, Franklin (D)
Conklin, Claudius (S)
Cook, Charles (R)
Crawford, James (S)
Davis, George C. (R)
Deiber, Charles (R)
Demain, John (S)
Denenger, Christian (S)
Dietrich, Ernst (S)
Dimond, James (R)
Dixon, George (S)
Eckhardt, Louis (R)
Ells, Hugo (S)
Emory, Robert (S)
Finlayson, Donald (S)
Fisher, Henry C. (R)
Fitzmyer, John (S)
Flynn, Thomas (R)
Foley, John (R)
Foster, Samuel B. (R)
Frederick, Adam (R)
Fredericks, Henry (R)***
Garton, Charles H. (R)
Gause, Lewis H. (R)

Gestenmier, Michael (R)
Gibson, Henry (S)
Giles, Isaac (R)
Gold, James (S)
Grinsley, George T. (S)
Gulick, Edward R. (R)
Haggerty, William R. (S)
Hart, George S. (R)
Hart, William (R)
Hass, Daniel (S)
Helier, John (R)
Hendrickson, Richard (R)***
Henlow, James (S)
Hennion, George W. (R)
Hoelzel, John (S)
Inmeyer, Robert (S)
Jemison, Joseph J. (R)
Johnson, John H. (R)
Kaiser, Harris (R)
Keegan, William (R)
Kelly, John E. (R)
Kenny, James (R)
King, William (R)
Kirsmire, Michael (R)
Lages, John H. (R)
Lindquest, Sion (S)
Long, Benjamin (R)
Loring, John A. (R)
Luderson, William (R)
Lynch, James (R)
Malew, Patrick (R)
Marsh, John (R)
Martin, James H. (S)
McAlney, William (D)
McDowell, Thomas (R)
Neary, Edward G. (S)***
Neirman, Joseph (R)
Nicholson, John (S)
Noll, August (R)
O'Donnell, John (S)
Perry, John (D)

Platt, Horace (D)
Price, Joseph (R)
Probst, Louis (R)
Prochaska, John (S)
Reis, Albert (R)
Scanlin, John (R)
Schleicher, Henry (R)
Sepp, Charles (R)
Sheidrick, Theodore (S)
Siegel, John (R)
Silvers, William H. (R)***
Smith, George A. (R)
Smith, Henry (S)
Snyder, Marshall (S)
Stopleman, Richard (S)
Strinning, Frederick (R)

Suydam, Jacob (S)
Thomas, James (R)
Thompson, Charles W. (R)
Traudt, Ernest (R)
Vanderveer, David G. (R)
Volz, John (S)
Warren, James (R)
Wenner, John (D)
Wheeland, Francis (R)
White, William (S)
Willetts, Jonathan (D)
Wolfe, Henry (D)
Wolfe, John (D)
Woodsides, Fenwick A. (R)
Yeager, Benjamin (R)
Zipfel, Matthias (R)

Company B

ORIGINAL ENLISTEES

Captain
Castner, Cornelius W.
First Lieutenant
Bartholomew, Luzerne
Second Lieutenant
Sofield, Charles H.
First Sergeant
Burnett, Thomas W.
Sergeants
Bradford, David C.
Dunham, James M.
Gordon, Isaac L.
Hubbs, Ethelbert E.
Corporals
Bennett, John
Blackeny, Moses C.
Currie, Edward
De Hart, Theodore
Hayes, Eugene M.***
Lawrence, John

Pierson, John L.
Strong, Silas P.**
Vanderhoef, Robert B.
White, Robert H.
Musician
Prall, James
Privates
Abrams, Cornell S.
Acker, Philip
Benjamin, John F.
Benjamin, Selah
Birney, Thomas
Bloodgood, Phineas F.
Booream, Edgar J.
Boudinot, William B.
Bough, Charles***
Breese, Henry
Buckley, Thomas
Butterworth, Jonathan
Cahill, Francis
Carter, John H.

Casler, John W.
Church, George W.
Cisco, William L.**
Clerkin, John
Coburn, Charles A.
Collins, William
Cosgrove, Daniel
Crawford, James
Daley, Michael
Danberry, Henry M.
Danberry, John
Danberry, William
Deady, John
Demot, George
Dennis, Charles*
Dennis, Daniel
Disbrow, Ferdinand*
Dock, Abraham
Dock, Isaac
Dow, William E.
Dye, Isaac S.
Dye, Walter
Dye, Walter J.
Egan, Thomas
Fowler, Joseph W.
Garretson, Dumont
Gibney, Joseph B.
Gould, Richard N.
Gray, David V. D.
Hagerty, Daniel
Hall, Ebenezer
Hoffman, John
Houghton, Michael
Hubbard, Seth R.
Hughes, Theodore V.
Irwin, Charles
Jackson, Matthew
Jayne, John S.
Johnson, William
King, C. Irwin
Knowles, David G.

Labone, Wallace W.
Lally, Patrick
Lare, William H.
Lawless, Peter
Lowton, John
McClay, James
Meagher, Peter
Meyers, John
Moore, Martin*
Moore, Thomas E.**
Moore, William H.
Morris, William
Munslow, Isaac P. H.
Murphy, James
Nichols, Sylvester
Numan, William H.
Penny, Jonathan R.
Reis, Christopher***
Reynolds, James
Roe, Edward***
Rule, William
Scheible, John***
Shardlow, William
Sheehan, John
Sherry, Peter
Silcox, Bergen
Skillman, Joakim
Smith, John H.
Soper, Charles D.***
Stryker, William H.
Sweeze, Warren W.
Tutenberg, Henry M.
Van Buskirk, James
Vandeventer, John
Vorhees, John C.
Youngs, John C.

LATER ADDITIONS

Privates

Acker, Francis (R)
Anderson, Thomas (R)

Avery, Edward F. (R)
Barker, Chauncey W. (R)
Barth, Joseph (R)
Bauer, Michael (R)
Bemspach, Michael (R)
Bender, John (R)
Bickel, Jacob (R)
Bolton, Levi (R)
Bonet, August (R)
Brennan, William (S)
Brown, Charles E. (R)
Brown, John B. (R)
Brown, Thomas H. (R)
Buckley, Daniel (R)
Burns, James (R)
Burns, John J. (R)
Caldwell, Thomas (R)
Carolan, Patrick (R)
Casey, James (R)
Chew, Eli (R)
Clark, Charles (R)
Clayton, Beverly (R)
Coeyman, Joseph O. (R)
Conover, Ananias M. (R)
Cook, Alfred (R)*
Cunningham, Lawrence (R)
Day, Samuel (R)
DeForrest, Charles (R)
Denton, Charles C. (D)
Devitt, William (R)
Dingler, Marcus (R)
Doldy, John M. (R)
Donnelly, William H. (R)
Driscoll, Timothy (R)
Dugan, Michael (R)
Dunn, William (R)
Eckert, Valentine (R)
English, Owen (R)
Ewing, Samuel A. (R)*
Faughy, John (R)
Gardner, Thomas C. (R)

Garrabrant, Edward (R)
Garrabrant, Minard (R)
Garrison, John C. (R)
Garrison, Menzies (D)
Gestenmier, Michael (R)
Giles, Runyon V. (R)
Givenwein, George (R)
Greathead, William (R)
Groff, Gustavus (R)*
Hall, Reuben (R)
Hamman, John (S)
Harrigan, William D. (S)
Harrison, James (R)
Harrison, Ralph (R)
Heary, James P. (R)
Hennion, George W. (R)
Herbert, Charles (R)
Hopkins, Simeon F. (S)
Howell, William (D)
Jacobs, Theodore (S)
Jerome, Frank (R)
Johnson, William (S)
Jones, John P. (D)
Jordan, John L. (R)
Jurgens, John R. (R)
Kelly, James (R)
Kenyon, Francis A. (R)
Kinkle, Charles (R)
Krum, Karl (S)
Lamair, Charles (S)
Larter, George E. (R)
Lloyd, John (R)
Lowton, George (R)
McAndrew, Allen (R)
McCollum, James (R)
McKloskey, Peter (R)
Meyer, Edward (R)
Miller, Edward (R)
Monahan, Thomas (S)
Montalvo, Frank (R)
Moss, Aaron (R)

Murray, George F. (R)
Nevins, Benjamin F. (R)
Newton, James (D)
Nicholson, John T. (R)
O'Conner, Daniel (R)
O'Rourke, Michael (R)
Osborne, Charles C. (R)
Owens, Francis (R)
Owens, Patrick (R)
Palmer, Benjamin F. (D)
Paul, George (R)
Perry, James A. (D)
Pierman, Garret V. (R)
Pierson, Wesley (D)
Prager, Frederick N. (R)
Putnam, Isaac F. (R)
Putnam, Thomas J. (R)*
Randall, William (R)
Reinhart, Henry (R)
Riley, Owen (R)

Rosser, Louis (R)
Ryno, Henry C. (R)
Shafer, Robert (R)
Shaw, Errick C. (D)
Smith, George (R)
Stout, John S. (S)
Taylor, William J. (R)
Thompson, Thomas (R)*
Thompson, Walter S. (R)
Thompson, William (R)
Van Brunt, Alfred (D)
Virtue, Thomas W. (R)
Vorhees, John H. (R)
Wagner, Jacob (D)
Walters, Gustavus (R)
Weatherby, Charles (R)
Wheeler, Frederick H. (R)
Williams, Charles E. (D)
Youmans, Manning (R)
Youmans, William G. (R)

Company C

ORIGINAL ENLISTEES

Captain
Hopkinson, Charles B.
First Lieutenant
Harris, Edwin S.*
Second Lieutenant
Clift, Joel W.
First Sergeants
Brown, A. Benson
Cowperthwaite, Dilwyn R.*
Sergeants
Hooper, William W.
Keller, John
Morrison, William M.
Rogers, William D.
Smith, Edward P.*
Thompson, Charles H.

Corporals
Clark, Isaac L. S.
Cline, Andrew S.
Corcoran, John
Gould, George C.
Hibbs, Theodore J.
Hudnut, John W.**
Thorn, Wesley
Van Brunt, William
Weinrich, Adam***
Wendell, William M.
Williams, Richard
Musicians
Knespel, Christian
McDonald, Patrick H.
Wagoner
Vorhees, Henry

Privates

Atkinson, John***
Bakely, Joseph W.
Barber, Charles W.
Blackfan, John W.
Blakely, George M.
Burch, David D.
Burton, John R.***
Carter, David J.
Cline, Joseph
Clinton, Benjamin
Conway, John
Cooper, Henry C.
Corson, Samuel D.
Craige, Josiah F.
Cunningham, Jerome B.
Dennis, John W.
Donaldson, Sylvanus
Dougherty, James***
Drost, Cornelius
Estlack, Edward H.
Forbes, Lorenzo
Garrigan, John
Garwood, Abraham
Hand, Enoch W.
Hendrickson, Daniel
Herbert, James*
Heritage, Job
Heritage, Richard
Hesley, Jacob
Hiers, John H.
Hiser, Christopher
Houk, George
Hurnburg, Christian
Hutton, Thomas
Jacobs, John H. A.
Johnson, Israel*
Kaiser, Charles
Lanagan, William N.
Lauer, Sebastian
Leming, Charles

Long, John D.
Manning, Benjamin
Martin, Theodore F.***
McCoy, Barney
Meyers, William
Mitchell, Reading B.***
Myers, Theodore***
Nelson, George
Page, Samuel
Poppy, John E.
Radrauff, Charles C.
Riker, Thomas
Roberts, Isaac H.
Rodney, Adam
Rogers, Elmer Q. C.
Ross, Alfred
Spalding, Augustus
Stagg, William W.
Stokes, James R.
Stout, William H.
Trout, William R.
Vanhise, Charles
Watson, Joseph L.***
Williams, Joseph H.
Wood, Thomas J.
Zane, William C.

LATER ADDITIONS

Privates

Bakley, Jesse (R)
Ball, William (R)
Bauman, Conrad (D)
Bohr, Niucholas (R)
Bonnefoy, Antoine (D)
Bradford, Jacob S. (R)
Bradley, John (R)***
Brick, Edward W. (R)
Brown, Charles (R)
Budding, Charles (R)
Cameron, John (R)
Chappins, Louis (R)***

Collins, Isaac (R)
Crane, Morris C. (D)
Dennis, Charles (R)
Dennis, Isaiah (R)
Doolin, John S. (R)
Dotson, Frederick (R)
Drake, Jacob V. (R)
Elsden, George (D)
Ely, Daniel E. (R)
Fisher, William (R)***
Flock, John, Jr. (R)
Garrison, Benjamin B. (R)***
Garrison, Jeremiah (R)
Gertner, Frederick (R)***
Giles, Asa (R)***
Gleisner, Benjamin (R)
Habig, Francis (R)
Habig, Leander (R)
Hancock, Thomas S. (R)
Hanno, George (R)***
Henry, Isaac (R)
Kane, John O. (R)***
Kelly, Francis (R)
Kirchner, August (R)
Koch, Charles (R)***
Koenig, Albert (R)
Kumpst, Leopold (R)
Lewis, Henry (R)
Lightkep, Andrew N. (R)
Long, William (R)
McCullough, Francis (R)
McKelvy, James F. (R)

Measey, William (R)
Miller, Charles (D)
Moore, Samuel B. (R)
Mosher, Isaac (R)
Mosher, Thompson (R)
O'Brien, Bernard (R)
Pflaum, Herman (S)
Pool, Alfred (R)
Powlmore, Pierson P. (R)
Quinn, John (R)
Rogers, Albin (R)
Sales, William (R)
Scherz, John (S)
Schmidt, Charles (R)
Shannon, Morris (R)***
Simmons, Frederick (R)
Smith, Joseph W. (R)
Spintil, Theodore (D)
Springer, Frederick (R)
Stockley, James H. (R)
Strudell, Charles (R)
Taylor, John (R)
Taylor, Peter (R)***
Taylor, Theodore O. (D)
Todd, Benjamin H. (R)
Tooker, Samuel (D)
Tumith, James (R)
Voegtlen, Jacob (R)
Voegtlen, Samuel (R)
Weigle, William (R)
Werner, Herman (R)

Company D

ORIGINAL ENLISTEES

Captain
Middleton, Thomas W.
First Lieutenant
Irons, George G.

Second Lieutenant
Kissam, Edgar
First Sergeant
Levey, Charles M.
Sergeants
Craft, Hiram

Elberson, Andrew J.
Hufty, Charles*
Wilkins, Jesse M.
Corporals
Bennett, Jesse L.***
Champion, Nicholas S.
Cranmer, Job L.
Cranmer, Joseph W.
Hulsart, Jesse R.
Johnston, James
Bennett, Jesse L.***
Penn, Redin N.
Smith, Charles P.*
Wagoner
Peck, William H.
Musician
Fithian, Napoleon B.
Privates
Ackerman, Jerry
Archer, Thomas
Ashton, Edward G.***
Atterson, Joseph*
Barclay, John W.
Beatty, Francis E.
Beatty, George
Benner, George
Brandt, Charles
Brindley, Charles
Brown, William
Cambren, Charles P.
Cambren, Henry A.
Chafey, Charles P.
Clark, James
Clayton, John M.
Clayton, William B.
Conklin, William B.
Cornelius, John
Crane, Eugene A.
Cranmer, Ezra***
Cranmer, Isaac
Dennis, William

Ellem, Joseph C.
Errickson, Horace G.
Errickson, John
Gregory, William H.
Hankins, David C.
Hazleton, Thomas
Herner, William
Hewitt, Henry
Heyers, Gilbert H.
Homan, Benjamin L.***
Hulse, James
Hulse, Joel*
Hurley, William H.
Hyers, Garrett V.
Imley, Orlando
Inman, Isaac M.
Inman, Oliver P.
Jeffrey, Noah E.
Johnson, Abraham T.***
Johnson, Barzillia
Johnson, Charles A.
Johnson, David A.
Johnson, Joseph
Johnson, William
Jones, Benjamin W.
Lachat, Henry*
Loveless, Joseph
McKelvy, David
Mount, Caleb H.***
Norcross, Wesley B.
Nutt, Albert S.*
Nutt, Henry W.*
Oakerson, John
Oakerson, Joseph
Osborne, Samuel***
Perrine, John W.
Phillips, Henry H.*
Randolph, Thomas S.
Reed, Alexander***
Riley, David
Robinson, Charles P.

Robinson, James H.
Rogers, Benjamin A.
Rogers, George W.
Rulay, Oscar J.***
Sharp, William H.
Shinn, Ezekiel
Steelman, John B.*
Truax, Charles W.
Truax, James
Vantilburg, Edgar
Westerman, Ferdinand
Worth, George R.
Yenny, Jacob

LATER ADDITIONS

Privates

Applegate, Edwin (R)
Beatty, George (R)
Beebe, William R. (D)
Biehl, Ernest (R)
Brawer, David (R)
Brindley, Samuel (R)
Bush, William (R)
Cambren, Benjamin B. (R)
Cambren, Francis E. (R)
Carr, William P. (R)
Carter, David S. (R)
Cavanagh, Joseph (R)
Chadwick, John R. (R)
Clark, Peter (R)
Clayton, John A (R).
Clevinger, Henry A. (R)
Collins, George (R)
Conncellor, Henry (R)
Craft, William H. (R)
Crossley, Robert (T)
Ely, Daniel E. (R)
Engles, George H. (R)
Errickson, Fuller B. (R)
Fagan, Francis (R)
Gant, Hance H. (R)

Gant, Joel H. (R)***
Gant, Stephen R. (R)
Gaston, Samuel B. (R)
Geimer, Simon (R)
Goodfellow, Samuel (R)
Gray, John (R)
Grover, Cornelius (R)
Hale, Banjamin V. (R)***
Hankins, Samuel W. (R)
Heider, William (D)
Hulse, Samuel (R)
Inman, Oliver P. (R)
Irons, Wallace (R)
Johnson, Abraham J. (R)
Johnson, John (R)
Johnson, Jonathan E. (R)***
Johnson, Thomas P. (R)***
Johnson, William F. (R)
Joslin, Thomas C. (R)
Ladow, Benjamin F. (D)
Martin, William W. (R)
McDonald, James (R)
McKelvy, James F. (R)
McKelvy, John S. (R)
McKelvy, John W. (R)
Moore, William H. (R)
Neal, James (R)
Norcross, Isaiah (R)
Norcross, Samuel V. (R)
Nutt, Henry W. (R)
Oakerson, John (R)
Osborne, Abram W. (R)
Osborne, Benjamin (R)
Parmer, James (S)
Penn, Samuel R. (R)
Phillips, Charles (T)
Polhemus, Herbert W. (R)***
Reynolds, Tylee (R)
Robinson, James H. (R)*
Rodgers, William H. (R)***
Roll, Charles W. (D)

Savage, Edwin W. (D)
Simpkins, Walker (D)
Simpson, James (D)
Spencer, Thomas (D)
Steelman, Andrew J. (R)
Street, John J. (R)***
Terry, David (D)
Tilton, Charles L. (R)
Tindle, Elihu (R)***

Tracy, Patrick (R)
Truax, William L. (R)
Vantilburg, John (R)**
Walter, Jacob (S)
Webb, Daniel (R)
Wilbur, Ivins (R)
Wirtz, Jacob (S)
Worth, Sydney (R)

Company E

ORIGINAL ENLISTEES

Captain
DeHart, Uriah
First Lieutenant
Abel, William H.
Second Lieutenant
Beach, Albert B.
First Sergeant
Goldsmith, James B.
Sergeants
Bonney, Charles F.
Coyte, Frederick G.
Hopper, Benjamin W.
King, Edo M.
Meyers, George
Wood, Robert
Corporals
Berdan, Richard J.
Fredenburg, Timothy G.
Hickman, James
June, Isaac
Keiler, Valentine
Monsch, John*
Senior, David J.
Suydam, Silas
Vorhees, Uriah D.
Wagoners
Crowell, Samuel S.
Raber, Henry

Bugler
Walmsley, Edward
Musicians
King, William H.
Tuttle, Edward C.
Privates
Ackerman, Jerry
Amerman, William P.
Breslin, Morris
Brown, John B.
Burris, Robert A.
Bush, Abraham A.
Carlough, John N.
Castmore, Samuel
Castmore, William
Cole, Alanson
Cole, Simon H.
Collins, Joseph
Cooper, George E.*
Cranmer, Isaac
Cummings, Lorenzo D.
Delaney, Tinton***
Dufford, Banjamin V.
Dunkerly, Enoch
Elmer, Joseph N.
Gilliam, George M.
Gilliam, Joseph M.
Gray, Hiram*
Havens, Horace

Hendershot, Obadiah
Hopper, Henry
Horner, William
Huff, John O.
Hufftellin, John D.
Hunt, Benjamin W.***
Inley, Orlando
Jennings, John D.
Johnson, Pierson
Johnson, William
Keefe, Daniel E.
Kent, James
Kimball, David
King, Michael
Lappin, Patrick
Lemons, William
Lenox, John H.
Love, George***
Lyons, John***
Lyons, Manning
Maxwell, Israel O.***
McClelland, James
Moore, William
Morrell, Isaac
Munson, William J.
Norman, William P.
Osborne, John H.
Pergdenkemper, Francis
Phillips, Henry H.
Post, Hulmuth
Post, Richard
Predmore, Theodore***
Prentiss, John
Prentiss, William
Ralfe, Jacob
Rankin, James
Reed, Alexander
Reed, William
Reid, William
Ries, Arthur
Riker, William B.

Rogers, Robert
Ross, Abraham H.
Rulay, Oscar J.
Ryerson, Cornelius
Sasson, Robert A.
Schilling, Ferdinand***
Sickles, James E.*
Simmons, George M.
Skill, John
Smith, Robert M.
Somers, William H.
Steelman, John B.
Stinard, James
Tierce, John
Tierce, Lucas***
Valentine, David
Van Etten, Joseph
Van Houten, Oscar
Van Riper, William T.
Van Schaick, Harry M.
Ward, Elias M.
Ward, Martin
Ware, Collins B.
Weaver, Ira
Westbrook, Daniel E.
Whitehead, Hampton*
Williams, James***
Winters, John

LATER ADDITIONS

Privates
   Ackerman, David D. (R)
   Alvord, Edward L. (R)
   Andrews, Henry (R)
   Applegate, Nathan S. (R)
   Banta, Charles G. (R)
   Barnes, Stephen A. (R)
   Bixby, Thomas (S)
   Bowen, Josiah E. (D)
   Brannan, William K. (S)
   Breslin, Morris (R)

Brooks, Abraham (R)
Brown, James (S)
Brown, James C. (S)
Brown, William J. (S)
Buckalew, Wesley (R)
Burke, John (S)
Burritt, Ely (R)
Burritt, John C. S. (R)
Butler, William (S)
Campbell, Henry (S)
Campbell, James (R)
Canar, William (S)
Cass, Richard (S)
Castmore, Charles R. (R)
Chapman, Thomas (S)
Clayhill, Henry (R)
Cody, Morris (S)
Cole, James H. (R)
Conrad, Lewis (R)
Decker, Andrew (R)
Dent, John (S)
Ellison, William (S)**
Emory, Aaron S. (R)
Emory, William (R)
Farley, Owen (S)
Feasler, Joseph (D)
Gillfeather, John (S)
Gordon, John C. (R)
Goss, Jacob (S)
Griffin, William (S)
Gunther, George (S)
Haling, Robert (S)
Haverty, John (S)
Hearon, Samuel (D)
Hewitt, Frank (R)
Higgins, Albert (S)
High, John (D)
Hines, Aaron P. (D)
Jenkins, Fayette (D)
Johnson, James (S)
Keefe, John (S)

Keisler, Jacob (R)
Keisler, Simpson (R)
Kenny, Peter (S)
Kerrigan, Patrick (S)
Kint, David (R)
Lee, George F. (S)
Lind, Adam (S)
Little, Joseph (R)
Lynch, Patrick (R)
Maines, William B. (R)
Marshall, Frederick (S)
Mather, William (S)
Morgan, David (R)
Morgan, John (R)
Murphy, Joseph (S)
Nan, Joseph (S)
Newhause, Charles (S)
Newman, Jacob (R)
Nichols, Henry (R)
Norfolk, Alexander (R)
O'Brien, James (S)
Owens, Thomas (S)
Parker, William (S)
Peterson, Elihu H. (D)
Pflum, John M. (S)
Pharo, Michael (D)
Plesch, Otto (S)
Politz, Edward (S)
Powers, Patrick (S)
Reed, Nathaniel (R)
Robbins, William (D)
Roberts, Richard (R)
Russell, Richard M. (R)
Sackville, Joseph (R)
Salifka, Otto (S)
Saville, John (S)
Sawyer, William (S)
Sayfried, John (S)
Scheick, Henry (S)
Schilling, Ferdinand (R)
Schnable, Otto (S)

Sheridan, John (R)
Sindle, John (R)
Slaven, James (S)
Sloan, Benjamin (D)
Small, Henry H. (R)
Smith, James F. (S)
Smith, John H. (S)
Smith, John P. (R)
Speer, Peter G. (R)

Steelman, Jonathan S. (D)
Street, Charles H. (S)
Taggart, William S. (R)
Van Gordon, Alexander M. (R)
Wagoner, Joseph (S)
Wainwright, Taylor (R)
Wallace, Charles D. (R)
Whitmore, Jacob (R)
Wolf, Joseph (R)

Company F

ORIGINAL ENLISTEES

Captain
Curlis, William B.
First Lieutenant
Thompson, Augustus
Second Lieutenant
Gibson, James W.
First Sergeant
Runyan, Morris C.
Sergeants
Burroughs, Clark N.
Evans, Amos H.
Sheppard, Lewis D.
Van Dewater, William L.
Corporals
Bailey, David S.
Benjamin, Frederick H.
Hopkins, Henry W.
Parker, William J.
Preston, Charles M.
Titus, George S.
Vandewater, Alexander
Van Nest, Henry V. D.
Wagoner
Scudder, Joseph P.
Musician
Wood, James
Privates
Acton, Edwin*

Aubick, Augustus
Auten, Abram M.
Bailey, Isaac P.
Baldwin, Ralph L.
Baner, James
Blackwell, Clayton E.
Blackwell, Isaac V. D.*
Blake, James
Blake, Samuel L.*
Blizzard, Franklin***
Boyle, Michael*
Brown, Aaron A.
Buckalew, Charles A.
Carlen, Edward
Chance, Edwin
Clark, John
Craig, John***
Cronce, Leonard F.
Cronce, Peter R.
Dalrymple, Jacob
Drost, Cornelius
Finan, James
Ford, Charles M.
French, John E.
Geary, Charles
Hall, George J.
Hall, Robert M.***
Harman, William*
Hellinger, Joseph

Hendershot, Obadiah
Hendershot, Philip
Hendershot, William
Hern, Thomas
Higgins, Barton
Housell, William H.***
Hughes, Simeon
Hurtt, Charles M.
Johnson, David
Johnson, Isaac**
Johnson, James
Kennedy, John***
Kitchen, John
Kline, William S.
Knowles, Joseph
Lanning, Henry B.
Larus, Watson S.
Leaming, Reuben H.
Lowe, Henry O.
Mailoff, James
McCready, David B.***
McGregor, John
McLarkin, Henry
McNeal, John
Metz, William M.
Mills, Samuel R.
Mitchell, Charles W.
Mitchell, James
Nelson, Harrison R.***
Nymaster, John D.*
Osborne, John***
Reading, Jonathan R.
Richman, Jonathan***
Sailor, Joseph
Salley, Benjamin Y.
Seals, Job*
Sheppard, Robert G.
Simpkins, Henry
Smith, John N.*
Smith, Jonathan
Smith, William G.

Sutphin, John V. M.
Suydam, Sydney B.
Suydam, William*
Thomas, Albert R.
Thompson, Joseph
Thompson, William J.
Tindall, John W.
Tooker, Theodore W.
Van Fleet, James O.
Van Syckle, John
Voit, Jacob
Vorhees, Hiram G.
Weaver, George V. H.
Webster, Samuel
Woodhull, Justus
Wright, Joseph

LATER ADDITIONS

Privates
Alkire, Samuel (R)
Bailey, Garrett T. (R)
Basch, Franz (R)
Benton, William (R)
Bierman, William (R)
Boyd, Charles (R)
Brestler, Frederick (R)
Buckalew, Wesley (R)***
Burns, Adam (D)
Cain, Bernard (R)
Carson, Samuel H. (R)
Clawson, Thomas J. (R)
Conover, George R. (R)
Cooley, Samuel (R)
Couchman, James (R)
Creed, William E. (R)
Cyphers, Philip (R)
Darling, Charles (R)
Deemer, Jefferson L. (R)***
Drost, John V. D. (R)
Everts, Hermann (R)
Fessol, Frederick (R)

Fitzgerald, Charles M. (R)
Gallagher, Hugh (R)
Gray, Matthew (R)
Hoagland, Asa P. (R)
Hough, Lewis S. (R)
Hulsizer, John W. (R)
Huth, Sebastian (D)
James, Thomas (R)
Kays, Oscar (R)
King, Robert (R)
Kitchen, Robert H. (R)
Koch, Jacob (D)
Lafont, Pierre (S)
Larue, Paul (S)
Leiseygang, Albert (D)
Lombart, Louis (S)
Lowe, John M. (R)
Lowe, Peter T. (R)***
McCausland, John A. (R)
McCormick, John (R)
Meir, William (D)
Morrison, Benjamin (R)
Mullniex, William (R)
Murat, Edward (S)
Nanman, Gustav (R)

Oldham, John (R)
Osborne, Lewis (R)
Quinse, Frederick (D)
Robertson, Henry H. (R)
Rooks, Jacob J. (R)
Sales, Thomas (R)*
Sargeant, Alexander (R)
Seeger, Adam (R)
Sheridan, John (S)
Smith, John (S)
Smith, Napoleon G. (R)***
Somet, Edwin H. (R)
Spangenberg, Alanson L. (R)
Steel, John (S)
Stewart, Edward C. (R)
Stryker, Andrew (R)
Sylvester, George (S)
Titus, Timothy (R)
Vanacker, William (R)
Veach, John P. (D)
Wakefield, Ralph (R)
Waters, Daniel (S)
Waters, John (S)
Whittaker, Jesse E. (D)
Williams, David (S)

Company G

ORIGINAL ENLISTEES

Captain
Ritter, John P.
First Lieutenant
Zimmerman, William
Second Lieutenant
Benton, William H.
First Sergeant
Hobart, Frederick
Sergeants
Brand, Frederick
Fatti, John H.
Hinds, Pulaski***

Meyer, Philip
Schnetzer, Joseph A.
Corporals
Beatty, Stephen
Beauman, Henry
Faczek, Charles A.
Garthwaite, Charles B.
Lauterback, Simon*
Peters, George
Raug, Antony***
Smith, William M.***
Tylee, George G.
Zimmerman, Charles

Wagoners
Agin, James H.
Murray, Samuel
Ward, Charles W.

Musicians
Muller, Johann***
Welch, Morris

Privates
Ash, George
Bopp, Jacob
Brondsteller, William
Brondsteller, William, Jr.
Byrne, Thomas
Commeford, Patrick*
Crowley, Thomas
Dickert, Adam
Dillon, Edward***
Dimler, David
Dolan, Michael*
Doty, Samuel R.
Downs, Patrick
Eckerson, Philip
Engle, Paul
Evans, Racey
Fitzpatrick, Thomas
Ford, Thomas
Fritz, John
Gaessler, Valentine
Godfrey, William
Hand, James
Happ, Henry
Keenan, Thomas
Knaben, Henry
Knapp, John
Kunkle, Michael
Lee, George
Lee, Patrick
Loetz, Henry*
Mahoney, Stephen
McBride, Patrick
McCandless, David

McCloskey, John
McCree, James
McGinn, Thomas
Moran, Patrick
Muller, Johann***
Mulvey, Timothy*
Newhoffer, Sebastian
Ott, Henry*
Rannard, John
Regenthall, William
Reidinger, Benjamin
Riley, Terence
Rosenbauer, Frederick
Rowe, Matthew
Saland, John P.
Sanders, Martin
Sauerbrunn, Jacob
Schardiam, Valentine
Scheller, Charles
Schmidt, Charles***
Schuldes, Joseph
Seidel, George
Simon, Samuel
Sloan, Robert J.*
Stiles, Amos B.
Stockman, Edward
Supple, Maurice
Terrell, William
Thiele, John
Vannest, Cornelius*
Wall, James
Ward, William
Waters, John J.***
Welsher, John***
Whitmore, Thomas
Whittemore, John
Williams, Victor
Wurst, Frederick
Zimmerman, William, Jr.

LATER ADDITIONS

Privates

Armstrong, William
Bauer, John (R)
Beck, Philip (R)***
Bemspacht, Michael (R)
Beri, Lewis (S)
Bieman, William (R)
Bierman, August (S)
Bolton, Levi (R)
Brook, Beaumont (R)
Chizzola, Achille (S)
Connolly, Mihael (R)
Conover, Jacob (R)
Corin, John J. (R)***
Corson, Joseph (D)
Coyle, Thomas (R)
Cutler, Charles (S)
Dalton, John (R)
Davis, Francis (S)
Dickey, Robert (R)
Dyer, Edward (R)
Ebert, Sebald (R)
Eckhardt, Henry (S)
Fahrer, Henry (S)
Fanorn, Henry (S)
Fessel, Frederick (R)
Frederick, William (R)
Frey, William (R)***
Gallagher, James (R)
Gardner, Amos H. (S)
Glaser, Frederick (S)
Graff, Peter (S)
Hamilton, James (S)
Hamlin, George (S)
Hegel, Paul (R)
Hill, Matthew (R)
Huber, Christian (R)*
Johnson, John (D)
Johnson, William H. (S)
Keinkerscht, Adolphus (D)

Kelly, Charles (R)
Kenley, Joseph (R)
Kennedy, Daniel (S)
Kerchgesner, Leopold (S)
King, James (S)
Kline, Jacob (R)
Knapp, Jon (R)
Kratz, Jacob (S)
Lanahan, William (S)
Lang, Albert (D)
Lang, Charles (S)
Lang, John (S)
Ludwig, Ludwig (R)
Manderville, James (R)
McCarty, John (S)
McDonald, John (R)
McJohn, Edward (R)
McMullin, James (R)
Michon, Alfred (S)
Miller, Jacob (R)
Moore, Joseph C. (D)
Morgan, Henry (S)
Muller, John (S)(
Newschafer, George (S)
Oliver, Edward (R)
Peach, Frederick G. (R)*
Raymond, John A. (R)
Reuss, Leopold (D)
Rhubart, George (D)
Rien, Lorenze (S)
Riley, James (S)
Ritchie, Valentine (S)
Sayre, James F. (R)
Scanlin, John (R)
Schafer, John (R)
Scheimer, George (D)
Schiller, Francis (S)
Schoen, John (R)
Seeger, Adam (R)
Shields, Michael (R)
Siebert, John (R)

Skunk, Jacob (D)
Smith, George (R)
Smith, George (S)
Sonst, Philip (S)
Sponheimer, Philip (R)
Struble, John H. (D)
Stubner, Theodore (R)
Terrell, Theodore (R)
Treen, John M. (R)

Violet, Lewis (S)
Weisler, Andrew (S)
Wentz, John (R)
Williams, James H. (R)
Wilson, Charles (R)
Wurgler, Rudolph (S)
Yaeder, James (R)
Zurfall, Augustus (R)

Company H

ORIGINAL ENLISTEES

Captain
Henry, Joseph J.*
First Lieutenant
Stewart, James, Jr.
Second Lieutenant
Lawrence, Joseph B.*
First Sergeant
McCue, Francis M.
Sergeants
Armstrong, Austin E.*
Carrell, Edward S.*
Hawk, Jacob L.
Littell, Cornelius P.
Corporals
Boyd, Augustus
Buckley, Samuel S.
Creveling, John W.
Duncan, Alfred L.
Hamilton, Lycidias
Matthews, John E.
Phillips, Robert R.***
Pullen, Edward S.
Shoemaker, Daniel W.
Wagoner
Dickey, John
Musicians
Houck, Allen G.
Miers, Isaac M.

Privates
Alstron, Charles
Ammick, Jacob
Aumick, John L.
Barrigan, James
Bean, Peter B.
Brown, John*
Brown, Samuel***
Burns, Thomas
Butler, John F.
Cahill, Patrick
Callahan, Timothy*
Clarke, William W.
Clayton, Edward
Comer, Wesley
Cook, Harvey
Cook, John E.***
Cooley, Elisha
Cooper, Thomas
Cramer, Nelson***
De Forest, Ammadee***
Decker, William H.
Devoe, Frederick M.
Donnelly, Francis
Donnelly, John
Duncan, Daniel L.
Durand, Joseph
Edmonds, John
Fiske, Marcus M.

Forgus, William***
Gillis, Frederick
Hadley, Jacob
Hagerman, Spencer A.***
Haggerty, Isaac W.
Hallowell, Daniel*
Harrison, Jeremiah
Hartzell, Benjamin
Higgins, Michael
Hirt, John*
Hoffman, James
Howell, Marshall
Hubbs, George
Johnson, David S.
Johnson, William H.
Ketcham, William G.
Levers, Charles P.
Levers, William
Loftus, John, Jr.
Lott, Augustus
McGraw, Jeremiah
Meyer, Jacob
Miller, George W.
Miller, John***
Moore, John
Osborne, John V.***
Parker, George W.
Phillips, Mulford B.***
Pittinger, Henry
Powers, Henry C.
Reichard, Harrison
Ribble, George F.
Scanlan, Morris
Schaeffer, John F.
Scofield, Edward
Shipman, Samuel Y.
Smith, John G.
Staples, Andrew D.***
Stout, George A.
Sutphin, John F.
Sylvester, Reuben F.
Taylor, George W.

Taylor, John F.
Van Gordon, Abraham
Van Gordon, Malifor***
Van Gordon, William
Van Norman, John B.
Vancampen, Jacob S.
Ward, William H.
Warner, Joseph***
Wilgus, Joseph R.
Witherill, Jeffrey W.
Wolverton, Charles A.
Worthington, Elijah
Worthington, Samuel
Yeomans, Jacob L.

LATER ADDITIONS

Privates
Barnes, Thomas (R)
Barron, Charles T. (R)
Barron, Tilghman A. (R)
Barron, William P. (R)***
Becht, John (D)
Beck, Henry (S)
Bosenbury, Joseph (R)
Burns, Thomas (R)
Butler, Edward (R)
Cannon, James (R)
Cartright, Samuel (R)
Cole, Samuel W. (R)
Cortwright, George (R)
Cougle, James (R)
Courtright, Thomas G. (R)
Crossman, William H. (R)
Daws, John (R)
Decker, George M. (R)
Deyer, Charles (D)
Dickson, George B. (R)*
Emory, Aaron S. (R)
Emory, William (R)
Fisher, Joseph (R)
Frank, John (S)
Garris, Jason (R)

Garrison, Philip S. (R)
Gilbeck, John (D)
Hardy, Thomas B. (R)
Hart, John F. (S)
Hummer, William (R)
Hussey, Michael (R)
Idesson, William (R)
Keenan, Henry F. (R)
King, George (R)
King, John H. (R)
Klapproth, Charles (R)
Koch, George (R)
Little, Andrew W. (R)
Losey, Casper (R)
Losey, Henry (R)***
Losey, Joseph (R)***
Matthews, James F. (R)
McCush, Robert (S)
McGhie, James (R)
Moore, William (R)
Muller, John (R)
Norton, Joseph (R)
Ozenbaugh, Jacob (R)
Poulmore, Pierson V. (R)
Ribble, Conrad (R)***
Ribble, George F. (R)
Rodenbough, Irvin (R)

Ryno, Henry C. (R)
Shipman, Samuel Y. (R)
Shuller, Andrew J. (R)
Smalley, Edward (R)
Smith, Jerome (R)
Snover, Zebedee (R)
Spangenberg, Andrew G. (R)
Speakman, William (R)
Surrey, William (R)
Terrell, Daniel H. (R)
Tinsman, Sylvester J. (R)
Valentine, Abraham H. (R)
Van Gordon, Amos J. (R)
Van Gordon, Jacob A. (R)
Van Gordon, James (R)
Van Gordon, Jonas S. (R)
Van Gordon, Mahlon (R)***
Vanaman, Charles (R)
Warford, William (R)
Warman, William H. H. (R)
Weaver, Richard (R)
Welsted, Edward W. (R)
Wheeler, George F. (R)
Wilson, James (R)
Winter, William O. (R)***
Woodruff, James (R)
Zane, Isaac B. (R)

Company I

ORIGINAL ENLISTEES

Captain
Chew, Henry F.
First Lieutenant
Hufty, Samuel
Second Lieutenant
Pinkard, Charles M.
First Sergeant
Swain, Robert D.
Sergeants
Bilderback, Smith

Bowker, Joseph C.
Harbison, Samuel B.
Mattson, Edward D.
Springer, C. Bayard***
Corporals
Birch, William P.
Goodwin, Charles P.
Kille, David
Lorch, Charles G.
Miller, John
Schweible, John

Shull, Jonathan
Tash, James W.
Whitney, Daniel
Wagoner
Tonkin, William H.
Bugler
Alcorn, Robert
Musician
Craig, Robert P.
Privates
Anderson, Joshua
Bennett, John
Brady, John
Bramble, Hugh
Brown, Charles***
Carney, Mark L.
Cawman, Albert C.
Clark, James V.
Cordrey, Enoch
Corliss, William F.
Daniels, James W.
Davis, Edward H.
Davis, William B.*
Eifert, Henry
Elkinton, James M.
Felney, Frederick
Gill, Benjamin
Green, Edward H.
Haines, Joshua D.
Hampton, John S.
Hanley, Andrew J.***
Harbert, Asa K.
Harbison, John W.
Hartline, William G.***
Hartranft, Henry A.
Harvey, John H.
Hepburn, Magnus***
Hilyard, Jolin W.
Hoffman, Charles*
Ireland, Richmond
Johnson, John E.*

Kauffman, Andrew
Keene, Charles
Kiger, Thomas H.
Layman, Samuel M.
Lester, Samuel
Loper, Henry
Loper, William B.
Lott, George H.
Lumis, Thomas W.
Matlock, Edward L.
Mattson, James P.
McGinn, Thomas***
Messick, Charles B.
Mickel, Lewis S.
Mifflin, Albert C.
Miller, Charles H.***
Mosure, Stephen M.*
Mulford, Charles D.
Murphy, Lewis
Newkirk, John
Nonamaker, William H.
Oatanger, Christian
Parsons, Thomas
Patton, John A.
Pittman, Reuben R.
Powell, John
Reeves, Isaac
Remming, Augustus*
Ross, Jacob
Segraves, Reuben***
Shepherd, Charles
Smith, John C.
Sparks, John***
Sparks, William C.
Stauleup, Samuel F.*
Taylor, Charles
Taylor, John E.
Taylor, Samuel B.
Townsend, George W.
Turnbull, George L.
Vanculen, Aaron***

Vining, Smith H.
Warfle, John
Wensell, David
Wensell, Josiah*
West, Joseph
White, George G.***
Williams, William
Zanes, Isaac***

LATER ADDITIONS

Privates

Albertson, Charles (R)
Babser, Frederick (R)
Ballinger, Joshua (R)
Beckett, Hiram B. (R)
Blackman, Malachi (R)
Butcher, Samuel T. (R)
Clark, John M. (R)***
Davis, George O. (R)
Davis, John M. (R)
Dickinson, Abram M. (R)
Dilmore, Benjamin H. (R)
Essex, Harry (R)
Estilow, Benjamin (R)
Evans, George B.
Fagan, Bernard (R)
Fagan, Francis (R)
Fannin, Thomas (R)
Floyd, William (R)
Gorman, John (R)
Grady, Thomas (R)
Graham, James (R)
Green, Robert (R)
Gumpert, Max (R)
Harper, William A. (R)
Harris, James J. (R)
Harris, William H. (R)
Hawthorn, James A. (R)
Hughes, William H. (R)***
Irelan, Enoch (R)
Kearley, Charles (R)

Kelcher, Daniel (R)
Kingston, John (R)
Madara, Eziekel (R)
Madara, Joseph (R)
Mailey, Frank E. (R)
Matlock, George W. (R)
McClay, James (R)
McDonald, John (R)
McDonald, Robert (R)
McFerrin, Henry (R)
Metzler, John (R)
Miller, August (R)
Miller, David T. (R)
Mitchell, John B. (R)
Myers, Daniel (R)
Newkirk, George M. (R)
Noll, August (R)
O'Neil, James (R)
Park, Stephen C. (R)
Parr, Daniel (R)*
Perkins, Samuel (R)
Pierce, Eli B. (R)
Schnabel, Charles (R)
Schroeder, Henry (S)
Shoemaker, Arthur F. (R)
Singwald, Francis H. (D)
Somers, James W. (R)
Strawn, Francis E. (R)
Stretch, William B. (R)
Strickland, Amos (R)
Sullivan, Eugene (R)
Thompson, William (R)
Van Gordon, James J. (R)
Warford, William (R)
Wax, Paul (R)
Webster, George L. (R)
Weitzell, Conrad (R)
Welch, John (R)
Woolbert, Edward S. (R)

Company K

Captain
Drake, Elias J.
First Lieutenant
Boudinot, William B. S.
Second Lieutenant
Townley, Jonathan
First Sergeant
Moffat, Edward S.
Sergeants
Drake, J. Madison
Hankins, Eleazer
Price, John E.
Wright, Joseph
Corporals
Bryant, George L.
Dilkes, Samuel J.
Dupue, Levi*
Good, John H.
Green, James W.
Lorence, John
Stearns, Joseph Q.
Wagoner
Lemon, John R.
Musician
Bell, John
Privates
Anderson, John
Ashley, William
Atchison, Moses
Ayres, Ezra F.
Babcock, William O.
Baldwin, Edward
Bellis, Henry W.
Berry, Alexander H.
Billings, Charles M.
Brown, James H.
Bural, Jonathan A.
Cadmus, Aaron S.

Campbell, Lewis
Carrigan, James
Chester, Reuben
Clark, Allen
Condelly, Edward
Conroy, John
Cook, Henry
Cook, James
Craig, Edmund T.
Crane, Stephen W.
Crowell, Jeremiah
Davis, Joseph H.
Davison, Luke
Decker, Jeremiah C.
Delaney, Thomas
Denman, Theodore***
Derbrow, John J.
Doran, Joseph
Doran, William J.
Ewing, Joseph F.
Fisher, Isaac*
Ford, William F.
Freeman, Thomas
Gafney, Andrew J.
Hale, Edward C.
Hamler, Abner
Hamler, James E.
Hankins, George S.
Hicks, Adam
Higgins, David S. C.
Hillyer, John E.
Hinton, Charles
Hoover, Absalom
Houghtaling, Henry
Huey, Isaac
Hughes, Robert
Hull, Benjamin
Knapp, William R.
Levy, William P.

MacQuaide, Thomas
Marshall, William D.
McCormick, Thomas
Moran, Edward
Parkhurst, John S.***
Purcell, Henry P.***
Randolph, Phineas
Ranear, John
Reeves, Jarvis
Robart, Vincent
Ross, Delaney M.
Ross, William H.
Shreve, Alexander***
Skillman, John G.
Smith, George H.*
Southard, William H.
Space, Henry***
Swain, Edward M.
Teates, George W.
Terrell, Samuel N.
Tonkin, George W.
Townley, Moses E.***
Van Arsdale, William H.
Ward, John
Watkins, Joseph S.
Weder, John*
Williams, Charles A.
Williams, Robert S.
Winans, Elias C.
Woolery, Jerome W.

LATER ADDITIONS

Privates
Anglo, Charles P. (R)
Ash, George W. (R)
Baker, John (S)
Bankson, Bernard (S)
Becker, August (S)
Bennett, William (R)
Bowers, Paul (R)
Brown, Charles (R)

Brown, Charles M. (R)
Brown, Henry L. (R)
Bryant, John J. (R)
Cass, Matthias (S)
Castlow, Bernard (R)
Ceasar, Christian (D)
Chew, William (R)
Cleveland, Edmund J. (R)
Cliff, John L. (R)
Colfer, James (R)
Condelly, Patrick (R)
Corcoran, John (S)
Covert, Louces C. (R)
Coyle, Michael (R)
Crist, John P. (R)
Davis, Joseph H. (R)
Davis, Luther (R)***
Dawson, John E. (R)
Delaney, John (R)
Devine, Isaac N. (D)
Fairbrother, John (S)
Dobbs, Joseph P. (R)
Doughty, Benjamin F. (R)
Douglass, Robert J. (R)
English, Henry B. (R)
English, Samuel W. (R)
Farron, John (S)
Force, Sobieski (D)
Forsyth, George (R)
Foster, Elvy (R)***
Franck, Emil (R)
Frank, Albert (S)
Fredericks, David (R)
Fredericks, Henry (R)***
Garrabrant, Andrew (D)
Giles, David S. (R)
Graham, Robert (R)
Hamler, William H. (R)
Harbert, David S. (D)
Harrison, James (S)
Hatfield, Ira, Jr. (R)

Herning, John (R)
Hinton, Thomas W. (R)
Hoffman, Charles (S)
Hoffman, John J. (R)
Holston, John M. (R)
Horton, William (S)
Hubert, Joseph C. (R)
Jackson, John R. (R)
Johnson, William M. (R)
Kane, John (S)
Kavanaugh, James (R)
Keene, George W. (R)
Kell, Nathan (R)
Kellum, Josiah (R)
Kneller, Frederick (R)
Kniller, William (R)
Lawrence, John (S)
Ledden, Nathan D. (R)
Ledden, Samuel (R)
Lidgett, James (R)***
Little, Isaac (R)
Longtin, Tenerel (S)
Longtin, Zotique (S)
Lutz, Joel E. (R)
Major, Timothy (R)
Malone, Peter (D)
Maloy, James (R)
Matthews, Thomas (R)
Maxwell, Henry (R)
McCarty, William (S)
McIlvaine, William (R)
McLaughlin, William (R)
Minnis, Robert (S)
Morris, William J. (S)
Murray, John (R)
Murray, Thomas (R)
Nelson, James H. C. (R)
Newbern, William H. (R)***
Park, William L. (S)
Parker, John (R)
Parker, Richard (R)

Peacock, John (R)
Peer, Tunis (R)***
Pettit, John (R)
Quinn, James (R)
Rame, Ferdinand (S)
Reed, David (R)
Reinhart, George A. (R)
Reitz, Francis (D)
Rice, James H. (S)
Ricketts, John W. (R)
Schneider, Frederick (S)
Seaman, Lansing (R)
Shields, George (R)
Simmerman, Abram (R)
Simmonds, John (R)***
Smith, David R. (R)
Smith, James (S)
Smith, James H. (R)
Smith, John (R)
Souders, George (R)
Stalford, William F. (R)
Sucke, Wenzell (S)
Sullivan, Francis (R)
Sweeney, Michael (R)
Thomas, Edwin W. (R)
Townley, George R. (R)
Trumbull, John (R)***
Vannaman, William (R)
Vaughn, John (S)
Von Cloedt, Julius (S)
Walker, George (S)
Weiss, Adolph (S)
Wellbrook, Henry (S)
Wescott, Daniel (R)
Whitney, George W. (R)
Williams, William (S)
Wilson, Charles (S)
Wilson, Cummings H. (R)

Company L

[Disbanded; enlisted men transferred to other companies, November 18, 1862]

ORIGINAL ENLISTEES

Captain
Erb, Charles H.
First Lieutenant
Heinold, Henry M.
Second Lieutenant
Adler, Francis A.
First Sergeant
Muller, John
Sergeants
Chiwitz, Axel
Mathes, Henry
Moll, Anton C.
Weinrich, Adam
Corporals
Binder, Gustav
Ebert, Philip
Hurnburg, Christian
Kraft, Conrad
Miller, John
Walker, John
Zorn, Edward***
Wagoner
Geroe, Daniel B.
Musician
Beyer, John
Privates
Barrett, John F.
Barrett, Joseph
Bauer, Andreas***
Benner, George
Bertrand, Albert
Bettinger, Jacob
Bettinger, John
Boucher, Henry
Brem, Frederick
Burgard, Daniel

Chiwitz, Axel***
Deishler, John
Dreher, August
Eckert, Leo***
Eier, Daniel
Ensle, Henry*
Frank, Anton
Graff, Christian
Green, Charles***
Hagel, Andreas
Hoffman, George
Hoyer, Gottleib
Jurgens, Martin
Kaiser, Charles
Kaiser, John
Karl, Michael A.***
Kirchguessner, Peter
Klaproth, Charles
Kuhn, Rudolph
Lauer, Sebastian
Lowe, Augustus
Meyers, John***
Moll, Christian
Muller, John
Nast, Rudolph
Neycomer, Conrad R.
Oberst, Charles
Pratsh, Thomas
Rink, John
Rothenholfer, George
Schmidt, Jacob
Schieck, Jacob
Schmidt, Philip
Schmitz, Joseph
Schwartz, John
Schweibel, John
Steiberts, Herman

Tenetus, Herman
Walters, Henry
Weber, Frederick
Weiser, Frederick
Wellendorf, Christian
Wirth, John

LATER ADDITIONS

Privates
Baden, Charles (R)
Brien, David (R)
Buck, John (R)
Dean, Ludwick (R)
Heilmann, John G. (R)

Heller, John (R)
Koenig, Albert (R)
Koenig, William (R)
Kramer, John (R)
Matzinger, John (R)
Merz, John (R)***
Ostertag, John (R)
Schaffer, Berghard (R)
Scherf, Ludwick A.
Scholz, Henry (R)
Stoll, Leonard (R)
Werner, Herman (R)
Yeager, Benjamin (R)

Company M

[Redesignated Company A, November 18, 1862]

ORIGINAL ENLISTEES

Captain
McChesney, Joseph M.
First Lieutenant
Smith, Thomas J.
Second Lieutenant
First Sergeant
Cause, Andrew, Jr.
Sergeants
Applegate, Arunah D.
Appleget, Thomas B.
Conover, Charles W.
Davies, John M.
Edwards, Albert
Corporals
Baricklow, Nelson
Bonham, Lucius C.
Burke, Thomas C.
Clayton, David C.
DeCamp, Mahlon
McDougal, John E.
Messeroll, Charles

Mount, John G.
Stillwell, Symmes H.
Wood, Reuben V. P.
Wagoner
Hoagland, Cornelius B.
Buglers
Albert, John*
Cox, Samuel F.
Musician
Hinton, William
Privates
Appleget, John
Arlow, Robert
Babst, Michael***
Barrett, John F.
Bauer, Andreas***
Baylis, Elias
Bendy, William H.
Brown, Samuel E.
Buckley, Nathan
Clayton, William***
Clevinger, Edward

Conover, Leonard
Cook, James
Cox, James
DeHart, David
Dobbs, Joseph P.
Dreher, August***
Dugan, Thomas***
Dunn, Andrew B.
Dunomore, James
Eldridge, Thomas S.
Evers, James
Flower, Charles
Garry, John
Giles, Enoch
Giles, John H.
Grover, Joseph
Haines, Charles G.
Hamilton, James
Handell, Michael
Harris, William
Hoagland, Calvin
Hubner, Charles
Hulfish, Caleb*
Hunt, William A.
Ingling, Ridgway S.*
Ives, Milton J.
Jackson, Thomas A.
Jones, Peter
Knoll, Herman***
Kuhn, Rudolph***
Leer, John
Macker, Francis*
Matthews, James
McElwee, Daniel
McGintay, Michael
McLarren, Thomas*
Messeroll, Isaac B.
Messeroll, Williamson
Morris, Michael
Muddell, Trayton
Muller, Charles

Muller, John
Mulligan, John
Nolan, John A.
Nulty, Bernard
Obert, Frederick
Perrine, Alfred***
Perrine, George
Perrine, Spafford***
Perrine, Thomas
Petty, Charles
Plondke, Julius
Qigley, Daniel A.
Reamer, John*
Rieger, Joseph*
Rolfe, George N.
Roxberry, Joseph
Rudolph, Augustus
Schmalstick, Charles***
Scholl, Frederick
Scully, John*
Selby, Richard
Shortell, Edward***
Slover, Abram
Slover, Stephen
Smith, Amzi W.
Smith, Jasper S.
Snediker, Howard
Snediker, Richard
Stout, William R.
Stults, Simeon
Stussy, Jacob
Trilk, Henry***
Van Nortwick, Nicholas
Vandewater, James
Vannise, Andrew M.
Vannote, Bartine
Voigt, Christian
Vorhees, John D.
Wade, William S.
Webb, William W.*
Wessels, Jacob H.

Williams, William H.
Witcraft, John
Zink, Henry

LATER ADDITIONS

Privates
  Bader, John (R)***
  Biehl, Ernest (R)

Heilman, John G. (R)***
Hopp, John (R)
Johnson, Thomas (R)
Marsh, George (R)*
Probst, Lewis (R)
Smith, George A. (R)
Stults, Salter S. (R)***

Regimental Band

[Mustered out, August 1862]

Band Leader
  Gahm, Peter
Bandsmen
  Gahm, John
  Gahm, George
  Konstenstatter, Godfried
  Lavere, Benjamin

Mohler, John
Saxon, William
Searing, Albert
Starner, Peter L.
Yaicht, John
Yost, Jacob

NOTES

INTRODUCTION

1. The two histories are: Hermann Everts, *A Complete and Comprehensive History of the Ninth Regiment New Jersey Vols. Infantry, from Its First Organization to Its Final Muster Out* (Newark NJ: A. Stephen Holbrook, 1865); and Lt. J. Madison Drake, *The History of the Ninth New Jersey Veteran Vols.: A Record of Its Service from Sept. 13th, 1861, to July 12th, 1865, with a Complete Official Roster, and Sketches of Prominent Members, with Anecdotes, Incidents and Thrilling Reminiscences* (Elizabeth NJ: Journal Printing House, 1889).
2. *Jersey City Daily Standard*, Mar. 2, 1863; *Newark Daily Journal*, Feb. 27, 1863.
3. Bilby and Goble, *"Remember You Are Jerseymen!,"* 161.
4. Barrett, *Civil War in North Carolina*, vii.

1. ATTENTION RIFLEMEN!

1. Richards, "Belvidere's Brief Secession"; Richards, "April 1861: First Call to Arms."
2. Wright, *Secession Movement in the Middle Atlantic States*, 114, 118, 122.
3. Wright, *Secession Movement in the Middle Atlantic States*, 106–8; Gillette, *Jersey Blue*, 58–60; Knapp, *New Jersey Politics*, 36.
4. Gillette, *Jersey Blue*, 1–7, 134–36; Wright, *Secession Movement in the Middle Atlantic States*, 98–101, 121–23; Knapp, *New Jersey Politics*, 3–7; Fleming, *New Jersey*, 115–16; Cunningham, *New Jersey*, 172–73, 188; Siegel, *For the Glory of the Union*, 15.
5. *War of the Rebellion: Official Records of the Union and Confederate Armies* [hereafter cited as OR], ser. 3, 1:67–68; Bilby and Goble, *"Remember You Are Jerseymen!,"* 3–5.
6. Longacre, *Early Morning of War*, 445.
7. OR, ser. 3, 1:365; Bilby and Goble, *"Remember You Are Jerseymen!,"* 6–7.
8. Bilby and Goble, *"Remember You Are Jerseymen!,"* 7; Stryker, *Record of Officers and Men of New Jersey*, 1:430.

9. *Newark Daily Mercury*, Aug. 20, 1861; Bilby and Goble, "Remember You Are Jerseymen!," 137, 204n; Stevens, *Berdan's United States Sharpshooters*, 1–5.

10. Scranton, *Attention Riflemen! . . . to Form a Company of Sharp Shooters* [broadside, Sept. 17, 1861]; Bilby and Goble, "Remember You Are Jerseymen!," 137; Charles M. Herbert to James S. Nevius, Sept. 17, 1861, Nevius Papers, Rutgers University Libraries; *Newark Daily Mercury*, Sept. 28, Oct. 8, 1861; *Newark Daily Advertiser*, Nov. 16, 1861; Stryker, *Record of Officers and Men of New Jersey*, 1:477.

11. Drake, *Ninth New Jersey*, 8, 10; Boa, "New Jersey Marksmen," 5. For information about the Ninth's training rendezvous see Seliga, *Search for Camp Olden*.

12. Drake, *Ninth New Jersey*, 8; Stryker, *Record of Officers and Men of New Jersey*, 1:430, 432.

13. Drake, *Ninth New Jersey*, 375–78; Everts, *Ninth New Jersey*, 132–35; *State Gazette and Republican* (Trenton NJ), Mar. 21, 1862; *Germantown* [PA] *Telegraph*, Jan. 18, 1896; Heitman, *Historical Record and Dictionary*, 1:519; Jackson, *New Jerseyans in the Civil War*, 84; Warner, *Generals in Blue*, 226–27.

14. Drake, *Ninth New Jersey*, 8–9.

15. Drake, *Ninth New Jersey*, 11, 374–75; Foster, *New Jersey and the Rebellion*, 206–7; *New Jersey Journal* (Elizabeth NJ), Nov. 19, 1861.

16. Stryker, *Record of Officers and Men of New Jersey*, 1:430; *Hunterdon County Democrat* (Flemington NJ), Dec. 11, 1861, Feb. 28, 1862; *State Gazette and Republican*, Feb. 14, 21, 1862.

17. Drake, *Ninth New Jersey*, 378–79; Everts, *Ninth New Jersey*, 110–15; Foster, *New Jersey and the Rebellion*, 264; *Memorial of Colonel Abram Zabriskie*, 6.

18. Charles Scranton to Joseph Thompson, Sept. 30, 1861, Thompson Papers, Rutgers University Libraries.

19. *New Jersey Journal*, Nov. 12, 1861; David C. Hankins to "Dear Sister," Oct. 14, 1861, Sarah Hankins Papers, Burlington County Historical Society. All soldiers' letters cited in this work are presented verbatim with two exceptions: the addition of essential punctuation and the standardizing of capitalization.

20. Symmes H. Stillwell to "Dear Mother," Nov. 5, 1861, Stillwell Papers, Princeton University Library. For more on that ubiquitous bread ration see "Hard to Swallow: A Brief History of Hardtack and Ship's Biscuit."

21. *Camden Democrat*, Oct. 19, 1861. For a good overview of the subject see Lord, *Civil War Sutlers and Their Wares*.

22. Drake, *Ninth New Jersey*, 336; *State Gazette and Republican*, July 19, 1865; *Report of Quartermaster General for 1862*, 44.

23. Drake, *Ninth New Jersey*, 12–13; *Belvidere Intelligencer*, Nov. 16, 1861.

24. Drake, *Ninth New Jersey*, 11; *Belvidere Intelligencer*, Dec. 6, 1861.

25. Drake, *Ninth New Jersey*, 13.

26. Drake, *Ninth New Jersey*, 11; *Princeton Standard*, Nov. 22, 1861; *Newark Daily Advertiser*, Dec. 2, 1861; William B. Curlis to Joseph Thompson, July 18, 1866, Thompson Papers.

27. *Somerset Messenger* (Somerville NJ), Oct. 10, 1861; *OR*, ser. 3, 1:592, 607.

28. Drake, *Ninth New Jersey*, 9–10; Bilby and Goble, *"Remember You Are Jerseymen!,"* 137; Bilby, *Civil War Firearms*, 15–22, 55.

29. *New Jersey Journal*, Nov. 12, 19, 1861; *State Gazette and Republican*, Nov. 15, 1861.

30. Bilby, *Civil War Firearms*, 55, 84; Drake, *Ninth New Jersey*, 10; Boa, "New Jersey Marksmen," 5.

31. *Newark Daily Mercury*, Oct. 7, 1861; Drake, *Ninth New Jersey*, 9; Symmes H. Stillwell to "Dear Mother," Oct. 13, 1861; *State Gazette and Republican*, Oct. 25, 1861.

32. Drake, *Ninth New Jersey*, 10.

33. Drake, *Ninth New Jersey*, 12–13; *New Jersey Journal*, Nov. 19, 1861.

34. *State Gazette and Republican*, Nov. 21, 1861.

35. Drake, *Ninth New Jersey*, 11–12; *Somerset Messenger*, Dec. 5, 1861.

36. Stryker, *Record of Officers and Men of New Jersey*, 1:430; Everts, *Ninth New Jersey*, 72; Drake, *Ninth New Jersey*, 13; *Hunterdon County Democrat*, Dec. 11, 1861; *Hunterdon Republican* (Flemington NJ), Dec. 13, 1861.

37. Drake, *Ninth New Jersey*, 13–14.

2. DOWN TO THE SEA IN TROOPSHIPS

1. David C. Hankins to "Dear Sister," Dec. 11, 1861; Drake, *Ninth New Jersey*, 14.

2. *Belvidere Intelligencer*, Dec. 13, 1861. For more on this soldiers' rest see Moore, *History of the Cooper Shop*.

3. Drake, *Ninth New Jersey*, 14; Edmund J. Cleveland diary, Mar. 15, 1864, Cleveland Papers, New Jersey Historical Society; *Belvidere Intelligencer*, Dec. 13, 1861.

4. Drake, *Ninth New Jersey*, 15. For details of the April 1861 incident see Emory, "Baltimore Riots."

5. *Belvidere Intelligencer*, Dec. 13, 1861.

6. Drake, *Ninth New Jersey*, 15-16; Jeffrey, Pension Claim, Feb. 2, 1883.

7. Stryker, *Record of Officers and Men of New Jersey*, 1:230; Drake, *Ninth New Jersey*, 376.

8. Everts, *Ninth New Jersey*, 72; Drake, *Ninth New Jersey*, 16–17.

9. Drake, *Ninth New Jersey*, 16; McWhiney and Jamieson, *Attack and Die*, 54–56.

10. Drake, *Ninth New Jersey*, 17; David C. Hankins to "Dear Sister," Dec. 22, 1861.

11. *Newark Daily Advertiser*, Jan. 15, 1862; Albert R. Thomas to Joseph Thompson, Dec. 9, 1861, Thompson Papers; *Princeton Standard*, Dec. 27, 1861. Drake, *Ninth*

New Jersey, 17–18, probably based on Everts, *Ninth New Jersey*, 72, dates the review as December 14. Sauers, *"Succession of Honorable Victories,"* 108, has it taking place on the seventeenth. However, Marvel, *Burnside*, 39, claims that on the seventeenth the general was still en route to Washington by train.

12. Drake, *Ninth New Jersey*, 17–18.

13. Drake, *Ninth New Jersey*, 17–18; *Hunterdon Republican*, Jan. 10, 1862; Marvel, *Burnside*, 32–33, 37–39; Sauers, *"Succession of Honorable Victories,"* 39–43, 50–59, 108.

14. Drake, *Ninth New Jersey*, 16–18; *State Gazette and Republican*, Dec. 20, 1861; *Princeton Standard*, Dec. 27, 1861; David C. Hankins to "Dear Sister," Dec. 22, 1861.

15. Everts, *Ninth New Jersey*, 72; Drake, *Ninth New Jersey*, 18.

16. David C. Hankins to "Dear Sister," Dec. 22, 1861.

17. James G. Van Fleet to "Dear Brother," Jan. 4, 1862, Van Fleet Papers, Rutgers University Libraries; Zachariah Hankins to "Dear Cousin," Jan. 15, 1862; John D. Nymaster to "Mrs T[h]om[p]son," Dec. 29, 1861, Thompson Papers.

18. Everts, *Ninth New Jersey*, 183; Drake, *Ninth New Jersey*, 10, 308; *State Gazette and Republican*, July 19, 1865.

19. Drake, *Ninth New Jersey*, 19–20.

20. Drake, *Ninth New Jersey*, 19–20; John D. Nymaster to "Mrs T[h]om[p]son," Dec. 29, 1861.

21. Drake, *Ninth New Jersey*, 21; Stryker, *Record of Officers and Men of New Jersey*, 1:431; *Newark Daily Journal*, Apr. 18, 1864; *State Gazette and Republican*, Apr. 21, 1864. Information on Pvt. Hoyer from *Sentinel of Freedom* (Newark NJ), Apr. 12, 1864, and courtesy of his descendant, Philip Koether of New York City.

22. Drake, *Ninth New Jersey*, 21; Henry Cook diary, Jan. 1, 1862, Gilder Lehrman Institute; C. Bayard Springer diary, Jan. 1, 1862, Southern Historical Collection, University of North Carolina at Chapel Hill.

23. Henry Cook diary, Jan. 2–3, 1861; James G. Van Fleet to "Dear Brother," Jan. 4, 1862.

24. Everts, *Ninth New Jersey*, 72; Drake, *Ninth New Jersey*, 21; Warner, *Generals in Blue*, 394–95. Reno's life and career are detailed in McConnell, *Remember Reno*.

25. Marvel, *Burnside*, 32–34; Sauers, *"A Succession of Honorable Victories,"* 17–20, 39–40, 43–45.

26. Everts, *Ninth New Jersey*, 72; Drake, *Ninth New Jersey*, 22–23; Foster, *New Jersey and the Rebellion*, 204; Henry Cook diary, Jan. 4–5, 1862; C. Bayard Springer diary, Jan. 5, 1862; *Newark Daily Advertiser*, Jan. 15, 1862.

27. Sauers, *"A Succession of Honorable Victories,"* 108–9; Everts, *Ninth New Jersey*, 72; Drake, *Ninth New Jersey*, 22.

28. Drake, *Ninth New Jersey*, 23–24; Henry Cook diary, Jan. 6, 1862.

29. Henry Cook diary, Jan. 7–8, 1862.

30. Marvel, *Burnside*, 43.

31. Henry Cook diary, Jan. 9–19, 1862; C. Bayard Springer diary, Jan. 9–10, 1862.

32. Drake, *Ninth New Jersey*, 24; *Paterson Daily Guardian*, Feb. 13, 1862; Henry Cook diary, Jan. 10–11, 1862; Symmes H. Stillwell to "Dear Mother," Jan. 16, 1862.

33. Henry Cook diary, Jan. 14, 1862; C. Bayard Springer diary, Jan. 14, 1862; Marvel, *Burnside*, 45; Sauers, "A Succession of Honorable Victories," 122; Luvaas, "Burnside's Roanoke Island Campaign," 9–10.

34. Luvaas, "Burnside's Roanoke Island Campaign," 9; Sauers, "A Succession of Honorable Victories," 122–23.

35. Drake, *Ninth New Jersey*, 25.

36. Drake, *Ninth New Jersey*, 26–28; Everts, *Ninth New Jersey*, 72–73; Foster, *New Jersey and the Rebellion*, 204–6; Symmes H. Stillwell to "Dear Mother," Jan. 16, 1862; *Newark Daily Advertiser*, Jan. 31, 1862; *Somerset Messenger*, Feb. 6, 1862; *Hunterdon Republican*, Feb. 7, 1862; *Camden Journal*, n.d. [ca. Feb. 1, 1862]; Drake, *Historical Sketches of Revolutionary and Civil Wars*, 245–47; *Memorial of Colonel Abram Zabriskie*, 7–8; Marvel, *Burnside*, 47; Sauers, "A Succession of Honorable Victories," 127–28. Foster and Drake agree that after being cast adrift, Zabriskie and/or Heckman managed to tie a piece of clothing—apparently a sailor's shirt—to the oar; by waving it back and forth they attracted the attention of a rescue ship. In his own description of the incident, however (Abram Zabriskie to A. O. Zabriskie, Jan. 17, 1862, William L. Dayton Papers, Princeton University Library, reprinted in *Newark Daily Advertiser*, Jan. 31, 1862), the adjutant makes no mention of this stratagem.

37. C. Bayard Springer diary, Jan. 16, 1862; Drake, *Ninth New Jersey*, 27, 30–31.

38. Drake, *Ninth New Jersey*, 27.

39. Drake, *Ninth New Jersey*, 27; C. Bayard Springer diary, Jan. 28, 1862; *State Gazette and Republican*, Feb. 14, 1862. Through the generosity of the officers of the Ninth, in January 1864 a monument to Allen's memory was erected over his grave in the cemetery of Grace Episcopal Church, in Bordentown. Details of the "elegant structure" are in Drake, *Ninth New Jersey*, 34–35, and Foster, *New Jersey and the Rebellion*, 207n.

40. Everts, *Ninth New Jersey*, 73, 81; OR, ser. 1, 9:83–84; *Hunterdon Republican*, Feb. 7, 1862; *State Gazette and Republican*, Feb. 14, 1862.

41. Everts, *Ninth New Jersey*, 73; Drake, *Ninth New Jersey*, 28–29; Symmes H. Stillwell to "Dear Mother," Jan. 31–Feb. 1, 1862; C. Bayard Springer diary, Jan. 16, 1862; Foster, *New Jersey and the Rebellion*, 206–7; *Somerset Messenger*, Feb. 6, 1862; *State Gazette and Republican*, Feb. 21, 1862; Henry Cook diary, Jan. 16, 1862.

42. Drake, *Ninth New Jersey*, 29–30.

43. Drake, *Ninth New Jersey*, 29–30, 31–32; Everts, *Ninth New Jersey*, 73; Henry Cook diary, Jan. 18–19, 1862; C. Bayard Springer diary, Jan. 19, 1862; *Trenton Evening Times*, Aug. 30, 1883; Symmes H. Stillwell to "Dear Mother," Jan. 31–Feb. 1, 1862.

44. Drake, *Ninth New Jersey*, 31–32; Symmes H. Stillwell to "Dear Mother," Jan. 31–Feb. 1, 1862.

45. Drake, *Ninth New Jersey*, 32.

3. JERSEY MUSKRATS

1. Drake, *Ninth New Jersey*, 35–39; Foster, *New Jersey and the Rebellion*, 204; Drake, *Historical Sketches of Revolutionary and Civil Wars*, 175–80; Henry Cook diary, Jan. 20–21, 1862.

2. Luvaas, "Burnside's Roanoke Island Campaign," 10; C. Bayard Springer diary, Jan. 21, 1862; Henry Cook diary, Jan. 30–31, 1862.

3. Henry Cook diary, Jan. 30–31, 1862.

4. Henry Cook diary, Jan. 20, 1862; Drake, *Ninth New Jersey*, 33.

5. Drake, *Ninth New Jersey*, 40; Henry Cook diary, Jan. 27–30, Feb. 4, 1862; C. Bayard Springer diary, Jan. 27, 1862. Although Cook makes it clear that the *Dragoon* was carried over the swash on January 30, Drake says both transports made it across on Feb. 5. This is probably a reference only to the *Ann E. Thompson*.

6. Everts, *Ninth New Jersey*, 73; Drake, *Ninth New Jersey*, 40; Henry Cook diary, Feb. 5, 1862; C. Bayard Springer diary, Feb. 5, 1862; Symmes H. Stillwell to "Dear Mother," Jan. 31–Feb. 1, 1862.

7. Drake, *Ninth New Jersey*, 39–40.

8. Drake, *Ninth New Jersey*, 40; Henry Cook diary, Feb. 6, 1862; C. Bayard Springer diary, Feb. 5–6, 1862.

9. Guernsey and Alden, *Harper's Pictorial History of the Civil War*, 242; Marvel, *Burnside*, 50–52; Luvaas, "Burnside's Roanoke Island Campaign," 7–8, 11, 43; Sauers, "*A Succession of Honorable Victories,*" 151–52.

10. *Official Records of the Union and Confederate Navies in the War of the Rebellion* [hereafter cited as OR-N], ser. 1, 6:570; *Hunterdon County Democrat*, Mar. 14, 1862.

11. Everts, *Ninth New Jersey*, 73; Drake, *Ninth New Jersey*, 40–42; Barrett, *Civil War in North Carolina*, 76–78; Marvel, *Burnside*, 52, 55; Luvaas, "Burnside's Roanoke Island Campaign," 43; Traver, *Burnside Expedition in North Carolina*, 16–22; Sauers, "*A Succession of Honorable Victories,*" 168–72; Symmes H. Stillwell to "Dear Mother," Feb. 13, 1862; OR-N, ser. 1, 6:612.

12. OR, ser. 1, 9:76, 86; Luvaas, "Burnside's Roanoke Island Campaign," 43–44; Barrett, *Civil War in North Carolina*, 77–78.

13. OR, ser. 1, 9:97–98; *Belvidere Intelligencer*, Mar. 28, 1862; Symmes H. Stillwell to "Dear Mother," Feb. 13, 1862.

14. *Hunterdon County Democrat*, Mar. 21, 1862; Drake, *Ninth New Jersey*, 41; Symmes H. Stillwell to "Dear Mother," Feb. 13, 1862.

15. OR, ser. 1, 9:77, 86, 97–98, 105.

16. Luvaas, "Burnside's Roanoke Island Campaign," 44–45; Marvel, *Burnside*, 56–57; Sauers, *"A Succession of Honorable Victories,"* 173–80.

17. OR, ser. 1, 9:77, 86, 96; Drake, *Ninth New Jersey*, 50; OR-N, ser. 1, 6:563, 579, 581.

18. OR, ser. 1, 9:86–87, 94, 97–98; Drake, *Ninth New Jersey*, 42.

19. Drake, *Ninth New Jersey*, 43; John Kitchen to Joseph Thompson, Mar. 4, 1862, Thompson Papers.

20. OR, ser. 1, 9:102; Sauers, *"A Succession of Honorable Victories,"* 188.

21. Drake, *Ninth New Jersey*, 43; *Hunterdon County Democrat*, Mar. 19, 1862; *Newark Daily Advertiser*, Feb. 24, 1862; *State Gazette and Republican*, Mar. 7, 1862.

22. Drake, *Ninth New Jersey*, 43–44; David C. Hankins to "Dear Sister," Feb. 18, 1862; Symmes H. Stillwell to "Dear Mother," Feb. 13, 1862.

23. Drake, *Ninth New Jersey*, 50–51; OR, ser. 1, 9:102.

24. Drake, *Ninth New Jersey*, 44; OR, ser. 1, 9:111–12, 156, 172; Sauers, *"A Succession of Honorable Victories,"* 193. An unidentified member of the Ninth, writing in the *State Gazette and Republican* for Mar. 21, 1862, claimed that Selden survived his wound long enough to assure his captors that "our regiment drove them out of the fort."

25. Drake, *Ninth New Jersey*, 44; *Hunterdon County Democrat*, Mar. 7, 1862.

26. Drake, *Ninth New Jersey*, 385–86; *Trenton Evening Times*, n.d. [ca. Mar. 1883]; *Newark Daily Mercury*, Feb. 28, 1862; *Newark Daily Advertiser*, Mar. 7, 1862; *Belvidere Intelligencer*, Feb. 28, Mar. 7, 1862; *Hunterdon County Democrat*, Mar. 7, 1862.

27. *Belvidere Intelligencer*, Feb. 28, Mar. 7, 1862. Capt. Henry's body was shipped by steamboat and railroad to the home of his sister at Oxford Furnace, where his funeral was held on February 23. The *Belvidere Intelligencer* described the ceremony as "the spontaneous outburst of feeling of our whole county, not less than 1000 to 1500 persons, from every part of the county, attending." Before the war Henry had spent most of his time in New York City and Washington and thus was relatively little known to the local people, "yet his character was so well established that everybody felt an interest in him."

28. Drake, *Ninth New Jersey*, 44; Henry Cook diary, Feb. 12, 1862; Barnes, *Medical and Surgical History of the War of the Rebellion*, 12:462. According to the *Woodbury Constitution*, "a pair of the best kind of artificial limbs," donated by the citizens of Jersey City, were made for Corp. Lorence (Stewart and Archut, *Gloucester County in the Civil War*, 1:38). Another source referred to the prosthesis as "cork legs" (*Newark Daily Mercury*, May 1, 1862). It is not known whether the wounded man was able to wear them; he was not using them five months later

when helping to recruit for the Twelfth New Jersey Volunteers (Longacre, *To Gettysburg and Beyond*, 9, 11).

29. Foster, *New Jersey and the Rebellion*, 210; *Hunterdon County Democrat*, Feb. 14, 1862; *State Gazette and Republican*, Mar. 21, 1862; *Newark Daily Advertiser*, Mar. 1, 1862; *Ocean Emblem* (Toms River NJ), Apr. 2, 1862; *Newark Daily Mercury*, May 1, 1862; *Paterson Daily Guardian*, May 2, 1862. A comrade of Lorence's, Pvt. Franz Muller of Company A, also had both of his legs amputated after being wounded on Roanoke Island (Stryker, *Record of Officers and Men of New Jersey*, 1:438). Unlike Lorence, Muller did not survive the operation and thus failed to receive the attention lavished on the Mullica Hill farmer. One example of the publicity given to Lorence was this poem, published in the *New Brunswick Daily Fredonian* for May 31, 1862, and later carried in the highly popular *Harper's Weekly*:

> Alas! Before the day was won,
> while fiercer grew the fray,
> and John was rushing on, a shot
> took both his legs away!
>
> ... At last the surgeon's task is o'er:
> the sleeper awakes. What sound
> has thrilled his soul, and made him glance
> so eagerly around?
>
> "Victory!" is the thrilling cry
> borne in upon the gale.
> The patriot rose upon his arm,
> his face, till now so pale.
> Flushed with new joy, he waved his cap,
> and gave three hearty cheers
> for Union and the glorious Ninth
> New Jersey Volunteers! ...

30. *Newark Daily Advertiser*, Feb. 24, 1862; *Belvidere Intelligencer*, Mar. 21, 28, 1862; John Kitchen to Joseph Thompson, Mar. 4, 1862.
31. Drake, *Ninth New Jersey*, 44–45; *Princeton Standard*, Mar. 7, 1862.
32. Drake, *Ninth New Jersey*, 45–46; Luvaas, "Burnside's Roanoke Island Campaign," 45–46; Sauers, "*A Succession of Honorable Victories*," 193–95, 463–78; *State Gazette and Republican*, Feb. 28; *Hunterdon County Democrat*, Mar. 19, 1862; *Belvidere Intelligencer*, Mar. 28, 1862; Bilby and Goble, "*Remember You Are Jerseymen!*," 680n; Symmes H. Stillwell to "Dear Mother," Mar. 20, 1862.

33. *Newark Daily Advertiser*, Mar. 14, 1862; *State Gazette and Republican*, Mar. 21, 1862; Sauers, *"A Succession of Honorable Victories,"* 195; John N. Smith to Joseph Thompson, Mar. 6, 1862, Thompson Papers.

34. Drake, *Ninth New Jersey*, 45; *Newark Daily Advertiser*, Feb. 24, 1861; David C. Hankins to "Dear Sister," Feb. 18, 1862.

35. Luvaas, "Burnside's Roanoke Island Campaign," 46; Sauers, *"A Succession of Honorable Victories,"* 196–99.

36. *OR*, ser. 1, 9:111, 158, 173; Symmes H. Stillwell to "Dear Mother," Feb. 13, 1862; *Hunterdon County Democrat*, Mar. 19, 1862.

37. Symmes H. Stillwell to "Dear Mother," Feb. 13, 1862; *Belvidere Intelligencer*, Mar. 28, 1862.

38. Henry Cook diary, Feb. 8, 1862; Drake, *Ninth New Jersey*, 46.

39. Symmes H. Stillwell to "Dear Mother," Mar. 20, 1862.

40. Drake, *Ninth New Jersey*, 47; *Jersey City Daily Standard*, Mar. 2, 1863.

41. *Newark Daily Advertiser*, Feb. 24, 1862; Symmes H. Stillwell to "Dear Mother," Mar. 20, 1862; John Kitchen to Joseph Thompson, Mar. 4, 1862, Thompson Papers.

4. "CHARGE, NINTH, CHARGE!"

1. *New York Times*, Feb. 21, 1862; *Hunterdon County Democrat*, Feb. 21, Mar. 21, 1862.

2. *OR*, ser. 1, 9:85.

3. Drake, *Ninth New Jersey*, 46.

4. *Hunterdon County Democrat*, Mar. 14, 1862.

5. Everts, *Ninth New Jersey*, 74–75; Stryker, *Record of Officers and Men of New Jersey*, 1:484; Symmes H. Stillwell to "Dear Mother," Mar. 20, Apr. 19, 1862; *State Gazette and Republican*, Mar. 7, 1862.

6. *OR*, ser. 1, 9:102–3.

7. Drake, *Ninth New Jersey*, 49–52.

8. Drake, *Ninth New Jersey*, 52–53.

9. *Belvidere Intelligencer*, Mar. 21, 1862; *New York Times*, Mar. 3, 1862 ("Correspondence of the *Newark Advertiser*").

10. Drake, *Ninth New Jersey*, 54.

11. *New York Times*, Mar. 3, 1862; Henry Cook diary, Feb. 9–10, 1862; *Newark Daily Advertiser*, Feb. 24, 1862.

12. *New York Times*, Mar. 3, 1862; Henry Cook diary, Feb. 22, 1862.

13. "Charlie" to anon., n.d. [ca. Feb. 9, 1862], in possession of Willard B. Green; Drake, *Ninth New Jersey*, 47, 55.

14. Henry Cook diary, Feb. 23–24, 1862; Drake, *Ninth New Jersey*, 47, 54.

15. Henry Cook diary, Feb. 10, 1862; Symmes H. Stillwell to "Dear Mother," Mar. 6, 1862.

16. Drake, *Ninth New Jersey*, 54–55; Stewart and Archut, *Gloucester County in the Civil War*, 1:9.

17. Henry Cook diary, Mar. 1 1862; C. Bayard Springer diary, Mar. 1, 1862; Symmes H. Stillwell to "Dear Mother," Mar. 6, 1862.

18. Henry Cook diary, Feb. 20, 25, 1862; C. Bayard Springer diary, Feb. 21, 1862.

19. Henry Cook diary, Feb. 29 [*sic*], 1862; Stryker, *Record of Officers and Men of New Jersey*, 1:444, 459, 463, 472, 482, 484; Longacre, *To Gettysburg and Beyond*, 11, 15.

20. Everts, *Ninth New Jersey*, 74; Drake, *Ninth New Jersey*, 55; Henry Cook diary, Mar. 3, 1862; C. Bayard Springer diary, Mar. 3, 1862.

21. Drake, *Ninth New Jersey*, 55–56; Henry Cook diary, Mar. 7, 9, 1862.

22. Barrett, *Civil War in North Carolina*, 27n, 31, 95–96; Sauers, "A Succession of Honorable Victories," 233; Henry Cook diary, Mar. 10, 1862; C. Bayard Springer diary, Mar. 11, 1862.

23. Drake, *Ninth New Jersey*, 56.

24. Marvel, *Burnside*, 66–67; Foster, *New Jersey and the Rebellion*, 212; Henry Cook diary, Mar. 13, 1862; OR, ser. 1, 9:198, 202, 212, 221, 233.

25. Drake, *Ninth New Jersey*, 57–58.

26. *American Standard* (Jersey City NJ), Dec. 30, 1862; *Woodbury Constitution*, Apr. 15, 1862; *Paterson Daily Guardian*, Mar. 27, 1862.

27. Barrett, *Civil War in North Carolina*, 95–100; Sauers, "A Succession of Honorable Victories," 249–52, 258–60; Clark, *Regiments and Battalions from North Carolina*, 2:321; OR, ser. 1, 9:240–44.

28. Drake, *Ninth New Jersey*, 58; OR, ser. 1, 9:198, 202–03, 212, 221; *Paterson Daily Guardian*, Mar. 27, 1862.

29. OR, ser. 1, 9:203, 221, 24–26; Marvel, *Burnside*, 72–73; Sauers, "A Succession of Honorable Victories," 271–75; Drake, *Ninth New Jersey*, 65.

30. OR, ser. 1, 9:221; *Woodbury Constitution*, Mar. 23, 1862.

31. Symmes H. Stillwell to "Dear Mother," Mar. 18, 1862; OR, ser. 1, 9:228, 231; Drake, *Ninth New Jersey*, 65.

32. Drake, *Ninth New Jersey*, 58–59, 65; Everts, *Ninth New Jersey*, 75; Houck, "Battle of New Bern," 7–8; OR, ser. 1, 9:228, 221–22.

33. Drake, *Ninth New Jersey*, 62.

34. Drake, *Ninth New Jersey*, 59–60, 65; Everts, *Ninth New Jersey*, 75; *Paterson Daily Guardian*, Mar. 27, 1862; *State Gazette and Republican*, Apr. 4, 1862; OR, ser. 1, 9:221, 228; Sauers, "A Succession of Honorable Victories," 290–91; Hill, *Bethel to Sharpsburg*, 224, 226.

35. Henry V. Van Nest to Joseph Thompson, Mar. 29, 1862, Thompson Papers; Houck, "Battle of New Bern," 14.

36. Drake, *Ninth New Jersey*, 61; Drake, *Historical Sketches of Revolutionary and Civil Wars*, 158–61; *Somerset Messenger*, Apr. 10, 1862; James Stewart, Jr.,

to N. J. Adj. Gen. R. Heber Breintnall, May 10, 1905, Record Book 420, New Jersey State Archives. Information on Capt. Martin can be found in Clark, *Regiments and Battalions from North Carolina*, 2:323, and *Raleigh* [NC] *Semi-Weekly Standard*, Apr. 9, 1862.

37. OR, ser. 1, 9:240–41, 244–45; Barrett, *Civil War in North Carolina*, 104–5; Wagstaff, "James A. Graham Papers," 117–18.

38. Drake, *Ninth New Jersey*, 62; OR, ser. 1, 9:199–200, 213, 245.

39. OR, ser. 1, 9:198, 211, 246; Drake, *Ninth New Jersey*, 59–61, 65.

40. David C. Hankins to "Dear Sister," Mar. 16, 1862; OR, ser. 1, 9:211; *Belvidere Intelligencer*, Mar. 28, 1862; *Princeton Standard*, Mar. 21, 1862; *American Standard*, May 7, 1862; *Sacramento* [CA] *Daily Union*, June 7, 1862. Numerous accounts, including the official reports of Heckman and Reno, have Lt. Walker killed in action at New Bern. However, Sgt. Drake, writing in the *State Gazette and Republican* for Apr. 4, 1862, noted that Walker had his "leg amputated—since died." Pvt. Benjamin Manning of Company C, in a letter to the *Paterson Daily Guardian*, Mar. 27, 1862, reported that "one Lieutenant was shot through the leg and had his leg cut off and bled to death." Walker was the only officer fatality.

41. *State Gazette and Republican*, Apr. 4, 1862; *Newark Daily Advertiser*, Apr. 9, 1862; *Newton Herald*, Aug. 9, 1862.

42. *Woodbury Constitution*, Mar. 23, 1862; Symmes H. Stillwell to "Dear Mother," Apr. 19, 1862.

43. Stryker, *Record of Officers and Men of New Jersey*, 1:482.

44. Drake, *Ninth New Jersey*, 61; OR, ser. 1, 9:228; *Newark Daily Mercury*, Mar. 19, Apr. 8, 1862; *Sacramento* [CA] *Daily Union*, Apr. 29, 1862; Riddle, "Beaufort Plow Boys Flag."

45. *New Brunswick Daily Times*, May 12, 1905; *Philadelphia Inquirer*, May 28, 1905; *Report of State Commission for Erection of Monument to Ninth New Jersey*, 89–90, 93.

5. WORKING ON THE RAILROAD

1. OR, ser. 1, 9:200, 276–77; Marvel, *Burnside*, 78–79; Barrett, *Civil War in North Carolina*, 109–10; Sauers, "A Succession of Honorable Victories," 309–10.

2. Drake, *Ninth New Jersey*, 66; Henry Cook diary, Mar. 15, 1862.

3. Henry Cook diary, Mar. 16, 18, 20, 31, 1862; *State Gazette and Republican*, Apr. 25, 1862; *Newark Daily Mercury*, Mar. 31, 1862; Stryker, *Record of Officers and Men of New Jersey*, 1:477.

4. *Hunterdon County Democrat*, June 6, 1862 ("Correspondence of *Newark Daily Advertiser*"); David C. Hankins to "Dear Sister," Apr. 6, 1862.

5. OR, ser. 1, 9:203, 221, 223; C. Bayard Springer diary, Mar. 18, 1862; Henry Cook diary, Mar. 19, 1862.

6. *State Gazette and Republican*, Feb. 14, 21, Mar. 21, Apr. 11, 1862; *Daily Progress* (New Bern NC), Apr. 26, 1862; C. Bayard Springer diary, Mar. 21, 1862. Detailed descriptions of the "most beautiful sword" can be found in *Hunterdon County Democrat*, May 30, 1862, and *Register and Times* (Rahway NJ), July 3, 1862, Drake, *Ninth New Jersey*, 86–87.

7. Drake, *Ninth New Jersey*, 68; *Paterson Daily Guardian*, July 29, 1862.

8. Stewart and Archut, *Gloucester County in the Civil War*, 1: 11–12; *Newark Daily Mercury*, Mar. 21, 1862. This flag was presented to the regiment on December 22, 1862.

9. *Newark Daily Mercury*, Apr. 17, 1862; *State Gazette and Republican*, Apr. 25, 1862.

10. Drake, *Ninth New Jersey*, 68; *Newark Daily Mercury*, Mar. 31, Apr. 1, 1862.

11. Everts, *Ninth New Jersey*, 77; Drake, *Ninth New Jersey*, 67–68, 390; Henry Cook diary, Mar. 23, 1862; C. Bayard Springer diary, Mar. 22, 1862; John N. Smith to Joseph Thompson, June 1, 1862, Thompson Papers; *American Standard*, June 17, Oct. 24, 1862; *Paterson Daily Guardian*, June 23, 1862; *Sentinel of Freedom*, Oct. 28, 1862.

12. Drake, *Ninth New Jersey*, 70–71, 74; Symmes H. Stillwell to "Dear Mother," Mar. 20, 1862; William B. Curlis to "Dear Sir," Mar. 21, 1862, Thompson Papers.

13. Henry Cook diary, Mar. 31, 1862; Drake, *Ninth New Jersey*, 69; OR, ser. 1, 9:206, 281, 283; Barrett, *Civil War in North Carolina*, 113–14; Sauers, "A Succession of Honorable Victories," 317.

14. Everts, *Ninth New Jersey*, 76; Drake, *Ninth New Jersey*, 69; Henry Cook diary, Apr. 1, 1862; C. Bayard Springer diary, Apr. 1, 1862; *Plainfield Union*, Oct. 28, 1862.

15. David C. Hankins to "Dear Sister," Apr. 6, 1862; *Hunterdon County Democrat*, June 6, 1862; Symmes H. Stillwell to "Dear Mother," Apr. 19, 1862; *American Standard*, Aug. 1, 1862.

16. Everts, *Ninth New Jersey*, 76; Drake, *Ninth New Jersey*, 70; Henry Cook diary, Apr. 2, 1863; C. Bayard Springer diary, Apr. 2–3, 1862; *Belvidere Intelligencer*, June 6, 1862; *Daily True American* (Trenton NJ), June 22, 1863; *State Gazette and Republican*, July 4, 1862; *Plainfield Union*, Oct. 28, 1862.

17. *Newark Daily Mercury*, Oct. 24, 1862; David C. Hankins to "Dear Sister," May 20, 1862.

18. Drake, *Ninth New Jersey*, 70–71; David C. Hankins to "Dear Sister," May 2, 1862.

19. Drake, *Ninth New Jersey*, 84–85; *Somerset Whig* (Somerville NJ), Sept. 18, 1862; *New Jersey Journal*, Oct. 7, 1862.

20. Everts, *Ninth New Jersey*, 76; Drake, *Ninth New Jersey*, 71; C. Bayard Springer diary, Apr. 7, 1862; OR, ser. 1, 9: 295–96; *Hunterdon County Democrat*, Apr. 25, 1862; *State Gazette and Republican*, Apr. 25, 1862; *Ocean Emblem*, Apr. 30, 1862; Sauers, "A Succession of Honorable Victories," 319.

21. Drake, *Ninth New Jersey*, 71–72, 75.

22. Drake, *Ninth New Jersey*, 72, 80; Symmes H. Stillwell to "Dear Mother," Apr. 19, 1862.

23. Drake, *Ninth New Jersey*, 75; C. Bayard Springer diary, May 30, 1862.

24. *OR*, ser. 1, 9:285; Symmes H. Stillwell to "Dear Mother," May 20, 1862; Drake, *Ninth New Jersey*, 73–74. The Ninth was issued five flags during the war, two national colors, two regimental colors, and a special flag presented by the State of New Jersey to honor the outfit's performance in its first two battles. The first national color, which is badly torn, appears to carry the following honors: "Roan[o]k[e] I[sland], Newb[ern], Fort Mac[on], Sou[thwest Creek], Kinsto[n]." The second national color, supplied to the Ninth in 1864, carried these same inscriptions along with the names of six other engagements ending with the skirmish at Cherry Grove, Virginia, April 14, 1864. It is not known why later honors were not added. Information courtesy of Brett Bondurant of Raleigh, North Carolina, who has made a detailed study of the subject.

25. David C. Hankins to "My Dear Sister," May 2, 1862.

26. C. Bayard Springer diary, Apr. 2, 1862; Drake, *Ninth New Jersey*, 74; Marvel, *Burnside*, 89.

27. Drake, *Ninth New Jersey*, 73–74.

28. Drake, *Ninth New Jersey*, 72.

29. Symmes H. Stillwell to "Dear Mother," May 20, 1864.

30. Everts, *Ninth New Jersey*, 77; Verter, "Disconsolations of a Jersey Muskrat," 251.

31. *Paterson Daily Guardian*, July 29, 1862; *Camden Democrat*, Aug. 16, 1862; *New Jersey Journal*, Oct. 7, 1862; Andrew J. Gafney to Marcus L. Ward, Sept. 15, 1862, Ward Papers, New Jersey Historical Society.

32. William P. Amerman to "Cousin Leta," June 9, 1862, Amerman Papers, U.S. Army Heritage and Education Center.

33. Symmes H. Stillwell to "Dear Mother," May 20, 1862; Barrett, *Civil War in North Carolina*, 127–28; Marvel, *Burnside*, 90–91.

34. Everts, *Ninth New Jersey*, 77–78; Drake, *Ninth New Jersey*, 75; David C. Hankins to "Dear Sister," June 23, 1862.

35. Drake, *Ninth New Jersey*, 75–76; Symmes H. Stillwell to "Dear Mother," June 15, 1862; *Paterson Daily Guardian*, June 23, 1862; *State Gazette and Republican*, June 27, 1862; *Hightstown Gazette*, July 3, 1862; *Somerset Whig*, July 17, 1862.

36. Everts, *Ninth New Jersey*, 78; Drake, *Ninth New Jersey*, 78–79; C. Bayard Springer diary, June 24, 1862.

37. *Paterson Daily Guardian*, July 10, 1862.

38. Everts, *Ninth New Jersey*, 79; Drake, *Ninth New Jersey*, 79–80. Various sources suggest that the men of the Ninth built blockhouses at Evans's Mill, near Havelock Station, at Gayles Creek, and on Bogue Sound. See Lt. Beach's account,

as well as *Paterson Daily Guardian*, July 22, 1862; *Camden Democrat*, Aug. 16, 1862; *Plainfield Union*, Dec. 16, 1862; and John Kitchen to Joseph Thompson, July 8, 1862, Thompson Papers.

39. *Paterson Daily Guardian*, July 29, 1862; *New Jersey Herald and Sussex County Democrat* (Newton NJ), Aug. 9, 1862; Drake, *Ninth New Jersey*, 80.

40. Barrett, *Civil War in North Carolina*, 128–31; Marvel, *Burnside*, 88, 92–93; John Kitchen to Joseph Thompson, July 8, 1862; Symmes H. Stillwell to "Dear Mother," July 18, 1862; David C. Hankins to "Dear Sister," July 21, 1862. For a full-length account of McClellan's failed campaign see Sears, *To the Gates of Richmond*.

41. Lindblade, *Fight as Long as Possible*, 33, 58–59.

42. *OR*, ser. 1, 33:85; *State Gazette and Republican*, Oct. 27, 1862; *Plainfield Union*, Dec. 16, 1862; *Newton Register*, Nov. 7, 1862.

43. *OR*, ser. 1, 33:81–82, 84–86.

44. *OR*, ser. 1, 9:412–13.

45. *OR*, ser. 1, 9:347–48; Everts, *Ninth New Jersey*, 79–80, 160; Drake, *Ninth New Jersey*, 81–82; Henry Cook diary, July 25–27, 1862; Foster, *New Jersey and the Rebellion*, 215–16; Symmes H. Stillwell to "Cousen Peter," Aug. 1, 1862; to "Dear Brother," Aug. 5–6, 1862; Andrew J. Gafney to Marcus L. Ward, Sept. 1, 1862, Ward Papers; *Camden Democrat*, Aug. 16, 1862; *Newark Daily Mercury*, Aug. 7, 13, 1862; *State Gazette and Republican*, Aug. 11, 1862; *Hunterdon Republican*, Aug. 22, 1862.

46. Everts, *Ninth New Jersey*, 80; Drake, *Ninth New Jersey*, 82–83; *OR*, ser. 1, 9:348; Henry Cook diary, July 28–30, 1862.

47. *OR*, ser. 1, 9:413; *Paterson Daily Guardian*, Aug. 8, 1862.

6. FAILED RAIDS AND FUTILE PURSUITS

1. Everts, *Ninth New Jersey*, 83; Drake, *Ninth New Jersey*, 85–88; Foster, *New Jersey and the Rebellion*, 217; *New Jersey Journal*, Oct. 7, 21, 1862; Edmund J. Cleveland diary, Sept. 16, Oct. 2, 26, 1862.

2. Symmes H. Stillwell to "Dear Mother," Aug. 5, 1862.

3. Everts, *Ninth New Jersey*, 83; Drake, *Ninth New Jersey*, 87; *Paterson Daily Guardian*, Sept. 30, 1862; *State Gazette and Republican*, Oct. 4, 1862.

4. David C. Hankins to "Dear Sister," Sept. 16, 1862; Symmes H. Stillwell to "Dear Mother," Oct. 3, 1862.

5. *New Jersey Journal*, Oct. 7, 1862.

6. Andrew W. Little to "Dear Sister," Sept. 20, Nov. 24, 1862, Little Papers, Hunterdon County Historical Society; *New Bern* [NC] *Weekly Progress*, Sept. 20, 1862; *Camden Democrat*, Aug. 16, 1862; Andrew J. Gafney to Marcus L. Ward, Sept. 15, 1862, Ward Papers; Symmes H. Stillwell to "Dear Mother," Oct. 9, 1862; David C. Hankins to "Dear Sister," Nov. 3, 1862. The private's

rank that Andrew Little assumed when joining the Ninth marked a steep decline in his military career; he had been a lieutenant colonel in the state's prewar militia.

7. *Camden Democrat*, Aug. 16, 1862; *Paterson Daily Guardian*, Aug. 4, 1862; Stryker, *Record of Officers and Men of New Jersey*, 1: 473; *Report of State Commission for Erection of Monument to Ninth New Jersey*, 110-12.

8. Everts, *Ninth New Jersey*, 83; Drake, *Ninth New Jersey*, 88; *Newark Daily Mercury*, Oct. 27, 1862; Foster, *New Jersey and the Rebellion*, 215n–216n, 233; *Newark Daily Journal*, Oct. 3, 1863; *Ocean Emblem*, Nov. 19, 1863.

9. Everts, *Ninth New Jersey*, 91, 97, 123, 137; Drake, *Ninth New Jersey*, 225, 253; *Ocean Emblem*, Nov. 19, 1863.

10. Drake, *Ninth New Jersey*, 382–83.

11. *State Gazette and Republican*, Aug. 15, 1862; *New Bern* [NC] *Weekly Progress*, Sept. 20, 1862; Andrew W. Little to "Dear Sister," Sept. 12, 20, 1862.

12. Everts, *Ninth New Jersey*, 83; *Newark Daily Advertiser*, Nov. 25, 1862.

13. Andrew J. Gafney to Marcus L. Ward, Sept. 15, 1862, Ward Papers; *New Jersey Journal*, Sept. 16, 1862; *Somerset Whig*, Sept. 18, 1862; *Hightstown Gazette*, Sept. 23, 1862.

14. Jonathan R. Reading to Joseph Thompson, Oct. 17, 1862, Thompson Papers.

15. David C. Hankins to "Dear Sister," Nov. 3, 1862; Stryker, *Record of Officers and Men of New Jersey*, 1:430, 432, 482. Everts, *Ninth New Jersey*, 86, reports that when the six supernumerary officers were mustered out in November 1862 so too were twenty-seven enlisted men. No details are provided.

16. Everts, *Ninth New Jersey*, 80–81; Drake, *Ninth New Jersey*, 83; OR, ser. 1, 9:350–51; *Jersey City Daily Standard*, Aug. 26, 1862.

17. Drake, *Ninth New Jersey*, 84; *State Gazette and Republican*, Aug. 29, Sept. 4, 5, 1862; Andrew J. Gafney to Marcus L. Ward, Sept. 1, 1862, Ward Papers.

18. Everts, *Ninth New Jersey*, 83; Drake, *Ninth New Jersey*, 87–88; *Paterson Daily Guardian*, Sept. 30, 1862. In his history Drake confuses the timing of the expedition to Adams Creek (September 16–19). On p. 81 he dates it as occurring in mid-July, but on pp. 87–88 he refers to it as taking place as of the correct date. Sgt. Goldsmith's letter of Sept. 22, published in the Sept. 30 issue of the *Paterson Daily Guardian*, positively dates it as starting on Sept. 16.

19. For a detailed study of the Antietam Campaign see Sears, *Landscape Turned Red*; for Second Bull Run (Second Manassas) see Hennessy, *Return to Bull Run*; and for the Kentucky Campaign see Hess, *Banners to the Breeze*.

20. *Newark Herald*, Sept. 27, 1862; McPherson, *Crossroads of Freedom*, 61–71; McPherson, *Tried by War*, 60–61, 127–34, 156–58.

21. *New Jersey Journal*, Oct. 21, 1862; *Sentinel of Freedom*, Oct. 28, 1862; *Newark Daily Journal*, Nov. 13, 1862.

22. *Newton Register*, Nov. 7, 1862; *Newark Daily Journal*, Nov. 13, Dec. 11, 1862.

23. Symmes H. Stillwell to "Dear Mother," Dec. 5–6, 1862; David C. Hankins to "Dear Sister," Nov. 3, 1862; *Paterson Daily Guardian*, Feb. 26, 1863.

24. Jonathan R. Reading to Joseph Thompson, Dec. 24, 1862, Thompson Papers.

25. *OR*, ser. 1, 18:469; Barrett, *Civil War in North Carolina*, 134–36.

26. *New Jersey Herald and Sussex County Democrat*, Nov. 22, 1862; Everts, *Ninth New Jersey*, 83–84; Drake, *Ninth New Jersey*, 88–89, 94.

27. Drake, *Ninth New Jersey*, 89–90, 94–95; Foster, *New Jersey and the Rebellion*, 217–18; *Newark Daily Mercury*, Nov. 28, 1862; *Plainfield Union*, Dec. 9, 1862.

28. Stewart and Archut, *Gloucester County in the Civil War*, 1:209.

29. Stewart and Archut, *Gloucester County in the Civil War*, 1:210; Drake, *Ninth New Jersey*, 90.

30. Everts, *Ninth New Jersey*, 84; Drake, *Ninth New Jersey*, 91–92, 95; Foster, *New Jersey and the Rebellion*, 218.

31. Everts, *Ninth New Jersey*, 85; Drake, *Ninth New Jersey*, 92; *Hightstown Gazette*, Nov. 27, 1862; *New Jersey Herald and Sussex County Democrat*, Nov. 22, 1862.

32. Drake, *Ninth New Jersey*, 92–93; *OR*, ser. 1, 18:25; John Bamford to "Dear Brother," Nov. 16, 1862, Bamford Papers, Rutgers University Libraries.

33. Everts, *Ninth New Jersey*, 85; Drake, *Ninth New Jersey*, 93; Edmund J. Cleveland diary, Nov. 11, 1862; *Newark Daily Advertiser*, Nov. 26, 1862.

34. Andrew W. Little to "Dear Mother," Nov. 12, 1862; Symmes H. Stillwell to "Dear Mother," Dec. 5, 1862.

35. Everts, *Ninth New Jersey*, 86; Drake, *Ninth New Jersey*, 5–6, 96; *Newark Daily Advertiser*, Dec. 4, 1862; *Newark Daily Journal*, Dec. 11, 1862; *Register and Times*, Jan. 1, 1863.

36. Drake, *Ninth New Jersey*, 96–97; *Newark Daily Advertiser*, Dec. 4, 1862; Edmund J. Cleveland diary, Dec. 9, 1862.

37. *OR*, ser. 1, 18:54; Barrett, *Civil War in North Carolina*, 139.

38. Everts, *Ninth New Jersey*, 86; Drake, *Ninth New Jersey*, 97; Barrett, *Civil War in North Carolina*, 139; Foster, *New Jersey and the Rebellion*, 219; David C. Hankins to "Dear Sister," Dec. 10, 1862; *State Gazette and Republican*, Dec. 30, 1862; *Newark Daily Mercury*, Dec. 15, 1862; *Plainfield Union*, Dec. 16, 1862; *Register and Times*, Jan. 1, 1863.

39. Edmund J. Cleveland diary, Dec. 12, 1862; Edmund J. Cleveland, "Personal Experiences on the Ten-Days' March in North Carolina . . . ," Cleveland Papers. Though written five months later, Cleveland's memoir is the most detailed and reliable eyewitness account of the Goldsboro Raid.

40. Everts, *Ninth New Jersey*, 87; Drake, *Ninth New Jersey*, 98–99; Foster, *New Jersey and the Rebellion*, 219; *OR*, ser. 1, 18:91–92, 101–2.

41. *OR*, ser. 1, 18:55, 91–92, 94; Drake, *Ninth New Jersey*, 99–100; *American Standard*, Dec. 29, 1862; *Democratic Banner* (Morristown NJ), Jan. 8, 1862; Barrett, *Civil War in North Carolina*, 140.

42. *Democratic Banner*, Jan. 8, 1863; Cleveland, "Personal Experiences on the Ten-Days' March in North Carolina."

43. OR, ser. 1, 18:91–92; Drake, *Ninth New Jersey*, 101–04, 116; Symmes H. Stillwell to "Dear Mother," Dec. 22, 1862; David C. Hankins to "Dear Sister," Dec. 25, 1862; Andrew W. Little to "Dear Sister," Dec. 28, 1862; *American Standard*, Dec. 29, 1862; *Democratic Banner*, Jan. 8, 1862.

44. Cleveland, "Personal Experiences on the Ten-Days' March in North Carolina."

45. Drake, *Ninth New Jersey*, 117; Jonathan R. Reading to Joseph Thompson, May 22, 1863, Thompson Papers.

46. Drake, *Ninth New Jersey*, 104–5.

47. *Democratic Banner*, Jan. 8, 1863; Drake, *Ninth New Jersey*, 106; Drake, *Historical Sketches of Revolutionary and Civil Wars*, 157. The Ninth's casualty figures (OR, ser. 1, 18:60) show that only one regiment of the thirty regiments, batteries, and separate companies involved in the Goldsboro Raid suffered heavier losses.

48. Drake, *Ninth New Jersey*, 105; Andrew W. Little to "Dear Sister," Dec. 28, 1862.

49. Drake, *Ninth New Jersey*, 107–12; OR, ser. 1, 18:93–95.

50. *Newark Daily Mercury*, Dec. 26, 1862; *Democratic Banner*, Jan. 8, 1862; Drake, *Ninth New Jersey*, 109.

51. Rogers, *Reminiscences of Military Service in the Forty-third Massachusetts*, 75.

52. OR, ser. 1, 18:93–95; Everts, *Ninth New Jersey*, 89; Drake, *Ninth New Jersey*, 109–11; Foster, *New Jersey and the Rebellion*, 225–26; David C. Hankins to "Dear Sister," Dec. 25, 1862; Bilby and Goble, *"Remember You Are Jerseymen!,"* 148; *Newark Daily Mercury*, Dec. 26, 1862; *Woodbury Constitution*, Jan. 6, 1863. Drake's history names Winans as the hero of the bridge burning; in his after-action report (OR, ser. 1, 18:93) Col. Heckman also cites Pvt. William Lemons of Company E and Lt. George W. Graham, his acting aide-de-camp. Apparently Heckman forgot Winans's name, as he left it blank in his report.

53. OR, ser. 1, 18:58; Barrett, *Civil War in North Carolina*, 147. Toward sundown on the seventeenth the Ninth, which had begun to leave the field, was rushed to the rear when that portion of Foster's column was attacked by Confederates ensconced behind a railroad embankment. Artillery fire mangled the assault force; as Sgt. Drake described the result, "whole platoons were swept off at a single discharge. The rebels lay in piles, presenting a horrible spectacle" (*New Jersey Journal*, Dec. 30, 1862). When he wrote his history, Drake compared the outcome to Pickett's Charge at Gettysburg as an example of wasted valor. In the end, the Ninth was not needed to repulse the effort.

54. *American Standard*, Dec. 29, 1862.

55. Andrew W. Little to "Dear Sister," Dec. 28, 1862, Jan. 1, 6, 1863; *Hunterdon Observer* (Flemington NJ), Mar. 3, 1990. The latter source, an article about

Sgt. Little and his wartime letters that repose in the county historical society, is entitled "Civil War Letters Tell a Grim Tale."

56. *American Standard*, Dec. 29, 1862.

7. SOUTHERN EXCURSION

1. David C. Hankins to "Dear Sister," Jan. 8, 1863, Apr. 4, 1864; McPherson, *Tried by War*, 103–5, 115.

2. Longacre, *Worthy Opponents*, 171–74. For more on the "hard war" concept see Grimsley, *Hard Hand of War*.

3. For a detailed account of Burnside's disastrous operations see O'Reilly, *Fredericksburg Campaign*. For Grant's initial struggles before Vicksburg see Bearss, *Vicksburg Is the Key*, and for Stones River see Cozzens, *No Better Place to Die*.

4. Knapp, *New Jersey Politics*, 74–75, 100; Gillette, *Jersey Blue*, 202–3.

5. *Plainfield Union*, Dec. 9, 1862; *Newark Daily Journal*, Dec. 11, 1862.

6. *Jersey City Daily Standard*, Dec. 29, 1862. In his report of the raid (OR, ser. 1, 18:53–59), Gen. Foster praised "Colonel Heckman, of the Ninth New Jersey, [who] was, with his admirable regiment, always in advance, and displayed the greatest courage and efficiency." Other ranking officers involved in the expedition mentioned "the Ninth New Jersey Volunteers with their usual intrepidity" (18:96), while describing the Ninth as "that gallant regiment" and "that brave regiment." (18:102).

7. Stryker, *Record of Officers and Men of New Jersey*, 1:430; Heitman, *Historical Register and Dictionary*, 1:519; Foster, *New Jersey and the Rebellion*, 226; *New Jersey Journal*, Dec. 30, 1862; *American Standard*, Dec. 30, 1862.

8. Drake, *Ninth New Jersey*, 120–21; Foster, *New Jersey and the Rebellion*, 227; *Newark Daily Advertiser*, Jan. 29, 1863; Edmund J. Cleveland diary, Jan. 2, 1863.

9. Drake, *Ninth New Jersey*, 120; Everts, *Ninth New Jersey*, 90; Jonathan R. Reading to Joseph Thompson, Dec. 24, 1862, Thompson Papers.

10. Boatner, *Civil War Dictionary*, 197; OR, ser. 1, 18:500–501; Bilby and Goble, *"Remember You Are Jerseymen!,"* 149.

11. Drake, *Ninth New Jersey*, 123; Fonville, *Wilmington Campaign*, 6–18, 52–53.

12. Longacre, "Profile of Major General David Hunter," 4, 6–9. The only modern biography of Hunter is Miller, *Lincoln's Abolitionist General*.

13. Everts, *Ninth New Jersey*, 90; Drake, *Ninth New Jersey*, 124; *Newark Daily Journal*, Jan. 30, 1863; Edmund J. Cleveland diary, Jan. 21, 1863; John Bamford to "Dear Brothers," Jan. 28, 1863; David C. Hankins to "Dear Sister," Jan. 29, 1863.

14. Drake, *Ninth New Jersey*, 124; *Paterson Daily Guardian*, Feb. 10, 1862; Symmes H. Stillwell to "Dear Mother," Feb. 1, 1863.

15. David C. Hankins to "Dear Sister," Nov. 3, 1862; *American Standard*, Dec. 30, 1862.

16. David C. Hankins to "Dear Sister," Jan. 8, 1863; *Newark Daily Journal*, Jan. 30, 1863.

17. Drake, *Ninth New Jersey*, 124–26; Everts, *Ninth New Jersey*, 90.

18. Drake, *Ninth New Jersey*, 126–27.

19. Edmund J. Cleveland diary, Jan. 31, 1863; Symmes H. Stillwell to "Dear Mother," Feb. 1, 1863.

20. Rose, *Rehearsal for Reconstruction*, provides a valuable overview of the interaction among the African American inhabitants of South Carolina's Sea Islands, Union military officers and civilian authorities, and Northern religious and educational officials.

21. Drake, *Ninth New Jersey*, 127; *Newark Daily Journal*, Feb. 27, 1863.

22. Drake, *Ninth New Jersey*, 128–30; *OR*, ser. 1, 14:394–96; Andrew W. Little to "Dear Sister," Feb. 18, 1863.

23. *OR*, ser. 1, 14:396–417, 423–24.

24. Burton, *Siege of Charleston*, 132–36.

25. *OR*, ser. 1, 14:469; *OR-N*, ser. 1, 14:32–35; *Newark Daily Advertiser*, Mar. 2, 1863; *New Jersey Journal*, Mar. 3, 17, 1863; Edmund J. Cleveland diary, Feb. 7, 8, 1863.

26. Drake, *Ninth New Jersey*, 127–28; Andrew W. Little to "Dear Sister," Feb. 9, 1863.

27. Everts, *Ninth New Jersey*, 90; Drake, *Ninth New Jersey*, 128; Edmund J. Cleveland diary, Feb. 11, 1863; *New Jersey Journal*, Mar. 17, 1863.

28. Andrew W. Little to "Dear Sister," Feb. 18, 1863; Edmund J. Cleveland diary, Feb. 11, 1863; *Newark Daily Journal*, Feb. 27, 1863. Although Drake, Everts, and other members of the regiment sought to exonerate the Ninth from complicity in the burning of the Negro village, an enlisted man from Gloucester County admitted in a letter printed in the May 5, 1863, issue of the *Woodbury Constitution* that soldiers of the Ninth were fully involved in the attack.

29. Everts, *Ninth New Jersey*, 90–91; Edmund J. Cleveland diary, Feb. 17, 1863.

30. Drake, *Ninth New Jersey*, 128; *Woodbury Constitution*, May 5, 1863; *New Jersey Journal*, Mar. 17, 1863.

31. *Freehold Democrat*, Mar. 19, 1863; Symmes H. Stillwell to "Dear Mother," Apr. 16, 1863.

32. *New Jersey Journal*, Mar. 3, 17, 1863; Symmes H. Stillwell to "Dear Mother," Mar. 8, 1863. The basis of Stillwell's "negative racial attitude" is explored in Verter, "Disconsolations of a Jersey Muskrat," 257–60.

33. *Newark Daily Journal*, Mar. 5, 1863; Symmes H. Stillwell to "Dear Mother," Mar. 8, 1863; David C. Hankins to "Dear Sister," Feb. 22, 1863.

34. Edmund J. Cleveland diary, Feb. 20, 21, 1863.

35. *Newton Register*, Mar. 6, 1863; Edmund J. Cleveland diary, Feb. 20, Mar. 7, 1863; *Newark Daily Advertiser*, Mar. 24, 1863.

36. Drake, *Ninth New Jersey*, 130–31; Edmund J. Cleveland diary, Feb. 11, 1863; Everts, *Ninth New Jersey*, 91; *New Jersey Journal*, Apr. 14, 1863.

37. Drake, *Ninth New Jersey*, 131; Symmes H. Stillwell to "Dear Mother," Mar. 8, 1863; *Plainfield Union*, Dec. 9, 1862; Edmund J. Cleveland diary, Mar. 5, 1863; *Newark Daily Advertiser*, Mar. 24, 1863; *New Jersey Journal*, Mar. 31, 1863; *Newark Daily Journal*, Apr. 2, 1863.

38. David C. Hankins to "Dear Sister," Mar. 26, 1863; Andrew W. Little to "Dear Sister," Mar. 12, 1863; Drake, *Ninth New Jersey*, 132; *OR*, ser. 1, 14:434–35; 18:577; Edmund J. Cleveland diary, Mar. 30, 1863; *New Jersey Journal*, Apr. 14, 1863; *Newark Daily Journal*, Mar. 17, 1863.

39. Andrew W. Little to "Dear Sister," Mar. 31, 1863; *New Jersey Journal*, Apr. 14, 1863.

40. Andrew W. Little to "Dear Sister," Apr. 12, 1863; Drake, *Ninth New Jersey*, 132.

41. Drake, *Ninth New Jersey*, 132; Everts, *Ninth New Jersey*, 91–92; Edmund J. Cleveland diary, Apr. 3–5, 1863; Symmes H. Stillwell to "Dear Mother," Apr. 4, 1863; Andrew W. Little to "Dear Sister," Apr. 12, 1863; David C. Hankins to "Dear Sister," Apr. 14, 1863; *OR-N*, ser. 1, 14:5; Burton, *Siege of Charleston*, 135.

42. Drake, *Ninth New Jersey*, 132; Edmund J. Cleveland diary, Apr. 6, 1863.

43. Drake, *Ninth New Jersey*, 132–33.

44. Burton, *Siege of Charleston*, 136–41; *OR-N*, ser. 1, 14:5–41, 75–78.

45. Andrew W. Little to "Dear Sister," Apr. 12, 1863; *Ocean Emblem*, May 14, 1863.

46. Drake, *Ninth New Jersey*, 133; *Woodbury Constitution*, May 5, 1863.

47. Everts, *Ninth New Jersey*, 92; Foster, *New Jersey and the Rebellion*, 229–30; *OR*, ser. 1, 14:440. Drake, *Ninth New Jersey*, 133–35, gives a highly dramatized account of the meeting between Hunter and Heckman, at which he was not present.

48. Drake, *Ninth New Jersey*, 135–36.

49. *Newark Daily Journal*, Apr. 22, 1863; *Newton Register*, May 1, 1863.

8. SWEET HOME NORTH CAROLINA

1. Barrett, *Civil War in North Carolina*, 149–56; Cormier, *Siege of Suffolk*, 298–99.

2. Drake, *Ninth New Jersey*, 137; Everts, *Ninth New Jersey*, 92; Edmund J. Cleveland diary, Apr. 16, 17, 1863; *Paterson Daily Guardian*, Apr. 28, 1863; *New Jersey Journal*, May 5, 1863; Barrett, *Civil War in North Carolina*, 157–61.

3. Symmes H. Stillwell to "Dear Mother," Apr. 16, 1863; Andrew W. Little to "Dear Sister," Apr. 17, 1863.

4. Drake, *Ninth New Jersey*, 138; Foster, *New Jersey and the Rebellion*, 232–33; *Woodbury Constitution*, May 5, 1863; *Ocean Emblem*, May 14, 1863.

5. *New Jersey Journal*, May 19, 1863; Robert B. Vanderhoef to "Dear Brothers," Apr. 27, 1863, Vanderhoef Papers, Rutgers University Libraries.

6. Everts, *Ninth New Jersey*, 93; Drake, *Ninth New Jersey*, 139–40; *Newark Daily Journal*, May 11, 1863.

7. Andrew W. Little to "Dear Sister," Apr. 25, 1863; Robert B. Vanderhoef to "Dear Brothers," Apr. 27, 1863; Edmund J. Cleveland diary, Apr. 26, 1863; Everts, *Ninth*

New Jersey, 94; Drake, *Ninth New Jersey*, 139, 142–43; *Newark Daily Journal*, June 23, July 13, 1863; *Ocean Emblem*, July 23, 1863.

8. Drake, *Ninth New Jersey*, 140; Everts, *Ninth New Jersey*, 93; *Newark Daily Journal*, June 2, 1863; Symmes H. Stillwell to "Dear Mother," May 6, 1863.

9. Andrew W. Little to "Dear Sister," May 3, 1863; David C. Hankins to "Dear Sister," May 4, 1863; Edmund J. Cleveland diary, Apr. 29, 30, May 1, 11, 15, 1863; William P. Amerman to "Dear Cousin," May 12, 1863.

10. *Ocean Emblem*, May 14, 1863; *Newton Register*, May 15, 1863; *New Jersey Journal*, May 26, 1863.

11. Edmund J. Cleveland diary, May 4, 19, 1863; *New Jersey Journal*, May 26, 1863; *Newark Daily Journal*, June 2, 1863; *Woodbury Constitution*, June 9, 1863. The most satisfactory modern account of Hooker's failed campaign is Sears, *Chancellorsville*. The eleven New Jersey regiments that fought at Chancellorsville, May 1–3, 1863, suffered a combined total of almost 1,000 officers and men killed, wounded, or missing (*OR*, ser. 1, 25, pt. 1:174–84).

12. Symmes H. Stillwell to "Dear Mother," Dec. 5–6, 1862.

13. Jonathan R. Reading to Joseph Thompson, May 22, 1863, Thompson Papers; *OR*, ser. 4, 1:1094–1100.

14. *OR*, ser. 4, 1:1094–1100; *Newark Daily Journal*, June 23, 1863; Edmund J. Cleveland diary, May 22, June 26, 1863; *New Jersey Journal*, June 16, 1863.

15. *OR*, ser. 3, 1:88–93; Faust, *Historical Times Illustrated Encyclopedia of the Civil War*, 160–61, 225–26.

16. *OR*, ser. 1, 18:737 and n; Warner, *Generals in Blue*, 467–68; Drake, *Ninth New Jersey*, 142; *Newark Daily Journal*, June 23, 1863; Edmund J. Cleveland diary, June 1, 1863; Andrew W. Little to "Dear Sister," June 19, 1863.

17. Edmund J. Cleveland diary, June 1, 1863; Symmes H. Stillwell to "Dear Mother," June 2, 1863; *Newark Daily Journal*, June 23, 1863.

18. *New Jersey Journal*, July 14, 1863.

19. Drake, *Ninth New Jersey*, 143; Everts, *Ninth New Jersey*, 94; Edmund J. Cleveland diary, June 26, 1863; Symmes H. Stillwell to "Dear Mother," July 2, 1863.

20. Drake, *Ninth New Jersey*, 143; Foster, *New Jersey and the Rebellion*, 233; *Newark Daily Journal*, July 13, 1863; *New Jersey Journal*, Aug. 11, 1863.

21. Drake, *Ninth New Jersey*, 143; Edmund J. Cleveland diary, July 4, 5, 1863; *Freehold Herald*, July 30, 1863; *Ocean Emblem*, July 23, 1863; *Newark Daily Journal*, July 13, 1863.

22. Drake, *Ninth New Jersey*, 143–44; *OR*, ser. 1, 27, pt. 2:859–65; Symmes H. Stillwell to "Dear Mother," July 8, 1863; *Newark Daily Advertiser*, July 20, 1863.

23. Drake, *Ninth New Jersey*, 144; Everts, *Ninth New Jersey*, 94; *Newark Daily Journal*, July 13, 1863; *Ocean Emblem*, July 23, 1863; Andrew W. Little to "Dear Sister," July 8, 1863.

24. Symmes H. Stillwell to "Dear Mother," June 21, July 8, 1863; *New Jersey Journal*, Aug. 11, 1863; Edmund J. Cleveland diary, July 11, 21, 1863.

25. Symmes H. Stillwell to "Dear Mother," Sept. 16, 1863.

26. Drake, *Ninth New Jersey*, 144–45; Everts, *Ninth New Jersey*, 95; Edmund J. Cleveland diary, July 14–17, 1863; Foster, *New Jersey and the Rebellion*, 231; OR, ser. 1, 27, pt. 2:874–75; *Newark Daily Mercury*, July 29, 1863; Andrew W. Little to "Dear Sister," July 17, 1863.

27. Edmund J. Cleveland diary, July 18, 1863; *Newark Daily Mercury*, July 29, 1863.

28. Edmund J. Cleveland diary, Aug. 1, 1863. For more on the New York draft riots see Cook, *Armies of the Streets*.

29. David C. Hankins to "Dear Sister," Aug. 15, 1863; *Newark Daily Mercury*, Sept. 12, 1863; Everts, *Ninth New Jersey*, 96; Drake, *Ninth New Jersey*, 148; Edmund J. Cleveland diary, Oct. 24, 1863.

30. Drake, *Ninth New Jersey*, 146; John Bamford to "Dear Brother," July 24, 1863; Everts, *Ninth New Jersey*, 95–96.

31. Drake, *Ninth New Jersey*, 146–48; Edmund J. Cleveland diary, July 26, 1863.

32. Drake, *Ninth New Jersey*, 146–47; Foster, *New Jersey and the Rebellion*, 234–35; Symmes H. Stillwell to "Dear Mother," Aug. 3, 1863; Edmund J. Cleveland diary, July 27, 1863; *Ocean Emblem*, Aug. 20, 1863.

33. Edmund J. Cleveland diary, July 28, 1863; Drake, *Ninth New Jersey*, 148; *Ocean Emblem*, Aug. 20, 1863.

34. Symmes H. Stillwell to "Dear Mother," Aug. 3, 1863.

35. *Medical and Surgical History of the War of the Rebellion*, 5:154. Everts, *Ninth New Jersey*, 194–97, presents a "Tabular List of Diseases" contracted by the men of the Ninth from 1863 to 1865, running the gamut from piles and carbuncles to dysentery and typhoid fever.

36. Andrew W. Little to "Dear Sister," Aug. 8, 1863.

37. David C. Hankins to "Dear Sister," Aug. 15, 1863; *Ocean Emblem*, Sept. 3, 1863; Edmund J. Cleveland diary, Aug. 10, 1863.

38. OR, ser. 1, 29, pt. 2:100.

39. Drake, *Ninth New Jersey*, 149; Symmes H. Stillwell to "Dear Mother," Aug. 30, 1863; Edmund J. Cleveland diary, Aug. 27, 1863.

40. Edmund J. Cleveland diary, Aug. 27, 1863; *New Jersey Journal*, Sept. 15, 1863; Symmes H. Stillwell to "Dear Mother," Sept. 16, 1863; *Newark Daily Journal*, Oct. 3, 28, 1863; *Newark Daily Mercury*, Oct. 6, 1863.

41. Drake, *Ninth New Jersey*, 149.

42. Andrew W. Little to "Dear Sister," Sept. 27, 1863; Edmund J. Cleveland diary, Aug. 24, Oct. 4, 1863.

43. Drake, *Ninth New Jersey*, 150; *Newark Daily Journal*, Oct. 3, 1863; Symmes H. Stillwell to "Dear Mother," Oct. 8, 1863.

44. Drake, *Ninth New Jersey*, 150.
45. Edmund J. Cleveland diary, Oct. 13–15, 1863.
46. *Newark Daily Journal*, Oct. 3, 1863; *New Jersey Journal*, Oct. 13, 1863.
47. *OR*, ser. 1, 29, pt. 2:267, 276–78, 301, 312.
48. *OR*, ser. 1, 29, pt. 2:277. The best book-length studies of the Chickamauga and Chattanooga Campaigns are Cozzens, *This Terrible Sound* and *Shipwreck of Their Hopes*, respectively.
49. *OR*, ser. 1, 29, pt. 2:352–53; Drake, *Ninth New Jersey*, 150; Foster, *New Jersey and the Rebellion*, 235; Edmund J. Cleveland diary, Oct. 19, 20–22, 1863; Andrew W. Little to "Dear Sister," Oct. 21, 1863; *State Gazette and Republican*, Oct. 23, 1863.
50. Drake, *Ninth New Jersey*, 151; Everts, *Ninth New Jersey*, 98; Symmes H. Stillwell to "Dear Mother," Oct. 23, 1863; *Paterson Daily Press*, Oct. 26, 1863.

9. VETERAN VOLUNTEERS

1. Symmes H. Stillwell to "Dear Mother," Oct. 23, 1863.
2. David C. Hankins to "Dear Sister," Nov. 6, 20, 1863; *Newark Daily Journal*, Nov. 5, 30, 1863; *OR*, ser. 1, 29, pt. 2:470; Drake, *Ninth New Jersey*, 151.
3. Everts, *Ninth New Jersey*, 98; *Newark Daily Journal*, Nov. 5, 1863; Edmund J. Cleveland diary, Oct. 31, 1863.
4. *Ocean Emblem*, Nov. 19, 1863, Jan. 21, 1864; Edmund J. Cleveland diary, Dec. 30, 1863; *Newark Daily Journal*, Jan. 22, 1864.
5. *Woodbury Constitution*, Dec. 1, 1863.
6. Drake, *Ninth New Jersey*, 151.
7. Drake, *Ninth New Jersey*, 151, 329–32; Symmes H. Stillwell to "Dear Mother," Oct. 23, 1863.
8. *Newark Daily Journal*, Oct. 26, 1863; David C. Hankins to "Dear Sister," Oct. 25, 1863.
9. *Ocean Emblem*, Nov. 19, 1863.
10. Symmes H. Stillwell to "Dear Mother," Feb. 10, 1864.
11. Symmes H. Stillwell to "Dear Mother," Feb. 10, 1864; Edmund J. Cleveland diary, Nov. 25, 1863.
12. Everts, *Ninth New Jersey*, 98; Drake, *Ninth New Jersey*, 151–52, 156; Symmes H. Stillwell to "Dear Mother," Nov. 24, 1863; *Newark Daily Journal*, Nov. 30, 1863; *New Jersey Journal*, Dec. 22, 1863; *Ocean Emblem*, Dec. 10, 1863.
13. Symmes H. Stillwell to "Dear Mother," Dec. 4, 1863.
14. Drake, *Ninth New Jersey*, 151; Everts, *Ninth New Jersey*, 98; Warner, *Generals in Blue*, 157; Boatner, *Civil War Dictionary*, 302; *New York Times*, Nov. 3, 1863; *New York Tribune*, Nov. 9, 1863.
15. *OR*, ser. 1, 29, pt. 2:397; Longacre, *Army of Amateurs*, 1–10.
16. Edmund J. Cleveland diary, Nov. 13, 1863; Andrew W. Little to "Dear Sister," Nov. 16, 1863.

17. Edmund J. Cleveland diary, Dec. 8, 1863; *Newark Daily Journal*, Dec. 16, 1863; Drake, *Ninth New Jersey*, 152. Drake misdates the review as December 1.

18. Edmund J. Cleveland diary, Dec. 20, 22, 1863; Symmes H. Stillwell to "Dear Mother," Dec. 25, 1863; Drake, *Ninth New Jersey*, 153.

19. *New Jersey Journal*, Jan. 5, 1864; Drake, *Ninth New Jersey*, 153; David C. Hankins to "Dear Sister," Jan. 10, 1864; Edmund J. Cleveland diary, Dec. 25, 1863. The "Army Hymn" by Oliver Wendell Holmes, Sr., published in 1861, begins: "O Lord of Hosts! Almighty King! / Behold the sacrifice we bring / To every arm thy strength impart, / Thy spirit shed through every heart!"

20. Drake, *Ninth New Jersey*, 153, 155; Edmund J. Cleveland diary, Jan. 2, 1864.

21. Edmund J. Cleveland diary, Nov. 6, 1863; *OR*, ser. 1, 29, pt. 2:565; ser. 3, 3:414–16, 785, 997–99; 4:930.

22. Edmund J. Cleveland diary, Nov. 28, 30, 1863.

23. Drake, *Ninth New Jersey*, 152–53; Andrew W. Little to "Dear Sister," Dec. 27, 1863; George V. H. Weaver to Joseph Thompson, Dec. 13, 1863, Thompson Papers; *Newark Daily Journal*, Dec. 16, 1863; *Newton Register*, Dec. 18, 1863. Bilby and Goble, *"Remember You Are Jerseymen!,"* 151–52, attribute the regiment's strong reenlistment rate to "the Ninth's high morale, linked to its elite status, combat successes and relatively low casualties."

24. *Newark Daily Journal*, Feb. 29, 1864; Symmes H. Stillwell to "Dear Mother," Nov. 7, 1863.

25. Drake, *Ninth New Jersey*, 157–58, 337; Edmund J. Cleveland diary, Jan. 13, 15, 1864; *American Standard*, Jan. 15, 16, 1864; *Daily True American*, Jan. 18, 1864; *Monmouth Herald-Inquirer* (Freehold NJ), Jan. 24, 1864; *Newark Daily Journal*, Jan. 23, 1864.

26. Everts, *Ninth New Jersey*, 99; Drake, *Ninth New Jersey*, 158–59; Foster, *New Jersey and the Rebellion*, 236; Edmund J. Cleveland diary, Jan. 21, 1864; Symmes H. Stillwell to "Dear Mother," Jan. 21, 1864; David C. Hankins to "Dear Sister," Apr. 4, 1864; *New Jersey Journal*, Feb. 23, 1864; *Trenton Times-Advertiser*, Jan. 26, 1864.

27. Everts, *Ninth New Jersey*, 99; Drake, *Ninth New Jersey*, 161, 163–65; *New Jersey Journal*, Feb. 23, 1864; Edmund J. Cleveland diary, Jan. 31–Feb. 4, 1864; *State Gazette and Republican*, Feb. 6, 12, 1864; *New Brunswick Daily Fredonian*, Feb. 8, 1864; *Paterson Daily Guardian*, Feb. 8, 1864; *Daily True American*, Feb. 9, 1864; *Sentinel of Freedom*, Feb. 9, 1864; *Hunterdon County Democrat*, Feb. 10, 1864; Bilby and Goble, *"Remember You Are Jerseymen!,"* 151.

28. *Paterson Press*, Feb. 9, 1864; *New Brunswick Daily Fredonian*, Feb. 10, 1864; *New Jersey Mirror and Burlington County Advertiser* (Mount Holly NJ), Feb. 11, 1864.

29. Drake, *Ninth New Jersey*, 161, 165–66, 337; Everts, *Ninth New Jersey*, 100–101; John Kitchen to Joseph Thompson, Feb. 24, 1864, Thompson Papers; *Newark Daily Journal*, Feb. 29, 1864; *Beacon* (Lambertville, NJ), Mar. 11, 1864.

30. Edmund J. Cleveland diary, Feb. 6–17, Mar. 7, 1864; Stryker, *Record of Officers and Men of New Jersey*, 1:481.

31. Everts, *Ninth New Jersey*, 98–99; Drake, *Ninth New Jersey*, 158–60; Foster, *New Jersey and the Rebellion*, 236; OR, ser. 1, 33:361; *Newark Daily Journal*, Jan. 22, 1864.

32. Drake, *Ninth New Jersey*, 160; Everts, *Ninth New Jersey*, 99; Symmes H. Stillwell to "Dear Mother," Jan. 21, 24, 1864; *Trenton Times-Advertiser*, Jan. 26, 1864; *New Jersey Journal*, Feb. 23, 1864; Edmund J. Cleveland diary, Jan. 30, 1864; OR, ser. 1, 33:483.

33. Symmes H. Stillwell to "Dear Mother," Jan. 21, 24, Feb. 7, 1864.

34. Everts, *Ninth New Jersey*, 100; Foster, *New Jersey and the Rebellion*, 236–37; *Beacon*, Mar. 11, 1864; *State Gazette and Republican*, Mar. 7, 1864; *Jersey City Daily Advocate and Hudson County Observer*, Mar. 8, 1864; *Ocean Emblem*, Mar. 31, 1864; Stryker, *Record of Officers and Men of New Jersey*, 1:452. According to Drake, *Ninth New Jersey*, 162, Pvt. Nutt's body was found the day after the skirmish "horribly mutilated." This cannot be confirmed; Drake himself was in New Jersey on leave at the time of the fight and thus was not a participant in or an observer of the skirmish. Also dubious is the claim made in Foster, *New Jersey and the Rebellion*, 237, that General Heckman, when pursuing the assailants, was "enraged by the wanton cruelty of the enemy."

35. OR, ser. 1, 33:225–27; David C. Hankins to "Dear Sister," Mar. 8, 1864.

36. Drake, *Ninth New Jersey*, 337–38; OR, ser. 1, 33:84–97; David C. Hankins to "Dear Sister," Mar. 8, 1864. For more on the Kilpatrick-Dahlgren raid see Venter, *Kill Jeff Davis*.

37. Gillette, *Jersey Blue*, 254–55; *State Gazette and Republican*, Apr. 5, 1864. Pvt. William H. Van Arsdale of Company K noted in his diary, Apr. 2, 1864 (in Van Arsdale Family Papers, Rutgers University Libraries), that other regiments in the department were granted mass furloughs "for the purpose of going home to vote . . . [during] their State election." New Jersey was one of only three Northern states (the others being Illinois and Indiana) to deny soldiers in the field the right to vote in the election (McPherson, *Tried by War*, 248–49).

38. *Ocean Emblem*, Mar. 31, 1864; *Belvidere Intelligencer*, Apr. 1, 1864.

39. Drake, *Ninth New Jersey*, 338; Edmund J. Cleveland diary, Nov. 25, 1863.

40. Composed by William Vincent Wallace with a libretto by Edward Fitzball, *Maritana* was first produced at Theatre Royal, Drury Lane, London, in November 1845.

41. Drake, *Ninth New Jersey*, 338–39.

42. Drake, *Ninth New Jersey*, 166; Everts, *Ninth New Jersey*, 102; Edmund J. Cleveland diary, Mar. 17, 1864; Andrew W. Little to "Dear Sister," Mar. 19, 1864; *Newark Daily Journal*, Mar. 24, 1864; David C. Hankins to "Dear Sister," Feb. 26, 1864.

43. Symmes H. Stillwell to "Dear Brother," Mar. 21, 1864; to "Dear Mother," Dec. 4, 1863.

44. Verter, "Disconsolations of a Jersey Muskrat," 268–69.

45. Everts, *Ninth New Jersey*, 102; Drake, *Ninth New Jersey*, 166, 340–41; *State Gazette and Republican*, Apr. 21, 1864; *Ocean Emblem*, Mar. 31, 1864; Edmund J. Cleveland diary, Mar. 22, 24, 27, 1864.

46. David C. Hankins to "Dear Sister," Apr. 4, 1864; Symmes H. Stillwell to "Dear Mother," Apr. 8, 1864.

47. Drake, *Ninth New Jersey*, 341–42.

48. Drake, *Ninth New Jersey*, 167–68, 341–43; Everts, *Ninth New Jersey*, 102–3; David C. Hankins to "Dear Sister," Apr. 16, 1864; Andrew W. Little to "Dear Sister," Apr. 17, 1864; Edmund J. Cleveland diary, Apr. 13–15, 1864; *State Gazette and Republican*, Apr. 21, 1864; *New Jersey Journal*, Apr. 26, 1864.

10. THE KILLING FIELDS

1. Smith, "Butler's Attack on Drewry's Bluff," 206 and 207; Longacre, *Army of Amateurs*, 33–39. Butler's command was officially known as the Army of the Department of Virginia and North Carolina. Its better-known appellation was bestowed on it by Brig. Gen. Rufus Ingalls, chief quartermaster of the armies besieging Richmond and Petersburg, as a means of distinguishing it from Ingalls's other customer, the Army of the Potomac.

2. Andrew W. Little to "Dear Sister," Apr. 23, 29, 1864; Everts, *Ninth New Jersey*, 102–3; Drake, *Ninth New Jersey*, 167, 170.

3. Everts, *Ninth New Jersey*, 103; Drake, *Ninth New Jersey*, 169, 343–44.

4. Drake, *Ninth New Jersey*, 169–70; Edmund J. Cleveland diary, Apr. 29–30, 1864.

5. Drake, *Ninth New Jersey*, 345; Symmes H. Stillwell to "Dear Mother," Apr. 30, 1864; Andrew W. Little to "Dear Sister," Apr. [May] 4, 1864; Edmund J. Cleveland diary, May 3, 1864; *OR*, ser. 1, 36, pt. 1:118.

6. Drake, *Ninth New Jersey*, 171, 345; Robertson, *Back Door to Richmond*, 60.

7. Drake, *Ninth New Jersey*, 171–72, 345; Robertson, *Back Door to Richmond*, 58–61; Schiller, *Bermuda Hundred Campaign*, 63–66.

8. Drake, *Ninth New Jersey*, 345; Robertson, *Back Door to Richmond*, 22; Smith, "Butler's Attack on Drewry's Bluff," 206; Longacre, *Army of Amateurs*, 74–75; Warner, *Generals in Blue*, 176–77.

9. Smith, "Butler's Attack on Drewry's Bluff," 207–8; Robertson, *Back Door to Richmond*, 78–80, 150–51, 158n; Longacre, *Army of Amateurs*, 87–88.

10. Longacre, "'A Perfect Ishmaelite,'" 10, 16; Robertson, *Back Door to Richmond*, 26–28, 35, 55–57.

11. Drake, *Ninth New Jersey*, 172, 198; Everts, *Ninth New Jersey*, 104; *OR*, ser. 1, 36, pt. 2:153–54; Edmund J. Cleveland diary, May 5, 1864; Andrew W. Little to "Dear

Sister," May 11, 1864; Robertson, *Back Door to Richmond*, 72, 79–80; Schiller, *Bermuda Hundred Campaign*, 77.

12. Drake, *Ninth New Jersey*, 173, 198; Everts, *Ninth New Jersey*, 104; Robertson, *Back Door to Richmond*, 79–80; Schiller, *Bermuda Hundred Campaign*, 77–81; Longacre, *Army of Amateurs*, 75–76.

13. Drake, *Ninth New Jersey*, 174, 198–99; *OR*, ser. 1, 36, pt. 2:154; Foster, *New Jersey and the Rebellion*, 238; Drake, *Fast and Loose in Dixie*, 13; Edmund J. Cleveland diary, May 6, 1864.

14. Drake, *Ninth New Jersey*, 174, 346–47. The soldier killed next to Pvt. Keenan on May 6 was Pvt. Timothy Callahan of Company H.

15. Drake, *Ninth New Jersey*, 175–76; Robertson, *Back Door to Richmond*, 82; *OR*, ser. 1, 36, pt. 2:154; Derby, *Bearing Arms in the Twenty-seventh Massachusetts*, 246; Schiller, *Bermuda Hundred Campaign*, 80 and n, 81 and n. The meritorious service that Drake performed was undoubtedly important, but no more so than that rendered by many another officer under similar conditions. Drake himself claimed (*Fast and Loose in Dixie*, 296) that "I was presented with a bronze medal by Congress (on the recommendation of General [James] Stewart to General Ulysses S. Grant) for 'gallantry and bravery.'" One wonders if Drake's subsequent suffering as a prisoner of war and his well publicized escape from captivity contributed to the War Department's decision to award him the medal in March 1873.

16. Robertson, *Back Door to Richmond*, 82–83, 88–90; Schiller, *Bermuda Hundred Campaign*, 81–82, 85–93, 96–98; Longacre, *Army of Amateurs*, 77–78; Klein, "Bottling Up Butler at Bermuda Hundred," 10.

17. Drake, *Ninth New Jersey*, 176–79, 199, 204; *OR*, ser. 1, 36, pt. 2:155; Andrew W. Little to "Dear Sister," May 11, 1864; Drake, *Fast and Loose in Dixie*, 14–16; Foster, *New Jersey and the Rebellion*, 238–39; Robertson, *Back Door to Richmond*, 88; Schiller, *Bermuda Hundred Campaign*, 87, 89; Edmund J. Cleveland diary, May 7, 1864.

18. Robertson, *Back Door to Richmond*, 88; Schiller, *Bermuda Hundred Campaign*, 92–93; *OR*, ser. 1, 36, pt. 2:124–25, 155.

19. Drake, *Ninth New Jersey*, 179, 199, 350; Edmund J. Cleveland diary, May 7, 1864.

20. Drake, *Ninth New Jersey*, 179; Robertson, *Back Door to Richmond*, 89.

21. Robertson, *Back Door to Richmond*, 109–116; Schiller, *Bermuda Hundred Campaign*, 122–34; Drake, *Ninth New Jersey*, 179–80, 199–200.

22. Drake, *Ninth New Jersey*, 350.

23. Drake, *Ninth New Jersey*, 182; Andrew W. Little to "Dear Sister," May 11, 1864.

24. Drake, *Ninth New Jersey*, 180; Robertson, *Back Door to Richmond*, 119–21.

25. Longacre, *Army of Amateurs*, 81–85.

26. Robertson, *Back Door to Richmond*, 146–53, 170–78.

27. Drake, *Ninth New Jersey*, 182–83, 200; Everts, *Ninth New Jersey*, 106–7; Drake, *Fast and Loose in Dixie*, 17–19.

28. Drake, *Ninth New Jersey*, 184–85; Bilby, *Civil War Firearms*, 203–4.

29. Drake, *Ninth New Jersey*, 185–89, 200–201, 205, 353–54; Everts, *Ninth New Jersey*, 107–8; Drake, *Fast and Loose in Dixie*, 20–22.

30. Robertson, *Back Door to Richmond*, 154, 175–76; Drake, *Ninth New Jersey*, 189–91.

31. Drake, *Ninth New Jersey*, 191, 201, 353–54; OR, ser. 1, 36, pt. 2:161–62; Robertson, *Back Door to Richmond*, 176, 178–79.

32. Drake, *Ninth New Jersey*, 190–91, 205; Robertson, *Back Door to Richmond*, 173.

33. Drake, *Ninth New Jersey*, 201, 205, 353–55.

34. Andrew W. Little to "Dear Sister," May 20, 1864; *Woodbury Constitution*, May 31, 1864.

35. Drake, *Ninth New Jersey*, 192–94, 201–2, 206, 254, 356–57; Andrew W. Little to "Dear Sir," May 21, 1864; *Woodbury Constitution*, May 31, 1864; OR, ser. 1, 36, pt. 2:162. A corrected handwritten copy of Lt. Col. Stewart's official report of the battle is in Record Book 421, New Jersey State Archives.

36. Drake, *Ninth New Jersey*, 357–58.

37. Drake, *Ninth New Jersey*, 195, 207–8.

38. Drake, *Ninth New Jersey*, 195–96, 201–2; Robertson, *Back Door to Richmond*, 184–85; Schiller, *Bermuda Hundred Campaign*, 233–34.

39. Robertson, *Back Door to Richmond*, 198–215; Schiller, *Bermuda Hundred Campaign*, 250–85.

40. Drake, *Ninth New Jersey*, 202–3; Everts, *Ninth New Jersey*, 108–10, 116; Andrew W. Little to "Dear Sister," May 20, 1864; Stryker, *Record of Officers and Men of New Jersey*, 1:430, 468; *Memorial of Colonel Abram Zabriskie*, 11–12; James Stewart, Jr., to anon., "List of Casualties among the Officers of the Ninth Regt New Jersey Vols, in the Late Engagement at Fort Drewry [*sic*] Va., May 16th 1864," June 4, 1864, Record Book 421, New Jersey State Archives. It is not known how many members of the Ninth fought at Drewry's Bluff. In his diary entry of May 12, 1864, Pvt. Cleveland claimed that half the regiment, being sick or otherwise unfit for field duty, was left at Bermuda Hundred when the army marched north that day.

41. J. Madison Drake, "How Prisoners Were Deprived of Comfort," *Elizabeth Leader*, Mar. 25, 1906; "General Heckman's Account of the Fighting of the 9th N.J. Vols at Drewry's Bluff, May 16 '64," Record Book 421, New Jersey State Archives. One of those captured on May 16 and sent to the notorious prison camp in Georgia was Company A's Pvt. Herman Knoll (misspelled as Noll in Stryker, *Record of Officers and Men of New Jersey*). Six days after the battle Knoll somehow sent a letter through the lines to his wife from his original place of confinement, Libby Prison in Richmond, where he claimed

to be "doing well." The letter reposes in the Marcus Ward Papers in the New Jersey Historical Society. Knoll would die of dysentery at Andersonville on August 25.

42. *Ocean Emblem*, Nov. 10, 1864; *Newark Daily Advertiser*, Dec. 1, 1864; *Democratic Banner*, Dec. 15, 1864; Drake, *Fast and Loose in Dixie*, 27–28. Another who was surprised to find Heckman among the prisoners of war was Archibald Gracie, who said to him: "I am right glad to meet you under these circumstances, and am proud to say that I have been fighting Jerseymen all day" (Foster, *New Jersey and the Rebellion*, 242).

11. DECLINE AND REVIVAL

1. Edmund J. Cleveland diary, May 17–19, 26, 1864. Details of Zabriskie's funeral in Jersey City and burial in Greenwood Cemetery can be found in *Memorial of Zabriskie*, 17–22; *New York Times*, May 30, 1864; and *American Standard*, June 1, 1864.

2. Drake, *Ninth New Jersey*, 211; William Arthur Conover to James S. Yard, May 23, 1864, Conover Papers, Rutgers University Libraries.

3. Amos H. Evans to "Dear Friend," June 20, 1864, William Frederick Allen Papers, Historical Society of Pennsylvania; Robertson, *Back Door to Richmond*, 170; Symmes H. Stillwell to "Dear Mother," May 21, 1864.

4. Andrew W. Little to "Dear Sir," May 21, 1864.

5. Drake, *Ninth New Jersey*, 211, 215; Everts, *Ninth New Jersey*, 116; Longacre, *Army of Amateurs*, 104; Warner, *Generals in Blue*, 471–72.

6. Andrew W. Little to "Dear Sister," May 26, 1864; Robertson, *Back Door to Richmond*, 219–23; Longacre, *Army of Amateurs*, 105–9; Klein, "Bottling Up Butler at Bermuda Hundred," 45–46.

7. Drake, *Ninth New Jersey*, 211–12; Foster, *New Jersey and the Rebellion*, 245; Jackson, *New Jerseyans in the Civil War*, 176.

8. Drake, *Ninth New Jersey*, 212–15; Everts, *Ninth New Jersey*, 117–18; Foster, *New Jersey and the Rebellion*, 245–46; Edmund J. Cleveland diary, May 23, 1864; Drake, *Historical Sketches of Revolutionary and Civil Wars*, 226–29. Although perhaps overly dramatic, the best source on this intelligence-gathering mission is the James Van Buskirk memoir, a typed copy of which is in the John Kuhl Collection. The original is in the possession of Gordon Simpson of Milford NJ.

9. Robertson, *Back Door to Richmond*, 224, 230–32; Longacre, *Army of Amateurs*, 111–13. Grant's Overland Campaign receives detailed coverage in three books by Gordon C. Rhea: *Battle of the Wilderness, Battles for Spotsylvania Court House and the Road to Yellow Tavern*, and *To the North Anna River*.

10. Everts, *Ninth New Jersey*, 118; Drake, *Ninth New Jersey*, 215; Edmund J. Cleveland diary, May 27, 1864.

11. Everts, *Ninth New Jersey*, 119; *OR*, ser. 1, 51, pt. 1:1253, 1260; Amos H. Evans to "Dear Friend," June 20, 1864, William Frederick Allen Papers; Edmund J. Cleveland diary, June 1, 1864; *Newark Daily Journal*, June 6, 1864; *Woodbury Constitution*, July 26, 1864; Drake, *Ninth New Jersey*, 215–16.

12. Longacre, *Army of Amateurs*, 116–23; Jonathan R. Reading to Joseph Thompson, June 10, 1864, Thompson Papers. Two worthy studies of the fighting of June 1–3 are Furgurson, *Not War but Murder*, and Rhea, *Cold Harbor*.

13. Everts, *Ninth New Jersey*, 119–20; Drake, *Ninth New Jersey*, 217; Amos H. Evans to "Dear Friend," June 20, 1864, William Frederick Allen Papers; Edmund J. Cleveland diary, June 5, 11, 1864.

14. Edmund J. Cleveland diary, June 5, 1864; Drake, *Ninth New Jersey*, 218–19; Drake, *Historical Sketches of Revolutionary and Civil Wars*, 152–54; Foster, *New Jersey and the Rebellion*, 247.

15. Everts, *Ninth New Jersey*, 121–22; Drake, *Ninth New Jersey*, 222–23; Edmund J. Cleveland diary, June 13, 1864.

16. *OR*, ser. 1, 51, pt. 1:255–56; Longacre, *Army of Amateurs*, 140–41; Jonathan R. Reading to Joseph Thompson, June 10, 1864, Thompson Papers.

17. Everts, *Ninth New Jersey*, 122; Drake, *Ninth New Jersey*, 223; Edmund J. Cleveland diary, June 15, 1864.

18. Longacre, *Army of Amateurs*, 143–47; Symmes H. Stillwell to "Dear Mother," Aug. 5, 1864.

19. Longacre, *Army of Amateurs*, 152–54; Klein, "Lost Opportunity at Petersburg," 42–50. The most satisfactory study of the Petersburg Campaign is Trudeau, *Last Citadel*.

20. Everts, *Ninth New Jersey*, 122–23; Drake, *Ninth New Jersey*, 223–24; Edmund J. Cleveland diary, June 16, 1864; Amos H. Evans to "Dear Friend," June 20, 1864, William Frederick Allen Papers; Foster, *New Jersey and the Rebellion*, 247–48; *OR*, ser. 1, 40, pt. 2:81–82, 153; *New Jersey Journal*, July 19, 1864; *Woodbury Constitution*, July 26, 1864; Longacre, *Army of Amateurs*, 154–57; Robertson, *Back Door to Richmond*, 241–42.

21. Everts, *Ninth New Jersey*, 123; Drake, *Ninth New Jersey*, 225; David C. Hankins to "Dear Sister," June 18, 1864; Edmund J. Cleveland diary, June 20, 1864.

22. *OR*, ser. 1, 40, pt. 2:224; Drake, *Ninth New Jersey*, 226; Edmund J. Cleveland diary, June 22, 1864; *New Jersey Journal*, July 19, 1864; *Woodbury Constitution*, July 26, 1864.

23. Amos H. Evans to "Dear Friend," June 20, 1864, William Frederick Allen Papers; Everts, *Ninth New Jersey*, 124; Edmund J. Cleveland diary, June 21, 1864, Drake, *Ninth New Jersey*, 226–27.

24. Drake, *Ninth New Jersey*, 227–28. On pp. 371–72, former Corp. Francis A. Kenyon, a veteran of Company B, tells the same story but identifies the unfortunate comrade as "Thomas Putnam," whose name cannot be found on the regiment's rolls.

25. Drake, *Ninth New Jersey*, 228–29, 370; Foster, *New Jersey and the Rebellion*, 248.

26. Drake, *Ninth New Jersey*, 228; Edmund J. Cleveland diary, July 1, 2, 1864.

27. Everts, *Ninth New Jersey*, 125, 128, 137, 139; Drake, *Ninth New Jersey*, 229, 237, 254; Stryker, *Record of Officers and Men of New Jersey*, 1:430; Foster, *New Jersey and the Rebellion*, 249, 251; *Hunterdon Republican*, July 1, 1864; *Princeton Standard*, Sept. 2, 1864; Edmund J. Cleveland, "Late Campaigns in North Carolina," 18.

28. Longacre, *Army of Amateurs*, 175–76, 183; *New York Times*, June 28, 1864.

29. *OR*, ser. 1, 40, pt. 1:266 and n; pt. 3:740; Everts, *Ninth New Jersey*, 129; Drake, *Ninth New Jersey*, 237; *Princeton Standard*, Aug. 5, 1864.

30. Longacre, *Army of Amateurs*, 187–91.

31. Symmes H. Stillwell to "Dear Mother," Aug. 5, 1864.

32. Edmund J. Cleveland diary, July 31, Aug. 1, 4, 1864; *New Jersey Journal*, Aug. 16, 1864; *Newark Daily Advertiser*, Aug. 3, 1864.

33. Edmund J. Cleveland diary, Aug. 15, 1864.

34. Edmund J. Cleveland diary, Aug. 1, 6, 1864; Drake, *Ninth New Jersey*, 238–39, 241–42; *Woodbury Constitution*, Aug. 16, 1864.

35. Edmund J. Cleveland diary, Aug. 13, 1864; *OR*, ser. 1, 42, pt. 2:500–501; David C. Hankins to "Dear Sister," Sept. 14, 1864.

36. Everts, *Ninth New Jersey*, 130; Drake, *Ninth New Jersey*, 242–43; David C. Hankins to "Dear Sister," Aug. 12, 1864.

37. Everts, *Ninth New Jersey*, 130–31; Drake, *Ninth New Jersey*, 243–44; Edmund J. Cleveland diary, Aug. 15, 1864; Andrew W. Little to "Dear Sister," Aug. 19, 1864; *Princeton Standard*, Sept. 2, 1864; Drake, *Historical Sketches of Revolutionary and Civil Wars*, 193–95.

38. Everts, *Ninth New Jersey*, 131–32; Drake, *Ninth New Jersey*, 245–47; Edmund J. Cleveland diary, Aug. 16–25, 1864; *New Jersey Journal*, Sept. 13, 1864; Foster, *New Jersey and the Rebellion*, 249. Heckman, who had been paroled, exchanged, and released from prison early in August, was assigned to the Virginia theater. In September he was given command of a division in the XVIII Corps and took part in an offensive against the outer works of Richmond. According to his corps commander, Maj. Gen. Edward O. C. Ord (successor to Baldy Smith, whom Grant had recently jettisoned), Heckman's maiden effort in division command was lacking. Though he succeeded Ord following the latter's wounding in the fight, Heckman later returned to divisional command. In January 1865 he was assigned to the newly formed XXV Corps, composed entirely of USCT units. Shortly before the commencement of the Appomattox Campaign, Heckman was relieved from duty for unspecified reasons and sent home. Late that May he resigned his brigadier's appointment (Warner, *Generals in Blue*, 227; Longacre, *Army of Amateurs*, 214–17, 219).

39. Foster, *New Jersey and the Rebellion*, 249; *New Jersey Journal*, Sept. 13, 1864; Gillette, *Jersey Blue*, 267–75.

40. Edmund J. Cleveland diary, Sept. 6, 1864.

41. Everts, *Ninth New Jersey*, 136; Drake, *Ninth New Jersey*, 249, 251; Edmund J. Cleveland diary, Sept. 17–18, 1864; *Newark Daily Advertiser*, Oct. 11, 1864; Symmes H. Stillwell to "Dear Mother," Aug. 29, 1864.

42. Edmund J. Cleveland, "Late Campaigns in North Carolina," 5, 11; *New Jersey Journal*, Sept. 22, 1864.

43. Drake, *Ninth New Jersey*, 251–53; Everts, *Ninth New Jersey*, 136; David C. Hankins to "Dear Sister," Oct. 6, 1864; Edmund J. Cleveland, "Late Campaigns in North Carolina," 5–6; *Newark Daily Advertiser*, Oct. 11, 1864.

44. Andrew W. Little to "Dear Sister," Sept. 24, 1864; *Woodbury Constitution*, Oct. 11, 1864.

45. Edmund J. Cleveland, "Late Campaigns in North Carolina," 7–8; Everts, *Ninth New Jersey*, 137–38, 160; Drake, *Ninth New Jersey*, 254–55; Amos H. Evans to "Friend Will," Oct. 6, 1864, William Frederick Allen Papers; Andrew W. Little to "Dear Sister," Oct. 10, 1864.

46. Edmund J. Cleveland, "Late Campaigns in North Carolina," 7, 10–11; Drake, *Ninth New Jersey*, 255.

47. Edmund J. Cleveland, "Late Campaigns in North Carolina," 10; Drake, *Ninth New Jersey*, 358.

48. Everts, *Ninth New Jersey*, 138–39; Drake, *Ninth New Jersey*, 255–56; Edmund J. Cleveland, "Late Campaigns in North Carolina," 14; *Newark Daily Advertiser*, Nov. 5, 1864; *Salem Standard*, Nov. 9, 1864.

49. *Woodbury Constitution*, Oct. 11, 1864; *New Jersey Journal*, Dec. 6, 1864.

50. *Trenton Daily Monitor*, Oct. 17, 1864.

51. Andrew W. Little to "Dear Sister," Nov. 3, 1864; *Newark Daily Journal*, Nov. 3, 1864.

52. Gillette, *Jersey Blue*, 285–94; McPherson, *Tried by War*, 248–50.

12. WAR'S END, AND AFTER

1. Drake, *Ninth New Jersey*, 272, 359; Everts, *Ninth New Jersey*, 158–59; Jonathan R. Reading to Joseph Thompson, Feb. 3, 1865, Thompson Papers; *Woodbury Constitution*, Feb. 15, 1865.

2. *OR*, ser. 1, 29, pt. 2:456; *OR-N*, ser. 1, 11:82–83, 180; Drake, *Ninth New Jersey*, 360.

3. Hunt and Brown, *Brevet Brigadier Generals in Blue*, 215; Stryker, *Record of Officers and Men of New Jersey*, 1:432.

4. Everts, *Ninth New Jersey*, 140–41; Drake, *Ninth New Jersey*, 257–58, 360; Foster, *New Jersey and the Rebellion*, 251–52; William B. Maines to William H. Van Arsdale, Dec. 14, 1864, Van Arsdale Family Papers; Edmund J. Cleveland, "Late Campaigns in North Carolina," 24–25; David C. Hankins to "Dear Sister," Dec. 8, 1864.

5. *OR-N*, ser. 1, 11:160–61, 177–78; Everts, *Ninth New Jersey*, 141–42; Drake, *Ninth New Jersey*, 258–59, Foster, *New Jersey and the Rebellion*, 252; *Newark Daily Advertiser*, Dec. 27, 1864; *State Gazette and Republican*, Jan. 30, 1865.

6. Everts, *Ninth New Jersey*, 142–43; Drake, *Ninth New Jersey*, 259–60; Foster, *New Jersey and the Rebellion*, 252; *Newark Daily Advertiser*, Dec. 27, 1864.

7. Everts, *Ninth New Jersey*, 143–44; Drake, *Ninth New Jersey*, 260–64, 360.

8. Drake, *Ninth New Jersey*, 266; Foster, *New Jersey and the Rebellion*, 253–54; *Newark Daily Advertiser*, Dec. 27, 1864; *OR-N*, ser. 1, 11:160–65, 177.

9. *OR-N*, ser. 1, 11:165, 177–81.

10. Drake, *Ninth New Jersey*, 266–67; David C. Hankins to "Dear Sister," Jan. 1, 1865.

11. Drake, *Ninth New Jersey*, 267, 269; Everts, *Ninth New Jersey*, 146.

12. Drake, *Ninth New Jersey*, 270–72; Jonathan R. Reading to Joseph Thompson, Feb. 3, 1865, Thompson Papers; *Newark Daily Advertiser*, Feb. 7, 1865.

13. Everts, *Ninth New Jersey*, 147–58; Drake, *Ninth New Jersey*, 271; Foster, *New Jersey and the Rebellion*, 254. Drake provides a detailed account of his imprisonment, escape, and return to the field in *Fast and Loose in Dixie* and in his *Historical Sketches of the Revolutionary and Civil Wars*, 128–50. Lt. Peters, captured along with Drake, also escaped from prison but was recaptured and incarcerated until paroled and exchanged in February 1865. His story is told in Drake, *Ninth New Jersey*, 289–93.

14. *State Gazette and Republican*, Jan. 14, 1865, carries an article by Drake about the accident.

15. Everts, *Ninth New Jersey*, 158; Drake, *Ninth New Jersey*, 271; Drake, *Fast and Loose in Dixie*, 295; Stryker, *Record of Officers and Men of New Jersey*, 1:477.

16. *OR*, ser. 1, 47, pt. 1:60; pt. 2:626; Everts, *Ninth New Jersey*, 158; Drake, *Ninth New Jersey*, 272; Stryker, *Record of Officers and Men of New Jersey*, 1:430, 432; *State Gazette and Republican*, Jan. 30, 1865.

17. *Newark Daily Advertiser*, Feb. 7, 1865. The regiment's first historian wrote that Woodhull's "indefatigable and patriotic labors, during four long years of war, exhibit a record which does him the greatest credit, and sheds luster on the State which he so ably represented in the field" (Everts, *Ninth New Jersey*, 161).

18. Longacre, *Army of Amateurs*, 245–67; McDonough, *Schofield*, 151, 153–55.

19. Longacre, *Worthy Opponents*, 302–4; Sherman, *Memoirs*, 2:299–300.

20. Andrew W. Little to "Dear Sister," Jan. 29, Feb. 12, 1865.

21. *Woodbury Constitution*, Feb. 15, 1865; Edmund J. Cleveland, "Late Campaigns in North Carolina," 40; *Minstrels! Grand Variety Entertainment by the 9th Regt. New Jersey Minstrels* (Office of the *North Carolina Times* (New Bern NC), Jan. 1865).

22. Drake, *Ninth New Jersey*, 273–74; Edmund J. Cleveland, "Late Campaigns in North Carolina," 42; *OR*, ser. 1:, 47, pt. 1:57n, 984.

23. Drake, *Ninth New Jersey*, 274; *OR*, ser. 1, 47, pt. 1:61, 974.

24. Everts, *Ninth New Jersey*, 162; Drake, *Ninth New Jersey*, 274–75; Longacre, *Worthy Opponents*, 305; *OR*, ser. 1, 47, pt. 1:980–81.

25. Drake, *Ninth New Jersey*, 275; Foster, *New Jersey and the Rebellion*, 255; *Camden Democrat*, Apr. 8, 1865; *OR*, ser. 1, 47, pt. 1:981–82, 984, 986.

26. For the most recent and most satisfactory account of the fighting of March 8–10, 1865, see Smith and Sokolosky, *"To Prepare for Sherman's Coming."*

27. Everts, *Ninth New Jersey*, 162; Barrett, *Civil War in North Carolina*, 287–88.

28. Drake, *Ninth New Jersey*, 276–78, 287.

29. Drake, *Ninth New Jersey*, 279; Everts, *Ninth New Jersey*, 162; Barrett, *Civil War in North Carolina*, 289–90.

30. *OR*, ser. 1, 47, pt. 1:61–62; Andrew W. Little to "Dear Sister," Mar. 11, 1865; Lt. Edward W. Welsted to N. J. Adj. Gen. Robert F. Stockton, Jr., Mar. 17, 1865, Record Book 420, New Jersey State Archives.

31. Everts, *Ninth New Jersey*, 162–63; Andrew W. Little to "Dear Sister," Mar. 11, 1865; Drake, *Ninth New Jersey*, 279–80, 361–62.

32. Everts, *Ninth New Jersey*, 163.

33. Everts, *Ninth New Jersey*, 164; Drake, *Ninth New Jersey*, 280–81; Foster, *New Jersey and the Rebellion*, 256; Andrew W. Little to "Dear Sister," Mar. 18, 1865; *Newark Daily Advertiser*, Apr. 5, 1865.

34. Drake, *Ninth New Jersey*, 282, 361.

35. Drake, *Ninth New Jersey*, 282–83, 363; Everts, *Ninth New Jersey*, 164–65; Foster, *New Jersey and the Rebellion*, 256–57; Andrew W. Little to "Dear Sister," Mar. 18, 1865; *Newark Daily Advertiser*, Apr. 5, 1865.

36. *Newark Daily Advertiser*, Apr. 5, 1865; Andrew W. Little to "Dear Sister," Apr. 2, 1865; Drake, *Ninth New Jersey*, 283–84, 288, 363–64; Edmund J. Cleveland, "Late Campaigns in North Carolina," 50, 70.

37. Drake, *Ninth New Jersey*, 284, 288; Everts, *Ninth New Jersey*, 166–67; Andrew W. Little to "Dear Sister," Apr. 2, 1865.

38. Everts, *Ninth New Jersey*, 168; Drake, *Ninth New Jersey*, 284–87; Edmund J. Cleveland, "Late Campaigns in North Carolina," 49.

39. Edmund J. Cleveland, "Late Campaigns in North Carolina," 50; Foster, *New Jersey and the Rebellion*, 257–58.

40. Drake, *Ninth New Jersey*, 289; *OR*, ser. 1, 47, pt. 1:59.

41. Drake, *Ninth New Jersey*, 293–94, 364; Everts, *Ninth New Jersey*, 173; Edmund J. Cleveland, "Late Campaigns in North Carolina," 52; Foster, *New Jersey and the Rebellion*, 258.

42. Andrew W. Little to "Dear Sister," Apr. 18, 1865; Drake, *Ninth New Jersey*, 297, 364–65; Edmund J. Cleveland, "Late Campaigns in North Carolina," 55, 57, 59.

43. Andrew W. Little to "Dear Sister," Apr. 18, 23, 1865.

44. Longacre, *Worthy Opponents*, 307–12. Typical of the regiment's reaction to Johnston's surrender was the April 27 diary entry of Pvt. Cleveland: "A nation's gratitude to God for the return of peace—Home, Home, Home Sweet Home!"

45. Drake, *Ninth New Jersey*, 298, 365; *OR*, ser. 1, 47, pt. 3:376.

46. Everts, *Ninth New Jersey*, 175–80; Drake, *Ninth New Jersey*, 299–301, 304; Edmund J. Cleveland, "Late Campaigns in North Carolina," 59–61.

47. Drake, *Ninth New Jersey*, 301; *OR*, ser. 1, 47, pt. 3:490–91; *Jersey City Daily Standard*, June 7, 1865; Runyan, *Eight Days with the Confederates*, 8–41.

48. Andrew W. Little to "Dear Mother," May 14, 1865.

49. Drake, *Ninth New Jersey*, 304, 365; Edmund J. Cleveland, "Late Campaigns in North Carolina," 66, 71.

50. *OR*, ser. 1, 47, pt. 3:614–15; Edmund J. Cleveland, "Late Campaigns in North Carolina," 69–70; Everts, *Ninth New Jersey*, 181; David C. Hankins to "Dear Sister," June 19, 1865; Drake, *Ninth New Jersey*, 305.

51. Edmund J. Cleveland, "Late Campaigns in North Carolina," 71–76.

52. Drake, *Ninth New Jersey*, 306–7, 365; Everts, *Ninth New Jersey*, 182–83; Stryker, *Record of Officers and Men of New Jersey*, 1:430.

53. Drake, *Ninth New Jersey*, 307; Everts, *Ninth New Jersey*, 182.

54. Edmund J. Cleveland, "Late Campaigns in North Carolina," 79–81.

BIBLIOGRAPHY

ARCHIVES/MANUSCRIPT MATERIALS

Amerman, William P. Correspondence. U.S. Army Heritage and Education Center, Carlisle Barracks PA.

Bamford, John. Correspondence. Rutgers University Libraries, New Brunswick NJ.

Boa, Joseph M. "Civil War Chronology as Related to the Service of Noah E. Jeffrey, Private, D Company, 9th Regiment NJ Volunteer Inf." Typescript in possession of the author.

"Charlie," Company I, Ninth New Jersey Volunteers. Letter of ca. February 9, 1862. In possession of Willard B. Green, Carneys Point NJ.

Cleveland, Edmund J. Diaries, 1862–64, and Papers. New Jersey Historical Society, Newark.

———. "The Late Campaigns in North Carolina as Seen through the Eyes of a New Jersey Soldier (Private Edmund J. Cleveland, Co. K., Ninth New Jersey Volunteers), September 20, 1864–July 4, 1865." Southern Historical Collection, Wilson Library, University of North Carolina, Chapel Hill.

Conover, William Arthur. Letter of May 23, 1864. Conover Papers, Rutgers University Libraries.

Cook, Henry. Diaries, 1862–64. Gilder Lehrman Institute, New York NY.

Curlis, William B. Correspondence. Joseph Thompson Papers. Rutgers University Libraries.

Drake, J. Madison. Scrapbook of "Civil War Reminiscences." New Jersey Historical Society.

Evans, Amos H. Letter of June 20, 1864. William Frederick Allen Papers. Historical Society of Pennsylvania, Philadelphia.

Gafney, Andrew J. Correspondence. Marcus Ward Papers. New Jersey Historical Society.

Gahm, Peter. Letter of January 27, 1863. Marcus Ward Papers. New Jersey Historical Society.

Hankins, David C. Correspondence. Sarah Hankins Papers. Burlington County Historical Society, Burlington NJ.

Henry, Joseph J. Letter of August 27, 1861. John Kuhl Collection, Pittstown NJ.

Herbert, Charles M. Letter of September 17, 1861. James M. Nevius Papers. Rutgers University Libraries.

Houck, John M. "The Battle of New Bern." Cornelia Berry Fore Papers. Charlotte and Mecklenburg County Library, Charlotte NC.

Jeffrey, Noah E. Pension Claim, February 2, 1883. In possession of Joseph M. Boa, Tinton Falls NJ.

Kitchen, John. Correspondence. Joseph Thompson Papers. Rutgers University Libraries.

Knoll, Herman. Letter of May 22, 1864. Marcus Ward Papers. New Jersey Historical Society.

Little, Andrew W. Correspondence. Hunterdon County Historical Society, Flemington NJ.

Maines, William B. Letter of December 14, 1864. Van Arsdale Family Papers. Rutgers University Libraries.

Ninth New Jersey Volunteers. Campaign Reports, Equipment and Ordnance Returns, Headquarters Correspondence, Muster Rolls, etc. New Jersey State Archives, Trenton.

Ninth New Jersey Volunteers, Companies B and D. Clothing Accounts, Company Correspondence, Court Martial Proceedings, Muster Rolls, Ordnance Returns, etc. Rutgers University Libraries.

Nymaster, John D. Letter of December 29, 1861. Joseph Thompson Papers. Rutgers University Libraries.

Reading, Jonathan R. Correspondence. Joseph Thompson Papers. Rutgers University Libraries.

Riddle, Gilbert V. "Beaufort Plow Boys Flag." PowerPoint presentation in possession of the compiler, Greenville NC.

Scranton, Charles. Letter of September 30, 1861. Joseph Thompson Papers. Rutgers University Libraries.

Smith, John N. Correspondence. Joseph Thompson Papers. Rutgers University Libraries.

Springer, C. Bayard. "Diary of Lieutenant C. Bayard Springer, Company I, 9th Regt. NJ. Vols., 1862." Southern Historical Collection, Wilson Library, University of North Carolina.

Stillwell, Symmes H. Correspondence and Diaries, 1862–64. Princeton University Library, Princeton NJ.

Thomas, Albert R. Letter of December 9, 1861. Joseph Thompson Papers. Rutgers University Libraries.

Van Arsdale, William H. Diary, 1864, and Letter of October 20, 1863. Rutgers University Libraries.

Van Buskirk, James. Memoirs. John Kuhl Collection.

Vanderhoef, Robert B. Correspondence. Rutgers University Libraries.

Van Fleet, James O. Letter of January 4, 1862. John E. Van Fleet Papers. Rutgers University Libraries.

Van Nest, Henry V. Correspondence. Joseph Thompson Papers. Rutgers University Libraries.

Weaver, Gorge V. H. Correspondence. Joseph Thompson Papers. Rutgers University Libraries.

Zabriskie, Abram. Letter of January 17, 1862. William L. Dayton Papers. Princeton University Library.

PUBLISHED WORKS

Annual Report of the Quartermaster General of the State of New Jersey, for the Year 1862. Trenton NJ: David Naar, 1863.

Barnes, Joseph K., ed. *The Medical and Surgical History of the War of the Rebellion (1861–65)*. 12 vols. Washington DC: Government Printing Office, 1870–88.

Barrett, John G. *The Civil War in North Carolina*. Chapel Hill: University of North Carolina Press, 1963.

Bearss, Edwin Cole. *Vicksburg Is the Key*. Vol. 1 of *The Campaign for Vicksburg*. Dayton OH: Morningside, 1985.

Bilby, Joseph G. *Civil War Firearms: Their Historical Background, Tactical Use and Modern Collecting and Shooting*. Conshohocken PA: Combined Publishing, 1996.

——. "No Way to Raise an Army: Recruiting in New Jersey during the Civil War." Master's thesis, Seton Hall University, 1982.

Bilby, Joseph G., and William C. Goble. *"Remember You Are Jerseymen!" A Military History of New Jersey Troops in the Civil War*. Hightstown NJ: Longstreet House, 1998.

Boa, Marty. "Evidence of Battle Survives on Roanoke Island in North Carolina." *Civil War News* 24 (July 1993): 44–45.

——. "New Bern Abounds with Civil War Lore." *Civil War News* 24 (December 1993): 53–54.

——. "New Bern—The Battle." *Atlanticville* 17 (May 21, 1992): 49.

——. "New Jersey Marksmen Rallied to the Cause in 1861." *Atlanticville* 17 (May 7, 1992), 38.

——. "Roanoke Island and New Bern—The Battles and the Battlefields." *Atlanticville* 17 (May 28, 1992): 34.

——. "Roanoke Island—The Battle." *Atlanticville* 17 (May 14, 1992): 36.

Boatner, Mark Mayo III. *The Civil War Dictionary*. New York: David McKay, 1959.

Burnside, Ambrose E. "The Burnside Expedition." In *Battles and Leaders of the Civil War*, edited by Robert U. Johnson and C. C. Buel, 2:660–69. New York: Century, 1887.

Bussanich, Leonard. "'To Reach Sweet Home Again': The Impact of Soldiering on New Jersey's Troops during the Civil War." *New Jersey History* 125 (2010): 37–60.

Clark, Walter, ed. *Histories of the Several Regiments and Battalions from North Carolina in the Great War, 1861–'65* . . . 5 vols. Goldsboro NC: E. M. Uzzell, 1901.

Clayton, W. Woodford, ed. *History of Union and Middlesex Counties, New Jersey with Biographical Sketches of Many of Their Pioneers and Prominent Men*. Philadelphia: Everts & Peck, 1882.

Clayton, W. Woodford, and William Nelson, comps. *History of Bergen and Passaic Counties, New Jersey, with Biographical Sketches of Many of Its Pioneers and Prominent Men*. Philadelphia: Everts & Peck, 1882.

Cook, Adrian. *The Armies of the Streets: The New York City Draft Riots of 1863*. Lexington: University Press of Kentucky, 1982.

Cormier, Steven A. *The Siege of Suffolk: The Forgotten Campaign, April 11–May 4, 1863*. Lynchburg VA: H. E. Howard, 1989.

Cozzens, Peter. *No Better Place to Die: The Battle of Stones River*. Urbana: University of Illinois Press, 1991.

———. *The Shipwreck of Their Hopes: The Battle for Chattanooga*. Urbana: University of Illinois Press, 1994.

———. *This Terrible Sound: The Battle of Chickamauga*. Urbana: University of Illinois Press, 1992.

Cunningham, John T. *New Jersey: America's Main Road*. Garden City NY: Doubleday, 1966.

Cushing, Thomas, and Charles E. Sheppard. *History of the Counties of Gloucester, Salem, and Cumberland, New Jersey, with Biographical Sketches of Their Prominent Citizens*. Philadelphia: Everts & Peck, 1883.

Denny, J. Waldo. *Wearing the Blue in the Twenty-fifth Mass. Volunteer Infantry* . . . Worcester MA: Putnam & Davis, 1879.

Derby, W. P. *Bearing Arms in the Twenty-seventh Massachusetts Regiment of Volunteer Infantry during the Civil War, 1861–1865*. Boston: Wright & Potter, 1883.

Drake, J. Madison. "Adventurous Escape from Prison Life: An Incident of the Late Civil War." *Magazine of American History* 14 (1885): 404–6.

———. *Fast and Loose in Dixie: An Unprejudiced Narrative of Personal Experience as a Prisoner of War at Libby, Macon, Savannah, and Charleston* . . . New York: Authors' Publishing, 1880.

———. *Historical Sketches of the Revolutionary and Civil Wars, with an Account of Author's Desperate Leap from a Swiftly Moving Train of Cars, and a Fatiguing Tramp of 1,000 Miles through Three Confederate States, in Making His Escape from a Prison-Pen*. New York: privately issued, 1908.

————. *The History of the Ninth New Jersey Veteran Vols.: A Record of Its Service from Sept. 13th, 1861, to July 12th, 1865, with a Complete Official Roster, and Sketches of Prominent Members, with Anecdotes, Incidents and Thrilling Reminiscences.* Elizabeth NJ: Journal Printing House, 1889.

————. *Narrative of the Capture, Imprisonment and Escape of J. Madison Drake, Captain Ninth New Jersey Veteran Volunteers* . . . n. p., privately issued, 1868.

————. "Out of Bondage." *Harper's Weekly* 9 (January 14, 1865): 30.

Emmerton, James A. *A Record of the Twenty-third Regiment Mass. Vol. Infantry in the War of the Rebellion, 1861–1865.* Boston: William Ware, 1886.

Emory, Frederick. "The Baltimore Riots." In *Annals of the War, Written by Leading Participants North and South,* 775–93. Philadelphia: Times Publishing, 1879.

Everts, Hermann. *A Complete and Comprehensive History of the Ninth Regiment New Jersey Vols. Infantry from Its First Organization to Its Final Muster Out.* Newark NJ: A. Stephen Holbrook, 1865.

Faust, Patricia L., ed., *Historical Times Illustrated Encyclopedia of the Civil War.* New York: Harper & Row, 1986.

Fleming, Thomas. *New Jersey: A Bicentennial History.* New York: W. W. Norton, 1977.

Fonville, Chris E., Jr. *The Wilmington Campaign: Last Rays of Departing Hope.* Mechanicsburg PA: Stackpole Books, 1997.

Foster, John Y. *New Jersey and the Rebellion: A History of the Services of the Troops and People of New Jersey in Aid of the Union Cause.* Newark NJ: Dennis, 1868.

Furgurson, Ernest B. *Not War but Murder: Cold Harbor, 1864.* New York: Alfred A. Knopf, 2000.

The Gazette Souvenir: Fifth Reunion of the Ninth Regt. New Jersey Vols., Held at Hightstown, N.J., September 16th, 1890. Hightstown: Hightstown Gazette, 1890.

Gillette, William. *Jersey Blue: Civil War Politics in New Jersey, 1854–1865.* New Brunswick NJ: Rutgers University Press, 1995.

Gillmore, Quincy A. "The Army before Charleston in 1863." In *Battles and Leaders of the Civil War,* edited by Robert U. Johnson and C. C. Buel, 4:52–71. New York: Century, 1888.

Gragg, Rod. *Covered with Glory: The 26th North Carolina Infantry at the Battle of Gettysburg.* New York: HarperCollins, 2000.

Grimsley, Mark. *The Hard Hand of War: Union Military Policy toward Southern Civilians, 1861–1865.* New York: Cambridge University Press, 1995.

Guernsey, Alfred H., and Henry M. Alden, eds. *Harper's Pictorial History of the Civil War.* New York: Harper & Brothers, 1866.

"Hard to Swallow: A Brief History of Hardtack and Ship's Biscuit." MilitaryHistoryNow.com. http://militaryhistorynow.com/2014/07/11/hard-to-swallow-a-brief-history-of-hardtack-and-ships-biscuit-2/.

Hawkins, Rush C. "Early Coast Operations in North Carolina." In *Battles and Leaders of the Civil War*, edited by Robert U. Johnson and C. C. Buel, 2:632–59. New York: Century, 1887.

Heitman, Francis B., comp. *Historical Register and Dictionary of the United States Army*. 2 vols. Washington DC: Government Printing Office, 1903.

Hennessy, John J. *Return to Bull Run: The Campaign and Battle of Second Manassas*. New York: Simon & Schuster, 1993.

Hess, Earl J. *Banners to the Breeze: The Kentucky Campaign, Corinth, and Stones River*. Lincoln: University of Nebraska Press, 2000.

Hill, Daniel Harvey. *Bethel to Sharpsburg*. Raleigh NC: Edwards & Broughton, 1926.

Hunt, Roger D., and Jack R. Brown. *Brevet Brigadier Generals in Blue*. Gaithersburg MD: Olde Soldier Books, 1990.

Jackson, William J. *New Jerseyans in the Civil War: For Union and Liberty*. New Brunswick NJ: Rutgers University Press, 2000.

Jordan, Weymouth T., Jr., and Louis H. Manarin, comps. *North Carolina Troops, 1861–1865: A Roster*. 18 vols. Raleigh: North Carolina Office of Archives and History, 1979.

Kinston, Whitehall and Goldsboro (North Carolina) Expedition, December, 1862. New York: W. W. Howe, 1890.

Klein, Frederic S. "Bottling Up Butler at Bermuda Hundred." *Civil War Times Illustrated* 6 (November 1967): 4–11, 45–47.

———. "Lost Opportunity at Petersburg." *Civil War Times Illustrated* 5 (August 1966): 39–50.

Knapp, Charles Merriam. *New Jersey Politics during the Period of the Civil War and Reconstruction*. Geneva NY: W. F. Humphrey, 1924.

Lindblade, Eric A. *Fight as Long as Possible: The Battle of Newport Barracks, North Carolina, February 2, 1864*. Gettysburg PA: Ten Roads Publishing, 2010.

Long, John D. *9th New Jersey Volunteer Regiment.—By J. D. Long, Private of Company C*. New York: H. De Marsan, 1862. [Broadside]

Longacre, Edward G. *Army of Amateurs: General Benjamin F. Butler and the Army of the James, 1863–1865*. Mechanicsburg PA: Stackpole Books, 1997.

———. *The Early Morning of War: Bull Run, 1861*. Norman: University of Oklahoma Press, 2014.

———. "'A Perfect Ishmaelite': General 'Baldy' Smith." *Civil War Times Illustrated* 15 (December 1976): 10–20.

———. "A Profile of Major General David Hunter." *Civil War Times Illustrated* 16 (January 1978): 4–9, 38–43.

———. *To Gettysburg and Beyond: The Twelfth New Jersey Volunteer Infantry, II Corps, Army of the Potomac, 1862–1865*. Hightstown NJ: Longstreet House, 1988.

————. *Worthy Opponents: General William T. Sherman, U.S.A., General Joseph E. Johnston, C.S.A.* Nashville TN. Rutledge Hill Press, 2006.

Lord, Francis A. *Civil War Sutlers and Their Wares.* New York: Thomas Yoseloff, 1969.

Luvaas, Jay. "Burnside's Roanoke Island Campaign." *Civil War Times Illustrated* 7 (December 1968): 4–11, 43–48.

Marvel, William. *Burnside.* Chapel Hill: University of North Carolina Press, 1991.

McConnell, William. *Remember Reno: A Biography of Major General Jesse Lee Reno.* Shippensburg PA: White Mane, 1996.

McDonough, James L. *Schofield: Union General in the Civil War and Reconstruction.* Tallahassee: Florida State University Press, 1972.

McPherson, James M. *Crossroads of Freedom: Antietam.* New York: Oxford University Press, 2002.

————. *Tried by War: Abraham Lincoln as Commander in Chief.* New York: Penguin Press, 2008.

McWhiney, Grady, and Perry D. Jamieson. *Attack and Die: Civil War Military Tactics and the Southern Heritage.* University: University of Alabama Press, 1982.

Memorial of Colonel Abram Zabriskie, by the Bar of Hudson County, New Jersey. Jersey City NJ: John H. Lyon, 1864.

Miers, Earl Schenck. *New Jersey and the Civil War: An Album of Contemporary Accounts.* Princeton NJ: D. Van Nostrand, 1964.

Miller, Edward A. *Lincoln's Abolitionist General: The Biography of David Hunter.* Columbia: University of South Carolina Press, 1997.

Minstrels! Grand Variety Entertainment by the 9th Regt. New Jersey Minstrels . . . [February 25, 1865]. Carolina City NC: Office of the North Carolina Times, 1865. [Broadside]

Moore, James. *History of the Cooper Shop Volunteer Refreshment Saloon.* Philadelphia: James B. Rodgers, 1866.

Nichols, Isaac T. *Historic Days in Cumberland County, New Jersey, 1855–1865.* Bridgeton NJ: privately issued, 1907.

Official Records of the Union and Confederate Navies in the War of the Rebellion. 2 series, 30 vols. Washington DC: Government Printing Office, 1894–1922.

O'Reilly, Francis Augustin. *The Fredericksburg Campaign: Winter War on the Rappahannock.* Baton Rouge: Louisiana State University Press, 2006.

Report of State Commission for Erection of Monument to Ninth New Jersey Volunteers, New Berne, North Carolina: Dedication, National Cemetery, New Berne, N.C., May 18, 1905. Philadelphia: John C. Winston, 1905.

Rhea, Gordon C. *The Battle of the Wilderness, May 5–6, 1864.* Baton Rouge: Louisiana State University Press, 1994.

————. *The Battles for Spotsylvania Court House and the Road to Yellow Tavern, May 7–12, 1864.* Baton Rouge: Louisiana State University Press, 1997.

————. *Cold Harbor: Grant and Lee, May 26–June 3, 1864*. Baton Rouge: Louisiana State University Press, 2002.

————. *To the North Anna River: Grant and Lee, May 13–25, 1864*. Baton Rouge: Louisiana State University Press, 2000.

Richards, Jay. "April 1861: First Call to Arms." *Civil War Warren County NJ* (blog). http://jayrichards-civilwarwarrencounty.blogspot.co.nz/2011/04/april-1861-first-call-to-arms.html.

————. "Belvidere's Brief Secession." *Civil War Warren County NJ* (blog). http://jayrichards-civilwarwarrencounty.blogspot.co.nz/2011/04/april-14-1861-bel videres-brief.html.

Robertson, William Glenn. *Back Door to Richmond: The Bermuda Hundred Campaign, April-June 1864*. Newark: University of Delaware Press, 1987.

Rodgers, C. R. P. "Du Pont's Attack at Charleston." In *Battles and Leaders of the Civil War*, edited by Robert U. Johnson and C. C. Buel, 4:32–47. New York: Century, 1888.

Rogers, Edward H. *Reminiscences of Military Service in the Forty-third Regiment, Massachusetts Infantry, during the Great Civil War, 1862–63*. Boston: Rand, Avery, 1883.

Rose, Willie Lee. *Rehearsal for Reconstruction: The Port Royal Experiment*. Indianapolis: Bobbs-Merrill, 1964.

Runyan, Morris C. *Eight Days with the Confederates and Capture of Their Archives, Flags, &c. by Company "G" Ninth New Jersey Vol.* Princeton NJ: Wm. C. C. Zapf, 1896.

Salter, Edwin. *A History of Monmouth and Ocean Counties* . . . Bayonne NJ: E. Gardner & Son, 1890.

Sauers, Richard A. *"A Succession of Honorable Victories": The Burnside Expedition in North Carolina*. Dayton OH: Morningside House, 1996.

Schiller, Herbert M. *The Bermuda Hundred Campaign: "Operations on the South Side of the James River, Virginia—May, 1864."* Dayton OH: Morningside, 1988.

Scranton, Charles. *Attention Riflemen! . . . to Form a Company of Sharp Shooters, September 17, 1861*. Cowan's Auctions, Cincinnati OH. [Broadside]

Sears, Stephen W. *Chancellorsville*. Boston: Houghton Mifflin, 1996.

————. *Landscape Turned Red: The Battle of Antietam*. New Haven: Ticknor & Fields, 1983.

————. *To the Gates of Richmond: The Peninsula Campaign*. New York: Ticknor & Fields, 1992.

Seliga, Joseph F. *The Search for Camp Olden, Hamilton Township*. Hightstown NJ: Longstreet House, 1995.

Sherman, William T. *Memoirs of General William T. Sherman*. 2 vols. New York: D. Appleton, 1875.

Siegel, Alan A. *For the Glory of the Union: Myth, Reality, and the Media in Civil War New Jersey.* Rutherford NJ: Fairleigh Dickinson University Press, 1984.

Smith, Mark, and Wade Sokolosky. *"To Prepare for Sherman's Coming": The Battle of Wise's Forks, March 1865.* El Dorado Hills CA: Savas Beatie, 2015.

Smith, William Farrar. "Butler's Attack on Drewry's Bluff." In *Battles and Leaders of the Civil War,* edited by Robert U. Johnson and C. C. Buel, 4:206–12. New York: Century, 1888.

——. "The Eighteenth Corps at Cold Harbor." In *Battles and Leaders of the Civil War,* edited by Robert U. Johnson and C. C. Buel, 4:221–30. New York: Century, 1888.

Soldiers Memorial: 9th Regiment, New Jersey Volunteers. Company C. New York: Sarony, Major & Knapp, 1863. [Broadside]

Stackpole, J. Lewis. "The Department of North Carolina under General Foster, July, 1862 to July, 1863." In *Papers of the Military Historical Society of Massachusetts,* 9:85–110. Boston: By the Society, 1887.

Stevens, C. A. *Berdan's United States Sharpshooters in the Army of the Potomac, 1861–1865.* Dayton OH: Morningside Bookshop, 1972.

Stewart, Frank H., and Raymond Archut, comps. *Gloucester County in the Civil War.* 3 vols. Woodbury NJ: Constitution Printing, 1941–43.

Stryker, William S., comp. *Record of Officers and Men of New Jersey in the Civil War, 1861–1865, Compiled in the Office of the Adjutant General.* 2 vols. Trenton NJ: John L. Murphy, 1876.

Traver, Lorenzo. *Burnside Expedition in North Carolina: Battles of Roanoke Island and Elizabeth City (Personal Narratives of the War of the Rebellion, Being Papers Read before the Rhode Island Soldiers and Sailors Historical Society, No. 5, Second Series).* Providence RI: Bangs Williams, 1880.

Trudeau, Noah Andre. *The Last Citadel: Petersburg, Virginia, June 1864–April 1865.* Boston: Little, Brown, 1991.

Twenty-Fifth Anniversary of the Battle of Roanoke Island: First Annual Reunion of the 9th New Jersey Veteran Volunteers at the Veteran Zouaves' Armory, Elizabeth, N.J. . . . Feb. 3, 1887. Elizabeth NJ: Cook & Hall, 1887.

Twenty-Sixth Anniversary of the Muster-in of the Regiment: Second Reunion of the Ninth N.J. Veteran Volunteers at the Rooms of Aaron Wilkes Post, no. 23, G. A. R., Trenton, N.J. . . . September 13, 1887. Elizabeth NJ: Cook & Hall, 1887.

Venter, Bruce M. *Kill Jeff Davis: The Union Raid on Richmond, 1864.* Norman: University of Oklahoma Press, 2016.

Verter, Bradford. "Disconsolations of a Jersey Muskrat: The Civil War Letters of Symmes H. Stillwell." *Princeton University Library Chronicle* 58 (1997): 231–72.

Wagstaff, H. M., ed. "The James A. Graham Papers, 1861–1864." *James Sprunt Historical Studies* 20 (1928): 89–223.

Warner, Ezra J. *Generals in Blue: Lives of the Union Commanders.* Baton Rouge: Louisiana State University Press, 1964.

War of the Rebellion: A Compilation of the Official Records of the Union and Confederate Armies. 4 series, 128 vols. Washington DC: Government Printing Office, 1880–1901.

Wright, William C. "New Jersey's Military Role in the Civil War Reconsidered." *New Jersey History* 92 (1974): 197–210.

———. *The Secession Movement in the Middle Atlantic States.* Rutherford NJ: Fairleigh Dickinson University Press, 1973.

Zatarga, Michael. *The Battle of Roanoke Island: Burnside and the Fight for North Carolina.* Charleston SC: Arcadia Publishing, 2015.

INDEX

Cameron, Simon, 15
Camp Allen, 24
Campbell, Edward L., 1
Camp Boudinot, 109–10, 115, 256
Camp Cameron, 28
Camp Olden, 7, 11–12
Camp Perrine, 201–2
Camp Reno, 89, 95, 98, 141
Cape Fear River, 146
Cape Hatteras, NC, 36, 146, 285
Cape May, NJ, 8
Carolina City, NC, 95, 109, 114–15, 166, 171, 183, 255, 266–67, 270–71
Carrell, Edward S., 68, 93, 138, 167, 233
Carrell, John J., 93, 194, 198
Carter, Samuel P., 272–74, 277, 285
Casement, John S., 279
Casey, Silas, 25–26
Castle Pinckney, 151
Castner, Cornelius W., 18, 40, 98
Cause, Andrew, Jr., 75
Cedar Grove Cemetery, 116
Cedar Landing, 265
Cedar Point, NC, 176
Central Railroad of New Jersey, 9
Chambers, John G., 174
Chancellorsville, Battle of, 168, 341n11
Charleston, SC, 146, 149, 151–52, 161, 267
Charlotte, NC, 282–83
Chase, Luke B., 55
Chattanooga, Siege of, 186, 194
Cherry Grove, skirmish at, 210–11
Chesapeake Bay, 35
Chesapeake Hospital, 233
Chester Station, 221
Chew, Henry F., 75–76
Chickamauga, Battle of, 186
Chickasaw Bayou, Battle of, 142
Chowan River, 37, 179, 181

Christian Commission, U.S., 93–94, 193
City of Richmond, 200
City Point, VA, 214, 241
Clark, John, 42
Cleveland, Edmund J., 113, 115, 124, 152–53, 155, 171, 172, 174, 187, 193, 198, 202, 214, 235–36, 243, 253–56, 283–84; on African Americans, 170, 251; at Cold Harbor, 242; complains about officers, 185; critiques Sherman's troops, 278; on draft riots, 177–78; on Goldsboro expedition, 133–35; on health of regiment, 182; homecoming of, 286–87, 355n44; on Lincoln's assassination, 280; at Port Walthall, 217–20; promotes Lincoln's reelection, 258; on reenlisting, 199–200
Clift, Joel W., 75–76
Coast Division, 27, 145
Cobb's Hill, 216, 237, 253
"Cockade City." See Petersburg, VA
Cold Harbor, Battles of, xvii, 241–43, 246
Cold Harbor, VA, 240–41
Columbia, SC, 267
Columbian College, 28
Company Shops, 283
Congaree River, 267
Congressional Medal of Honor, 219, 347n15
conscription, 169–70
Convoy, 179, 254
Cook, Henry, 31–32, 35–36, 42, 46–47, 75, 77, 90; at Roanoke Island, 64, 72
Cook, James, 32
Cook, Jonathan, 32
Cooper Shop Saloon, 21–22
Copperheads, 141, 281

regiments, infantry (*cont.*)

soldiers, xv, 72, 85, 274; at Crater mine explosion, 249–51; at Deep Creek, 204–5, 345n34; denied right to vote, 206, 258, 345n37; departure of "anti-veterans," 257; discipline in, 101, 103, 157; discord in, 100–103, 131, 155–57; dubbed "Jersey Muskrats," 65–66; ethnic bias of, 87, 99, 120; flags of, 14–15, 99, 137, 144–45, 204, 232, 257, 277, 332n8, 333n24; follows military developments, 123, 168, 172, 175, 177, 194; follows political developments, 124–26, 143, 171, 177–78, 194, 206, 254, 257–59; and fugitive slaves, xv, 78, 94, 97, 175; and General Hunter, 153–54, 162–63; on Goldsboro expedition, 132–40, 336n39, 337n47; guards railroad, 94–99, 113–14; health of, 24, 27–28, 74, 90–91, 115–16, 119, 130, 155, 182–85, 197–98, 247–48, 256, 269, 342n35; as independent command, 129, 132; infiltrates enemy lines, 238–39; on Kenansville scout, 173–75; left behind by Burnside, 107–8; and Lincoln's assassination, 280–81; on Little Washington expedition, 165–66; marksmanship of, xvi, 17, 29, 156, 189, 227, 246, 263; mass furlough of, 200–202; medical care of, 28, 39–41, 116–17, 182, 184–85, 197, 205, 219; meets Sherman's forces, 277; moves to North Carolina, 33; moves to South Carolina, 147–49; moves to Virginia, 186–87; moves to Washington, DC, 20–23; muster-out of, 284–85; near-shipwreck of, 41–43; at Newport News, 188–98; occupies Goldsboro, 276–79;

pacifies Greensboro area, 282–83; performs minstrel concert, 270; in Petersburg siege, xvii, 245–54; at Port Walthall, 216–21; at Portsmouth, 203–4, 207–10; postwar homecoming of, 286–87; praised for valor, 65, 70, 72, 91–92, 99, 128–29, 138, 143–45, 172, 223, 236, 267, 285–86, 338n6; publishes newspaper, 278–79; purses minister's kidnappers, 105–6; racial attitudes of, xv, 94, 99–100, 124–26, 129, 143, 148–49, 151–55, 162, 169–70, 240, 244, 250–51, 258; on Rainbow Bluff expedition, 260–66; rations of, 11–12, 28, 34, 36, 46, 73, 96–97, 167, 185, 248, 256, 275; recruiting of, 6–7, 117–19, 178; reenlistment of, 198–201, 344n23; religious activities of, 31, 93–94, 105, 194, 198; returns to North Carolina, 162–63, 165, 254–55; at Rowell's Mill, 127–28, 337nn52–53; scouts to Adams Creek, 121–23, 335n18; scouts to Lewis's plantation, 106–7; scouts to Swansborough, 120–21; scouts to Young's Cross Roads, 110–12; and Southern civilians, xiv, 94, 97, 100, 124, 168–69, 278, 283; at Southwest Creek, 133–34; staffing of, 8–9; strength of, 6, 17, 100, 119–20, 131, 335n15; strikes railroad to Petersburg, 245; and sutlers, 12–13, 157, 184; on Tarboro expedition, 126–30; training of, 7, 8, 18, 25, 75; transportation of, 19–20; on Weldon expedition, 179–81; 9th New York, 53, 61–62, 70; 10th Connecticut, 135; 12th New Jersey, 76, 328n28; 13th Indiana, 226; 17th Massachusetts, 132, 138, 179–80; 17th North

Van Fleet, James, 28
Van Nest, Henry V., 83–84
Veteran Reserve Corps, 269
veteran volunteers, 199
Vicksburg Campaign, 142, 172, 175
Virginia and North Carolina, Department of, 182–83, 195
Virginia Peninsula, 213

Walker, William S., 238
Walker, William Z., 86, 331n40
Walthall/Dunn house, 217, 220
Ward, Marcus L., 143
War Democrats, 143, 257
Ware Bottom Church, 245
Warren Guards, 1
Washington, DC, 23–32
Washington, NC, 126–27
Washington, NJ, 84
Webbtown, NC, 276, 278
Weder, John, 218
Weehawken, 160
Weitzel, Godfrey, 213, 216
Weldon, NC, 179, 181
Weller, Frederick S., 28, 38–39, 40
Welles, Gideon, 160
Wessells, Henry W., 134
White, Robert H., 239
Whitehall, NC, 137, 275–76
Whitehall, skirmish at, 137–38
White House Landing, 243
White Oak River, 120–21, 176
Whitford, John N., 107
Whiting, William H. C., 225, 233
Wilborn, Edward, 120
Wilcox Bridge, 174
Wild, Edward A., 169–70
Wilderness, Battle of the, 224, 240
Wilkins, Jesse, 211
Williamsburg, VA, 213
Williamston, NC, 128, 263

Willis house, 228–29
Wilmington, DE, 285
Wilmington, NC, 146, 164, 260–61, 269–70
Wilmington and Weldon Railroad, 132, 139
Wilson, James, 24–25, 34, 46–47, 91–93, 95–96, 98, 101, 131
Winans, Elias, 138–39, 337n52
Winton, NC, 179
wire entanglements, 228
Wise, Henry A., 49–50, 53
Wise, O. Jennings, 64
Wise Legion, 53
Wise's Forks, Battle of, 272–74
Wistar, Isaac J., 228
Woodhull, Addison W., 40, 74, 111, 116–17, 167, 182, 197, 233, 353n17; inspects regiment's tents, 184; issues medical statistics, 268–69; joins regiment, 89–90
Wright, Joseph, 274

Yanceyville, NC, 282
yellow fever, 256
York River, 213–14, 241, 243
Yorktown, VA, 104, 213
Young Men's Christian Association (YMCA), 14, 93–94
Young's Cross Roads, skirmish at, 111

Zabriskie, Abram, 10, 31, 38–39, 93, 100–101, 106, 111, 131, 159, 166–67, 180, 183, 191, 325n36, 349n1; at Bermuda Hundred, 227, 230–31, 233; on Goldsboro expedition, 132, 134; mourned by regiment, 235; promotions of, 92, 144; receives gift sword, 201–2; at Roanoke Island, 60, 70; urges men to reenlist, 201
Zimmerman, William, 102

CPSIA information can be obtained
at www.ICGtesting.com
Printed in the USA
LVOW07*2255071116
511989LV00007B/8/P